Cooking Light
◆ the essential
dinner
tonight
cookbook

Oxmoor House®

Shrimp Caesar Salad,
page 107

Cooking Light

◆ the essential
dinner
tonight
cookbook

compiled and edited by
Heather Averett

OXMOOR
HOUSE®

©2009 by Time Home Entertainment Inc.
Book Division of Southern Progress Corporation
P.O. Box 2262, Birmingham, Alabama 35201-2262

ISBN-13: 978-0-8487-3644-6
ISBN-10: 0-8487-3644-3
Library of Congress Control Number: 2009928804

Printed in the United States of America
Second printing 2012

Be sure to check with your health-care provider before making any changes in your diet.

Oxmoor House, Inc.

VP, Publishing Director: Jim Childs
Brand Manager: Allison Long Lowery
Managing Editor: L. Amanda Owens

Cooking Light® *Essential Dinner Tonight*

Editor: Heather Averett
Nutrition Editors: Andrea C. Kirkland, M.S., R.D.; Rachel Quinlivan, R.D.
Project Editor: Vanessa Lynn Rusch
Director, Test Kitchens: Elizabeth Tyler Austin
Assistant Director, Test Kitchens: Julie Christopher
Test Kitchens Professionals: Kathleen Royal Phillips, Catherine Crowell Steele, Ashley T. Strickland
Photography Director: Jim Bathie
Senior Photo Stylist: Kay E. Clarke
Associate Photo Stylist: Katherine Eckert Coyne
Production Manager: Theresa Beste-Farley

Contributors
Designer and Compositor: Carol Damsky
Copy Editor: Norma Butterworth-McKittrick
Indexer: Mary Ann Laurens
Interns: Emily Chappell, Anne-Harris Jones, Shea Staskowski

Cooking Light®

Editor in Chief: Mary Kay Culpepper
Executive Editor: Billy R. Sims
Creative Director: Susan Waldrip Dendy
Managing Editor: Maelynn Cheung
Senior Editor: Phillip Rhodes
Projects Editor: Mary Simpson Creel, M.S., R.D.
Food Editor: Ann Taylor Pittman
Associate Food Editors: Timothy Q. Cebula; Kathy Kitchens Downie, R.D.; Julianna Grimes
Associate Editors: Cindy Hatcher, Brandy Rushing
Test Kitchens Director: Vanessa Taylor Johnson
Assistant Test Kitchens Director: Tiffany Vickers
Senior Food Stylist: Kellie Gerber Kelley
Test Kitchens Professionals: Mary Drennen Ankar, SaBrina Bone, Mike Wilson
Art Director: Maya Metz Logue
Associate Art Directors: Fernande Bondarenko, J. Shay McNamee
Senior Designer: Brigette Mayer
Senior Photographer: Randy Mayor
Senior Photo Stylist: Cindy Barr
Photo Stylists: Jan Gautro, Leigh Ann Ross
Copy Chief: Maria Parker Hopkins
Assistant Copy Chief: Susan Roberts
Copy Editor: Johannah Gilman Paiva
Copy Researcher: Michelle Gibson Daniels
Production Manager: Liz Rhoades
Production Editor: Hazel R. Eddins
Cookinglight.com Editor: Kim Cross
Administrative Coordinator: Carol D. Johnson
Editorial Assistant: Jason Horn
Intern: Holly V. Kapherr

To order additional publications, call 1-800-765-6400
For more books to enrich your life, visit **oxmoorhouse.com**

To search, savor, and share thousands of recipes, visit **myrecipes.com**

Cover: Greek Salad with Shrimp, page 109

Back Cover: (left to right) Turkey Noodle Soup, page 32; Fresh Herb-Coated Beef Tenderloin Steaks with Mushroom Gravy, page 245; Egg Salad BLTs, page 47

Tex-Mex Flank Steak and Vegetables, page 233

Turkey Curry, page 351

Marble Cheesecake Squares, page 389

Contents

Welcome

Cooking Light magazine reaches more than 1.7 million households and 11.9 million readers each month—more than any other food magazine in the country. And among all the columns featured, Dinner Tonight consistently remains one of the most popular. It has even become one of the most searched features on **myrecipes.com.** In addition, Dinner

Tonight has also been the inspiration for our latest book, *Cooking Light Essential Dinner Tonight,* which boasts more than 500 great-tasting and healthy recipes to help you eat smart, be fit, and live well.

Readers, like you, often tell us that deciding what to cook is more challenging than actually cooking it. But if someone does the planning for the side dishes, shortcuts, and substitution possibilities for you, then it seems like half your work is done. And that's what we want *Cooking Light Essential Dinner Tonight* to do for you, whether you're looking for dinner tonight or planning ahead for a special weekend meal.

Busy days call for relaxing evenings and a chance to enjoy a leisurely dinner and time to catch your breath. You don't want to deal with a fussy meal, and you certainly don't want to sacrifice flavor for health. *Cooking Light Essential Dinner Tonight* solves these dilemmas. With recipes, menus, game plans, complete nutritional analyses, and big beautiful photographs, you can make smart dinner decisions quickly and easily without sacrificing time or flavor.

"Weeknight Meals," the first section of *Cooking Light Essential Dinner Tonight,* offers easy entrées paired with quick side dishes, each in a menu than can be prepared in about 45 minutes or less. "Weekend Menus," on the other hand, offers ideas for more ambitious fare, such as brunches, casual get-togethers, and special occasions when you've got a little more time to spare. Regardless of which you choose for your particular meal, you can be sure that *Cooking Light Essential Dinner Tonight* offers rich, delicious food at its finest, allowing you to get a meal on the table quickly and easily.

We hope these easy menus help take the guesswork out of meal planning, inspire your creativity in the kitchen, and bring exciting new possibilities to your dining table. Here's to cooking dinner tonight!

Mary Kay Culpepper
Editor in Chief

Cooking with Options

The recipes in *Cooking Light Essential Dinner Tonight* can be used exactly as is, or you may choose to improvise, taking full advantage of ingredients you have on hand or to suit particular family preferences. When improvising, here are some tips to keep in mind:

Take stock. Many of our quick weeknight dinner entrées are inspired by world cuisines, which use bold-flavored sauces and condiments. Consider including these ingredients in your refrigerator: Thai fish sauce, oyster sauce, capers, chile paste with garlic, and sun-dried tomatoes. Keep fresh lemons, limes, garlic, green onions, fresh parsley (and other fresh herbs), and fresh gingerroot on hand. All of the above deliver a lot of flavor with minimal effort.

Choose recipes with make-ahead potential. Appetizers, salads, breads, and desserts are examples of dishes that can be prepared in advance to free you up to prepare the rest of the meal.

Take advantage of summer's best. Shop the markets for seasonal fruits, vegetables, and fresh herbs while they're abundant and at their peak flavor for recipes like Shortcakes with Fresh Berries (page 399) and Orecchiette with Fresh Fava Beans, Ricotta, and Mint (page 140).

Multitask to save time. Many of our menus include dishes with procedures that can be completed concurrently. Cut and measure other ingredients while you start a pan of water to boil for pasta, rice, or couscous. Take advantage of the waiting time when something is marinating, simmering, or baking to prepare a salad or to heat the bread.

Take shortcuts. If you're pressed for time, use our serving suggestions as a guide and make substitution choices using convenience products that suit your schedule. Boil-in-bag instant rice, refrigerated potatoes, bottled salad dressings, and rotisserie chicken make do in a pinch.

Just try it. The best way to improvise is to just do it. Here are some great dishes to get you started.

Garlicky Pasta with Fresh Tomatoes and Basil, page 136

Portobello Cheeseburgers, page 51

Greek Salad with Grilled Chicken, page 121

Asian Rice with Shrimp and Snow Peas, page 204

Chicken, Peppers, Onions, and Mushrooms
with Marsala Wine, page 312

Weeknight Meals

Prepare any of these delicious meals with a side dish, salad, or dessert in less than 45 minutes.

Spiced Salmon with Mustard Sauce, page 182

Chile-Spiced Tenderloin Steaks, page 244

Chicken, Rice, and Tropical Fruit Salad, page 85

Soups

Beef and Beer Chili,
page 24

MENU *serves 6*

Broccoli and Cheese Soup

Broiled plum tomatoes
Preheat broiler. Cut 9 plum tomatoes in half lengthwise; scoop out and discard seeds. Place tomato halves on a jelly-roll pan coated with cooking spray. Sprinkle ½ teaspoon seasoned dry breadcrumbs over each tomato half, and top with 1 teaspoon shredded part-skim mozzarella cheese. Coat tomatoes lightly with cooking spray. Broil 2 to 3 minutes or until cheese bubbles.

Baked potatoes

Game Plan

1 Preheat broiler for tomatoes.

2 While broth for soup comes to a boil, prepare tomatoes.

3 While broccoli boils:
•Microwave potatoes.
•Combine milk and flour for soup.
•Cube cheese for soup.
•Broil tomatoes.

Broccoli and Cheese Soup

Processed cheese melts beautifully, giving this soup a smooth texture and mild flavor.

Cooking spray
1 cup chopped onion
2 garlic cloves, minced
3 cups fat-free, less-sodium chicken broth
1 (16-ounce) package broccoli florets
2½ cups 2% reduced-fat milk
⅓ cup all-purpose flour
¼ teaspoon black pepper
8 ounces light processed cheese, cubed (such as Velveeta Light)

❶ Heat a large nonstick saucepan over medium-high heat; coat with cooking spray. Add onion and garlic; sauté 3 minutes or until tender. Add broth and broccoli, and bring mixture to a boil over medium-high heat. Reduce heat to medium; cook 10 minutes.
❷ Combine milk and flour, stirring with a whisk until well blended. Add milk mixture to broccoli mixture. Cook 5 minutes or until slightly thick, stirring constantly. Stir in pepper. Remove from heat; add cheese, stirring until cheese melts.
❸ Place one-third of soup in a blender or food processor, and process until smooth. Return pureed soup mixture to pan. Yield: 6 servings (serving size: 1½ cups).

CALORIES 203 (28% from fat); FAT 6.3g (sat 4g, mono 1.8g, poly 0.4g); PROTEIN 15.6g; CARB 21.7g; FIBER 2.9g; CHOL 24mg; IRON 1.2mg; SODIUM 897mg; CALC 385mg

Quick Tip: Packaged broccoli florets, found with bagged salads in the produce section of most supermarkets, eliminate cutting and cleanup.

Potato, Corn, and Leek Chowder

This soup is a good source of 3 blood pressure-lowering minerals: calcium, potassium, and magnesium. Serve with hot sauce.

2	tablespoons butter
1	tablespoon olive oil
1½	cups coarsely chopped leek (about 1 large)
½	cup finely chopped celery
½	cup finely chopped red bell pepper
2	cups whole milk
3	tablespoons all-purpose flour
3	cups fat-free, less-sodium chicken broth
2	cups fresh corn kernels (about 4 ears)
2	pounds cubed peeled Yukon gold or red potatoes
1	teaspoon salt
¼	teaspoon freshly ground black pepper
¼	cup finely chopped fresh parsley
3	tablespoons chopped fresh chives

❶ Heat butter and oil in a large Dutch oven over medium heat. Add leek, celery, and bell pepper; cook 4 minutes or until vegetables are tender, stirring frequently. Combine milk and flour in a small bowl; stir with a whisk. Slowly add milk mixture to pan, stirring constantly. Stir in broth and next 4 ingredients; bring to a boil. Reduce heat, and simmer 20 minutes or until potato is tender. Stir in parsley and chives. Yield: 6 servings (serving size: 1⅓ cups).

CALORIES 331 (26% from fat); FAT 9.5g (sat 4.4g, mono 3.4g, poly 0.9g); PROTEIN 9.8g; CARB 54.9g; FIBER 5.3g; CHOL 18mg; IRON 1.8mg; SODIUM 701mg; CALC 127mg

Sweet Corn Chowder with Hot-Smoked Salmon

Salty, smoky salmon and tangy goat cheese offset sweet notes from the corn and roasted pepper. The fish, used in place of the bacon often found in traditional chowder recipes, adds heart-healthy fats and protein. Great made ahead, this soup gets even better with time.

1 tablespoon butter
2 cups chopped onion
3 cups fat-free, less-sodium chicken broth
1½ cups cubed peeled baking potato
1½ cups fresh corn kernels (about 3 ears)
1 (15-ounce) can no-salt-added cream-style corn
¼ teaspoon freshly ground black pepper
⅛ teaspoon ground red pepper
2 (4.5-ounce) packages hot-smoked salmon, flaked
4 teaspoons chopped fresh chives

❶ Melt butter in a large saucepan over medium-high heat. Add onion; sauté 4 minutes. Add broth and potato; bring to a boil. Reduce heat, and simmer 10 minutes or until potato is tender. Add corn kernels and cream-style corn; cook 5 minutes. Stir in peppers. Ladle 1¼ cups chowder into each of 4 soup bowls. Divide salmon evenly among bowls. Garnish each serving with 1 teaspoon chives. Yield: 4 servings.

CALORIES 310 (21% from fat); FAT 7.4g (sat 2.6g, mono 2.3g, poly 1.2g); PROTEIN 18.6g; CARB 45.5g; FIBER 6g; CHOL 22mg; IRON 1.8mg; SODIUM 832mg; CALC 43mg

Game Plan

1 Chop vegetables and cut corn kernels off the cob for soup.

2 While broth mixture comes to a boil:
- Slice red onion for sandwiches.

3 While soup simmers:
- Prepare sandwiches.

4 Flake salmon for soup.

MENU *serves 6*

Golden Gazpacho

Grilled pepper cheese sandwiches

Combine ½ cup shredded sharp cheddar cheese, ¼ cup diced pimientos, 2 tablespoons chopped fresh cilantro, 4 ounces softened ⅓-less-fat cream cheese, and 1 seeded minced jalapeño. Spread about 2 tablespoons cheese mixture on each of 6 (½-inch-thick) slices crusty bread; top each with another bread slice. Heat a nonstick skillet over medium-high heat; coat pan with cooking spray. Cook each sandwich 3 minutes on each side or until golden.

Lemon sorbet

Game Plan

1 Prepare soup; cover and chill.

2 While soup chills:

•Prepare sandwiches.

Golden Gazpacho

This is a perfect light meal for summer. For a little more zip, add some jalapeño peppers.

3½ cups chopped seeded yellow tomato (about 1½ pounds)

2 cups chopped seeded peeled cucumber (about 1)

1 cup chopped yellow bell pepper (about 1 medium)

½ cup chopped red bell pepper (about ½ medium)

½ cup chopped green bell pepper (about ½ medium)

½ cup chopped red onion

2 garlic cloves, chopped

2 tablespoons white wine vinegar

1 tablespoon chopped fresh mint

1 tablespoon chopped fresh cilantro

1 tablespoon honey

2 teaspoons extra-virgin olive oil

¾ teaspoon salt

¼ teaspoon ground cumin

❶ Place first 7 ingredients in a blender or food processor; process until smooth. Add vinegar and remaining ingredients; pulse 5 times or until well combined. Cover and chill at least 1 hour or overnight. Yield: 6 servings (serving size: 1 cup).

CALORIES 77 (27% from fat); FAT 2.3g (sat 0.3g, mono 1.2g, poly 0.4g); PROTEIN 2.9g; CARB 13.9g; FIBER 2.7g; CHOL 0mg; IRON 1.4mg; SODIUM 342mg; CALC 37mg

Quick Tip: It's really rather easy to seed a cucumber. Simply cut the cucumber in half lengthwise, and scrape the seeds out with a spoon.

Tomato-Basil Soup

This quick version of a classic soup makes a refreshingly light supper. Toasted French bread spread with light Boursin cheese is a tasty stand-in for the standard grilled cheese sandwich.

2 teaspoons olive oil
3 garlic cloves, minced
3 cups fat-free, less-sodium chicken broth
¾ teaspoon salt
3 (14.5-ounce) cans no-salt-added diced tomatoes, undrained
2 cups fresh basil leaves, thinly sliced
Basil leaves (optional)

1 Heat oil in a large saucepan over medium heat. Add garlic; cook 30 seconds, stirring constantly. Stir in broth, salt, and tomatoes; bring to a boil. Reduce heat; simmer 20 minutes. Stir in sliced basil.

2 Place half of soup in a blender or food processor, and process until smooth. Pour pureed soup into a bowl, and repeat procedure with remaining soup. Garnish with basil leaves, if desired. Yield: 4 servings (serving size: 1½ cups).

CALORIES 103 (24% from fat); FAT 2.8g (sat 0.4g, mono 1.7g, poly 0.4g); PROTEIN 5.8g; CARB 15.9g; FIBER 4g; CHOL 0mg; IRON 2.4mg; SODIUM 809mg; CALC 129mg

Quick Tip: To easily slice the basil, stack several leaves on top of one another. Roll the leaves together tightly, and slice the roll thinly. The ribbonlike slices are called chiffonade.

MENU *serves 4*

Tomato-Basil Soup

Cheese toast
Preheat broiler. Spread each of 8 (½-inch-thick) slices French bread baguette with 1 teaspoon light Boursin cheese. Broil 2 minutes or until lightly browned.

Green salad

Game Plan

1 Mince garlic and slice basil for soup.

2 Preheat broiler for cheese toast.

3 While soup simmers:

• Prepare salad.

• Broil cheese toast.

Winter Potage

A hearty combination of 6 vegetables gives layers of flavor to this soup. A squeeze of fresh lemon and a little cracked black pepper delivered at the table brighten each bowl. Substitute Gruyère or Monterey Jack cheese for the cheddar in the grilled cheese sandwiches, if desired.

 1 teaspoon olive oil
 1 teaspoon butter
 1 cup thinly sliced leek (about 1 large)
 ½ cup sliced celery
 2 garlic cloves, minced
 2 cups chopped broccoli florets
 2 cups baby spinach leaves
 1 cup frozen shelled edamame (fresh soybeans)
 1 cup frozen petite green peas
 1 tablespoon rice
 ⅛ teaspoon ground red pepper
 3 cups fat-free, less-sodium chicken broth
 1½ cups water
 1½ teaspoons fresh lemon juice
 ¼ teaspoon salt
 ¼ teaspoon black pepper
Lemon wedges (optional)
Cracked black pepper (optional)

1 Heat oil and butter in a Dutch oven over medium-high heat. Add leek and celery; sauté 4 minutes or until tender. Stir in garlic; cook 1 minute. Add broccoli and next 5 ingredients. Stir in broth and water; bring to a boil. Reduce heat, cover, and simmer 20 minutes or until vegetables are tender.

2 Place one-third of vegetable mixture in a food processor or blender; process until smooth. Pour pureed mixture into a large bowl; repeat procedure with remaining vegetable mixture. Stir in lemon juice, salt, and ¼ teaspoon black pepper. Garnish with lemon wedges and cracked black pepper, if desired. Yield: 4 servings (serving size: 1½ cups).

CALORIES 152 (25% from fat); FAT 4.2g (sat 0.9g, mono 1.5g, poly 1.2g); PROTEIN 10g; CARB 19.3g; FIBER 6.4g; CHOL 3mg; IRON 3.2mg; SODIUM 540mg; CALC 101mg

---

MENU *serves 4*

Winter Potage

Grilled cheese sandwiches

Heat a medium nonstick skillet over medium-high heat; coat pan with cooking spray. Sauté ½ cup thinly sliced onion 6 minutes or until golden. Remove from pan; set aside. Spread each of 4 slices of rustic sourdough bread with 1 teaspoon Dijon mustard; top each with 1 tablespoon onion and 3 tablespoons reduced-fat shredded sharp cheddar cheese. Top each with 1 bread slice. Reduce heat to medium. Recoat pan with cooking spray; cook sandwiches 2 minutes on each side or until cheese melts.

Light pound cake

Game Plan

1 Slice leek and celery, mince garlic, and chop broccoli for soup.

2 While soup simmers:
  • Squeeze lemon to get juice for soup.
  • Prepare sandwiches.

MENU *serves 8*

Leek and Lima Bean Soup with Bacon

Crunchy chopped salad

Combine 6 cups chopped romaine lettuce, 2 cups chopped cucumber, 2 cups sugar snap peas (sliced in half crosswise), 2 cups chopped plum tomato, and 1 cup chopped green onions. Combine ¼ cup cider vinegar, 1½ tablespoons sugar, 1 tablespoon olive oil, and ¾ teaspoon salt; stir with a whisk. Drizzle over salad; toss gently to coat. Sprinkle with 3 tablespoons toasted sliced almonds.

Pumpernickel toast

Lemon sorbet with mixed berries

Game Plan

1 Chop leeks and slice green onions for soup.

2 While soup simmers:

- •Prepare salad.
- •Squeeze lemon to get juice for soup.
- •Toast pumpernickel bread slices.

3 Prepare dessert.

Leek and Lima Bean Soup with Bacon

For a casual gathering with friends, serve this light meal. The slightly sweet salad is a nice complement to the smoky-savory soup. Fresh limas are at their peak from June to September; thawed frozen beans substitute well for fresh. Here, the beans are pureed in a creamy soup garnished with bacon, sour cream, and onions.

- 3 bacon slices
- 2 cups chopped leek (about 2 leeks)
- 4 cups fresh baby lima beans
- 4 cups fat-free, less-sodium chicken broth
- 1 cup water
- 2 tablespoons fresh lemon juice
- ½ teaspoon salt
- ¼ teaspoon freshly ground black pepper
- ½ cup thinly sliced green onions
- ½ cup reduced-fat sour cream

1 Cook bacon in a large saucepan over medium heat until crisp. Remove bacon from pan, reserving 1 tablespoon drippings in pan. Crumble bacon; set aside. Add leek to drippings in pan; cook 7 minutes or until tender, stirring frequently. Stir in beans, broth, and water; bring to a boil. Reduce heat, and simmer 10 minutes or until beans are tender.

2 Place half of bean mixture in a blender. Remove center piece of blender lid (to allow steam to escape); secure lid on blender. Place a clean towel over opening in blender lid (to avoid splatters), and blend until smooth. Pour pureed bean mixture into a large bowl; repeat procedure with remaining bean mixture. Stir in lemon juice, salt, and pepper. Ladle about 1 cup soup into each of 8 bowls; top each serving with 1 tablespoon onions, 1 tablespoon sour cream, and about 1 teaspoon bacon. Yield: 8 servings.

CALORIES 170 (26% from fat); FAT 5g (sat 2.4g, mono 1.8g, poly 0.5g); PROTEIN 8.9g; CARB 22.6g; FIBER 6.1g; CHOL 10mg; IRON 2.3mg; SODIUM 440mg; CALC 55mg

Lentil Soup with Balsamic-Roasted Winter Vegetables

The flavor of this dish improves on the second day, so it's ideal to make in advance. Add the chard just before serving to preserve its color. The roasted root vegetables in the soup balance the sharp flavors of endive and radicchio in the salad. Stir in a little water when you reheat the soup if it's too thick.

1⅔ cups cubed peeled sweet potato (about 8 ounces)
1⅔ cups cubed peeled parsnip (about 8 ounces)
1⅔ cups cubed peeled carrot (about 8 ounces)
2 tablespoons balsamic vinegar
2 tablespoons olive oil
⅛ teaspoon kosher salt
1 cup (4 ounces) chopped pancetta
1 cup chopped shallots (about 6 large)
1 cup chopped red onion (about 1 medium)
1 tablespoon fresh thyme leaves
1 tablespoon minced garlic
1 tablespoon balsamic vinegar
½ teaspoon black pepper
¼ cup dry white wine
1¼ cups dried lentils
6 cups fat-free, less-sodium chicken broth, divided
8 cups Swiss chard, trimmed and chopped (about 9 ounces)

❶ Preheat oven to 375°.
❷ Combine first 6 ingredients in a large bowl; toss well. Arrange vegetable mixture in a single layer on a foil-lined jelly-roll pan; bake at 375° for 30 minutes or until lightly browned, stirring occasionally. Set aside.
❸ Cook pancetta in a Dutch oven over medium-high heat 8 minutes or until crisp. Remove from pan with a slotted spoon; set aside. Add shallots and onion to drippings in pan; cook 15 minutes or until golden. Add thyme, garlic, 1 tablespoon vinegar, and pepper, and cook 1 minute. Add wine, scraping pan to loosen browned bits. Add pancetta, lentils, and 4 cups broth to pan; bring to a boil. Cover, reduce heat, and simmer 30 minutes. Add remaining 2 cups broth and roasted vegetables to pan, and simmer, uncovered, 15 minutes. Add chard, and cook 2 minutes or until wilted. Yield: 6 servings (serving size: about 1½ cups).

CALORIES 373 (28% from fat); FAT 11.7g (sat 3.5g, mono 6.4g, poly 1.6g); PROTEIN 18.8g; CARB 51g; FIBER 15.3g; CHOL 14mg; IRON 6.4mg; SODIUM 875mg; CALC 118mg

---

MENU *serves 6*

Lentil Soup with Balsamic-Roasted Winter Vegetables

Radicchio-endive winter salad
Combine 3 cups chopped radicchio and 3 cups chopped endive in a large bowl. Combine 2 tablespoons orange juice, 2 teaspoons extra-virgin olive oil, ¼ teaspoon salt, and ⅛ teaspoon freshly ground black pepper in a small bowl; stir with a whisk. Drizzle over salad greens; toss gently to coat.

Coffee and almond biscotti

Game Plan

1 Preheat oven for vegetables.

2 While oven heats:
  • Cube and peel sweet potato, parsnip, and carrot for soup.

3 While vegetables bake:
  • Prepare pancetta mixture.

4 While soup simmers:
  • Trim and chop Swiss chard.
  • Prepare salad.
  • Make coffee.

MENU *serves 5*

White Bean-Rajas Soup

Chicken and cheese quesadillas

Heat a medium nonstick skillet over medium heat; coat with cooking spray. Working with 1 (6-inch) corn tortilla at a time, place tortilla in pan; cook 30 seconds. Turn tortilla; sprinkle 1 tablespoon shredded queso chihuahua on half of tortilla. Top cheese with 2 tablespoons shredded cooked chicken breast and 1 teaspoon chopped green onions. Sprinkle 1 tablespoon shredded queso chihuahua evenly over onions. Fold tortilla in half; turn and cook 1 minute or until lightly browned and cheese melts. Repeat procedure to yield 5 quesadillas; cut each quesadilla into 3 wedges.

Green salad with bottled salsa

Game Plan

1 While broth mixture simmers:

- Squeeze lime to get juice for soup.

- Shred cheese for soup and quesadillas.

- Preheat skillet for quesadillas.

2 While soup stands for 5 minutes:

- Prepare quesadillas.

- Spoon salsa over salad.

White Bean-Rajas Soup

The soup gets its name from the cooked peppers, which are called rajas in Spanish. Sour cream helps mellow the heat and rounds out the flavors.

Cooking spray
- 2 cups chopped white onion
- 2 cups chopped seeded poblano chile
- 1 cup chopped red bell pepper
- 4 garlic cloves, minced
- 2 (14-ounce) cans fat-free, less-sodium chicken broth
- 2 (15-ounce) cans navy beans, rinsed and drained
- ¼ cup fresh lime juice
- 2 tablespoons ground cumin
- 1 cup (4 ounces) shredded queso chihuahua or Monterey Jack cheese
- 2½ tablespoons reduced-fat sour cream

❶ Heat a Dutch oven over medium-high heat; coat with cooking spray. Add onion, chile, bell pepper, and garlic; sauté 5 minutes. Add broth; bring to a boil. Cover, reduce heat, and simmer 10 minutes. Remove from heat. Add beans, juice, and cumin. Cover and let stand 5 minutes. Ladle about 1½ cups soup into each of 5 bowls; top each serving with about 3 tablespoons cheese and 1½ teaspoons sour cream. Yield: 5 servings.

CALORIES 373 (22% from fat); FAT 9.2g (sat 5.1g, mono 2g, poly 0.7g); PROTEIN 22.8g; CARB 52.5g; FIBER 12.1g; CHOL 28mg; IRON 5.1mg; SODIUM 968mg; CALC 291mg

Quick Tip: To save time, use prechopped onions, found in the produce section of supermarkets.

North Woods Bean Soup

Pureeing some of the soup lends body to the dish. Stir in fresh spinach after the soup is removed from the heat so it won't overcook and lose its bright color.

Cooking spray
- 1 cup baby carrots, halved
- 1 cup chopped onion
- 2 garlic cloves, minced
- 7 ounces turkey kielbasa, halved lengthwise and cut into ½-inch pieces
- 4 cups fat-free, less-sodium chicken broth
- ½ teaspoon dried Italian seasoning
- ½ teaspoon black pepper
- 2 (15.8-ounce) cans Great Northern beans, drained and rinsed
- 1 (6-ounce) bag fresh baby spinach leaves

❶ Heat a large saucepan over medium-high heat; coat with cooking spray. Add carrots, onion, garlic, and kielbasa; sauté 3 minutes, stirring occasionally. Reduce heat to medium; cook 5 minutes. Add broth, Italian seasoning, pepper, and beans. Bring to a boil; reduce heat, and simmer 5 minutes.

❷ Place 2 cups of soup in a food processor or blender, and process until smooth. Return pureed mixture to pan, and simmer 5 minutes. Remove soup from heat. Add spinach, stirring until spinach wilts. Yield: 5 servings (serving size: about 1½ cups).

CALORIES 227 (15% from fat); FAT 3.9g (sat 1.2g, mono 1.3g, poly 1.2g); PROTEIN 18.1g; CARB 30.8g; FIBER 6.7g; CHOL 26mg; IRON 3.5mg; SODIUM 750mg; CALC 112mg

MENU *serves 5*

North Woods Bean Soup

Country apple coleslaw

Combine ¼ cup red wine vinegar, 3 tablespoons brown sugar, 1 teaspoon canola oil, and ¼ teaspoon salt in a microwave-safe bowl. Microwave at HIGH 1 minute. Add 1 (10-ounce) package coleslaw, 2 cups chopped apple, and ½ cup raisins; toss well to coat. Serve chilled or at room temperature.

Pumpernickel bread with honey butter

Game Plan

1 Cut kielbasa and vegetables for soup.

2 While kielbasa and vegetables cook:
   - Microwave dressing for slaw.

3 While soup simmers:
   - Chop apple for slaw.

Quick Fall Minestrone

This easy soup brims with fresh vegetables. Canned beans and orzo make it hearty and filling.

1 tablespoon canola oil
1 cup chopped onion
2 garlic cloves, minced
6 cups vegetable broth
2½ cups (¾-inch) cubed peeled butternut squash
2½ cups (¾-inch) cubed peeled baking potato
1 cup (1-inch) cut green beans (about ¼ pound)
½ cup chopped carrot
1 teaspoon dried oregano
½ teaspoon freshly ground black pepper
¼ teaspoon salt
4 cups chopped kale
½ cup uncooked orzo (rice-shaped pasta)
1 (16-ounce) can cannellini beans or other white beans, rinsed and drained
½ cup (2 ounces) grated fresh Parmesan cheese

1 Heat oil in a large Dutch oven over medium-high heat. Add onion and garlic; sauté 2½ minutes or until tender. Add broth and next 7 ingredients; bring to a boil. Reduce heat, and simmer 3 minutes. Add kale, orzo, and beans; cook 5 minutes or until orzo is done and vegetables are tender. Sprinkle with cheese. Yield: 8 servings (serving size: 1½ cups soup and 1 tablespoon cheese).

CALORIES 212 (21% from fat); FAT 5g (sat 1.6g, mono 1g, poly 1.2g); PROTEIN 9.6g; CARB 36g; FIBER 3.9g; CHOL 5mg; IRON 1.9mg; SODIUM 961mg; CALC 164mg

Ingredient Tip: To quickly remove the skin from the squash, use a vegetable peeler.

Moroccan Chickpea Chili

This recipe comes together quickly and proves you don't need meat to make a hearty chili.

2 teaspoons olive oil
1 cup chopped onion
¾ cup chopped celery
½ cup chopped carrot
1 teaspoon bottled minced garlic
2 teaspoons ground cumin
2 teaspoons paprika
1 teaspoon ground ginger
½ teaspoon ground turmeric
¼ teaspoon freshly ground black pepper
¼ teaspoon salt
⅛ teaspoon ground cinnamon
⅛ teaspoon ground red pepper
1½ cups water
2 tablespoons no-salt-added tomato paste
2 (15½-ounce) cans chickpeas (garbanzo beans), rinsed and drained
1 (14.5-ounce) can no-salt-added diced tomatoes, undrained
2 tablespoons chopped fresh cilantro
1 tablespoon fresh lemon juice

1 Heat oil in a large saucepan over medium-high heat. Add onion, celery, carrot, and garlic; sauté 5 minutes. Stir in cumin and next 7 ingredients; cook 1 minute, stirring constantly. Add 1½ cups water, tomato paste, chickpeas, and tomatoes; bring to a boil. Cover, reduce heat, and simmer 20 minutes. Stir in cilantro and juice. Yield: 4 servings (serving size: 1½ cups).

CALORIES 215 (23% from fat); FAT 5.5g (sat 0.4g, mono 2.9g, poly 1.9g); PROTEIN 7.7g; CARB 36.3g; FIBER 9.8g; CHOL 0mg; IRON 3.4mg; SODIUM 534mg; CALC 102mg

MENU *serves 4*

Beef and Beer Chili

Monterey Jack and red pepper quesadillas
Preheat oven to 400°. Coat 1 side of each of 4 (6-inch) whole wheat tortillas with cooking spray. Place tortillas, coated side down, on a large baking sheet. Sprinkle each tortilla with 2 tablespoons shredded Monterey Jack cheese, 2 tablespoons chopped bottled roasted red bell peppers, 1 tablespoon chopped cilantro, and 2 teaspoons sliced green onions. Fold each tortilla in half. Bake at 400° for 5 minutes or until cheese melts. Cut into wedges.

Mixed green salad with bottled cilantro dressing

Game Plan

1 While oven preheats for quesadillas:

  • Chop ingredients for chili.

2 While chili simmers:

  • Squeeze lime for juice for chili.

  • Assemble quesadillas.

3 While quesadillas bake:

  • Toss salad.

Beef and Beer Chili

Cornmeal absorbs some of the liquid to help thicken the chili to a satisfying consistency.

1½ cups chopped red onion (about 1 medium)
1   cup chopped red bell pepper (about 1 small)
8   ounces ground beef, extra lean
2   garlic cloves, minced
1½ tablespoons chili powder
2   teaspoons ground cumin
1   teaspoon sugar
½   teaspoon salt
½   teaspoon dried oregano
1   (19-ounce) can red kidney beans, rinsed and drained
1   (14.5-ounce) can no-salt-added diced tomatoes, undrained
1   (14-ounce) can low-sodium beef broth
1   (12-ounce) bottle beer (such as Budweiser)
1   tablespoon yellow cornmeal
1   tablespoon fresh lime juice

❶ Combine first 4 ingredients in a large Dutch oven over medium-high heat. Cook 5 minutes or until beef is browned, stirring to crumble. Stir in chili powder, cumin, sugar, and salt; cook 1 minute. Add oregano and next 4 ingredients; bring to a boil. Reduce heat; simmer 15 minutes. Stir in cornmeal; cook 5 minutes. Stir in juice. Yield: 4 servings (serving size: 1½ cups).

CALORIES 261 (20% from fat); FAT 5.7g (sat 2.1g, mono 2g, poly 0.2g); PROTEIN 18.3g; CARB 30.3g; FIBER 8.3g; CHOL 30mg; IRON 3.7mg; SODIUM 799mg; CALC 74mg

Make-Ahead Tip: Prepare an extra batch of the chili; freeze in single-serving zip-top plastic bags up to 3 months. Thaw overnight in the refrigerator, and reheat in the microwave.

Nonstop, No-Chop Chili

Ground round combines effortlessly with the robust flavors of salsa, chili powder, cumin, and dried oregano for a savory dinner in a flash.

¾ pound ground round
Cooking spray
2 cups water
1½ cups frozen whole-kernel corn
1 cup bottled salsa
2 tablespoons chili powder
1 tablespoon sugar
2½ teaspoons ground cumin
1½ teaspoons dried oregano
¼ teaspoon salt
1 (16-ounce) can chili beans, undrained
1 (14.5-ounce) can no-salt-added diced tomatoes, undrained

❶ Cook ground round in a large Dutch oven coated with cooking spray over medium-high heat 4 minutes or until beef is browned, stirring occasionally. Stir in water and remaining ingredients, and bring to a boil. Reduce heat, and simmer 25 minutes, stirring occasionally. Yield: 6 servings (serving size: about 1 cup).

CALORIES 254 (28% from fat); FAT 8g (sat 2.8g, mono 2.4g, poly 0.6g); PROTEIN 18g; CARB 30.5g; FIBER 7.2g; CHOL 24mg; IRON 3.9mg; SODIUM 649mg; CALC 96mg

MENU *serves 6*

Nonstop, No-Chop Chili

Colby-Jack chiles
Cut a lengthwise slit down center of each of 6 (4-inch-long) Anaheim chiles; discard seeds and membranes. Arrange chiles in a 9-inch pie plate. Cover with heavy-duty plastic wrap. Microwave at HIGH 3 minutes or until crisp-tender; drain. Return chiles to pie plate. Split 3 colby-Jack cheese sticks (such as Sargento) in half lengthwise; stuff each chile with 1 piece of cheese. Microwave at HIGH 30 seconds or until cheese melts.

Corn bread twists (such as Pillsbury)

Game Plan

1 Preheat oven for corn bread twists.

2 Cook ground round mixture.

3 While soup simmers:

  • Bake corn bread twists.

  • Prepare chiles.

MENU *serves 4*

Pork and Hominy Chili

Strawberry agua fresca

Combine 2 cups quartered strawberries, 1 cup cold water, 2 tablespoons sugar, and 1 tablespoon chopped fresh mint in a blender or food processor; process 2 minutes or until smooth. Strain strawberry mixture through a sieve into a bowl; discard solids. Add 2 cups cold water and 2 teaspoons fresh lemon juice; chill. Serve over ice.

Blue corn tortilla chips

Game Plan

1 Trim and chop pork and vegetables.

2 While pork and vegetables sauté:

• Quarter strawberries for agua fresca.

3 While chili simmers:

• Blend ingredients for agua fresca; chill.

Pork and Hominy Chili

You can also prepare this recipe by substituting turkey or chicken breast for the pork chops.

2 teaspoons canola oil
8 ounces boneless center-cut pork chops, trimmed and cubed
1 cup chopped onion (about 1 medium)
¾ cup chopped green bell pepper
2 teaspoons bottled minced garlic
1 tablespoon chili powder
2 teaspoons ground cumin
¼ teaspoon salt
¼ teaspoon freshly ground black pepper
⅛ teaspoon ground red pepper
¼ cup no-salt-added tomato paste
1 (15.5-ounce) can golden hominy, rinsed and drained
1 (14.5-ounce) can no-salt-added diced tomatoes, undrained
1 (14-ounce) can fat-free, less-sodium chicken broth
¼ cup light sour cream

❶ Heat oil in a large saucepan over medium-high heat. Add pork to pan; sauté 5 minutes or until lightly browned. Add onion, bell pepper, and garlic; sauté 5 minutes or until tender. Stir in chili powder and next 4 ingredients. Cook 1 minute, stirring constantly. Stir in tomato paste, hominy, tomatoes, and broth; bring to a boil. Reduce heat, and simmer 10 minutes. Serve with sour cream. Yield: 4 servings (serving size: about 1½ cups chili and 1 tablespoon sour cream).

CALORIES 238 (29% from fat); FAT 7.8g (sat 2.5g, mono 3g, poly 1.3g); PROTEIN 17.6g; CARB 24.6g; FIBER 5.2g; CHOL 33mg; IRON 2.1mg; SODIUM 650mg; CALC 61mg

Shrimp and Egg Flower Soup

Better than takeout, this fast Cantonese-style menu works both for weeknight dining and impromptu entertaining. Drizzle the egg into the soup while stirring to create "flowers."

- 2 tablespoons cornstarch
- 2 tablespoons water
- 5 cups fat-free, less-sodium chicken broth
- 1 tablespoon dry sherry
- 1 tablespoon low-sodium soy sauce
- 1½ teaspoons grated peeled fresh ginger
- 1 teaspoon dark sesame oil
- 2 cups (4 ounces) presliced mushrooms
- 1 cup shredded carrot
- 1 cup frozen petite peas, thawed
- ¾ pound peeled and deveined medium shrimp, cut lengthwise
- 2 large eggs, lightly beaten
- ¼ cup thinly sliced green onions

❶ Combine cornstarch and water in a small bowl, stirring with a whisk.
❷ Combine cornstarch mixture, broth, and next 4 ingredients in a large saucepan; bring to a boil. Add mushrooms and carrot; cook 2 minutes. Add peas and shrimp; cook 3 minutes or until shrimp are done. Remove from heat. Slowly drizzle egg into broth mixture, stirring constantly. Stir in onions. Yield: 4 servings (serving size: 2 cups).

CALORIES 226 (23% from fat); FAT 5.7g (sat 1.4g, mono 1.3g, poly 1.1g); PROTEIN 26.7g; CARB 15.6g; FIBER 4g; CHOL 235mg; IRON 4.1mg; SODIUM 841mg; CALC 104mg

Quick Tip: To save time, purchase frozen, peeled, and deveined shrimp.

MENU *serves 4*

Shrimp and Egg Flower Soup

Snow pea and water chestnut salad
Combine 4 cups fresh snow peas, 2 tablespoons chopped green onions, and 1 (5-ounce) can drained, sliced water chestnuts in a large bowl. Combine 2 tablespoons rice wine vinegar, 1 tablespoon low-sodium soy sauce, 2 teaspoons toasted sesame seeds, 1 teaspoon sugar, and 2 teaspoons dark sesame oil; stir with a whisk. Drizzle over snow pea mixture; toss well to coat.

Store-bought almond cookies

Game Plan

1 While broth mixture comes to a boil:
- Prepare salad.
- Shred carrot, slice green onions, and beat eggs.

Shrimp and Crab Gumbo

Combine 2 cups zinfandel or other fruity dry red wine and ¼ cup sugar in a small saucepan. Boil 10 to 12 minutes or until reduced to ½ cup. Remove from heat; stir in 2 cups frozen pitted dark cherries. Serve over vanilla frozen yogurt.

Game Plan

1 While water for rice comes to a boil:
  - Chop onion and bell pepper.
  - Slice celery and mince garlic.

2 While rice cooks:
  - Brown flour in skillet.

3 While gumbo simmers:
  - Cook bacon.
  - Bring zinfandel syrup to a boil and reduce.
  - Add cherries.

Traditionally, gumbo begins with a roux of butter and flour. Toasting the flour in a dry pan on the stove provides a flavorful, low-fat substitute for a roux in this Creole specialty.

⅓ cup all-purpose flour
3 bacon slices, diced
2 cups finely chopped onion
1½ cups finely chopped green bell pepper (about 1 large)
4 celery stalks, thinly sliced
4 garlic cloves, minced
1 cup water
2 (14-ounce) cans fat-free, less-sodium chicken broth, divided
2 teaspoons salt-free Cajun seasoning
½ teaspoon salt
¼ teaspoon crushed red pepper
1 (16-ounce) bag frozen cut okra, thawed
1 pound peeled and deveined medium shrimp
2 (6-ounce) cans lump crabmeat, drained
3 cups hot cooked long-grain white rice
Hot pepper sauce (optional)

❶ Place flour in a small skillet; cook 5 minutes over medium heat or until brown, stirring constantly. Place in a small bowl; cool.

❷ Cook bacon in a Dutch oven over medium-high heat 3 minutes. Add onion, bell pepper, celery, and garlic; sauté 10 minutes or until vegetables are tender and lightly browned. Add water, and cook 1 minute, stirring constantly.

❸ Combine toasted flour and 1 can chicken broth in a medium bowl, stirring with a whisk. Gradually pour broth mixture into pan. Stir in 1 can chicken broth, Cajun seasoning, salt, crushed red pepper, and okra; bring to a boil. Cover, reduce heat, and simmer 15 minutes.

❹ Add shrimp; cook 3 minutes or until done. Gently stir in crabmeat. Remove from heat; serve gumbo over rice with hot pepper sauce, if desired. Yield: 6 servings (serving size: ½ cup rice and 1¼ cups gumbo).

CALORIES 464 (28% from fat); FAT 9g (sat 2.9g, mono 3.4g, poly 1.7g); PROTEIN 33.8g; CARB 60.2g; FIBER 5.4g; CHOL 160mg; IRON 5.5mg; SODIUM 955mg; CALC 192mg

Chipotle Chicken and Tomato Soup

A chipotle chile (canned smoked jalapeño pepper) adds heat to this soup. If you want to tame the spice, substitute ½ teaspoon smoked paprika for the chile.

½   teaspoon ground cumin
1   (15.5-ounce) can navy beans, rinsed and drained
1   (14.5-ounce) can no-salt-added stewed tomatoes
1   (14-ounce) can fat-free, less-sodium chicken broth
1   chipotle chile, canned in adobo sauce, finely chopped
2   cups chopped cooked chicken breast (about ½ pound)
1   tablespoon extra-virgin olive oil
½   cup reduced-fat sour cream
¼   cup chopped fresh cilantro

❶ Combine first 5 ingredients in a large saucepan; bring to a boil. Cover, reduce heat, and simmer 10 minutes. Partially mash tomatoes and beans with a potato masher. Stir in chicken; cook 2 minutes or until thoroughly heated. Remove from heat; stir in oil. Place 1¼ cups soup in each of 4 bowls. Top each serving with 2 tablespoons sour cream and 1 tablespoon cilantro. Yield: 4 servings.

CALORIES 325 (28% from fat); FAT 10g (sat 3.6g, mono 4.4g, poly 1.1g); PROTEIN 28.9g; CARB 30.4g; FIBER 7.5g; CHOL 58mg; IRON 3.1mg; SODIUM 741mg; CALC 120mg

Ingredient Tip:
Jicama, a round root vegetable commonly found in supermarkets and Latin groceries, adds crunch to the salad.

MENU *serves 4*

Chipotle Chicken and Tomato Soup

Orange and jicama salad

Combine 2 cups orange sections, 1 cup julienne-cut jicama, and ½ cup vertically sliced red onion in a large bowl. Combine 2 tablespoons fresh lime juice, 1 tablespoon extra-virgin olive oil, 1 tablespoon honey, and ¼ teaspoon salt; stir with a whisk. Drizzle over salad; toss gently to coat. Sprinkle with 1 tablespoon chopped chives.

Baked tortilla chips

Game Plan

1   Rinse and drain beans, and chop chipotle chile for soup.

2   While bean mixture comes to a boil:
•Chop chicken and cilantro for soup.

3   While bean mixture simmers:
•Prepare salad.

MENU *serves 4*

Spicy Mulligatawny

Pita wedges

Ice cream with sautéed pears

Toss 2 cups sliced peeled pear with 1 teaspoon lemon juice. Heat 1 tablespoon butter in a nonstick skillet over medium-high heat. Add pear; sauté 6 minutes or until tender. Stir in 2 tablespoons brown sugar. Serve over vanilla low-fat ice cream; top with crushed gingersnaps.

Game Plan

1. Chop and measure ingredients for soup.

2. While soup simmers:
   - Prepare and sauté pear for dessert; keep warm.
   - Crush gingersnaps for dessert.
   - Cut pitas into wedges.

Spicy Mulligatawny

The name of this highly seasoned Indian soup means "pepper water." It gets quite a kick from the combination of curry powder, ground ginger, and crushed red pepper, but you can halve those ingredients if you don't like spicy foods.

- 1 tablespoon canola oil, divided
- ½ pound skinless, boneless chicken breast, cut into bite-sized pieces
- 1 cup chopped peeled Gala or Braeburn apple
- ¾ cup chopped onion
- ½ cup chopped carrot
- ½ cup chopped celery
- ½ cup chopped green bell pepper
- 2 tablespoons all-purpose flour
- 1 tablespoon curry powder
- 1 teaspoon ground ginger
- ½ teaspoon crushed red pepper
- ¼ teaspoon salt
- 2 (14-ounce) cans fat-free, less-sodium chicken broth
- ⅓ cup mango chutney
- ¼ cup tomato paste

Chopped fresh parsley (optional)

1 Heat 1 teaspoon oil in a Dutch oven over medium-high heat. Add chicken, and sauté 3 minutes. Remove from pan; set aside.

2 Heat 2 teaspoons oil in pan. Add apple and next 4 ingredients; sauté 5 minutes, stirring frequently. Stir in flour and next 4 ingredients; cook 1 minute. Stir in broth, chutney, and tomato paste; bring to a boil.

3 Reduce heat; simmer 8 minutes. Return chicken to pan; cook 2 minutes or until mixture is thoroughly heated. Sprinkle with parsley, if desired. Yield: 4 servings (serving size: 1¼ cups).

CALORIES 236 (18% from fat); FAT 4.8g (sat 0.8g, mono 1.1g, poly 2.3g); PROTEIN 18g; CARB 31g; FIBER 4.9g; CHOL 33mg; IRON 1.9mg; SODIUM 599mg; CALC 42mg

Quick Tip: Slightly frozen chicken cuts quickly and easily. Place raw chicken in the freezer 20 minutes before cutting into bite-sized pieces.

Quick Avgolemono, Orzo, and Chicken Soup

Avgolemono (ahv-goh-LEH-moh-noh) is a tangy Greek soup that combines chicken broth, eggs, and lemon juice. Traditional versions include rice; our interpretation uses orzo.

6 cups fat-free, less-sodium chicken broth
1 teaspoon finely chopped fresh dill
½ cup uncooked orzo
4 large eggs
⅓ cup fresh lemon juice
1 cup shredded carrot
¼ teaspoon salt
¼ teaspoon pepper
8 ounces skinless, boneless chicken breast, cut into bite-sized pieces

1 Bring broth and dill to a boil in a large saucepan. Add orzo. Reduce heat; simmer 5 minutes or until orzo is slightly tender. Remove pan from heat.

2 Place eggs and juice in a blender; process until smooth. Remove 1 cup broth from pan with a ladle, making sure to leave out orzo. With blender on, slowly add broth; process until smooth.

3 Add carrot, salt, pepper, and chicken to pan. Bring to a simmer over medium-low heat, and cook 5 minutes or until chicken and orzo are done. Reduce heat to low. Slowly stir in egg mixture; cook 30 seconds, stirring constantly (do not boil). Yield: 4 servings (serving size: 2 cups).

CALORIES 228 (25% from fat); FAT 6.3g (sat 1.9g, mono 2.2g, poly 1g); PROTEIN 25.3g; CARB 16.6g; FIBER 2.9g; CHOL 244mg; IRON 2.6mg; SODIUM 855mg; CALC 68mg

MENU *serves 4*

Quick Avgolemono, Orzo, and Chicken Soup

Ricotta-garlic pita wedges

Preheat broiler. Combine ⅓ cup part-skim ricotta cheese, 1 teaspoon chopped fresh oregano, ⅛ teaspoon salt, ⅛ teaspoon freshly ground black pepper, and 1 minced garlic clove in a small bowl. Place 8 pita wedges on a baking sheet; broil 2 minutes or until toasted. Top each wedge with 4 teaspoons ricotta mixture. Broil 1 minute or until cheese is lightly browned.

Tossed salad with bottled Greek dressing

Game Plan

1 While broiler preheats:

- Prepare ricotta mixture for pita wedges.
- Boil broth for soup.
- Squeeze lemon for juice for soup.
- Shred carrot and cut chicken into bite-sized pieces for soup.

2 While soup simmers:

- Prepare salad.
- Broil pita wedges.

Turkey Noodle Soup

Enjoy a soup full of tender noodles, fresh veggies, and juicy turkey in just 35 minutes. It's an
easy year-round soup, and you can substitute shredded chicken for the turkey, if you prefer.

Cooking spray
  1 cup (¼-inch-thick) slices carrot
  ¾ cup chopped onion
  4 garlic cloves, minced
  1 cup (¼-inch-thick) slices celery
  ¼ teaspoon salt
  ¼ teaspoon freshly ground black pepper
  6 cups fat-free, less-sodium chicken broth
  2 cups (3 ounces) uncooked egg noodles
  1 tablespoon low-sodium soy sauce
  1 bay leaf
  2 cups shredded cooked turkey
Coarsely ground black pepper (optional)

❶ Heat a large saucepan over medium-high
heat; coat with cooking spray. Add carrot,
onion, and garlic; sauté 5 minutes or until
onion is lightly browned. Add celery, salt,
and ¼ teaspoon pepper; sauté 3 minutes. Add
broth and next 3 ingredients; bring to a boil.
Reduce heat, and simmer 5 minutes. Add
turkey; cook 3 minutes. Discard bay leaf.
Sprinkle with coarsely ground black pepper,
if desired. Yield: 4 servings (serving size:
2 cups).

CALORIES 280 (23% from fat); FAT 7.2g (sat 2.6g, mono 1.1g,
poly 1.4g); PROTEIN 29.1g; CARB 24.3g; FIBER 2.3g; CHOL 80mg;
IRON 2.6mg; SODIUM 544mg; CALC 79mg

Quick Tip: Purchase prechopped onion,
bottled minced garlic, and presliced celery and
carrots in the supermarket produce section.

Udon-Beef Noodle Bowl

This entrée falls somewhere between a soup and a noodle dish that can easily be enjoyed using either chopsticks or a fork.

8 ounces uncooked udon noodles (thick, round fresh Japanese wheat noodles) or spaghetti
1½ teaspoons bottled minced garlic
½ teaspoon crushed red pepper
2 (14¼-ounce) cans low-sodium beef broth
3 tablespoons low-sodium soy sauce
3 tablespoons sake (rice wine) or dry sherry
1 tablespoon honey
Cooking spray
2 cups sliced shiitake mushroom caps (about 4 ounces)
½ cup thinly sliced carrot
8 ounces top round, thinly sliced
¾ cup diagonally cut green onions
1 (6-ounce) bag prewashed baby spinach

❶ Cook noodles according to package directions; drain, and set aside.
❷ Place garlic, pepper, and broth in a large saucepan. Bring to a boil; reduce heat, and simmer 10 minutes.
❸ Combine soy sauce, sake, and honey in a small bowl; stir with a whisk.
❹ Heat a large nonstick skillet over medium-high heat; coat with cooking spray. Add mushrooms and carrot; sauté 2 minutes. Stir in soy sauce mixture, and cook 2 minutes, stirring constantly. Add vegetable mixture to broth mixture. Stir in beef; cook 2 minutes or until beef loses its pink color. Stir in noodles, green onions, and spinach. Serve immediately. Yield: 5 servings (serving size: about 1½ cups).

CALORIES 306 (16% from fat); FAT 5.6g (sat 1.8g, mono 2g, poly 0.4g); PROTEIN 22.4g; CARB 36.6g; FIBER 2.4g; CHOL 39mg; IRON 3.4mg; SODIUM 707mg; CALC 59mg

Quick Tip:
To speed the slicing of the shiitakes, stack a few caps on top of one another, and then slice the entire stack.

MENU

Udon-Beef Noodle Bowl

Steamed edamame (fresh soybeans)

Gingered wonton chips with ice cream
Preheat oven to 400°. Cut 10 wonton wrappers into thin strips. Combine wonton strips and ½ teaspoon dark sesame oil in a small bowl, tossing to coat. Add 2 teaspoons sugar and ½ teaspoon ground ginger, tossing to coat. Arrange strips on a baking sheet. Bake at 400° for 8 minutes or until crisp, turning once. Serve wonton chips with vanilla low-fat ice cream.

Game Plan

1 Preheat oven for wonton chips.

2 While water for noodles and broth mixture come to a boil:
  • Prepare wontons for baking.
  • Slice mushrooms, carrot, and beef.

3 While noodles cook and broth mixture simmers:
  • Bake wonton chips.
  • Steam edamame until tender.
  • Sauté vegetables for noodle bowl.

Southwest Cilantro Fish Stew

A generous squeeze of lime juice enhances the flavors of this dish inspired by the Baja Coast.

1   tablespoon olive oil
2   cups chopped onion
1   cup (¼-inch-thick) slices carrot
1   cup (¼-inch-thick) slices celery
3   garlic cloves, minced
1   jalapeño pepper, sliced
4   cups fat-free, less-sodium chicken broth
2   cups cubed peeled Yukon gold or red potato
1   cup dry white wine
½   cup chopped fresh cilantro
1   (15-ounce) can crushed tomatoes, undrained
1   pound halibut, cut into bite-sized pieces
½   pound peeled and deveined large shrimp
Cilantro sprigs (optional)

❶ Heat oil in a large Dutch oven over medium-high heat. Add onion and next 4 ingredients to pan; sauté 5 minutes or until tender. Stir in broth and next 4 ingredients; bring to a boil. Reduce heat, and simmer 15 minutes or until potato is tender. Add fish and shrimp; cook an additional 5 minutes or until fish and shrimp are done. Ladle 2½ cups stew into each of 4 bowls. Garnish with cilantro sprigs, if desired. Yield: 4 servings.

CALORIES 372 (18% from fat); FAT 7.6g (sat 1.2g, mono 3.6g, poly 1.8g); PROTEIN 42.1g; CARB 32.8g; FIBER 5.7g; CHOL 122mg; IRON 5.4mg; SODIUM 684mg; CALC 167mg

White Bean and Sausage Ragout with Tomatoes, Kale, and Zucchini

Chock-full of vegetables, this colorful ragout will warm you up on a chilly winter evening.

1 tablespoon olive oil
½ cup chopped onion
2 (4-ounce) links chicken sausage, cut into ½-inch slices
1 zucchini, quartered and cut into ½-inch slices (about 2 cups)
3 garlic cloves, peeled and crushed
6 cups chopped trimmed kale (about ½ pound)
½ cup water
¼ teaspoon salt
¼ teaspoon freshly ground black pepper
2 (16-ounce) cans cannellini beans or other white beans, rinsed and drained
1 (14.5-ounce) can diced tomatoes, undrained

❶ Heat oil in a large skillet over medium-high heat. Add onion and sausage; sauté 4 minutes or until sausage is browned. Add zucchini and garlic; cook 2 minutes. Add kale and remaining ingredients; bring to a boil. Cover, reduce heat, and simmer 10 minutes or until thoroughly heated. Serve immediately. Yield: 4 servings (serving size: 1¾ cups).

CALORIES 467 (20% from fat); FAT 10.2g (sat 2.3g, mono 4.6g, poly 2.5g); PROTEIN 28.5g; CARB 71.8g; FIBER 15.4g; CHOL 42mg; IRON 8.8mg; SODIUM 764mg; CALC 370mg

Quick Tip: Look for bags of trimmed and washed kale at the supermarket.

MENU *serves 4*

White Bean and Sausage Ragout with Tomatoes, Kale, and Zucchini

Garlic-rosemary bruschetta
Cut a 4-ounce French bread baguette into ¼-inch slices; broil 3 minutes or until golden brown. Cut 1 peeled garlic clove in half; rub cut sides of garlic clove and a sprig of rosemary over bread. Brush with 2 teaspoons olive oil; sprinkle with ¼ teaspoon salt and ⅛ teaspoon freshly ground black pepper.

Green salad with bottled low-fat vinaigrette

Game Plan

1 Chop vegetables and sausage for ragout.

2 While ragout simmers:
•Prepare bruschetta.
•Toss salad.

MENU *serves 6*

Duck Stew

Goat cheese crostini
Combine 1 tablespoon chopped bottled roasted red bell peppers, 1 tablespoon chopped fresh parsley, 1½ teaspoons chopped fresh rosemary, and 1 (3-ounce) package goat cheese in a small bowl; stir with a whisk. Cut 1 (8-ounce) French bread baguette into 8 slices; lightly toast bread slices. Spread goat cheese mixture evenly over toasted bread slices.

Spinach salad with low-fat bottled vinaigrette

Game Plan

1 While duck and sausage cook:

- Rinse and drain beans.
- Chop celery, carrot, and onion.

2 While stew cooks:

- Prepare goat cheese mixture for crostini; slice and toast bread slices.
- Toss salad.

Duck Stew

For a thicker consistency, coarsely mash 1 can of beans with a fork or potato masher before adding to Dutch oven. Enjoy leftover stew for lunch the next day.

2 teaspoons canola oil
1 pound boneless duck breast halves, skinned and cut into 1-inch pieces
½ pound smoked turkey sausage, sliced
1 cup chopped celery
1 cup chopped carrot
1 cup chopped onion
1½ teaspoons bottled minced garlic
1 cup fat-free, less-sodium chicken broth
2 (15.8-ounce) cans Great Northern beans, rinsed and drained
1 (14.5-ounce) can diced tomatoes, undrained

❶ Heat oil in a Dutch oven over medium-high heat. Add duck and sausage; cook 7 minutes or until browned. Remove duck and sausage from pan. Add celery and next 3 ingredients to pan; sauté 7 minutes. Return duck mixture to pan. Add broth, beans, and tomatoes; bring to a boil. Reduce heat, and simmer 10 minutes. Yield: 6 servings (serving size: about 1⅓ cups).

CALORIES 296 (24% from fat); FAT 7.8g (sat 2.3g, mono 2.7g, poly 1.5g); PROTEIN 27.5g; CARB 30g; FIBER 8.6g; CHOL 71mg; IRON 8.9mg; SODIUM 712mg; CALC 107mg

Quick Tip: Buy prechopped celery, onions, and carrots for the stew and prewashed fresh spinach for the salad, if you're making the entire menu.

Ropa Vieja

This Cuban stew is made by braising beef until it can be shredded—thus the recipe name which means "old clothes." Serve with tortillas, and add hot sauce on the side for those who like it fiery. Because the meat is shredded, it's also suitable for tacos and burritos.

Cooking spray
- 2 (1-pound) flank steaks, trimmed
- 3 cups thinly vertically sliced red onion
- 2 cups red bell pepper strips (about 2 peppers)
- 2 cups green bell pepper strips (about 2 peppers)
- 4 garlic cloves, minced
- 6 tablespoons thinly sliced pitted green olives
- 1 teaspoon salt
- 1 teaspoon dried oregano
- 1 teaspoon ground cumin
- ½ teaspoon dried rosemary, crushed
- ½ teaspoon freshly ground black pepper
- 6 tablespoons sherry vinegar
- 3 cups fat-free, less-sodium beef broth
- 1 tablespoon no-salt-added tomato paste
- 2 bay leaves
- ½ cup chopped fresh cilantro

❶ Heat a large Dutch oven over medium-high heat; coat with cooking spray. Add 1 steak to pan; cook 2½ minutes on each side or until browned. Remove steak from pan; repeat procedure with cooking spray and remaining steak.

❷ Reduce heat to medium. Add onion, bell peppers, and garlic to pan; cook 7 minutes or until tender, stirring frequently. Stir in olives and next 5 ingredients; cook 30 seconds or until fragrant. Stir in vinegar, scraping pan to loosen browned bits; cook 2 minutes or until liquid almost evaporates. Stir in broth, tomato paste, and bay leaves. Add steaks; bring to a simmer. Cover, reduce heat, and cook 1½ hours or until steaks are very tender. Discard bay leaves.

❸ Remove steaks from pan; shred with 2 forks. Add shredded beef and cilantro to pan; stir to mix. Yield: 8 servings (serving size: about ¾ cup).

CALORIES 229 (36% from fat); FAT 9.1g (sat 3.4g, mono 3.9g, poly 0.6g); PROTEIN 26g; CARB 9.6g; FIBER 2g; CHOL 40mg; IRON 2.4mg; SODIUM 614mg; CALC 53mg

MENU *serves 8*

Ropa Vieja

Grapefruit-avocado salad

Combine 4 cups pink grapefruit sections, 1 cup diced peeled avocado, and ½ cup thinly vertically sliced red onion in a large bowl. Combine 2 tablespoons chopped fresh cilantro, 2 tablespoons fresh lime juice, 1 tablespoon canola oil, ½ teaspoon sugar, ¼ teaspoon salt, and ¼ teaspoon ground red pepper; stir with a whisk. Drizzle dressing over salad; toss gently to coat.

Warm tortillas

Game Plan

1 Prepare vegetables, garlic, and olives for stew.

2 While stew cooks:
- •Prepare salad.
- •Chop cilantro for soup.
- •Warm tortillas.

Sandwiches

Steak Sandwiches with
Worcestershire Mayonnaise,
page 73

Salad Niçoise in Pita Pockets

Fresh green beans give these tuna sandwiches, inspired by the classic French salad, an interesting crunch. Cook the beans in the microwave to save time in the kitchen.

1 cup (1-inch) cut fresh green beans (about 4 ounces)
1 tablespoon water
¼ cup niçoise olives, pitted and chopped (about 18 olives)
1 tablespoon capers
1 (12-ounce) can solid white tuna in water, drained
1 tablespoon extra-virgin olive oil
1 tablespoon fresh lemon juice
½ teaspoon salt
2 (6-inch) whole wheat pita rounds, halved
4 curly leaf lettuce leaves

❶ Combine beans and water in a microwave-safe bowl; cover with plastic wrap. Microwave at HIGH 1½ minutes or until beans are crisp-tender; drain. Rinse with cold water; drain well, and cool. Stir in olives, capers, and tuna.
❷ Combine oil, juice, and salt; stir with a whisk. Pour oil mixture over tuna mixture; toss gently to coat.
❸ Line each pita half with 1 lettuce leaf; spoon about ½ cup tuna mixture into each lettuce-lined pita half. Yield: 4 servings (serving size: 1 pita half).

CALORIES 253 (30% from fat); FAT 8.3g (sat 1.5g, mono 4.4g, poly 1.7g); PROTEIN 24.1g; CARB 21.6g; FIBER 4.2g; CHOL 36mg; IRON 2.6mg; SODIUM 702mg; CALC 48mg

MENU *serves 4*

Salad Niçoise in Pita Pockets

Potato salad
Combine 2 tablespoons fresh lemon juice, 2 tablespoons light mayonnaise, 2 tablespoons fat-free sour cream, ½ teaspoon salt, and ¼ teaspoon pepper in a large bowl; stir with a whisk. Add 2 pounds cooked quartered small red potatoes, ½ cup chopped green onions, and 2 strips of bacon, cooked and crumbled; stir to combine.

Lemonade

Game Plan

1 While potatoes cook:
  • Chop green onions.
  • Cook bacon.
  • Prepare mayonnaise mixture.
  • Pit and chop olives.
2 While green beans cool:
  • Combine tuna, olives, and capers.
  • Prepare dressing.

MENU *serves 6*

Summer Crab Rolls

Coleslaw

Limeade
Combine ¾ cup sugar and ¾ cup water in a microwave-safe dish; microwave at HIGH 3 minutes or until sugar dissolves. Cool. Add 2 cups water and ½ cup fresh lime juice. Serve over ice.

Game Plan

1 Prepare vegetables and chives for sandwiches.

2 While skillet heats:
  • Prepare crab mixture.

3 While water and sugar microwave:
  • Assemble sandwiches.
  • Squeeze limes for juice for drink.

4 Prepare limeade.

Summer Crab Rolls

These crab sandwiches are a snap to prepare. You can find a 12-pack of dinner rolls in the bakery section of your supermarket. Pick up a package of cabbage-and-carrot coleslaw mix, and toss it with light coleslaw dressing for a quick side.

¼ cup finely chopped Vidalia or other sweet onion
¼ cup low-fat mayonnaise
2 tablespoons chopped fresh chives
1 tablespoon Dijon mustard
1 teaspoon fresh lemon juice
½ teaspoon hot pepper sauce (such as Tabasco)
1 pound lump crabmeat, drained and shell pieces removed
1½ tablespoons butter, softened
12 (1-ounce) dinner rolls, cut in half horizontally
12 Boston lettuce leaves (about 1 small head)
6 plum tomatoes, each cut into 4 slices

❶ Combine first 7 ingredients in a large bowl; toss well.

❷ Heat a large nonstick skillet over medium heat. Spread butter onto cut sides of rolls. Place 6 roll halves, cut sides down, in pan, and cook 1 minute or until toasted. Repeat procedure with remaining roll halves. Spoon ¼ cup crab mixture onto each bottom roll half. Top each with 1 lettuce leaf and 2 tomato slices; top with remaining roll halves. Yield: 6 servings (serving size: 2 rolls).

CALORIES 320 (23% from fat); FAT 8.3g (sat 2g, mono 1.2g, poly 3.2g); PROTEIN 22.2g; CARB 40.8g; FIBER 2.9g; CHOL 83mg; IRON 3.4mg; SODIUM 696mg; CALC 132mg

Ingredient Tip: Substitute lobster or chopped shrimp for crab, if desired.

Shrimp and Crab Salad Rolls

We loved the kick of the horseradish. For milder flavor, use 1 teaspoon horseradish. If you can't find crabmeat, double the amount of coarsely chopped cooked shrimp.

3 tablespoons chopped green onions
3 tablespoons light mayonnaise
1 tablespoon prepared horseradish
2 teaspoons Dijon mustard
¼ teaspoon hot sauce
8 ounces coarsely chopped cooked shrimp (about 1½ cups chopped)
8 ounces lump crabmeat, drained and shell pieces removed
4 small whole wheat hoagie rolls, split and toasted
4 small Boston lettuce leaves

❶ Combine first 5 ingredients in a large bowl, and stir well. Add shrimp and crabmeat, stirring to combine. Line each hoagie roll with 1 lettuce leaf. Place ⅔ cup shrimp mixture in each bun. Yield: 4 servings.

CALORIES 331 (24% from fat); FAT 8.7g (sat 1.3g, mono 1g, poly 1.9g); PROTEIN 29.7g; CARB 35.6g; FIBER 5.4g; CHOL 172mg; IRON 4.2mg; SODIUM 777mg; CALC 153mg

Quick Tip: Get a head start by using frozen, thawed, cooked, peeled shrimp, available near the meat department or in the frozen foods aisle of supermarkets.

MENU *serves 4*

Shrimp and Crab Salad Rolls

Quick corn and potato chowder
Combine 2 cups refrigerated hash brown potatoes with onions and peppers (such as Simply Potatoes), 1½ cups 1% low-fat milk, 1 (14¾-ounce) can cream-style corn, ¾ teaspoon salt, and ¼ teaspoon black pepper in a saucepan. Bring to a boil, stirring occasionally. Reduce heat, and simmer 8 minutes or until thickened, stirring occasionally. Ladle chowder into bowls; top each serving with 1½ teaspoons chopped fresh chives.

Strawberry sorbet

Game Plan

1 While chowder cooks:
 • Combine mayonnaise mixture for sandwiches.
 • Chop shrimp.
2 While buns toast:
 • Combine mayonnaise mixture with shrimp and crabmeat.
 • Wash lettuce leaves, and pat dry.
3 Assemble sandwiches.

Roast Chicken and Cranberry Sandwiches

Ripe tomato salad
Combine 2 tablespoons balsamic vinegar with 2 tablespoons brown sugar, and microwave at MEDIUM (50% power) until mixture comes to a boil (about 1½ to 2 minutes). Let stand until cool and slightly thick (about 5 minutes). Place ¾ cup salad greens on each of 4 plates. Slice 1 large yellow and 1 large red tomato; arrange on top of salad greens. Sprinkle ¼ teaspoon salt evenly over tomatoes. Drizzle with vinaigrette, and sprinkle evenly with 1 tablespoon pine nuts, if desired.

Game Plan

1 While vinaigrette microwaves:
- Prepare cream cheese mixture.

2 While vinaigrette cools:
- Chop chicken.
- Prepare vegetables for sandwiches and salad.
- Assemble sandwiches.

3 Assemble salads.

Roast Chicken and Cranberry Sandwiches

Cranberry chutney adds a pleasing sweetness to this new twist to chicken sandwiches.

¼   cup (2 ounces) ⅓-less-fat cream cheese
¼   cup bottled cranberry chutney (such as Crosse & Blackwell)
8   (1-ounce) slices multigrain bread
½   cup thinly sliced radishes
½   cup trimmed arugula or spinach
2   cups chopped roasted skinless, boneless chicken breast (about 2 breast halves)

❶ Combine cream cheese and cranberry chutney in a small bowl. Spread 1 tablespoon cream cheese mixture over each bread slice. Arrange one-fourth of radishes, arugula, and chicken on each of 4 bread slices. Top with remaining bread slices. Yield: 4 servings (serving size: 1 sandwich).

CALORIES 361 (23% from fat); FAT 9.1g (sat 3.6g, mono 3.2g, poly 1.2g); PROTEIN 30.3g; CARB 39.7g; FIBER 3.2g; CHOL 76mg; IRON 2.7mg; SODIUM 459mg; CALC 63mg

Quick Tip: Microwaving the liquid to dissolve the sugar in the dressing for the tomato salad helps the sugar granules disappear faster than whisking the mixture by hand.

Curried Chicken Salad in Naan

This fruited sandwich filling is a natural for breads such as naan (an Indian flatbread) or pita. It's also tasty on pumpernickel or sourdough bread.

- 6 tablespoons reduced-fat mayonnaise
- ½ teaspoon grated orange rind
- 1½ teaspoons orange juice
- 1 teaspoon curry powder
- ½ teaspoon grated peeled fresh ginger
- 2½ cups diced roasted skinless, boneless chicken breast (about ¾ pound)
- ¾ cup green seedless grapes, halved
- ¼ cup diced dried apricots
- ¼ cup thinly sliced green onions
- 2 tablespoons chopped, unsalted cashews
- 1 tablespoon chopped fresh parsley
- 4 (6-inch) naan breads
- 3 cups trimmed watercress

❶ Combine first 5 ingredients in a large bowl, and stir with a whisk. Add chicken and next 5 ingredients, tossing to coat.
❷ Heat naan according to package directions, if desired.
❸ Spoon about ¾ cup chicken mixture onto each naan. Top with ¾ cup watercress, and fold over. Yield: 4 servings (serving size: 1 sandwich).

CALORIES 458 (24% from fat); FAT 12.2g (sat 3g, mono 4.1g, poly 3.8g); PROTEIN 35.5g; CARB 52.7g; FIBER 5.5g; CHOL 72mg; IRON 3.8mg; SODIUM 602mg; CALC 83mg

Quick Tip: To chop dried apricots, coat the knife blade with cooking spray to keep the fruit from sticking to the blade. You can also use a sharp pair of kitchen shears.

MENU *serves 4*

Curried Chicken Salad in Naan

Baked sweet potato chips

Cranberry spritzers
Combine 2 cups cranberry juice with 1 cup sparkling water, and 1 cup orange juice in a small pitcher; chill until ready to serve. Pour 1 cup cranberry mixture into each of 4 ice-filled glasses.

Game Plan

1 Prepare cranberry spritzers.

2 While spritzers chill:
- Prepare salad.
- Assemble sandwiches.

Chicken and Bacon Roll-Ups

MENU *serves 4*

Chicken and Bacon Roll-Ups

Sweet potato chips

Mixed berry parfaits
Combine 2 cups blueberries and 2 cups sliced strawberries in a medium bowl. Combine 1/2 cup vanilla yogurt, 1 tablespoon honey, and 1/4 teaspoon grated lemon rind in a small bowl. Place 1/2 cup fruit mixture in each of 4 parfait glasses. Spoon 2 tablespoons yogurt mixture into each glass. Top each serving with 1/2 cup fruit mixture. Garnish with fresh mint sprigs, if desired. Refrigerate until ready to serve.

Game Plan

1 Assemble parfaits, and refrigerate.

2 Make mayonnaise mixture.

3 Shred lettuce and chicken; chop tomato.

4 Assemble wraps.

Ripe summer tomatoes are essential here. Cut the wraps in half crosswise to serve. For a smoky taste, try an applewood-smoked bacon (such as Nueske's).

1/2 cup reduced-fat mayonnaise
1 teaspoon minced fresh tarragon
2 teaspoons fresh lemon juice
4 (2.8-ounce) whole wheat flatbreads (such as Flatout)
2 cups shredded romaine lettuce
2 cups chopped tomato (about 2 medium)
4 center-cut bacon slices, cooked and drained
2 cups shredded skinless, boneless rotisserie chicken breast

1 Combine first 3 ingredients in a small bowl. Spread 2 tablespoons mayonnaise mixture over each flatbread. Top each with 1/2 cup lettuce, 1/2 cup tomato, 1 bacon slice, crumbled, and 1/2 cup chicken. Roll up. Yield: 4 servings (serving size: 1 wrap).

CALORIES 433 (27% from fat); FAT 13g (sat 2.6g, mono 2g, poly 0.9g); PROTEIN 34.8g; CARB 44.2g; FIBER 5.5g; CHOL 66mg; IRON 3.1mg; SODIUM 925mg; CALC 49mg

Flavor Tip: Substitute 1 teaspoon chopped fresh basil or chives for tarragon in the mayonnaise mixture, if you prefer.

Smoky Bacon and Blue Cheese Chicken Salad Pitas

The BLT sandwich is the inspiration for this tangy salad. You can make the chicken salad ahead, and place it in the pita halves just before serving.

¾ cup plain fat-free yogurt
¼ cup (1 ounce) crumbled blue cheese
2 tablespoons light mayonnaise
½ teaspoon freshly ground black pepper
3 cups shredded romaine lettuce
1½ cups shredded cooked chicken (about 6 ounces)
4 bacon slices, cooked and crumbled
2 tomatoes, seeded and chopped
4 (6-inch) whole wheat pitas, cut in half

❶ Combine first 4 ingredients in a small bowl. Combine lettuce, chicken, bacon, and tomatoes in a medium bowl. Drizzle yogurt mixture over chicken mixture; toss gently to coat. Spoon ½ cup chicken salad into each pita half. Serve immediately. Yield: 4 servings (serving size: 2 stuffed pita halves).

CALORIES 375 (29% from fat); FAT 12.1g (sat 3.7g, mono 3.6g, poly 3.1g); PROTEIN 26.1g; CARB 43.8g; FIBER 6.3g; CHOL 55mg; IRON 3.5mg; SODIUM 696mg; CALC 130mg

MENU *serves 4*

Smoky Bacon and Blue Cheese Chicken Salad Pitas

Herbed carrots
Cook 3 cups (1½-inch) pieces peeled carrots in boiling water 5 minutes or until crisp-tender; drain well. Rinse with cold water; drain. Combine 3 tablespoons white wine vinegar, 1 tablespoon extra-virgin olive oil, 1 teaspoon dried oregano, 1 teaspoon salt, ½ teaspoon freshly ground black pepper, and 1 minced garlic clove; drizzle over carrots. Cover and chill until ready to serve.

Fresh berries

Game Plan

1 Prepare carrots; cover and chill.

2 While carrots chill:
 •Prepare salad.
 •Place salad in pita halves.

Turkey-Vegetable Wraps

These easy, tasty wraps make a great weeknight meal. The bell pepper and corn add a nice crunch.

2 cups coarsely chopped smoked turkey breast (about 8 ounces)
2 cups gourmet salad greens
½ cup fresh corn kernels (about 1 ear)
½ cup chopped red bell pepper
¼ cup thinly sliced green onions
3 tablespoons light ranch dressing
4 (8-inch) flour tortillas

❶ Combine first 6 ingredients in a large bowl, tossing well to coat. Warm tortillas according to package directions. Top each tortilla with 1 cup turkey mixture; roll up. Cut each wrap in half diagonally. Yield: 4 servings (serving size: 1 wrap).

CALORIES 252 (26% from fat); FAT 7.2g (sat 1.2g, mono 2.3g, poly 3.3g); PROTEIN 18.2g; CARB 29.8g; FIBER 3g; CHOL 32mg; IRON 2.4mg; SODIUM 741mg; CALC 76mg

Quick Tip: Using bagged salad greens cuts down on preparation time.

Egg Salad BLTs

The slaw tastes better if you prepare it in advance. *Cornichon* is French for "gherkin," meaning a small pickle.

¼ cup fat-free mayonnaise
3 tablespoons thinly sliced green onions
3 tablespoons reduced-fat sour cream
2 teaspoons whole-grain Dijon mustard
½ teaspoon freshly ground black pepper
¼ teaspoon grated lemon rind
8 hard-cooked large eggs
8 (1½-ounce) slices peasant bread or firm sandwich bread, toasted
4 center-cut bacon slices, cooked and cut in half crosswise
8 (¼-inch-thick) slices tomato
4 large Boston lettuce leaves

❶ Combine first 6 ingredients in a medium bowl.
❷ Cut 2 eggs in half lengthwise, and reserve 2 yolks for another use. Coarsely chop remaining egg whites and whole eggs. Add eggs to mayonnaise mixture; stir gently to combine.
❸ Arrange 4 bread slices on a cutting board or work surface. Top each with ½ cup egg mixture, 2 bacon pieces, 2 tomato slices, 1 lettuce leaf, and 1 bread slice. Serve immediately. Yield: 4 servings (serving size: 1 sandwich).

CALORIES 371 (28% from fat); FAT 11.7g (sat 4.1g, mono 4.4g, poly 1.4g); PROTEIN 21.9g; CARB 44g; FIBER 2.4g; CHOL 329mg; IRON 4mg; SODIUM 892mg; CALC 70mg

MENU *serves 4*

Egg Salad BLTs

Slaw with feta
Combine 1 tablespoon white wine vinegar, 1 tablespoon fresh lemon juice, 1 tablespoon extra-virgin olive oil, 1 teaspoon sugar, ½ teaspoon salt, and ½ teaspoon freshly ground black pepper. Combine 4 cups packaged angel hair slaw, ½ cup chopped green onions, and ⅓ cup crumbled feta cheese. Drizzle dressing over slaw; toss to combine.

Cornichons

Game Plan

1 **Prepare slaw.**
2 **Cook eggs.**
3 **While eggs cook:**
   • Cook bacon.
   • Prepare vegetables and lemon rind for sandwiches.
   • Toast peasant bread slices.
4 **Combine ingredients for egg salad.**
5 **Assemble sandwiches.**

Falafel-Stuffed Pitas

The patties will seem small when you're forming them, but they fit perfectly in the pita halves. To prevent the falafel mixture from sticking to your hands, dip your hands into water before forming the patties. Look for tahini near the peanut butter and other nut butters in the supermarket.

FALAFEL:
- ¼ cup dry breadcrumbs
- ¼ cup chopped fresh cilantro
- 1½ teaspoons ground cumin
- ½ teaspoon salt
- ¼ teaspoon ground red pepper
- 2 garlic cloves, crushed
- 1 large egg
- 1 (15-ounce) can chickpeas (garbanzo beans), drained
- 1 tablespoon olive oil

SAUCE:
- ½ cup plain low-fat yogurt
- 2 tablespoons fresh lemon juice
- 2 tablespoons tahini (sesame-seed paste)
- 1 garlic clove, minced

REMAINING INGREDIENTS:
- 4 (6-inch) whole wheat pitas, cut in half
- 8 curly leaf lettuce leaves
- 16 (¼-inch-thick) slices tomato

❶ To prepare falafel, place first 8 ingredients in a food processor; process mixture until smooth. Divide mixture into 16 equal portions, and shape each portion into a ¼-inch-thick patty. Heat olive oil in a large nonstick skillet over medium-high heat. Add patties, and cook 5 minutes on each side or until browned.

❷ To prepare sauce, combine yogurt, lemon juice, tahini, and 1 garlic clove; stir with a whisk. Spread about 1½ tablespoons tahini sauce into each pita half. Fill each pita half with 1 lettuce leaf, 2 tomato slices, and 2 patties. Yield: 4 servings (serving size: 2 stuffed pita halves).

CALORIES 403 (28% from fat); FAT 12.6g (sat 1.9g, mono 5.6g, poly 3.9g); PROTEIN 15g; CARB 59g; FIBER 6.8g; CHOL 56mg; IRON 4.4mg; SODIUM 901mg; CALC 188mg

MENU *serves 4*

Falafel-Stuffed Pitas

Grape and walnut salad

Combine ½ cup plain low-fat yogurt, 2 tablespoons brown sugar, and a dash of ground cinnamon in a bowl. Add 3 cups halved red seedless grapes and 3 tablespoons chopped walnuts; stir well. Cover and chill until ready to serve.

Iced mint tea

Game Plan

1 Prepare grape salad; cover and chill.

2 While falafel patties cook:
- •Prepare sauce.
- •Wash lettuce.
- •Slice tomato.
- •Prepare tea.
- •Assemble sandwiches.

Southwest Pinto Bean Burgers with Chipotle Mayonnaise

Featuring fresh cilantro, jalapeños, and corn kernels, these hearty bean burgers are made even more memorable with a tongue-tingling chipotle mayo.

BURGERS:
- ½ cup diced onion
- ½ cup dry breadcrumbs
- ¼ cup chopped fresh cilantro
- 2 tablespoons minced seeded jalapeño pepper
- 2 tablespoons reduced-fat sour cream
- 1 teaspoon hot pepper sauce
- ½ teaspoon ground cumin
- ¼ teaspoon freshly ground black pepper
- ⅛ teaspoon salt
- 1 large egg, lightly beaten
- 1 (15-ounce) can pinto beans, rinsed and drained
- 1 (8¾-ounce) can no-salt-added whole-kernel corn, drained

CHIPOTLE MAYONNAISE:
- ¼ cup low-fat mayonnaise
- 1 teaspoon canned minced chipotle chile in adobo sauce

REMAINING INGREDIENTS:
- 1 tablespoon canola oil
- 4 (1½-ounce) whole wheat hamburger buns, toasted
- 4 romaine lettuce leaves

❶ To prepare burgers, combine first 10 ingredients in a large bowl. Add pinto beans and corn; partially mash with a fork. Divide bean mixture into 4 equal portions, shaping each into a 3½-inch patty, and refrigerate 10 minutes.
❷ To prepare chipotle mayonnaise, combine mayonnaise and chipotle in a small bowl; set aside.
❸ Heat oil in a large nonstick skillet over medium-high heat. Add patties to pan, and cook 4 minutes on each side or until thoroughly heated. Place patties on bottom halves of buns; top each patty with 1 tablespoon mayonnaise, 1 lettuce leaf, and top half of bun. Yield: 4 servings.

CALORIES 411 (23% from fat); FAT 10.7g (sat 1.9g, mono 3.2g, poly 3.2g); PROTEIN 15.2g; CARB 63.1g; FIBER 9.1g; CHOL 57mg; IRON 3.9mg; SODIUM 837mg; CALC 153mg

Portobello Cheeseburgers

Meaty mushrooms and garlicky aïoli sauce update traditional diner fare. Portobello mushrooms are well-paired with pungent Gorgonzola cheese. Or you can substitute crumbled blue cheese for Gorgonzola, if you like.

2 teaspoons olive oil
4 (4-inch) portobello caps
¼ teaspoon salt
¼ teaspoon black pepper
1 tablespoon bottled minced garlic
¼ cup (1 ounce) crumbled Gorgonzola cheese
3 tablespoons reduced-fat mayonnaise
4 (2-ounce) sandwich rolls
2 cups trimmed arugula
½ cup sliced bottled roasted red bell peppers

❶ Heat oil in a large nonstick skillet over medium-high heat. Sprinkle mushrooms with salt and black pepper. Add mushrooms to pan; sauté 4 minutes or until tender, turning once. Add garlic; sauté 30 seconds. Remove mushroom mixture from heat.
❷ Combine cheese and mayonnaise. Spread about 2 tablespoons mayonnaise mixture over bottom half of each roll; top each serving with ½ cup arugula and 2 tablespoons bell peppers. Place 1 mushroom on each serving, and top with top halves of rolls. Yield: 4 servings (serving size: 1 burger).

CALORIES 278 (32% from fat); FAT 9.9g (sat 3g, mono 1.7g, poly 0.4g); PROTEIN 9.3g; CARB 33.7g; FIBER 2.4g; CHOL 6mg; IRON 1.7mg; SODIUM 726mg; CALC 129mg

MENU *serves 4*

Portobello Cheeseburgers

Oven fries with aïoli
Preheat oven to 400°. Cut 2 pounds peeled baking potatoes into ¼-inch-thick strips. Place potatoes on a jelly-roll pan. Drizzle with 1 tablespoon canola oil and sprinkle with ½ teaspoon salt; toss to coat. Bake at 400° for 20 minutes or until tender and golden. Toss with 1½ tablespoons melted butter and 1½ tablespoons chopped fresh parsley. Combine ¼ cup reduced-fat mayonnaise, 2 teaspoons fresh lemon juice, ⅛ teaspoon ground red pepper, and 1 minced garlic clove. Serve with fries.

Vanilla low-fat ice cream with hot fudge sauce

Game Plan

1 While oven preheats:
  • Cut potatoes.
2 While potatoes cook:
  • Chop parsley and prepare aïoli.
  • Prepare vegetables for sandwich.
  • Cook mushrooms.
  • Assemble sandwiches.
3 Toss fries with butter and parsley.

Asian Catfish Wraps

Asian-flavored wraps and crunchy wonton chips elevate sandwich night to a new level. Catfish nuggets are fresh catfish pieces that are less expensive than fillets. If they're not available, buy fillets and cut them into bite-sized pieces.

- 1 teaspoon dark sesame oil, divided
- 1 pound catfish nuggets
- 3 cups thinly sliced napa (Chinese) cabbage
- 1 cup thinly sliced shiitake mushroom caps
- ¾ cup preshredded carrot
- ½ cup sliced green onions
- 1 tablespoon bottled minced fresh ginger
- 1 tablespoon bottled minced garlic
- ¼ cup hoisin sauce
- 1 teaspoon chili garlic sauce (such as Lee Kum Kee)
- 4 (8-inch) fat-free flour tortillas

1 Heat ½ teaspoon oil in a large nonstick skillet over medium-high heat. Add catfish; cook 3 minutes or until done, stirring frequently. Remove from pan.

2 Add ½ teaspoon oil to pan. Add cabbage and next 5 ingredients; sauté 2 minutes or until carrot is crisp-tender. Stir in catfish nuggets, hoisin sauce, and chili garlic sauce, and cook 1 minute or until thoroughly heated. Remove from heat.

3 Warm tortillas according to package directions. Divide catfish mixture evenly among tortillas; roll up. Yield: 4 servings (serving size: 1 wrap).

CALORIES 344 (27% from fat); FAT 10.4g (sat 2.3g, mono 4.7g, poly 2.6g); PROTEIN 22.8g; CARB 37.8g; FIBER 3.7g; CHOL 54mg; IRON 0.9mg; SODIUM 650mg; CALC 58mg

Game Plan

1 While skillet and oven heat:
   - Slice cabbage, shiitake mushrooms, and green onion.
   - Cut wonton wrappers.

2 Cook fish and cabbage mixture.

3 Bake wontons.

4 While wontons bake:
   - Steam edamame.
   - Warm tortillas.
   - Assemble wraps.

Baked Cornmeal-Crusted Grouper Sandwiches with Tartar Sauce

Oven-frying grouper fillets in a cornmeal batter gives the fish its crispy exterior. For a little extra crunch, try adding slaw on the sandwich.

GROUPER:
- ½ cup yellow cornmeal
- ½ teaspoon salt
- ¼ teaspoon ground red pepper
- ¼ cup 2% reduced-fat milk
- 4 (6-ounce) grouper fillets

Cooking spray

TARTAR SAUCE:
- ½ cup low-fat mayonnaise
- 2 tablespoons chopped green onions
- 1 tablespoon sweet pickle relish
- 1½ teaspoons capers
- 1½ teaspoons fresh lemon juice
- ½ teaspoon Worcestershire sauce

REMAINING INGREDIENT:
- 4 (1½-ounce) hamburger buns, split

1 Preheat oven to 450°.

2 To prepare grouper, combine cornmeal, salt, and red pepper in a shallow dish, stirring well with a fork. Place milk in a shallow bowl.

3 Dip each fillet in milk; dredge in cornmeal mixture. Place fish on a baking sheet coated with cooking spray. Bake at 450° for 10 minutes or until fish is done, turning once.

4 To prepare tartar sauce, combine mayonnaise and next 5 ingredients; stir with a whisk.

5 Spread about 2 tablespoons tartar sauce over cut sides of each bun; place 1 fish fillet on bottom half of each bun. Top fillets with remaining bun halves. Yield: 4 servings.

CALORIES 443 (29% from fat); FAT 14.3g (sat 2.6g, mono 4.5g, poly 6.6g); PROTEIN 38.5g; CARB 38.3g; FIBER 2.5g; CHOL 75mg; IRON 3.2mg; SODIUM 961mg; CALC 110mg

Quick Tip: To save time, buy bagged preshredded cabbage.

MENU *serves 4*

Baked Cornmeal-Crusted Grouper Sandwiches with Tartar Sauce

Asian-style coleslaw

Combine 3 cups shredded cabbage, 1 cup snow peas, ½ cup julienne-cut red bell pepper, and 3 tablespoons chopped green onions in a large bowl. Combine 1½ tablespoons rice vinegar, 1 teaspoon vegetable oil, 1 teaspoon dark sesame oil, 1 teaspoon less-sodium soy sauce, ¼ teaspoon sugar, and ⅛ teaspoon pepper; stir with a whisk. Add to cabbage mixture, tossing well to coat.

Lemon sorbet

Game Plan

1 While oven preheats:
- Bread fish fillets.

2 While fish cooks:
- Prepare tartar sauce.
- Prepare coleslaw.

3 Assemble sandwiches.

MENU *serves 4*

Wasabi Salmon Sandwiches

Miso soup

Bring 3 cups water to a boil. Combine 3 tablespoons boiling water and 2 tablespoons white miso in a medium bowl, stirring to form a paste. Add remaining boiling water, 1 tablespoon slivered green onions, 1 teaspoon low-sodium soy sauce, and ½ teaspoon fish sauce; stir well.

Sliced cucumbers and red onions tossed with seasoned rice vinegar and black pepper

Game Plan

1 While salmon marinates:

- Prepare ginger-garlic mayonnaise.
- Whisk sesame oil into shallot mixture for dressing.
- Prepare cucumbers; chill until ready to serve.

2 While salmon cooks:

- Toss greens and dressing.
- Prepare miso soup.

3 Assemble sandwiches.

Wasabi Salmon Sandwiches

Wasabi is a welcome addition to the ginger-garlic mayonnaise. It gives it a nice spicy kick.

FISH:

- ⅓ cup rice vinegar
- ¼ cup minced shallots
- 2 tablespoons brown sugar
- 2 tablespoons minced peeled fresh ginger
- 1 tablespoon minced garlic (about 3 cloves)
- 3 tablespoons low-sodium soy sauce
- 1½ teaspoons wasabi paste
- 4 (6-ounce) salmon fillets (about 1 inch thick), skinned

GINGER-GARLIC MAYONNAISE:

- 2 tablespoons low-fat mayonnaise
- 2 tablespoons plain fat-free yogurt
- 1 teaspoon wasabi paste
- ¾ teaspoon grated peeled fresh ginger
- ½ teaspoon rice vinegar
- 1 garlic clove, minced

REMAINING INGREDIENTS:

- 1 tablespoon dark sesame oil
- 4 cups baby spinach leaves
- 8 (1-ounce) slices ciabatta bread, toasted

1 To prepare fish, combine first 7 ingredients. Place ¾ cup shallot mixture in a large zip-top plastic bag. Set remaining shallot mixture aside. Add fish to bag; seal and marinate in refrigerator 30 minutes, turning once.

2 To prepare ginger-garlic mayonnaise, combine mayonnaise and next 5 ingredients.

3 Preheat broiler.

4 Remove fish from bag; discard marinade. Place fish on a broiler pan; broil 10 minutes or until fish flakes easily when tested with a fork.

5 Combine reserved shallot mixture and sesame oil in a large bowl; stir with a whisk. Add spinach; toss well.

6 Spread about 1 tablespoon ginger-garlic mayonnaise evenly over each of 4 bread slices; top each with 1 fillet and about 1 cup spinach mixture. Top with remaining bread slices. Yield: 4 servings (serving size: 1 sandwich).

CALORIES 434 (33% from fat); FAT 15.7g (sat 3.3g, mono 6.5g, poly 4.5g); PROTEIN 33.8g; CARB 37.6g; FIBER 2.6g; CHOL 65mg; IRON 2.8mg; SODIUM 682mg; CALC 103mg

Quick Tip: The shallot mixture does double duty as a marinade for the fish and dressing for the spinach.

Salmon Burgers

Dress up these burgers with baby spinach and bottled tomato chutney for a tasty alternative.

- 1   cup finely chopped red onion
- ¼   cup thinly sliced fresh basil
- ¼   teaspoon salt
- ¼   teaspoon freshly ground black pepper
- 1   (1-pound) salmon fillet, skinned and chopped
- 1   tablespoon hot pepper sauce
- 1   large egg white
- Cooking spray
- 8   (¾-ounce) slices focaccia, toasted

1 Combine red onion, fresh basil, salt, black pepper, and salmon in a large bowl. Combine hot pepper sauce and egg white in a small bowl; add egg white mixture to salmon mixture, stirring well to combine.

2 Divide mixture into 4 equal portions, shaping each into a ½-inch-thick patty. Heat a large nonstick skillet over medium-high heat; coat with cooking spray. Add salmon patties, and cook 3 minutes on each side or until desired degree of doneness. Serve patties on toasted focaccia. Yield: 4 servings (serving size: 1 burger).

CALORIES 190 (42% from fat); FAT 8.8g (sat 2.1g, mono 3.8g, poly 2.1g); PROTEIN 25.2g; CARB 1.1g; FIBER 0.3g; CHOL 58mg; IRON 0.6mg; SODIUM 236mg; CALC 21mg

MENU *serves 4*

Salmon Burgers

Summer fruit
Combine 1 cup fresh blackberries, 1 cup fresh blueberries, and 2 nectarines cut into ½-inch pieces. Combine 2 tablespoons lime juice and 1 tablespoon honey; drizzle over fruit, tossing gently.

Cold beer

Game Plan

1. Preheat oven for focaccia.
2. Chop red onion and slice basil.
3. Prepare salmon patties.
4. While salmon patties cook:
   - Toast focaccia slices.
   - Prepare summer fruit.
5. Assemble burgers.

MENU *serves 4*

Shrimp Po'boy with Spicy Ketchup

Corn salad

Heat a nonstick skillet over medium heat. Add 2 cups fresh corn kernels; cook 5 minutes, stirring often. Combine corn, ½ cup chopped red bell pepper, 2 tablespoons chopped fresh parsley, 2 tablespoons chopped red onion, 1½ tablespoons fresh lime juice, 1 teaspoon olive oil, ¼ teaspoon salt, and ⅛ teaspoon pepper in a large bowl; toss gently.

Fresh strawberries

Game Plan

1 Prepare corn salad.

2 While broiler heats:

- •Prepare breadcrumb mixture.
- •Toss shrimp in oil.
- •Coat shrimp in bread crumb mixture.

3 While shrimp cooks:

- •Prepare ketchup mixture.
- •Slice rolls.
- •Tear lettuce and slice onion.
- •Wash and halve strawberries.

4 Assemble sandwiches.

Shrimp Po'boy with Spicy Ketchup

A New Orleans specialty, this sandwich is often made with deep-fried shrimp. Broiling the shrimp, which is coated in garlicky breadcrumbs, delivers big flavor without the fat.

- 3 tablespoons dry breadcrumbs
- ¼ teaspoon salt
- ¼ teaspoon black pepper
- 1 garlic clove, minced
- 1 tablespoon olive oil
- 1 pound large shrimp, peeled and deveined
- ¼ cup ketchup
- 1½ teaspoons fresh lemon juice
- ½ teaspoon Worcestershire sauce
- ¼ teaspoon chili powder
- ¼ teaspoon hot sauce
- 2 (10-inch) submarine rolls, split
- 2 cups torn curly leaf lettuce
- ½ cup thinly sliced red onion

❶ Preheat broiler.
❷ Line a baking sheet with heavy-duty aluminum foil. Combine first 4 ingredients in a medium bowl; stir with a fork. Combine oil and shrimp; toss well. Place half of shrimp in breadcrumb mixture; toss well to coat. Place breaded shrimp in a single layer on prepared baking sheet. Repeat procedure with remaining shrimp and breadcrumb mixture. Broil 4 minutes or until shrimp are done.
❸ Combine ketchup and next 4 ingredients in a small bowl; stir with a whisk.
❹ Spread 2 tablespoons ketchup mixture over cut side of each roll half. Place 1 cup lettuce over bottom half of each roll; top with ¼ cup onion. Arrange 1 cup shrimp on each sandwich; top with remaining roll halves. Cut sandwiches in half. Yield: 4 servings (serving size: 1 sandwich half).

CALORIES 401 (20% from fat); FAT 9.1g (sat 1.7g, mono 4.6g, poly 1.7g); PROTEIN 30g; CARB 48.9g; FIBER 3g; CHOL 172mg; IRON 5.3mg; SODIUM 864mg; CALC 183mg

Quick Tip: Buy peeled and deveined shrimp to save time in the kitchen.

Chinese Chicken and Persimmon Lettuce Wraps

Asian preparations are a natural match for persimmons, which complement this menu well.

1½ teaspoons peanut oil
½ cup minced green onions
2 teaspoons cornstarch
1 pound ground chicken
1 cup chopped peeled ripe Fuyu persimmon (about 2)
½ cup chopped water chestnuts
1 tablespoon grated peeled fresh ginger
3 tablespoons low-sodium soy sauce
2 tablespoons fresh orange juice
1 tablespoon oyster sauce
12 Boston lettuce leaves

❶ Heat oil in a large skillet over medium-high heat. Add onions, cornstarch, and chicken to pan; sauté 4 minutes or until chicken is done, stirring to crumble. Add persimmon, water chestnuts, ginger, soy sauce, juice, and oyster sauce to pan; cook 2 minutes. Remove from heat. Spoon ¼ cup chicken mixture into center of each lettuce leaf; roll up jelly-roll fashion. Yield: 4 servings (serving size: 3 wraps).

CALORIES 247 (40% from fat); FAT 11g (sat 2.8g, mono 4g, poly 2.7g); PROTEIN 20.2g; CARB 19.3g; FIBER 3.4g; CHOL 75mg; IRON 2.1mg; SODIUM 392mg; CALC 34mg

Game Plan

1 Prepare grill or preheat broiler.

2 Prepare and refrigerate avocado mayonnaise.

3 Prepare burgers.

4 While burgers cook:

  •Prepare salad.

  •Toast onion rolls.

  •Prepare pineapple-coconut coolers.

5 Assemble burgers.

Chicken-Chorizo Burgers with Avocado Mayonnaise

Bite-sized pieces of corn tortillas act as a binder in these tempting burgers.

AVOCADO MAYONNAISE:

- 1/3 cup fat-free mayonnaise
- 1/4 cup fresh cilantro leaves
- 2 tablespoons fresh lime juice
- 1/4 teaspoon salt
- 1/2 ripe peeled avocado, seeded

BURGERS:

- 1/2 pound Spanish chorizo sausage (such as Usinger's)
- 1/4 teaspoon salt
- 5 (6-inch) corn tortillas, torn into bite-sized pieces
- 1 1/2 pounds skinless, boneless chicken breast, coarsely chopped
- 1 jalapeño pepper, seeded and chopped

Cooking spray

- 8 (2-ounce) onion rolls, toasted
- 8 (1/4-inch-thick) slices tomato

❶ Prepare grill or preheat broiler.

❷ To prepare mayonnaise, combine first 5 ingredients in a food processor; pulse 10 times or until combined. Cover and chill.

❸ To prepare burgers, remove casings from sausage. Place sausage, salt, tortillas, chicken, and jalapeño in food processor; process 30 seconds or until mixture is coarsely ground. Divide mixture into 8 equal portions, shaping each into a 1/2-inch-thick patty.

❹ Place patties on a grill rack or broiler pan coated with cooking spray; cook 7 minutes on each side or until done.

❺ Cut rolls in half horizontally, and spread 1 1/2 tablespoons mayonnaise mixture over top half of each roll. Place tomato slices on bottom halves of rolls; top each with 1 patty and top half of roll. Yield: 8 servings.

CALORIES 385 (29% from fat); FAT 12.6g (sat 4.4g, mono 4.8g, poly 2.3g); PROTEIN 29.2g; CARB 39.5g; FIBER 3g; CHOL 63mg; IRON 2.8mg; SODIUM 735mg; CALC 111mg

Quick Tip: To remove sausage from its casing, cut the casing lengthwise with kitchen scissors and squeeze sausage out from casing.

Grilled Chicken and Tapenade Sandwiches

Robust olives, balsamic vinegar, and feta cheese convey Mediterranean flavors.

1½ cups diced seeded tomato
2 tablespoons balsamic vinegar
2 tablespoons finely chopped pitted kalamata olives
1 tablespoon chopped fresh basil
1 tablespoon chopped fresh flat-leaf parsley
1 teaspoon chopped fresh oregano
½ teaspoon minced garlic
5 teaspoons extra-virgin olive oil, divided
1 pound skinless, boneless chicken breast
½ teaspoon kosher salt, divided
½ teaspoon freshly ground black pepper
Cooking spray
¼ cup (1 ounce) crumbled feta cheese
4 (2-ounce) ciabatta sandwich rolls, halved

❶ Combine first 7 ingredients in a small bowl, and add 2 teaspoons oil. Toss tomato mixture gently to combine. Let stand 15 minutes.
❷ Prepare grill.
❸ Brush chicken evenly with 1 tablespoon oil, and sprinkle with ¼ teaspoon salt and pepper. Place chicken on a grill rack coated with cooking spray; grill 6 minutes on each side or until done. Remove from grill. Let stand 5 minutes before cutting into thin slices.
❹ Add cheese and ¼ teaspoon salt to tomato mixture; stir gently to combine. Arrange sliced chicken evenly on bottom halves of rolls. Top each with one-fourth of tomato mixture, and cover with top halves of rolls. Serve immediately. Yield: 4 servings (serving size: 1 sandwich).

CALORIES 369 (30% from fat); FAT 12.3g (sat 3g, mono 7g, poly 1.6g); PROTEIN 33.2g; CARB 30.1g; FIBER 1.5g; CHOL 79mg; IRON 2.7mg; SODIUM 815mg; CALC 63mg

MENU *serves 4*

Grilled Chicken and Tapenade Sandwiches

Grilled vegetable skewers

Prepare grill. Cut 2 zucchini, 1 red bell pepper, and 1 red onion into 1½-inch pieces. Thread vegetables alternately onto 4 skewers, brush with olive oil, and sprinkle with ½ teaspoon kosher salt and ¼ teaspoon freshly ground black pepper. Grill 15 minutes or until crisp-tender and lightly charred. Brush evenly with 1 tablespoon balsamic vinegar just before serving.

Cubed cantaloupe drizzled with port

Game Plan

1 Prepare tomato topping for sandwiches.

2 While topping stands:
- Prepare vegetable skewers.
- Prepare grill.
- Grill chicken and vegetables.

3 While chicken stands:
- Add cheese and remaining ingredients to topping.

4 Cut chicken into thin slices; assemble sandwiches.

59

MENU *serves 4*

Balsamic-Glazed Chicken Sandwiches with Red Onions and Goat Cheese

Antipasto salad
Combine 1 cup quartered mushrooms, ½ cup sliced bottled roasted red bell peppers, 1 (15-ounce) can drained chickpeas, ¼ cup low-fat balsamic vinaigrette, and 1 (14-ounce) can drained and halved artichoke hearts in a medium bowl; toss well to coat.

Cubed winter pears

Game Plan

1 While vinegar mixture cooks:
  • Slice onion.
  • Cook chicken and thinly slice.
  • Cook onion.
2 Prepare salad.
3 Cube pears.
4 Assemble sandwiches.

Balsamic-Glazed Chicken Sandwiches with Red Onions and Goat Cheese

These tangy chicken sandwiches take less than a half-hour to prepare from pan to plate. The addition of antipasto salad and pears rounds them out into a full meal.

¾   cup balsamic vinegar
½   cup dry red wine
2   teaspoons brown sugar
1   teaspoon low-sodium soy sauce
Cooking spray
2   (6-ounce) skinless, boneless chicken breast halves
½   teaspoon salt
¼   teaspoon freshly ground black pepper
1   tablespoon olive oil
1½ cups thinly vertically sliced red onion
1   (3-ounce) package goat cheese
4   (2-ounce) hoagie or Kaiser rolls
1   cup trimmed arugula

❶ Combine first 4 ingredients in a small saucepan over medium heat. Bring mixture to a boil, stirring until sugar dissolves. Cook until reduced to ⅓ cup (about 12 minutes). Remove from heat; cool slightly.

❷ While vinegar mixture cooks, heat a large nonstick skillet over medium-high heat; coat with cooking spray. Sprinkle chicken with salt and pepper. Add chicken to pan; cook 4 minutes on each side or until done. Remove chicken from pan, and cut into thin slices. Cover and keep warm.

❸ Add oil to pan; reduce temperature to medium-low. Add onion; cook 5 minutes or until onion is soft and beginning to brown, stirring frequently. Remove pan from heat.

❹ Spread about 1½ tablespoons goat cheese evenly over bottom half of each roll; arrange chicken and onion evenly over cheese. Drizzle each serving with about 1 tablespoon balsamic mixture, and top with ¼ cup arugula and top half of a roll. Serve immediately. Yield: 4 servings (serving size: 1 sandwich).

CALORIES 424 (25% from fat); FAT 11.6g (sat 4.2g, mono 4.4g, poly 1.7g); PROTEIN 30.1g; CARB 43.9g; FIBER 2.2g; CHOL 59mg; IRON 3.7mg; SODIUM 796mg; CALC 129mg

Hot Turkey Sandwiches

Serve these quick-to-make sandwiches for lunch on the Friday after Thanksgiving or any-time you have turkey leftovers and crave a hearty sandwich. Cranberry-shallot chutney adds a sweet, tangy flavor. Bottled gravy works fine in this recipe.

8   (1-ounce) slices French bread
2   tablespoons light mayonnaise
¼   cup turkey gravy
4   reduced-sodium bacon slices, cooked and cut in half
12 ounces sliced cooked turkey breast
2   slices provolone cheese, halved
1   cup arugula
1   tablespoon cranberry-shallot chutney (see recipe at right)

1 Preheat oven to 400°.
2 Place bread on a baking sheet. Spread mayonnaise evenly over 4 slices. Spread turkey gravy evenly over remaining 4 slices. Top mayonnaise-spread slices evenly with bacon, turkey, and cheese. Bake at 400° for 10 minutes or until cheese melts. Top cheese evenly with arugula. Drizzle with cranberry-shallot chutney. Top with gravy-spread bread slices; press sandwiches together. Yield: 4 servings (serving size: 1 sandwich).

CALORIES 402 (25% from fat); FAT 11g (sat 4.5g, mono 3.5g, poly 1.2g); PROTEIN 38.2g; CARB 35.1g; FIBER 2.1g; CHOL 89mg; IRON 3.3mg; SODIUM 787mg; CALC 174mg

Flavor Tip: Experiment with different cheeses in this sandwich. Swiss, sharp cheddar, or Monterey Jack cheese would all be delicious substitutes.

MENU *serves 4*

Hot Turkey Sandwiches

Cranberry-shallot chutney
Combine ¼ cup cranberry sauce, 1 tablespoon minced shallots, 1 tablespoon cider vinegar, and 1 teaspoon Dijon mustard in a small bowl.

Sour cream and onion-flavored baked potato chips

Game Plan

1 While bacon for sandwiches cooks:
  • Slice bread.
  • Rinse arugula and pat dry.

2 While sandwiches bake:
  • Prepare chutney.

3 Assemble sandwiches.

Game Plan

1 While oven preheats:

  •Halve cherry tomatoes.

  •Chop parsley, onion, and avocado.

  •Prepare mayonnaise mixture.

2 While French bread toasts:

  •Slice tomato for sandwiches.

  •Prepare pesto mixture.

  •Heat grill pan.

3 While panini cook:

  •Assemble salad.

  •Slice peaches.

Turkey and Cheese Panini

In Italian, *panini* means "small bread" and refers to a pressed sandwich. Using a grill pan gives these sandwiches a nice appearance, but the recipe works just as well in a regular nonstick skillet. If you don't have provolone cheese, you can use mozzarella.

 2 tablespoons fat-free mayonnaise
 4 teaspoons basil pesto
 8 (1-ounce) thin slices sourdough bread
 8 ounces sliced cooked turkey breast
 2 ounces thinly sliced provolone cheese
 8 (⅛-inch-thick) slices tomato
Cooking spray

1 Combine mayonnaise and pesto. Spread 1 tablespoon mayonnaise mixture on each of 4 bread slices; top each slice with 2 ounces turkey, ½ ounce cheese, and 2 tomato slices. Top with remaining bread slices.

2 Heat grill pan or large nonstick skillet over medium heat; coat with cooking spray. Add sandwiches to pan; top with another heavy skillet. Cook 3 minutes on each side or until golden brown. Yield: 4 servings.

CALORIES 257 (29% from fat); FAT 8.2g (sat 2.9g, mono 0.2g, poly 0.1g); PROTEIN 18.4g; CARB 30.4g; FIBER 4.1g; CHOL 30mg; IRON 2.4mg; SODIUM 1,208mg; CALC 204mg

Quick Tip: You can find prepared pesto in jars, tubs, or tubes at most supermarkets.

Italian Burgers

These slightly messy, robust burgers are just as delicious and satisfying as meatball subs.

Cooking spray
- 4 cups red bell pepper strips
- 2 cups green bell pepper strips
- 2 cups vertically sliced onion
- 1½ cups fat-free Italian herb pasta sauce (such as Muir Glen)
- 12 ounces hot turkey Italian sausage
- 12 ounces ground turkey breast
- 6 (2-ounce) whole wheat hamburger buns
- ¾ cup (3 ounces) shredded sharp provolone cheese

❶ Prepare grill or preheat broiler.
❷ Heat a large nonstick skillet over medium-high heat; coat with cooking spray. Add bell peppers and onion; sauté 10 minutes. Add pasta sauce, and cook 1 minute or until thoroughly heated; keep warm.

❸ Remove casings from sausage. Combine sausage and turkey in a large bowl. Divide mixture into 6 equal portions, shaping each into a ½-inch-thick patty.
❹ Place patties on a grill rack or broiler pan coated with cooking spray; cook 4 minutes on each side or until done.
❺ Place 1 patty on bottom half of each bun; top each patty with ⅔ cup bell pepper mixture, 2 tablespoons cheese, and top half of a bun. Yield: 6 servings.

CALORIES 428 (27% from fat); FAT 13g (sat 4.6g, mono 3.9g, poly 2.4g); PROTEIN 34.7g; CARB 42.1g; FIBER 5.6g; CHOL 93mg; IRON 4.4mg; SODIUM 860mg; CALC 233mg

Quick Tip: To remove sausage from its casing, cut the casing lengthwise with kitchen scissors and squeeze sausage out from casing.

MENU serves 6

Italian Burgers

Chickpea-artichoke salad

Combine 1 cup halved grape tomatoes; ½ cup finely chopped celery; ¼ cup finely chopped red onion; 1 (15½-ounce) can chickpeas, drained; and 1 (6-ounce) jar marinated artichoke hearts, undrained, in a large bowl. Cover and chill until ready to serve.

Strawberries with mascarpone cheese

Game Plan

1. Prepare grill or preheat broiler.
2. Slice bell peppers and onion for burgers.
3. While peppers and onion cook:
   - Prepare patties.
   - Grate cheese for burgers.
4. While burgers cook:
   - Prepare salad.
   - Halve strawberries to serve with mascarpone cheese.

MENU *serves 2*

Larb

Hot cooked rice

Spicy sesame snow peas
Heat ½ teaspoon sesame oil in a nonstick skillet over medium-high heat. Add ½ pound trimmed snow peas; sauté 1 minute. Add 1 tablespoon rice vinegar, 1½ teaspoons low-sodium soy sauce, and ¼ teaspoon crushed red pepper, stirring to combine; cook 4 minutes or until peas are crisp-tender. Sprinkle with 2 teaspoons sesame seeds.

Game Plan

1 While water for rice comes to a boil:
- Prepare juice mixture for larb.
- Chop mint.
- Core and halve cabbage.
- Heat skillet for larb.

2 While rice and turkey cook:
- Prepare snow peas.

Larb

Larb is a traditional Thai dish of spicy ground chicken, but ground turkey breast is leaner and just as tasty. Place the cooked turkey mixture in cabbage leaves for a delicious wrap.

2	teaspoons grated lime rind
1	teaspoon grated lemon rind
¼	cup fresh lime juice
1	tablespoon fresh lemon juice
1	tablespoon fish sauce
2	teaspoons brown sugar
½	teaspoon finely chopped serrano chile
¼	teaspoon crushed red pepper
1	teaspoon canola oil
12	ounces ground turkey breast
1	tablespoon chopped shallots
½	cup coarsely chopped fresh mint
½	head green cabbage, cored and halved

❶ Combine first 8 ingredients; stir with a whisk until sugar dissolves.

❷ Heat oil in a large nonstick skillet over medium-high heat. Add turkey and shallots; sauté 5 minutes or until browned, stirring to crumble. Drizzle with juice mixture, stirring to coat. Sprinkle with mint. Serve with cabbage. Yield: 2 servings (serving size: about ²⁄₃ cup larb and 1 cabbage wedge).

CALORIES 305 (12% from fat); FAT 4.2g (sat 0.9g, mono 1.3g, poly 1.4g); PROTEIN 46.6g; CARB 21.3g; FIBER 7.3g; CHOL 105mg; IRON 6.3mg; SODIUM 829mg; CALC 184mg

Ingredient Tip: If you can't find ground turkey breast, you can use ground chicken breast.

Curried Duck Sandwiches

If you don't have white wine on hand, use 2 tablespoons chicken broth, white cranberry juice, or apple juice instead. The filling can also be served with crackers or fruit salad.

Cooking spray
- ¾ pound boneless duck breast halves, skinned (about 2 breast halves)
- ½ cup chopped celery
- ¼ cup golden raisins
- 3 tablespoons low-fat mayonnaise
- 2 tablespoons mango chutney
- 2 tablespoons dry white wine
- 2 tablespoons chopped dry-roasted cashews
- 1 tablespoon curry powder
- 1 tablespoon chopped green onions
- 4 (6-inch) pitas, cut in half
- 8 small lettuce leaves

1 Heat a small nonstick skillet over medium-high heat; coat with cooking spray. Add duck; cook 4 minutes on each side or until a thermometer inserted into thickest portion registers 170°. Cool slightly; coarsely chop duck.
2 Combine duck, celery, and next 7 ingredients in a large bowl. Line each pita half with 1 lettuce leaf; spoon duck mixture evenly into pita halves. Yield: 4 servings (serving size: 2 pita halves).

CALORIES 382 (14% from fat); FAT 5.8g (sat 1g, mono 2g, poly 1g); PROTEIN 28.4g; CARB 52.4g; FIBER 2.5g; CHOL 111mg; IRON 6.2mg; SODIUM 651mg; CALC 83mg

Ingredient Tip: You can substitute 2 cups cooked chicken, turkey, or shrimp for duck.

MENU *serves 4*

Curried Duck Sandwiches

Quick creamy tomato soup
Combine 2 (14.5-ounce) cans undrained petite diced tomatoes; 2 (10¾-ounce) cans undiluted fat-free, less-sodium condensed tomato soup; ¼ cup buttermilk; and ¼ teaspoon freshly ground black pepper in a large saucepan. Cook over medium heat 8 minutes or until thoroughly heated, stirring frequently. Sprinkle with sliced fresh basil, if desired.

Sliced fresh fruit

Game Plan

1 While duck cooks:
- •Combine soup ingredients.

2 While soup cooks:
- •Prepare duck mixture.
- •Halve pitas.

3 Assemble sandwiches.

Sloppy Joes with Corn

If you need less than 6 servings for dinner, leftovers are great for lunch the next day. The meat mixture will keep in the refrigerator for a few days stored in an airtight container. Reheat it in a saucepan, adding water to thin as necessary.

1   teaspoon canola oil
1   cup finely chopped onion
1   cup finely chopped green bell pepper
2   garlic cloves, minced
1½ pounds lean ground beef
1   (6-ounce) can no-salt-added tomato paste
2   teaspoons chili powder
1   teaspoon ground cumin
½   teaspoon salt
1   (14-ounce) can fat-free, less-sodium chicken broth
1   (15-ounce) can no-salt-added corn, rinsed and drained
6   (1½-ounce) whole wheat hamburger buns, toasted

❶ Heat oil in a large nonstick skillet over medium-high heat. Add onion, bell pepper, and garlic; sauté 3 minutes. Add meat to pan; cook 5 minutes or until browned, stirring to crumble. Stir in tomato paste; cook 2 minutes. Add chili powder, cumin, salt, and broth; reduce heat, and simmer 12 minutes or until thick, stirring occasionally. Stir in corn; cook 2 minutes or until thoroughly heated.
❷ Spoon about 1 cup meat mixture on bottom half of each bun, and cover with top half of each bun. Yield: 6 servings (serving size: 1 sandwich).

CALORIES 338 (20% from fat); FAT 7.5g (sat 2g, mono 2.5g, poly 1.7g); PROTEIN 31.7g; CARB 40g; FIBER 6.2g; CHOL 61mg; IRON 4.1mg; SODIUM 638mg; CALC 72mg

Meat Loaf Burgers with Caramelized Onions

Meat loaf is shaped into individual burgers that are just as comforting as their namesake. The burgers are delicate, so take extra care when flipping them.

ONIONS:
- 1 teaspoon olive oil
- 4½ cups vertically sliced red onion (about 2 medium onions)
- ¼ teaspoon salt
- 1 tablespoon sugar
- 2 tablespoons balsamic vinegar

BURGERS:
- Cooking spray
- 1 cup finely chopped green bell pepper
- 1 cup finely chopped celery
- 1 cup crushed whole wheat crackers (about 20 crackers)
- ⅓ cup ketchup, divided
- ½ teaspoon dried thyme
- ¼ teaspoon salt
- 1 pound ground sirloin
- 1 large egg, lightly beaten
- 12 (1¼-ounce) slices rye bread, toasted

❶ Prepare grill or preheat broiler.
❷ To prepare onions, heat oil in a large non-stick skillet over medium-high heat. Add onion and ¼ teaspoon salt; sauté 12 minutes or until golden brown. Stir in sugar and vinegar; cook 30 seconds. Remove from pan. Wipe pan with paper towels.
❸ To prepare burgers, heat pan over medium-high heat; coat with cooking spray. Add bell pepper and celery; sauté 3 minutes or until tender.
❹ Combine bell pepper mixture, crackers, ¼ cup ketchup, thyme, ¼ teaspoon salt, beef, and egg in a large bowl. Divide mixture into 6 equal portions, shaping each into a ½-inch-thick patty.
❺ Place patties on a grill rack or broiler pan coated with cooking spray; cook 5 minutes. Carefully turn patties over; brush with 4 teaspoons ketchup. Cook 5 minutes or until done.
❻ Place 1 patty on each of 6 bread slices. Top each patty with ¼ cup onion mixture and 1 bread slice. Yield: 6 servings.

CALORIES 419 (29% from fat); FAT 13.4g (sat 4.3g, mono 6g, poly 1.3g); PROTEIN 23.1g; CARB 51.8g; FIBER 6.6g; CHOL 86mg; IRON 4.2mg; SODIUM 906mg; CALC 92mg

Quick Tip: To crush crackers (or cookies), place them in a large zip-top plastic bag, and pound with a meat mallet or rolling pin.

MENU *serves 6*

Meat Loaf Burgers with Caramelized Onions

Corn on the cob

Quick peach crisp
Preheat oven to 400°. Arrange 1 (29-ounce) can sliced peaches in light syrup, drained, in an 8-inch square baking dish. Combine ¾ cup crushed gingersnaps and 2 tablespoons brown sugar; sprinkle over peaches. Bake at 400° for 15 minutes.

Game Plan

1 **Prepare grill or preheat broiler.**

2 **While onions cook:**
- •Chop bell pepper and celery.
- •Crush crackers.
- •Cook corn on the cob.

3 **While bell pepper and celery cook:**
- •Measure and combine remaining ingredients for burgers.

4 **While burgers cook:**
- •Assemble and bake peach crisp.

5 **Assemble burgers.**

Red Wine-Marinated Steak Sandwiches

Prepare the marinade the night before and refrigerate; in the morning, marinate the steak until you're ready to make dinner.

BEEF:
- ½ cup dry red wine
- 3 tablespoons low-sodium soy sauce
- 2 tablespoons Worcestershire sauce
- 2 tablespoons fresh lemon juice
- 2 tablespoons Dijon mustard
- 1½ teaspoons coarsely ground black pepper
- 1 teaspoon dried thyme
- 1 pound flank steak, trimmed

HORSERADISH CREAM:
- ¼ cup fat-free sour cream
- 1 tablespoon prepared horseradish
- 1 tablespoon Dijon mustard

GREENS:
- 1 tablespoon minced shallots
- ¼ teaspoon grated lemon rind
- 1 tablespoon fresh lemon juice
- 1 teaspoon Dijon mustard
- ½ teaspoon extra-virgin olive oil
- ⅛ teaspoon black pepper
- 3 cups mixed salad greens

REMAINING INGREDIENTS:
- 8 (1-ounce) slices diagonally cut French bread, toasted
- ½ cup (2 ounces) shaved fresh Parmesan cheese

1 To prepare beef, combine first 7 ingredients in a large zip-top plastic bag. Add steak; seal. Marinate in refrigerator 8 hours or overnight.

2 Heat a grill pan or large nonstick skillet over medium-high heat. Remove steak from marinade, and discard marinade. Add steak to pan; cook 4 minutes on each side or until desired degree of doneness. Let stand 5 minutes; cut into thin slices.

3 To prepare horseradish cream, combine sour cream, horseradish, and 1 tablespoon mustard.

4 To prepare greens, combine shallots and next 5 ingredients in a large bowl. Add salad greens; toss to coat.

5 Spread about 1 tablespoon horseradish cream evenly over each of 4 bread slices; arrange steak and greens evenly over bread slices. Top each serving with 2 tablespoons cheese and 1 bread slice. Yield: 4 servings (serving size: 1 sandwich).

CALORIES 432 (32% from fat); FAT 15.2g (sat 6.6g, mono 5.9g, poly 1.1g); PROTEIN 35.6g; CARB 36.6g; FIBER 3.3g; CHOL 69mg; IRON 4.9mg; SODIUM 889mg; CALC 292mg

---

MENU *serves 4*

Red Wine-Marinated Steak Sandwiches

Roasted herbed potatoes

Preheat oven to 375°. Combine 1 (1¼-pound) package refrigerated new potato wedges (such as Simply Potatoes), 1 tablespoon olive oil, ½ teaspoon dried thyme, ¼ teaspoon garlic powder, ¼ teaspoon salt, and ¼ teaspoon black pepper in a large bowl, tossing well; place on a jelly-roll pan coated with cooking spray. Bake at 375° for 30 minutes or until lightly browned, turning after 15 minutes.

Steamed baby carrots

Game Plan

1 Marinate steak 8 hours or overnight.

2 While potatoes roast:
- Make vinaigrette and prepare greens.
- Cook steak.

3 While steak stands:
- Toss greens with dressing.
- Prepare horseradish cream.

4 Assemble sandwiches.

MENU *serves 4*

Grilled Beef and Pepper Sandwich

Vegetable chips

Pineapple shake

Place 4 scoops vanilla low-fat ice cream, 3 cups 2% reduced-fat milk, 2 cups chopped fresh pineapple, 3 tablespoons brown sugar, and ½ teaspoon vanilla extract in a blender; process until smooth.

Game Plan

1 While grill heats:
- Prepare seasoning mixture for steak.
- Season steak.
- Let steak stand.
- Halve and seed peppers.

2 While steak and peppers cook:
- Prepare mayonnaise mixture.

3 While steak and peppers stand:
- Prepare shake.

4 Assemble sandwiches.

Grilled Beef and Pepper Sandwich

It's better to let the steak rest 10 minutes after it's grilled, but if you need to shave time off preparing this recipe, omit the resting time beforehand. This stand time allows the juices to redistribute throughout the steak.

2 teaspoons grated lemon rind
1 teaspoon dried rosemary
1 teaspoon olive oil
1 teaspoon Dijon mustard
½ teaspoon freshly ground black pepper
¼ teaspoon salt
2 garlic cloves, minced
1 (1-pound) flank steak, trimmed
Cooking spray
2 red bell peppers
⅓ cup reduced-fat mayonnaise
3 tablespoons finely grated Parmesan cheese
1 tablespoon fresh lemon juice
1 garlic clove, minced
1 (10-ounce) round focaccia bread, cut in half horizontally

❶ Prepare grill.

❷ Combine first 7 ingredients in a small bowl. Rub spice mixture over one side of steak; let stand 10 minutes.

❸ Place steak on grill rack coated with cooking spray, and grill 8 minutes on each side or until desired degree of doneness. Let steak stand 10 minutes; cut diagonally across grain into thin slices.

❹ Cut bell peppers in half lengthwise; discard seeds and membranes. Flatten peppers with hand. Place peppers, skin-side down, on grill rack; grill 12 minutes or until blackened. Place peppers in a zip-top plastic bag; seal. Let stand 10 minutes. Peel and cut each half into quarters.

❺ Combine mayonnaise, cheese, juice, and 1 garlic clove in a small bowl, stirring well. Spread about ¼ cup mayonnaise mixture onto cut side of each bread half. Arrange beef evenly over bottom half; top with peppers. Cover with top bread half, pressing gently. Cut sandwich into 4 wedges. Yield: 4 servings (serving size: 1 wedge).

CALORIES 427 (29% from fat); FAT 13.9g (sat 4.6g, mono 5.9g, poly 2.4g); PROTEIN 31g; CARB 45.3g; FIBER 2.8g; CHOL 47.9mg; IRON 4.2mg; SODIUM 719mg; CALC 69mg

Greek Steak Pitas with Dill Sauce

The lemon juice marinade quickly penetrates the steak, so a 10-minute soak is enough to flavor the meat. Try crumbled goat or blue cheese in place of the feta.

SAUCE:
- ½ cup plain fat-free yogurt
- 2 teaspoons chopped fresh dill
- ¼ teaspoon salt
- ¼ teaspoon black pepper
- 1 garlic clove, minced

STEAK:
- ½ cup fresh lemon juice
- 1 teaspoon dried oregano
- ½ teaspoon black pepper
- 2 garlic cloves, minced
- 1 (1-pound) flank steak, trimmed

Cooking spray

REMAINING INGREDIENTS:
- 4 (6-inch) pitas, cut in half
- 4 romaine lettuce leaves, halved
- ¼ cup (1 ounce) crumbled feta cheese

1 Prepare grill or preheat broiler.

2 To prepare sauce, combine first 5 ingredients in a small bowl; stir with a whisk.

3 To prepare steak, combine juice and next 4 ingredients in a large zip-top plastic bag; seal. Marinate in refrigerator 10 minutes, turning once. Remove steak from bag; discard marinade.

4 Place steak on grill rack or broiler pan coated with cooking spray; cook 6 minutes on each side or until desired degree of doneness. Let steak stand 5 minutes; cut diagonally across the grain into thin slices. Line each pita half with 1 lettuce leaf half. Divide steak evenly among pita halves. Spoon 1 tablespoon sauce and 1½ teaspoons cheese into each pita half. Yield: 4 servings (serving size: 2 stuffed pita halves).

CALORIES 386 (25% from fat); FAT 10.9g (sat 4.9g, mono 3.9g, poly 0.7g); PROTEIN 31.6g; CARB 38.4g; FIBER 1.7g; CHOL 64mg; IRON 4.2mg; SODIUM 643mg; CALC 165mg

Quick Tip: Use bagged hearts of romaine lettuce, which you don't have to wash and dry.

MENU *serves 4*

Greek Steak Pitas with Dill Sauce

Grape tomato salad
Combine 2 cups grape tomatoes, 1¼ cups chopped English cucumber, and 2 tablespoons chopped green onions in a medium bowl; toss gently. Combine ¼ cup balsamic vinegar, 1 teaspoon sugar, 2 teaspoons olive oil, ¼ teaspoon black pepper, and ⅛ teaspoon salt in a small bowl; stir with a whisk. Drizzle vinaigrette over salad; toss gently to coat.

Prepared hummus with baby carrots

Game Plan

1 While steak marinates:
- Prepare sauce.

2 While steak cooks:
- Prepare salad.

3 Slice steak and assemble sandwiches.

MENU *serves 6*

Thai Beef Salad Wraps

Grilled soy-glazed eggplant

Prepare grill. Slice 4 Japanese eggplants crosswise into ¼-inch-thick slices. Combine 1½ tablespoons low-sodium soy sauce, 2 teaspoons fresh lime juice, and 1 teaspoon dark sesame oil; brush evenly over both sides of eggplant. Place on a grill rack coated with cooking spray; grill 1 minute on each side or until tender.

Iced green tea

Game Plan

1 While grill heats:

- Chop cucumber and herbs for wraps.

- Squeeze lime for juice for wraps and eggplant.

- Halve tomatoes and slice shallots for wraps.

- Prepare soy sauce mixture for wraps.

2 While steak grills:

- Slice eggplant.

- Brush eggplant slices with soy sauce glaze.

3 While steak rests:

- Grill eggplant.

4 Assemble wraps.

Thai Beef Salad Wraps

This recipe has all the bright, fresh flavors and crunchy textures of summer harvest. The tortilla wrappers make it a satisfying main dish.

- 1 (1-pound) flank steak, trimmed
- ¼ teaspoon salt
- ¼ teaspoon black pepper
- Cooking spray
- 1 cup cubed peeled cucumber
- ½ cup grape or cherry tomato halves
- ¼ cup thinly sliced shallots
- 1 tablespoon chopped fresh mint
- 1 tablespoon chopped fresh basil
- 1 tablespoon chopped fresh cilantro
- 3 tablespoons low-sodium soy sauce
- 2 tablespoons fresh lime juice
- 2 tablespoons brown sugar
- ½ teaspoon crushed red pepper
- 6 (10-inch) flour tortillas
- 12 Bibb lettuce leaves

1 Prepare grill to medium-high heat.

2 Sprinkle steak with salt and black pepper. Place steak on a grill rack coated with cooking spray, and grill 4 minutes on each side or until desired degree of doneness. Let steak stand 5 minutes; cut diagonally across grain into thin slices. Combine sliced steak, cucumber, and next 5 ingredients in a large bowl. Combine soy sauce, juice, sugar, and red pepper in a small bowl; stir with a whisk. Drizzle over steak mixture; toss well to coat.

3 Warm tortillas according to package directions. Arrange 2 lettuce leaves on each tortilla. Spoon ⅔ cup steak mixture into center of each tortilla; roll up. Yield: 6 servings (serving size: 1 wrap).

CALORIES 399 (28% from fat); FAT 12.4g (sat 4.3g, mono 5.6g, poly 1.1g); PROTEIN 22.4g; CARB 48.5g; FIBER 3.1g; CHOL 39mg; IRON 4.4mg; SODIUM 760mg; CALC 113mg

Quick Tip: If the tortillas are dry, revive them by wrapping in damp paper towels and microwaving at HIGH 10 seconds. This will keep them from cracking when you roll them up.

Steak Sandwiches with Worcestershire Mayonnaise

Mayonnaise, Worcestershire sauce, and whole-grain mustard combine for a tangy, slightly smoky sandwich spread. Arugula is a peppery salad green. Substitute your favorite lettuce, if you like.

Cooking spray
- 2 (8-ounce) boneless ribeye steaks, trimmed
- ½ teaspoon kosher salt
- ½ teaspoon freshly ground black pepper
- 2 tablespoons fat-free mayonnaise
- 1 teaspoon whole-grain mustard
- 2 teaspoons Worcestershire sauce
- 1 garlic clove, minced
- 8 (1-ounce) slices crusty whole-grain bread, toasted
- 1 cup arugula leaves

① Heat a grill pan or large nonstick skillet over medium-high heat; coat with cooking spray. Sprinkle both sides of steaks evenly with salt and pepper. Add steaks to pan; cook 4 minutes on each side or until desired degree of doneness.

Let steaks stand 5 minutes; cut diagonally across grain into thin slices.
② Combine mayonnaise and next 3 ingredients in a small bowl; stir with a whisk. Spread about 1 tablespoon mayonnaise mixture on each of 4 slices of bread; divide steak evenly among bread slices. Top each serving with ¼ cup arugula and 1 bread slice. Yield: 4 servings (serving size: 1 sandwich).

CALORIES 383 (38% from fat); FAT 16.2g (sat 5.8g, mono 6.5g, poly 1.1g); PROTEIN 28.1g; CARB 31.3g; FIBER 4.2g; CHOL 103mg; IRON 3.9mg; SODIUM 688mg; CALC 87mg

Ingredient Tip: Purchase a loaf of crusty whole-grain bread from the bakery. It will add flavor, and the substantial texture will hold up to the steak in the sandwiches.

MENU *serves 4*

Steak Sandwiches with Worcestershire Mayonnaise

Sweet potato oven fries

Preheat oven to 425°. Cut 2 medium peeled sweet potatoes lengthwise into wedges; place on a baking sheet. Drizzle potatoes with 1½ tablespoons olive oil. Sprinkle with 1 teaspoon salt and ½ teaspoon freshly ground black pepper; toss to coat. Bake at 425° for 20 minutes or until golden, turning after 10 minutes.

Apple slices with bottled caramel topping

Game Plan

1 While oven preheats for fries:
- Prepare potatoes.
- Season steaks.
- Prepare mayonnaise mixture for sandwiches.

2 While fries bake:
- Grill steaks.
- Toast bread for sandwiches.

3 Assemble sandwiches.

4 Slice apples.

MENU *serves 4*

Gyros

Mediterranean salad

Combine 2 teaspoons olive oil, 1 teaspoon fresh lemon juice, ½ teaspoon salt, and ¼ teaspoon freshly ground black pepper in a small bowl; stir with a whisk. Combine 6 cups mixed salad greens, 2 cups chopped tomato, and ¼ cup (1 ounce) crumbled feta cheese in a large bowl. Add oil mixture; toss gently to coat. Serve immediately.

Fresh peaches with vanilla yogurt and honey

Game Plan

1 While broiler heats:

 • Prepare meat mixture.

 • Drain cucumber and onion for sauce.

2 While meat cooks:

 • Prepare sauce for gyros.

 • Prepare salad.

Gyros

A Greek specialty, gyros are traditionally made from spiced, spit-roasted lamb. Here, we mold a ground lamb mixture into loaves. The yogurt dressing is a variation on traditional tzatziki.

LOAVES:

 1 teaspoon onion powder
 1 teaspoon garlic powder
 1 teaspoon dried oregano
 2 teaspoons fresh lemon juice
 ¼ teaspoon salt
 3 garlic cloves, minced
 6 ounces ground lamb
 6 ounces ground sirloin
Cooking spray
 ⅛ teaspoon ground red pepper

SAUCE:

 1 cup shredded peeled cucumber
 ¼ cup vertically sliced red onion
 1 tablespoon chopped fresh mint
 ½ teaspoon garlic powder
 ½ teaspoon fresh lemon juice
 ⅛ teaspoon salt
 ⅛ teaspoon black pepper
 1 (8-ounce) carton plain fat-free yogurt

REMAINING INGREDIENT:

 4 pocketless pitas

① Preheat broiler.

② To prepare loaves, combine first 8 ingredients. Divide mixture in half, forming each half into a 6 x 3-inch loaf. Place loaves on a broiler pan coated with cooking spray; broil 7 minutes on each side or until done.

③ Sprinkle loaves with red pepper. Cut each loaf crosswise into ⅛-inch slices.

④ To prepare sauce, place cucumber and onion on several layers of heavy-duty paper towels. Cover with additional paper towels; let stand 5 minutes.

⑤ Combine cucumber mixture, mint, and next 5 ingredients. Divide meat slices evenly among pitas; top each serving with about ¼ cup sauce. Yield: 4 servings.

CALORIES 375 (28% from fat); FAT 11.6g (sat 4.4g, mono 4.7g, poly 1g); PROTEIN 25g; CARB 42.4g; FIBER 2.3g; CHOL 61mg; IRON 3.5mg; SODIUM 627mg; CALC 158mg

Quick Tip: Lemon juice is used in the meat mixture, sauce, and salad, so squeeze enough for all at one time.

Lamb Pitas with Lemon-Mint Sauce

A chilled yogurt sauce is a refreshing contrast to the zesty seasoned meat mixture.

SAUCE:
- ²⁄₃ cup plain low-fat yogurt
- 2 tablespoons chopped fresh mint
- 2 teaspoons grated lemon rind
- ¼ teaspoon ground black pepper
- ⅛ teaspoon salt

SANDWICHES:
- 6 ounces ground lamb
- 6 ounces ground sirloin
- Cooking spray
- ½ cup finely chopped red onion
- 1 teaspoon minced fresh thyme
- ¼ teaspoon ground cumin
- ¼ teaspoon salt
- ⅛ teaspoon crushed red pepper
- 2 garlic cloves, minced
- ¼ cup minced fresh parsley
- 4 (6-inch) pitas, cut in half
- 1 cup peeled seeded thinly sliced cucumber
- 2 bottled roasted red bell peppers, cut into ¼-inch strips (about ½ cup)

1 To prepare sauce, combine first 5 ingredients in a small bowl; cover and chill until ready to serve.

2 To prepare sandwiches, heat a large non-stick skillet over medium-high heat. Add lamb and beef to pan; cook 5 minutes or until browned, stirring to crumble. Drain well, and set aside. Wipe pan dry with a paper towel.

3 Lightly coat pan with cooking spray; return to heat. Add onion; sauté 3 minutes or until tender. Stir in meat mixture, thyme, cumin, ¼ teaspoon salt, crushed red pepper, and garlic. Reduce heat to low; cook 2 minutes, stirring occasionally. Remove from heat; stir in parsley. Fill each pita half with ¼ cup lamb mixture, 2 tablespoons cucumber, about 1 tablespoon roasted peppers, and about 1 tablespoon sauce. Yield: 4 servings (serving size: 2 stuffed pita halves).

CALORIES 381 (28% from fat); FAT 11.8g (sat 4.7g, mono 4.5g, poly 1.2g); PROTEIN 27.1g; CARB 40.9g; FIBER 2.4g; CHOL 66mg; IRON 3.8mg; SODIUM 680mg; CALC 163mg

Flavor Tip: Heat pitas 1 minute on each side in a small skillet before preparing the meat filling; wrap them in foil to keep warm.

MENU *serves 4*

Lamb Pitas with Lemon-Mint Sauce

Spinach and tomato salad

Combine 4 cups fresh baby spinach; 1 cup peeled diced cucumber; ⅓ cup thinly sliced red onion; 2 tablespoons sliced ripe olives; 2 tablespoons crumbled feta cheese; and 4 plum tomatoes, cut into wedges, in a large bowl. Combine 3 tablespoons lemon juice, 1 tablespoon olive oil, 2 teaspoons minced fresh oregano, ⅛ teaspoon salt, and ⅛ teaspoon black pepper in a small bowl; stir with a whisk. Add dressing to spinach mixture; toss well.

Vanilla frozen yogurt with honey

Game Plan

1 Prepare lemon-mint sauce for sandwiches.

2 Prepare ingredients for Greek salad.

3 Simmer meat mixture; toss salad.

4 Assemble sandwiches.

Lamb Burgers with Fennel Salad

A crunchy yet creamy mixture of fennel, sour cream, yogurt, and mint tops these Greek-style burgers served in pitas. Seasoned feta and olives flavor the patties.

Greek potatoes

Combine 2 tablespoons olive oil, 1 tablespoon fresh lemon juice, 1 teaspoon bottled minced garlic, ½ teaspoon salt, ½ teaspoon dried oregano, and ¼ teaspoon black pepper in a small bowl; stir with a whisk. Arrange 3 pounds quartered small red potatoes in an 11 x 7-inch baking dish; drizzle with oil mixture, tossing to coat. Cover with plastic wrap; vent. Microwave at HIGH 15 minutes or until potatoes are tender.

Baby carrots with commercial hummus

Game Plan

1 Prepare grill or preheat broiler.

2 Prepare fennel salad.

3 Prepare potatoes.

4 While potatoes cook:

  • Prepare and grill burgers.

  • Assemble burgers.

SALAD:

- 2 cups thinly sliced fennel bulb (about 1 [8-ounce] bulb)
- ½ cup fat-free sour cream
- ½ cup plain fat-free yogurt
- ¼ cup finely chopped red onion
- 2 tablespoons chopped fresh mint
- 1 tablespoon grated lemon rind
- 1 tablespoon honey
- ¼ teaspoon salt
- ¼ teaspoon black pepper
- 1 garlic clove, minced

BURGERS:

- ½ cup (2 ounces) crumbled feta cheese with basil and garlic
- ¼ cup chopped pimiento-stuffed olives
- 2 tablespoons Greek seasoning (such as McCormick)
- ¼ teaspoon salt
- 1 pound lean ground lamb
- 1 pound ground turkey breast
- Cooking spray
- 4 (6-inch) pitas, cut in half

1 Prepare grill or preheat broiler.

2 To prepare salad, combine first 10 ingredients in a large bowl and set aside.

3 To prepare burgers, combine cheese and next 5 ingredients in a large bowl. Divide mixture into 8 equal portions, shaping each into a ½-inch-thick patty.

4 Place patties on a grill rack or broiler pan coated with cooking spray; cook 4 minutes on each side or until done. Cut patties in half. Place 2 patty halves and ¼ cup salad in each pita half. Yield: 8 servings.

CALORIES 316 (30% from fat); FAT 10.7g (sat 4.6g, mono 4.1g, poly 0.9g); PROTEIN 29g; CARB 24.7g; FIBER 1.5g; CHOL 81mg; IRON 2.1mg; SODIUM 616mg; CALC 133mg

Quick Tip: Use a mandoline or food processor to slice the fennel thinly and easily.

Pacific Rim Pork Sandwiches with Hoisin Slaw

Since the pork marinates for 1 to 2 hours, add it to the marinade as early as possible before preparing dinner. The pork is also delicious stir-fried with vegetables and served over rice.

PORK:

- 3 tablespoons low-sodium soy sauce
- 3 tablespoons dry sherry
- 3 tablespoons hoisin sauce
- 2 tablespoons minced peeled fresh ginger
- 1 tablespoon dark sesame oil
- 1½ teaspoons hot Chinese mustard
- ¼ teaspoon five-spice powder
- 1 garlic clove, minced
- 1 pound pork tenderloin, trimmed and cut into ¼-inch slices

SLAW:

- 2 tablespoons seasoned rice wine vinegar
- 1 tablespoon hoisin sauce
- 2 teaspoons dark sesame oil
- 1 teaspoon low-sodium soy sauce
- 1 teaspoon minced peeled fresh ginger
- ¼ teaspoon hot Chinese mustard
- 1 garlic clove, minced
- 2½ cups packaged cabbage-and-carrot coleslaw
- ¼ cup sliced green onions

REMAINING INGREDIENTS:

Cooking spray
- 4 (2-ounce) sesame seed buns, toasted

❶ To prepare pork, combine first 8 ingredients in a large zip-top plastic bag. Add pork, and seal. Marinate in refrigerator 1 to 2 hours, turning occasionally.

❷ To prepare slaw, combine vinegar and next 6 ingredients in a large bowl. Add coleslaw and green onions; toss well. Chill until ready to serve.

❸ Heat a large nonstick skillet over medium-high heat; coat with cooking spray. Remove pork from bag, and discard marinade. Add pork to pan; cook 2 minutes on each side or until done.

❹ Divide pork evenly among bottom halves of buns. Top each serving with about ½ cup slaw mixture and top half of bun. Yield: 4 servings (serving size: 1 sandwich).

CALORIES 360 (23% from fat); FAT 9.2g (sat 2.1g, mono 3.5g, poly 2.6g); PROTEIN 30.4g; CARB 37.1g; FIBER 2.8g; CHOL 74mg; IRON 3.6mg; SODIUM 697mg; CALC 84mg

Ingredient Tip: Pork tenderloin cooks quickly, especially when cut into thin slices and pan-fried.

MENU *serves 4*

Pacific Rim Pork Sandwiches with Hoisin Slaw

Sesame noodle salad
Combine 2 cups cooked soba noodles (2 ounces uncooked), ⅓ cup diced red bell pepper, ⅓ cup shredded carrot, ¼ cup sliced green onions, and 3 tablespoons bottled light soy-sesame dressing (such as Tamari Sesame Asian Dressing); toss well. Sprinkle with 1 teaspoon toasted sesame seeds. Chill until ready to serve.

Orange and grapefruit slices

Game Plan

1 While pork marinates:
- •Prepare slaw; chill until ready to serve.
- •Prepare noodle salad; chill until ready to serve.

2 While pork cooks:
- •Slice fruit.
- •Assemble sandwiches.

Spicy Pork and Sauerkraut Sandwiches

Vegetables with roasted garlic dip

Combine ¼ cup (2 ounces) fat-free cream cheese, 2 tablespoons low-fat mayonnaise, 1 tablespoon minced green onions, 1½ teaspoons bottled minced roasted garlic, and ⅛ teaspoon salt in a small bowl; beat with a mixer at medium speed until well blended. Refrigerate dip until ready to serve. Serve with assorted raw vegetables.

Strawberry sorbet

Game Plan

1 Prepare and refrigerate dip for vegetables.

2 Prepare spice mixture for pork.

3 While pork cooks:

• Measure sauerkraut ingredients.

• Cook sauerkraut.

4 Assemble sandwiches.

Spicy Pork and Sauerkraut Sandwiches

Using packaged coleslaw mix offers an easy, speedy alternative that's more colorful and less salty than traditional sauerkraut recipes.

½ teaspoon salt, divided
½ teaspoon dried oregano
½ teaspoon dried thyme
½ teaspoon black pepper
1 pound pork tenderloin, trimmed and cut crosswise into ¼-inch-thick slices
1 tablespoon canola oil, divided
Cooking spray
4 cups packaged cabbage-and-carrot coleslaw (about 8 ounces)
1 tablespoon prepared horseradish
1 tablespoon red wine vinegar
1½ teaspoons Worcestershire sauce
½ teaspoon crushed red pepper
⅓ cup fat-free mayonnaise
1 tablespoon Dijon mustard
4 (2-ounce) Kaiser rolls or hamburger buns
16 (⅛-inch-thick) slices cucumber

❶ Combine ¼ teaspoon salt, oregano, thyme, and black pepper; sprinkle pork with spice mixture. Heat 1½ teaspoons oil in a large non-stick skillet coated with cooking spray over medium-high heat. Add pork; cook 2 minutes on each side or until done. Remove pork from pan; keep warm.

❷ Heat 1½ teaspoons oil in pan over medium-high heat. Add ¼ teaspoon salt, coleslaw, and next 4 ingredients; cook 2 minutes, stirring frequently. Remove from heat.

❸ Combine mayonnaise and mustard; spread mixture evenly over cut sides of rolls. Divide coleslaw mixture, pork, and cucumber slices evenly among bottom halves of rolls. Cover with top halves of rolls. Yield: 4 servings.

CALORIES 366 (27% from fat); FAT 10.8g (sat 2.6g, mono 3.2g, poly 3.8g); PROTEIN 29.9g; CARB 37.5g; FIBER 4.1g; CHOL 76mg; IRON 3.7mg; SODIUM 989mg; CALC 108mg

Croque Monsieur

Similar to a Monte Cristo, a croque monsieur is a French-style grilled ham and cheese sandwich that is dipped into egg batter and then cooked in a skillet. Keep the finished sandwiches warm in a 200° oven while cooking the others.

4   (1½-ounce) slices French bread
4   teaspoons honey mustard
6   ounces reduced-fat deli ham, thinly sliced
4   (1-ounce) slices reduced-fat Swiss cheese
½   cup fat-free milk
3   large egg whites
Cooking spray

1 Cut a slit in each bread slice to form a pocket. Spread 1 teaspoon honey mustard into each bread pocket. Divide ham and cheese evenly among bread pockets.

2 Combine milk and egg whites in a shallow bowl; stir with a whisk. Dip sandwiches, 1 at a time, in milk mixture, turning to coat.

3 Heat a large nonstick skillet over medium-high heat; coat with cooking spray. Add 2 sandwiches; cook 3 minutes on each side or until golden brown. Repeat procedure with remaining sandwiches. Yield: 4 servings (serving size: 1 sandwich).

CALORIES 293 (30% from fat); FAT 9.8g (sat 5.2g, mono 0.8g, poly 0.8g); PROTEIN 22.3g; CARB 27.9g; FIBER 1.3g; CHOL 40mg; IRON 1.6mg; SODIUM 649mg; CALC 475mg

MENU *serves 4*

Croque Monsieur

Raspberry smoothies
Place 2 cups fat-free milk, 1 cup frozen raspberries, 1 cup raspberry sorbet, and 1 (8-ounce) carton vanilla low-fat yogurt in a blender; process until smooth. Serve immediately in chilled glasses.

Game Plan

1 Chill glasses for smoothies.

2 Prepare sandwiches.

3 While sandwiches cook:
   •Prepare smoothies.

Salads

Shrimp Caesar Salad,
page 107

Chickpea-Vegetable Salad with Curried Yogurt Dressing

To cut prep time, pick up packages of shredded carrots and torn romaine lettuce in the produce section of your supermarket. In addition, if you are preparing the entire menu, we recommend preparing the dressing and salad ingredients while the pita wedges bake.

DRESSING:

⅓ cup chopped fresh cilantro
2 tablespoons olive oil
1 tablespoon lemon juice
1½ teaspoons curry powder
¾ teaspoon salt
½ teaspoon bottled minced garlic
¼ teaspoon freshly ground black pepper
1 (8-ounce) carton plain fat-free yogurt

SALAD:

2 cups finely shredded carrot
1½ cups thinly sliced yellow or red bell pepper
1½ cups chopped plum tomato
½ cup golden raisins
¼ cup finely chopped red onion
2 (15½-ounce) cans chickpeas (garbanzo beans), drained
12 cups chopped romaine lettuce

❶ To prepare dressing, combine first 8 ingredients in a small bowl; stir with a whisk.

❷ To prepare salad, combine carrot and next 5 ingredients in a large bowl. Pour ½ cup dressing over carrot mixture, tossing gently to coat. Place 2 cups lettuce on each of 6 plates, and drizzle each serving with about 1 tablespoon dressing. Top each serving with 1⅓ cups carrot mixture. Yield: 6 servings.

CALORIES 337 (21% from fat); FAT 8g (sat 1.1g, mono 4.1g, poly 2g); PROTEIN 15.4g; CARB 55.4g; FIBER 8.9g; CHOL 1mg; IRON 5.7mg; SODIUM 573mg; CALC 201mg

---

MENU *serves 6*

Chickpea-Vegetable Salad with Curried Yogurt Dressing

Spiced pita wedges
Preheat oven to 350°. Combine 1 tablespoon melted butter and ¼ teaspoon each of coriander, cumin, and turmeric. Brush evenly over rough sides of an 8-inch split pita. Cut each pita half into 6 wedges; place on a baking sheet. Bake at 350° for 12 minutes or until toasted.

Game Plan

1 While oven heats for pita wedges:

•Prepare butter mixture.

•Cut pita rounds into wedges.

2 While pita wedges bake:

•Prepare salad dressing.

•Prepare vegetables for salad.

3 Assemble salad.

Tuscan Panzanella

This classic bread salad, full of juicy tomatoes, is like summer on a plate. It's best when the toasted bread is still crisp, so serve immediately after tossing.

4 (1-ounce) slices Italian bread
Cooking spray
1 cup torn fresh basil leaves
½ cup thinly sliced red onion
⅓ cup pitted kalamata olives, halved
2 pounds ripe tomatoes, cored and cut into 1-inch pieces
1 (16-ounce) can cannellini beans or other white beans, rinsed and drained
3 tablespoons red wine vinegar
1 tablespoon water
1 tablespoon extra-virgin olive oil
1 teaspoon bottled minced garlic
½ teaspoon freshly ground black pepper
¼ teaspoon salt

1 Preheat oven to 350°.
2 Trim crusts from bread slices; discard crusts. Cut bread into 1-inch cubes. Arrange bread cubes in a single layer on a baking sheet; coat bread with cooking spray. Bake at 350° for 15 minutes or until toasted.
3 Combine basil and next 4 ingredients in a large bowl. Combine vinegar and remaining 5 ingredients in a small bowl; stir with a whisk. Pour over tomato mixture; toss to coat. Add bread cubes; toss well. Serve immediately. Yield: 4 servings (serving size: 2 cups).

CALORIES 255 (29% from fat); FAT 8.1g (sat 1g, mono 4.9g, poly 1.1g); PROTEIN 9.8g; CARB 39.9g; FIBER 8.2g; CHOL 0mg; IRON 3.4mg; SODIUM 708mg; CALC 83mg

Quick Tip: To core a tomato easily, cut it into quarters and then slice the core out of each quarter.

Warm Lentil-Ham Salad with Dijon Cream

Serve this main dish salad as an alternative to potato salad at potluck dinners and picnics.

1 cup dried lentils
½ cup reduced-fat sour cream
2 tablespoons Dijon mustard
2 tablespoons fat-free milk
1 tablespoon white wine vinegar
1 teaspoon chopped fresh or ¼ teaspoon dried thyme
¼ teaspoon black pepper
1⅓ cups chopped cooked ham
¾ cup chopped celery
¾ cup chopped red onion

1 Place lentils in a large saucepan, and cover with water to 2 inches above lentils. Bring to a boil; cover, reduce heat, and simmer 20 minutes or until tender. Drain well.

2 Combine sour cream and next 5 ingredients in a large bowl. Add lentils, ham, celery, and onion; toss well. Yield: 4 servings (serving size: about 1⅓ cups).

CALORIES 291 (20% from fat); FAT 6.6g (sat 3.1g, mono 1.2g, poly 0.6g); PROTEIN 24.4g; CARB 35.6g; FIBER 15.8g; CHOL 37mg; IRON 5.5mg; SODIUM 649mg; CALC 114mg

Quick Tip: Dried lentils are ideal for weeknight dinners because they require no soaking and cook in about 20 minutes.

MENU *serves 4*

Warm Lentil-Ham Salad with Dijon Cream

Sautéed Swiss chard
Heat 1 tablespoon olive oil in a large nonstick skillet over medium-high heat. Add 12 ounces torn Swiss chard; sauté 3 minutes or until chard begins to wilt. Stir in 1 teaspoon sugar, 1 teaspoon white wine vinegar, and ¼ teaspoon salt; sauté 1 minute or until done.

Crusty French rolls

Game Plan

1 While lentils cook:
• Chop thyme, ham, celery, and onion.
• Measure ingredients for salad.
• Warm French rolls.
• Prepare Swiss chard.

2 Assemble salad.

Lemon-Dill Bulgur Salad with Scallops

Watercress is a pungent green with a peppery bite. Generally sold in small bunches, its dark green leaves are small and crisp. Wash and shake dry just before serving.

- 2 cups water
- 1 cup uncooked bulgur
- Cooking spray
- 1½ pounds sea scallops
- 2 cups chopped seeded cucumber
- 1½ cups chopped plum tomato
- 1 cup frozen corn kernels, thawed
- ¼ cup chopped fresh or 1 tablespoon dried dill
- ¼ cup lemon juice
- 2 tablespoons olive oil
- 1½ teaspoons salt
- 1 teaspoon sugar
- 1 teaspoon bottled minced garlic
- ¼ teaspoon freshly ground black pepper
- 6 cups trimmed watercress (about 2 bunches) or baby spinach

❶ Bring 2 cups water to a boil in a medium saucepan. Add bulgur; partially cover, reduce heat, and simmer 5 minutes. Drain; cool.

❷ While bulgur cooks, heat a medium non-stick skillet over medium-high heat; coat with cooking spray. Add scallops, and cook 3 minutes, turning once. Remove from heat; place scallops in a large bowl.

❸ Add bulgur, cucumber, and next 9 ingredients to scallops; toss well to coat. Place 1 cup watercress on each of 6 plates; top each serving with 1 cup scallop mixture. Yield: 6 servings.

CALORIES 275 (21% from fat); FAT 6.5g (sat 0.8g, mono 3.5g, poly 1g); PROTEIN 24.4g; CARB 32.4g; FIBER 6.9g; CHOL 37mg; IRON 1.7mg; SODIUM 795mg; CALC 103mg

Quick Tip: To seed a cucumber, cut in half lengthwise, and scoop out seeds with a spoon. Chop as directed. Peeling is optional and based on personal preference.

Chicken, Rice, and Tropical Fruit Salad

Serve this salad chilled or at room temperature, depending on your preference. You can also substitute lime juice for lemon.

1 cup uncooked basmati rice
2 cups cubed skinless, boneless rotisserie chicken breast
1 cup cubed fresh pineapple
1 cup bottled sliced peeled mango, drained and chopped
½ cup seedless red grapes, halved
¼ cup sliced almonds, toasted
2 tablespoons finely chopped fresh mint
1½ tablespoons fresh lemon juice
1½ tablespoons canola oil
¼ teaspoon salt
¼ teaspoon freshly ground black pepper
4 romaine lettuce leaves
Mint sprigs (optional)

❶ Cook rice according to package directions, omitting salt and fat. Cool. Combine rice and next 5 ingredients.

❷ Combine chopped mint, juice, oil, salt, and pepper in a small bowl; stir with a whisk. Drizzle mint mixture over rice mixture; toss well. Cover and chill. Place 1 lettuce leaf on each of 4 plates. Spoon 1½ cups rice mixture onto each lettuce leaf. Garnish with mint sprigs, if desired. Refrigerate until ready to serve. Yield: 4 servings.

CALORIES 346 (30% from fat); FAT 11.5g (sat 1.4g, mono 6.2g, poly 3g); PROTEIN 25.5g; CARB 36.1g; FIBER 2.8g; CHOL 60mg; IRON 1.6mg; SODIUM 199mg; CALC 45mg

Quick Tip: Look for peeled, cored, and cubed fresh pineapple in the produce section of your supermarket.

MENU *serves 4*

Chicken, Rice, and Tropical Fruit Salad

Herbed green beans
Cook 1 pound trimmed green beans in boiling water 7 minutes or until crisp-tender; drain. Place green beans in a medium bowl. Add 1 tablespoon minced fresh tarragon, 1 tablespoon minced fresh flat-leaf parsley, 2 teaspoons extra-virgin olive oil, ¼ teaspoon salt, and ⅛ teaspoon freshly ground black pepper; toss well.

Iced tea

Game Plan

1 While rice cooks:
  • Chop pineapple and mango.
  • Halve grapes.
  • Prepare mint mixture.

2 Assemble salad, and refrigerate.

3 While beans cook:
  • Chop herbs for beans.

MENU *serves 4*

**Chicken and
Couscous Salad**

Pita crisps

Preheat oven to 350°. Split 1 pita in half horizontally; cut each half into 6 wedges. Place wedges in a single layer on a baking sheet. Lightly coat with cooking spray; sprinkle with ⅛ teaspoon salt and ⅛ teaspoon freshly ground black pepper. Bake at 350° for 15 minutes or until pita wedges are crisp and golden brown.

Lemon sorbet

Game Plan

1 While oven heats:
- Prepare couscous.
- Prepare dressing.
- Season pita wedges.

2 While pita wedges cook:
- Prepare salad.

Chicken and Couscous Salad

If you can't find the specified box size of couscous, use 1 cup uncooked couscous. Take any leftover salad to work the next day for a light lunch.

SALAD:

- 1¼ cups fat-free, less-sodium chicken broth
- 1 (5.7-ounce) box uncooked couscous
- 1½ cups cubed cooked chicken (about 6 ounces)
- ½ cup thinly sliced green onions
- ½ cup diced radishes (about 3 large)
- ½ cup chopped seeded peeled cucumber
- ¼ cup chopped fresh flat-leaf parsley
- 2 tablespoons pine nuts, toasted

DRESSING:

- ¼ cup white wine vinegar
- 1½ tablespoons extra-virgin olive oil
- 1 teaspoon ground cumin
- ½ teaspoon salt
- ⅛ teaspoon freshly ground black pepper
- 1 garlic clove, minced

❶ To prepare salad, bring broth to a boil in a medium saucepan; gradually stir in couscous. Remove from heat; cover and let stand 5 minutes. Fluff with a fork. Spoon couscous into a large bowl; cool slightly. Add chicken and next 5 ingredients; toss gently.

❷ To prepare dressing, combine vinegar and remaining 5 ingredients; stir with a whisk. Drizzle dressing over salad; toss to combine. Yield: 4 servings (serving size: 1½ cups).

CALORIES 334 (29% from fat); FAT 10.9g (sat 2g, mono 5.9g, poly 2.1g); PROTEIN 20.9g; CARB 35.8g; FIBER 2.9g; CHOL 39mg; IRON 1.8mg; SODIUM 484mg; CALC 23mg

Quick Tip: You can toast pine nuts quickly in a dry skillet over medium-high heat. Stir frequently, and as soon as the pine nuts become fragrant, remove them from the pan.

Couscous Salad with Chicken, Tomato, and Basil

We used packaged roasted chicken to save time preparing this dish. It's available in the meat department of your supermarket.

2 tablespoons extra-virgin olive oil, divided
2 garlic cloves, minced
1 (15.75-ounce) can fat-free, less-sodium chicken broth
1½ cups uncooked couscous
2 cups chopped tomato (about 1¼ pounds)
2 cups chopped roasted skinless, boneless chicken breast (about 2 breast halves)
⅓ cup thinly sliced fresh basil
2 tablespoons balsamic vinegar
½ teaspoon salt
¼ teaspoon black pepper
¼ cup (1-ounce) crumbled feta cheese

❶ Combine 1 tablespoon olive oil and garlic in a large microwave-safe bowl, and microwave at HIGH 45 seconds. Add broth; microwave at HIGH 4 minutes or until mixture simmers. Gradually stir in couscous; cover and let stand 5 minutes. Fluff with a fork. Stir in tomato, chicken, basil, vinegar, salt, and pepper. Drizzle with 1 tablespoon oil, and sprinkle with cheese. Yield: 4 servings (serving size: 1½ cups).

CALORIES 487 (23% from fat); FAT 12.7g (sat 3g, mono 6.5g, poly 1.5g); PROTEIN 34.7g; CARB 57.5g; FIBER 3.7g; CHOL 71mg; IRON 2.8mg; SODIUM 718mg; CALC 60mg

MENU *serves 4*

Couscous Salad with Chicken, Tomato, and Basil

Cucumber-dill soup
Combine 1¾ cups chopped seeded peeled cucumber and ½ cup sliced green onions in a food processor; process until minced. Add 2 tablespoons chopped fresh or 2 teaspoons dried dill, ¾ teaspoon salt, ¾ teaspoon sugar, ¼ teaspoon white pepper, and 1 (16-ounce) carton plain low-fat yogurt; process until smooth. Ladle ¾ cup soup into each of 4 bowls. Top each serving with ½ teaspoon fresh dill and ½ teaspoon low-fat sour cream.

Toasted pita triangles

Game Plan

1 Preheat oven for pita wedges.

2 While broth mixture microwaves:
   • Chop tomato and chicken, and slice basil.

3 While couscous mixture stands:
   • Prepare soup.
   • Toast pita triangles.

4 Assemble salad.

MENU *serves 6*

Summer Farfalle Salad with Smoked Salmon

Artichoke-Parmesan cream cheese with crackers

Combine ¾ cup tub-style light cream cheese, ¼ cup chopped canned artichoke hearts, 3 tablespoons grated Parmesan cheese, and ¼ teaspoon garlic salt. Serve with crackers.

Sliced peaches

Game Plan

1 While water for pasta comes to a boil:

- Halve cherry tomatoes.
- Chop dill.
- Prepare artichoke-Parmesan cream cheese.

2 While pasta cooks:

- Prepare dressing for salad.
- Cut salmon.
- Slice peaches.

Summer Farfalle Salad with Smoked Salmon

You may substitute leftover cooked salmon for the sliced smoked salmon, if you prefer.

    3   cups uncooked farfalle (bow tie pasta)
    2   cups cherry tomatoes, halved
    ¼   cup chopped fresh dill
    1   (6-ounce) bag baby spinach
    1   teaspoon grated lemon rind
    2   tablespoons fresh lemon juice
    2   tablespoons cold water
    1½ tablespoons extra-virgin olive oil
    ½   teaspoon salt
    ¼   teaspoon black pepper
    4   ounces (about 8 slices) smoked salmon, cut into thin strips

❶ Cook pasta according to package directions, omitting salt and fat. Drain and rinse with cold water; drain.

❷ Combine pasta, tomatoes, dill, and spinach in a large bowl; toss gently.

❸ Combine lemon rind and next 5 ingredients in a small bowl; stir with a whisk. Drizzle over pasta mixture; toss gently to coat. Top with salmon. Yield: 6 servings (serving size: 2 cups).

CALORIES 206 (23% from fat); FAT 5.3g (sat 0.9g, mono 3.1g, poly 1.1g); PROTEIN 9.8g; CARB 31.4g; FIBER 2.7g; CHOL 4mg; IRON 2.3mg; SODIUM 603mg; CALC 43mg

Quick Tip: Look for sliced smoked salmon near the gourmet cheeses or in the seafood department. Freeze leftover salmon for later use on scrambled eggs or add to a toasted bagel with light cream cheese.

Greek Pasta Salad

A citrus dressing brightens this Greek-inspired salad. Great-tasting leftovers are an added bonus to this recipe, so take any extra to work the next day.

SALAD:
- 3 cups uncooked farfalle (bow tie pasta)
- Cooking spray
- 1 (8-ounce) tuna steak (about ¾ inch thick)
- ⅛ teaspoon salt
- 1½ cups sliced peeled cucumber
- ¾ cup (3 ounces) crumbled feta cheese with peppercorns
- ¼ cup coarsely chopped red onion
- ¼ cup sliced kalamata olives
- ¼ teaspoon freshly ground black pepper
- 12 cherry tomatoes, halved

DRESSING:
- ¼ cup fresh lemon juice
- 2 teaspoons extra-virgin olive oil
- 1 teaspoon dried oregano
- ¼ teaspoon freshly ground black pepper
- ⅛ teaspoon salt

❶ To prepare salad, cook pasta according to package directions, omitting salt and fat. Drain and rinse with cold water. Drain; place in a large bowl.

❷ Heat a large grill pan over high heat, and coat with cooking spray. Sprinkle tuna with ⅛ teaspoon salt. Add tuna to pan; cook 5 minutes on each side or until desired degree of doneness. Remove from pan; cool slightly. Cut tuna into 1-inch pieces. Add tuna, cucumber, and next 5 ingredients to pasta.

❸ To prepare dressing, combine lemon juice and remaining 4 ingredients; stir with a whisk. Drizzle over salad, and toss gently to coat. Yield: 4 servings (serving size: 2 cups).

CALORIES 352 (30% from fat); FAT 11.8g (sat 4.1g, mono 5g, poly 1.2g); PROTEIN 23.2g; CARB 39.6g; FIBER 2.8g; CHOL 44mg; IRON 2.5mg; SODIUM 567mg; CALC 144mg

Quick Tip: To save time, buy sliced olives and crumbled cheese.

MENU *serves 4*

Greek Pasta Salad

Pita crisps
Preheat broiler. Cut each of 4 pitas into 8 wedges. Arrange wedges in a single layer on a baking sheet coated with cooking spray. Lightly brush with 2 teaspoons olive oil; sprinkle with ½ teaspoon dried basil and 2 tablespoons freshly grated Parmesan cheese. Broil 2 minutes or until cheese is melted and pita is lightly browned.

Orange sorbet

Game Plan

1 While pasta cooks:
- •Preheat broiler.
- •Heat grill pan.
- •Slice cucumber, chop onion and olives, and halve tomatoes.

2 While tuna cooks:
- •Prepare dressing.

3 While tuna cools:
- •Prepare pita crisps.

MENU *serves 4*

Chicken and Farfalle Salad with Walnut Pesto

Strawberries in balsamic vinegar with angel food cake

Combine 4 cups hulled, halved strawberries and 2 teaspoons sugar; let stand 30 minutes. Drizzle with 2 tablespoons balsamic vinegar; toss gently to coat. Let stand 15 minutes; serve over slices of angel food cake.

White wine

Game Plan

1 While strawberries and sugar stand:

- •Bring water for farfalle to a boil.

2 While pasta cooks:

- •Prepare pesto.

3 Toss pasta salad.

4 Drizzle strawberries with vinegar; toss.

Chicken and Farfalle Salad with Walnut Pesto

To make sure the walnut pesto ingredients are evenly minced, stop the food processor halfway through processing, and scrape down the sides.

SALAD:

- 2 cups uncooked farfalle (bow tie pasta; about 6 ounces)
- 2 cups cubed cooked skinless, boneless chicken breast
- 1 cup quartered cherry tomatoes
- 2 tablespoons chopped pitted kalamata olives

WALNUT PESTO:

- 1 cup basil leaves
- ½ cup fresh parsley leaves
- 3 tablespoons coarsely chopped walnuts, toasted
- 1½ tablespoons extra-virgin olive oil
- 1 tablespoon white wine vinegar
- ½ teaspoon salt
- 1 garlic clove

REMAINING INGREDIENT:

- 4 curly leaf lettuce leaves

❶ To prepare salad, cook pasta according to package directions, omitting salt and fat. Drain; rinse with cold water. Combine pasta, chicken, tomatoes, and olives in a large bowl.
❷ To prepare walnut pesto, combine basil and next 6 ingredients in a food processor; pulse 6 times or until finely minced. Add pesto to pasta mixture, tossing gently to coat. Place 1 lettuce leaf on each of 4 plates, and top with salad mixture. Yield: 4 servings (serving size: 1½ cups salad and 1 lettuce leaf).

CALORIES 374 (30% from fat); FAT 12.5g (sat 2g, mono 5.5g, poly 3.9g); PROTEIN 29.4g; CARB 36.3g; FIBER 3g; CHOL 60mg; IRON 3.6mg; SODIUM 393mg; CALC 62mg

Ingredient Tip: Keep kalamata olives on hand to add zesty saltiness to salads, sandwiches, and spreads.

Chicken-Penne Salad with Green Beans

To quickly prepare the beans, trim just the stem ends, leaving the tapered blossom ends intact. Line up 5 or 6 beans at a time, and cut them roughly the same length as the pasta.

- 2 cups uncooked penne (tube-shaped pasta)
- 2 cups (1-inch) cut green beans (about ½ pound)
- 2 cups shredded cooked chicken breast
- ½ cup vertically sliced red onion
- ¼ cup chopped fresh basil
- 1½ teaspoons chopped fresh flat-leaf parsley
- 1 (7-ounce) bottle roasted red bell pepper, drained and cut into thin strips
- 2 tablespoons extra-virgin olive oil
- 2 tablespoons red wine vinegar
- 1 tablespoon cold water
- ½ teaspoon salt
- ½ teaspoon bottled minced garlic
- ¼ teaspoon black pepper

❶ Cook pasta in boiling water 7 minutes. Add green beans; cook 4 minutes. Drain and rinse with cold water; drain.

❷ Combine pasta mixture, chicken, and next 4 ingredients in a large bowl; toss gently to combine.

❸ Combine oil and remaining 5 ingredients in a small bowl; stir with a whisk. Drizzle over pasta mixture; toss gently to coat. Yield: 4 servings (serving size: 2 cups).

CALORIES 384 (23% from fat); FAT 9.7g (sat 1.8g, mono 5.7g, poly 1.5g); PROTEIN 26.9g; CARB 47.8g; FIBER 2.6g; CHOL 49mg; IRON 3.2mg; SODIUM 866mg; CALC 59mg

Quick Tip: Use 2 forks to shred the chicken breast. The texture of shredded chicken allows it to hold the dressing more easily.

MENU *serves 4*

Chicken-Penne Salad with Green Beans

Mozzarella toasts
Preheat oven to 350°. Place 4 (½-inch-thick) diagonally cut slices French bread baguette on a baking sheet. Sprinkle each bread slice with 1 tablespoon shredded part-skim mozzarella cheese. Bake at 350° for 12 minutes or until bread is golden and cheese is melted.

Mixed berries dolloped with vanilla yogurt

Game Plan

1 While water for pasta comes to a boil and oven preheats for toasts:
- Prepare toasts.
- Trim and cut green beans.
- Shred chicken.

2 While pasta and beans cook:
- Slice onion and bell pepper.
- Chop basil and parsley.
- Prepare dressing.
- Prepare berries.

Orzo Salad with Chickpeas, Dill, and Lemon

If you're not a big dill fan, use half of the amount called for in the recipe. Quick-cooking couscous can replace the orzo.

- 1 cup uncooked orzo (rice-shaped pasta)
- ½ cup thinly sliced green onions
- ½ cup (2 ounces) crumbled feta cheese
- ¼ cup chopped fresh dill
- 1 (19-ounce) can chickpeas (garbanzo beans), drained
- 3 tablespoons fresh lemon juice
- 1½ tablespoons extra-virgin olive oil
- 1 tablespoon cold water
- ½ teaspoon salt
- ½ teaspoon bottled minced garlic

❶ Cook pasta according to package directions, omitting salt and fat. Drain and rinse with cold water; drain.

❷ Combine pasta, onions, cheese, dill, and chickpeas in a large bowl; toss gently.

❸ Combine juice and remaining 4 ingredients in a small bowl; stir with a whisk. Drizzle over pasta mixture; toss gently to coat. Yield: 4 servings (serving size: 1¼ cups).

CALORIES 327 (29% from fat); FAT 10.4g (sat 2.9g, mono 5.1g, poly 1.8g); PROTEIN 10.8g; CARB 47.6g; FIBER 4.9g; CHOL 13mg; IRON 3mg; SODIUM 641mg; CALC 107mg

Quick Tip: To get more juice from a lemon, be sure the lemon is at room temperature. Then, before juicing, roll the lemon across the countertop while applying pressure with the palm of your hand.

MENU *serves 4*

Orzo Salad with Chickpeas, Dill, and Lemon

Sliced romaine with mint
Combine 4 cups thinly sliced romaine lettuce and ½ cup chopped fresh mint in a bowl. Combine 1 tablespoon fresh lemon juice, 2 teaspoons olive oil, and ⅛ teaspoon salt in a small bowl; stir with a whisk. Drizzle over salad; toss to combine.

Garlic breadsticks

Game Plan

1 While water for pasta comes to a boil and oven preheats for breadsticks:
  - Slice green onions.
  - Chop dill.
  - Drain chickpeas.

2 While pasta cooks:
  - Bake breadsticks.
  - Prepare romaine salad.
  - Prepare dressing for orzo salad.

MENU *serves 4*

Mediterranean Orzo Salad with Feta Vinaigrette

Pita wedges

Mint iced tea
Combine 1 quart cold water, ¾ cup fresh mint leaves, and 5 regular-sized tea bags in a saucepan; bring to a simmer. Remove from heat; cover and steep 3 minutes. Strain mixture, discarding mint and tea bags. Add 3 table-spoons sugar, stirring to dissolve. Serve over ice.

Game Plan

1 While water for orzo and water for tea comes to a boil:

- Chop spinach, sun-dried tomatoes, red onion, and kalamata olives.

2 While orzo cooks:

- Steep tea bags and mint in water.

- Chop marinated artichokes.

3 Prepare salad.

4 Strain tea, and add sugar.

Mediterranean Orzo Salad with Feta Vinaigrette

This salad is chock-full of zesty ingredients. If pitted kalamata olives aren't available, press each pitted olive with the flat side of a wide chef's knife to loosen the pits for easy removal.

1 cup uncooked orzo (rice-shaped pasta; about 8 ounces)
2 cups bagged prewashed baby spinach, chopped
½ cup chopped drained oil-packed sun-dried tomato halves
3 tablespoons chopped red onion
3 tablespoons chopped pitted kalamata olives
½ teaspoon freshly ground black pepper
¼ teaspoon salt
1 (6-ounce) jar marinated artichoke hearts, undrained
¾ cup (3 ounces) feta cheese, crumbled and divided

❶ Cook orzo according to package directions, omitting salt and fat. Drain and rinse with cold water; drain. Combine cooked orzo, spinach, and next 5 ingredients in a large bowl. ❷ Drain artichokes, reserving marinade. Coarsely chop artichokes; add artichokes, reserved marinade, and ½ cup feta cheese to orzo mixture, tossing gently to coat. Place salad on serving plates. Sprinkle each serving with feta cheese. Yield: 4 servings (serving size: 1¼ cups salad and about 1 tablespoon cheese).

CALORIES 338 (29% from fat); FAT 11g (sat 3.8g, mono 2.7g, poly 0.5g); PROTEIN 11.9g; CARB 52g; FIBER 5.1g; CHOL 19mg; IRON 3mg; SODIUM 620mg; CALC 138mg

Quick Tip:
The marinade from the artichokes does double duty: It saturates the artichokes and becomes a quick vinaigrette for the salad.

Rotini, Summer Squash, and Prosciutto Salad with Rosemary Dressing

Using white balsamic vinegar in this recipe maintains the salad dressing's pure golden color.

3 cups uncooked rotini (corkscrew pasta; about 8 ounces)
1½ cups coarsely chopped yellow squash
1½ cups coarsely chopped zucchini
4 ounces thinly sliced prosciutto, chopped
3 tablespoons chopped red onion
2 ounces fresh mozzarella cheese, chopped
¼ teaspoon salt
¼ teaspoon freshly ground black pepper
2 tablespoons white balsamic vinegar
1 tablespoon extra-virgin olive oil
1½ teaspoons Dijon mustard
½ teaspoon finely chopped fresh rosemary

❶ Cook pasta according to package directions, omitting salt and fat. Add squash and zucchini during last minute of cooking. Drain and rinse with cold water; drain.
❷ Heat a large nonstick skillet over medium-high heat until hot. Add prosciutto; cook 5 minutes or until crisp, stirring frequently.
❸ Combine pasta mixture, prosciutto, onion, and cheese in a large bowl; sprinkle with salt and pepper. Combine vinegar, oil, mustard, and rosemary in a small bowl; stir with a whisk. Add vinegar mixture to pasta mixture; toss gently to coat. Yield: 4 servings (serving size: 2¼ cups).

CALORIES 359 (28% from fat); FAT 11.1g (sat 4g, mono 2.8g, poly 0.4g); PROTEIN 18.7g; CARB 46.3g; FIBER 2.4g; CHOL 36mg; IRON 2.5mg; SODIUM 771mg; CALC 103mg

MENU *serves 4*

Rotini, Summer Squash, and Prosciutto Salad with Rosemary Dressing

Tomato bruschetta
Preheat broiler. Combine 1 cup cherry tomatoes, 1 teaspoon olive oil, 4 fresh basil leaves, and a dash of salt and pepper in a food processor; process until coarsely chopped. Coat 8 (½-ounce) French bread baguette slices with cooking spray. Broil 2 minutes or until lightly browned. Spoon 2 tablespoons cherry tomato mixture onto each baguette slice.

Fresh blueberries with low-fat vanilla yogurt

Game Plan

1 While water for rotini comes to a boil:
   • Chop yellow squash, zucchini, prosciutto, and red onion.
   • Cook prosciutto.
2 While pasta cooks:
   • Prepare bruschetta.
   • Combine ingredients for balsamic vinegar mixture.
3 Assemble salad.

MENU *serves 4*

Lemon-Splashed Shrimp Salad

Spicy Broccolini
Cook 1 pound Broccolini in boiling water 2 minutes. Drain and plunge into ice water; drain. Heat 1 tablespoon olive oil in a skillet over medium heat. Add 2 thinly sliced garlic cloves; cook 1 minute. Add Broccolini and ¼ teaspoon crushed red pepper; cook 1 minute or until thoroughly heated.

Angel food cake with berries

Game Plan

1 Peel and devein shrimp.

2 While water for pasta, shrimp, and Broccolini comes to a boil:
  • Prepare vegetables, cilantro, and lemon for salad.

3 While pasta cooks:
  • Cook Broccolini.

4 Add shrimp to pasta.

5 Assemble salad.

6 Prepare dessert.

Lemon-Splashed Shrimp Salad

Purchase peeled and deveined shrimp to save prep time. Chock-full of colorful ingredients, this makes a summery one-dish meal. Spicy Broccolini provides a flavorful counterpoint to the cold shrimp salad. However, you could serve the side dish cold and pack up the meal for a picnic.

8 cups water
⅔ cup uncooked rotini (corkscrew pasta)
1½ pounds large shrimp, peeled and deveined
1 cup halved cherry tomatoes
¾ cup sliced celery
½ cup chopped avocado
½ cup chopped seeded poblano chile
2 teaspoons grated lemon rind
3 tablespoons fresh lemon juice
2 tablespoons chopped fresh cilantro
2 teaspoons extra-virgin olive oil
¾ teaspoon kosher salt

❶ Bring 8 cups water to a boil in a large saucepan. Add pasta; cook 5 minutes or until almost tender. Add shrimp; cook 3 minutes or until done. Drain. Rinse with cold water; drain. Combine pasta mixture, tomatoes, and remaining ingredients in a bowl; toss well to combine. Yield: 4 servings (serving size: about 1¾ cups).

CALORIES 250 (25% from fat); FAT 6.9g (sat 1.2g, mono 3.8g, poly 1.2g); PROTEIN 30.3g; CARB 17g; FIBER 2.6g; CHOL 252mg; IRON 5.1mg; SODIUM 667mg; CALC 74mg

Wine Tip: The dominant green flavors in this salad (celery and avocado) along with a nice hint of heat (poblanos) and citrus (lemon) all point to a perfect wine partner: sauvignon blanc. Sassy and herbal, sauvignon blanc's splash of lemon makes it a great complement to these flavors.

Asian Beef-Noodle Salad

Bottled fresh ground ginger is a speedy way to invigorate this salad; look for it in the produce section of larger supermarkets. You may also substitute an equal amount of grated fresh ginger.

- 1 (3.75-ounce) package bean threads (cellophane noodles)
- 8 ounces sliced deli roast beef, cut lengthwise into thin strips
- 1 cup snow peas, trimmed and cut lengthwise into thin strips
- ½ cup julienne-cut carrot
- ½ cup low-sodium teriyaki sauce
- 2 tablespoons fresh lime juice
- 2 teaspoons dark sesame oil
- 2 teaspoons chile paste with garlic
- ½ teaspoon bottled fresh ground ginger (such as Spice World)
- 6 cups torn spinach
- ¼ cup chopped fresh cilantro

❶ Cover noodles with boiling water in a bowl. Let stand 15 minutes or until tender; drain.
❷ Combine beef, snow peas, and carrot in a microwave-safe bowl. Combine teriyaki sauce and next 4 ingredients, and pour over beef mixture. Microwave at HIGH 2 minutes or until thoroughly heated. Add noodles; toss well. Serve over spinach. Sprinkle with cilantro. Yield: 6 servings (serving size: 1 cup beef mixture and 1 cup spinach).

CALORIES 173 (26% from fat); FAT 5g (sat 1g, mono 1.5g, poly 0.8g); PROTEIN 10g; CARB 22.8g; FIBER 2.8g; CHOL 32mg; IRON 2.9mg; SODIUM 653mg; CALC 58mg

MENU *serves 6*

Asian Beef-Noodle Salad

Fresh fruit salad
Combine 1 mango, cut into ½-inch cubes; 1 Granny Smith apple, cut into ½-inch cubes; 1 sliced banana; and 1 cup seedless grapes. Combine 2 tablespoons fresh lime juice, 2 tablespoons honey, and 2 teaspoons chopped fresh mint; stir with a whisk. Drizzle over fruit. Cover and chill.

Game Plan

1 Bring water for noodles to a boil.

2 While noodles stand:
- •Prepare fruit salad, and chill.

3 Prepare noodle salad.

MENU *serves 4*

Asian Chicken, Noodle, and Vegetable Salad

Wonton crisps
Preheat oven to 375°. Stack 12 wonton wrappers; cut in half diagonally. Arrange wonton halves in a single layer on a foil-lined baking sheet. Coat with cooking spray; sprinkle with ¼ teaspoon kosher salt. Bake at 375° for 10 minutes or until lightly browned.

Cucumber spears

Game Plan

1 While noodles cook:

- Prepare chili sauce mixture for salad.
- Cut cucumber spears.

2 While oven preheats:

- Cut and season wonton wrappers.
- Chop vegetables for salad.

3 While wonton crisps bake:

- Assemble salad.

Asian Chicken, Noodle, and Vegetable Salad

Mix dark meat with the breast meat, if you like. Look for Thai sweet chili sauce in Asian and gourmet markets or in the supermarket's ethnic section.

6 ounces uncooked rice noodles
2 cups cubed skinless, boneless rotisserie chicken breast
½ cup matchstick-cut carrots
½ cup chopped green bell pepper
⅓ cup chopped green onions (about 3)
¼ cup canned sliced water chestnuts, drained
¼ cup Thai sweet chili sauce (such as Mae Ploy)
2 tablespoons canola oil
1½ tablespoons rice wine vinegar
1½ tablespoons fresh lemon juice
2 teaspoons low-sodium soy sauce
½ teaspoon grated peeled fresh ginger
2 tablespoons chopped unsalted, dry-roasted peanuts

❶ Prepare noodles according to package directions. Drain and cool. Combine noodles, chicken, and next 4 ingredients in a large bowl; toss well.

❷ Combine chili sauce and next 5 ingredients in a small bowl; stir with a whisk. Drizzle chili sauce mixture over noodle mixture; toss gently to coat. Sprinkle with peanuts. Serve immediately. Yield: 4 servings (serving size: 2 cups).

CALORIES 373 (29% from fat); FAT 11.9g (sat 1.5g, mono 6.1g, poly 3.4g); PROTEIN 23.6g; CARB 43.7g; FIBER 1.8g; CHOL 60mg; IRON 2.1mg; SODIUM 368mg; CALC 37mg

Quick Tip: Spend less time chopping by purchasing matchstick-cut carrots and chopped green bell pepper from the supermarket produce section.

Soba Noodle Salad with Vegetables and Tofu

Soba noodles are Japanese noodles made with a combination of buckwheat flour, wheat flour, and water. This is one of the few Asian noodles for which there is no suitable substitute.

DRESSING:
- ½ cup low-sodium soy sauce
- ¼ cup packed brown sugar
- 1 tablespoon sesame seeds, toasted
- 2 tablespoons orange juice
- 1 tablespoon bottled minced or minced peeled fresh ginger
- 1 tablespoon rice vinegar
- 2 teaspoons dark sesame oil
- 1 teaspoon bottled minced garlic
- 1 teaspoon chile paste with garlic

SALAD:
- 4 cups hot cooked soba (about 8 ounces uncooked buckwheat noodles) or whole wheat spaghetti
- 3 cups very thinly sliced napa (Chinese) cabbage
- 2 cups fresh bean sprouts
- 1 cup shredded carrot
- ½ cup chopped fresh cilantro
- 1 (12.3-ounce) package firm tofu, drained and cut into 1-inch cubes

1 To prepare dressing, combine first 9 ingredients in a small bowl; stir with a whisk.

2 To prepare salad, combine noodles and remaining 5 ingredients in a large bowl. Drizzle with dressing, tossing well to coat. Yield: 5 servings (serving size: 2 cups).

CALORIES 336 (19% from fat); FAT 7g (sat 1g, mono 1.8g, poly 3g); PROTEIN 15.1g; CARB 53.8g; FIBER 2.8g; CHOL 0mg; IRON 6.6mg; SODIUM 850mg; CALC 169mg

Quick Tip:
Napa cabbage is traditionally used in Asian-inspired salads, but if you're short on time, substitute bagged sliced cabbage or coleslaw mix.

MENU *serves 5*

Soba Noodle Salad with Vegetables and Tofu

Sesame crisps
Preheat oven to 375°. Combine 2 tablespoons sesame seeds, ½ teaspoon garlic salt, and ½ teaspoon paprika in a small bowl. Stack 15 wonton wrappers; cut in half diagonally, and place on a baking sheet. Brush evenly with 1 tablespoon sesame oil, and sprinkle with sesame seed topping. Bake at 375° for 4 minutes or until crisp.

Game Plan

1 While oven heats and water comes to a boil:
- Prepare sesame mixture for wontons.
- Cut wontons in half diagonally.

2 While soba noodles cook:
- Prepare salad dressing.
- Prepare vegetables for salad.
- Drain tofu.
- Bake wontons.

3 Assemble salad.

MENU *serves 4*

Soba and Slaw Salad with Peanut Dressing

Melon and lime compote
Peel and cut 1 honeydew melon into 1-inch pieces. Drizzle with ½ cup fresh lime juice, tossing gently to coat. Sprinkle with 1 tablespoon grated lime rind.

Fortune cookies

Game Plan

1 While water for soba noodles comes to a boil:

• Prepare compote.

• Shred cabbage and grate carrot.

2 While noodles cook:

• Prepare soy sauce mixture.

• Chop shrimp and slice green onions.

3 Assemble salad.

Soba and Slaw Salad with Peanut Dressing

Look for soba noodles, rice vinegar, chile paste, and soy sauce in the specialty-foods aisle of your supermarket or in Asian markets. Use packaged slaw mix in place of the red cabbage and carrot if you're in a hurry. Try this recipe with coarsely chopped rotisserie chicken instead of shrimp.

6 ounces uncooked soba (buckwheat) noodles, broken in half
6 cups shredded red cabbage
2 cups grated carrot
¾ cup thinly sliced green onions, divided
½ pound coarsely chopped cooked shrimp
3 tablespoons low-sodium soy sauce
3 tablespoons rice vinegar
2½ tablespoons creamy peanut butter
1 tablespoon canola oil
2 teaspoons Thai chile paste with garlic
2 tablespoons chopped dry-roasted peanuts

❶ Cook noodles according to package directions, omitting salt and fat. Drain and rinse with cold water; drain.

❷ Combine noodles, shredded cabbage, carrot, ½ cup green onions, and shrimp in a large bowl.

❸ Combine soy sauce and next 4 ingredients in a small bowl; stir with a whisk. Add soy sauce mixture to noodle mixture, tossing gently to coat. Sprinkle with ¼ cup green onions and peanuts. Yield: 4 servings (serving size: 2½ cups salad, 1 tablespoon onions, and 1½ teaspoons peanuts).

CALORIES 393 (30% from fat); FAT 12.9g (sat 1.8g, mono 5.8g, poly 3.5g); PROTEIN 24.6g; CARB 47.7g; FIBER 4.7g; CHOL 111mg; IRON 5.5mg; SODIUM 753mg; CALC 127mg

Quick Tip:
Use the shredding attachment of a food processor to make quick work of preparing the cabbage and carrots.

Sizzling Salmon-and-Spinach Salad with Soy Vinaigrette

The presentation of this salad is beautiful, and the flavors blend together perfectly. It is the ideal light dinner to eat outside on a summer evening.

DRESSING:

- 3 tablespoons thinly sliced green onions
- 3 tablespoons rice vinegar
- 3 tablespoons low-sodium soy sauce
- 1 tablespoon water
- 1 teaspoon sesame seeds, toasted
- 1 teaspoon bottled minced garlic
- 1 teaspoon dark sesame oil
- ½ teaspoon chile paste with garlic or ¼ teaspoon crushed red pepper

SALAD:

- 2 teaspoons dark sesame oil, divided
- 4 cups thinly sliced shiitake or button mushroom caps (about 8 ounces)
- 1 cup (1-inch) sliced green onions
- 1 cup fresh or frozen corn kernels, thawed
- 4 (6-ounce) salmon fillets (about 1 inch thick)
- 8 cups baby spinach
- 1 cup fresh bean sprouts
- 1 cup red bell pepper strips

1 Preheat broiler.

2 To prepare dressing, combine first 8 ingredients in a small bowl; stir with a whisk.

3 To prepare salad, heat 1 teaspoon oil in a large nonstick skillet over medium-high heat. Add mushrooms and 1 cup onions; sauté 8 minutes. Stir in corn; remove from heat.

4 Place fillets on a foil-lined baking sheet; brush evenly with 1 teaspoon oil. Broil 8 minutes or until fish flakes easily when tested with a fork.

5 Place 2 cups spinach on each of 4 plates; top each serving with ¼ cup bean sprouts, ¼ cup red bell pepper, ½ cup mushroom mixture, and 1 fillet. Drizzle about 2 tablespoons dressing over each salad. Yield: 4 servings.

CALORIES 418 (40% from fat); FAT 18.8g (sat 3.2g, mono 8.3g, poly 5.1g); PROTEIN 42.9g; CARB 21.8g; FIBER 7.8g; CHOL 111mg; IRON 6.1mg; SODIUM 549mg; CALC 163mg

MENU *serves 4*

Sizzling Salmon-and-Spinach Salad with Soy Vinaigrette

Sesame-garlic braid
Preheat oven to 350°. Unroll 1 (11-ounce) can refrigerated French bread dough on a baking sheet coated with cooking spray; cut into thirds lengthwise. Braid portions together; pinch loose ends to seal. Combine 2 tablespoons melted butter and 1 teaspoon bottled minced garlic; brush over braid, and sprinkle with 1 tablespoon sesame seeds. Bake at 350° for 25 minutes or until loaf sounds hollow when tapped.

Game Plan

1 While bread bakes:
- •Prepare salad dressing.
- •Prepare vegetables.

2 Remove bread from oven and keep warm.

3 While mushrooms, onions, and corn cook:
- •Broil fish.

4 Assemble salad.

MENU *serves 4*

Grilled Tuna Niçoise Salad

Crusty whole wheat rolls

Blueberry-yogurt sundaes
Combine 2 tablespoons blueberry spread (such as Polaner All-Fruit) and 1 tablespoon warm water, stirring until blended. Stir in 2 cups fresh or frozen, thawed, blueberries. Scoop ½ cup vanilla low-fat frozen yogurt into each of 4 serving bowls; top with blueberry sauce. Garnish with fresh mint leaves, if desired.

Game Plan

1 While grill heats:

- Microwave potatoes and green beans.

- Combine dressing and tarragon.

2 While tuna cooks:

- Slice potatoes.

- Divide vegetables, egg, and olives evenly among 4 plates.

- Prepare topping for sundaes.

Grilled Tuna Niçoise Salad

Niçoise olives are smaller than the more familiar green or ripe black olives. If you can't find niçoise, choose kalamata olives (which are available with and without pits).

¾ pound small red potatoes
½ pound green beans, trimmed
⅓ cup reduced-fat Italian dressing
2 teaspoons chopped fresh or ½ teaspoon dried tarragon
4 (6-ounce) tuna steaks (about ¾ inch thick)
Cooking spray
8 cups mixed salad greens
1 hard-cooked large egg, chopped
16 niçoise olives
2 tablespoons capers

❶ Prepare grill.
❷ Scrub potatoes. Place wet potatoes in an 8-inch square baking dish; cover with wax paper. Microwave at HIGH 3 minutes. Add beans to dish; cover. Microwave at HIGH 3 minutes or until vegetables are tender; drain. Rinse with cold water.
❸ While vegetables cook, combine dressing and tarragon. Set aside ¼ cup dressing mixture;

brush remaining dressing mixture over fish. Place fish on grill rack coated with cooking spray; grill 3 minutes on each side or until medium-rare (140° to 145°) or desired degree of doneness. (Do not overcook or fish will be tough.)
❹ Arrange greens on 4 serving plates. Drain potatoes and green beans; thinly slice potatoes. Arrange potatoes, green beans, egg, and olives over greens. Top each salad with a steak; sprinkle with capers. Drizzle evenly with reserved dressing. Yield: 4 servings (serving size: 1 tuna steak, 2 cups salad greens, 4 olives, and 1½ teaspoons capers).

CALORIES 437 (22% from fat); FAT 10.6g (sat 1.9g, mono 4g, poly 3.5g); PROTEIN 57.3g; CARB 26.1g; FIBER 6.2g; CHOL 152mg; IRON 4.2mg; SODIUM 706mg; CALC 146mg

Quick Tip: If you buy frozen tuna steaks, thaw them in the refrigerator 1 day ahead. Keep hard-cooked eggs on hand to make this salad anytime.

Lump Crab Salad

Though it can be expensive, crabmeat is great for quick and delicious dinners. Substitute canned lump crabmeat for fresh, if you prefer, but avoid using regular canned crabmeat; the meat is too flaky for this dish. Rinse canned lump crabmeat for the best flavor.

DRESSING:
- ½ teaspoon grated lime rind
- 3 tablespoons fresh lime juice
- 1½ tablespoons extra-virgin olive oil
- 1 teaspoon sugar
- 1 teaspoon Thai fish sauce (such as Three Crabs)
- ¼ teaspoon salt
- ⅛ teaspoon ground red pepper

SALAD:
- ¾ cup finely chopped celery
- ⅔ cup finely chopped red bell pepper
- ⅓ cup thinly sliced green onions
- 3 tablespoons chopped fresh mint
- 1 pound lump crabmeat, shell pieces removed
- 4 Boston lettuce leaves

1 To prepare dressing, combine first 7 ingredients; stir with a whisk.

2 To prepare salad, combine celery and next 4 ingredients in a medium bowl; toss gently. Drizzle dressing over salad; toss gently to coat. Place 1 lettuce leaf on each of 4 plates; spoon 1 cup salad into each leaf. Yield: 4 servings.

CALORIES 202 (29% from fat); FAT 6.6g (sat 0.7g, mono 3.7g, poly 0.6g); PROTEIN 27.8g; CARB 5.3g; FIBER 1.3g; CHOL 128mg; IRON 1.5mg; SODIUM 730mg; CALC 160mg

Ingredient Tip:
To get more juice from a lime, microwave it at HIGH 10 seconds before cutting it open.

MENU *serves 4*

Lump Crab Salad

Marinated cucumbers
Combine 2 cups thinly sliced English cucumber, 3 tablespoons rice vinegar, 1½ teaspoons sugar, ½ teaspoon dark sesame oil, ¼ teaspoon salt, and ¼ teaspoon crushed red pepper. Cover and chill.

Sesame crackers

Game Plan
1 Prepare and refrigerate marinated cucumbers.
2 Prepare crab salad.
3 Spoon salad into lettuce leaves just before serving.

Shellfish and Bacon Spinach Salad

MENU *serves 4*

Shellfish and Bacon Spinach Salad

Herb and Parmesan breadsticks
Preheat oven to 375°. Unroll 1 (11-ounce) can refrigerated breadstick dough, and separate into 12 pieces. Combine 3 tablespoons grated Parmesan cheese and 2 teaspoons herbes de Provence on a plate. Coat each piece of dough lightly with cheese mixture. Twist each piece several times, forming a spiral; place on an ungreased baking sheet, pressing down lightly on both ends. Bake at 375° for 13 minutes or until lightly browned. Serve warm.

Oatmeal-raisin cookies

Game Plan

1 While breadsticks bake:
- Cook bacon.
- Scrub and debeard mussels.
- Mince garlic.

2 While mussels cook:
- Slice onion.

Gently rinse mussels under cold running water, and discard any opened mussels before you cook them. After cooking, be sure to discard any unopened shells.

2 thick slices applewood-smoked bacon, diced (such as Neuske's)
2 garlic cloves, minced
¼ cup riesling or other dry white wine
⅛ teaspoon crushed red pepper
3 pounds mussels, scrubbed and debearded
⅓ cup thinly sliced red onion, separated into rings
2 (6-ounce) packages prewashed baby spinach

1 Cook bacon in a Dutch oven over medium heat until crisp. Remove bacon from pan, reserving 1 tablespoon drippings in pan. Crumble bacon; set aside.

2 Add garlic to drippings in pan; cook over medium heat 1 minute. Add wine and crushed red pepper. Add mussels; cover and cook 6 minutes or until shells open. Remove from heat; discard any unopened shells. Place mussels in a bowl. Add onion and spinach to wine mixture in pan; cook 1 minute or until spinach wilts. Divide spinach mixture among 4 plates; sprinkle evenly with bacon. Arrange mussels over spinach mixture; drizzle evenly with remaining wine mixture. Yield: 4 servings (serving size: about 2 dozen mussels, 2 cups spinach mixture, and 1 tablespoon bacon).

CALORIES 165 (25% from fat); FAT 4.6g (sat 1.5g, mono 0.6g, poly 0.7g); PROTEIN 16.7g; CARB 14.9g; FIBER 4.2g; CHOL 37mg; IRON 7.3mg; SODIUM 586mg; CALC 96mg

Caribbean Grilled Scallop Salad

Boston lettuce is pale green with a mild taste and tender texture. To prep it perfectly, rinse gently, pat dry, and refrigerate in moistened paper towels until ready to assemble salad.

12 large sea scallops (about 1½ pounds)
2 teaspoons fish rub, divided (such as Emeril's)
Cooking spray
5 (½-inch) slices fresh pineapple
4 cups gourmet salad greens or mixed salad greens
4 cups torn Boston lettuce (about 2 small heads)
⅓ cup diced peeled avocado
2 tablespoons mango chutney
2 tablespoons fresh lime juice
2 teaspoons olive oil

❶ Prepare grill.
❷ Pat scallops dry with a paper towel. Sprinkle 1½ teaspoons fish rub evenly over scallops. Coat scallops with cooking spray. Place scallops on grill rack; grill 3 minutes on each side or until done. Remove scallops. Add pineapple to grill rack; grill 2 minutes on each side. Remove pineapple from grill, and chop.
❸ Combine pineapple, salad greens, lettuce, and avocado in a large bowl.
❹ Chop large pieces of mango chutney. Combine ½ teaspoon fish rub, chutney, lime juice, and oil. Add to salad; toss well. Place 1½ cups salad in each of 4 bowls. Arrange 3 scallops over each salad. Yield: 4 servings.

CALORIES 264 (20% from fat); FAT 5.8g (sat 0.8g, mono 3g, poly 1.1g); PROTEIN 30.8g; CARB 22.8g; FIBER 3.4g; CHOL 56mg; IRON 2.3mg; SODIUM 559mg; CALC 101mg

Quick Tip: Speed up preparation by purchasing peeled and cored pineapple and prewashed salad greens in the produce section of your supermarket.

MENU *serves 4*

Caribbean Grilled Scallop Salad

Grilled baguette
Prepare grill. Cut 1 (8-ounce) French baguette into ½-inch-thick slices. Brush both sides of bread evenly with 2 table-spoons olive oil. Grill both sides of bread 1 minute or until golden.

Coconut sorbet

Game Plan

1 While grill heats:
   •Peel, core, and slice pineapple.
   •Slice baguette; brush with oil.
   •Season scallops.

2 While scallops and pineapple cook:
   •Place salad greens and avocado in bowl.
   •Prepare dressing.

MENU *serves 4*

Coconut Crab and Shrimp Salad

Spicy pita wedges
Preheat oven to 450°. Cut 4 (6-inch) pita breads into wedges; arrange wedges in a single layer on a baking sheet. Lightly coat wedges with cooking spray. Combine 2 teaspoons sesame seeds, ½ teaspoon ground cumin, ¼ teaspoon salt, ¼ teaspoon garlic powder, and ¼ teaspoon ground red pepper. Sprinkle evenly over wedges. Bake at 450° for 5 minutes or until lightly browned.

Pineapple sorbet

Game Plan

1 While pita wedges bake:
- •Toast coconut.
- •Chop cilantro and jalapeño.
- •Chop onion and dice avocado.

2 While shrimp cooks:
- •Tear lettuce.

3 Assemble salad.

4 Scoop sorbet; freeze until time to serve.

Coconut Crab and Shrimp Salad

This fresh, colorful seafood salad also makes a terrific appetizer. For added heat, add the jalapeño pepper seeds or use 2 peppers.

Cooking spray
- ½ pound medium shrimp, peeled and deveined
- ½ teaspoon salt, divided
- 1 cup fresh (about 2 ears) or frozen corn kernels, thawed
- ⅓ cup finely chopped onion
- ⅓ cup chopped fresh cilantro
- ⅓ cup diced peeled avocado
- ½ pound lump crabmeat, drained and shell pieces removed
- 1 jalapeño pepper, seeded and chopped
- 3 tablespoons fresh lemon juice
- 2 teaspoons extra-virgin olive oil
- 6 cups torn Boston lettuce (about 3 small heads)
- ¼ cup flaked sweetened coconut, toasted

❶ Heat a medium nonstick skillet over medium-high heat; coat with cooking spray. Add shrimp and ¼ teaspoon salt; cook 4 minutes or until shrimp are done, turning once. Remove from pan. Coarsely chop shrimp.

❷ Combine corn and next 5 ingredients in a medium bowl. Gently stir in shrimp. Combine juice, oil, and ¼ teaspoon salt; stir with a whisk. Drizzle juice mixture over shrimp mixture; toss gently to coat. Place lettuce on each of 4 plates; top with shrimp mixture. Sprinkle with coconut. Yield: 4 servings (serving size: 1½ cups lettuce, about 1 cup shrimp mixture, and 1 tablespoon coconut).

CALORIES 223 (34% from fat); FAT 8.5g (sat 2.2g, mono 3.6g, poly 1.3g); PROTEIN 24g; CARB 16g; FIBER 3g; CHOL 124mg; IRON 3mg; SODIUM 613mg; CALC 94mg

Quick Tip: To avoid using 2 pans, toast the coconut over medium-high heat until golden before cooking the shrimp.

Shrimp Caesar Salad

Using precooked shrimp speeds up preparation. If you purchase raw shrimp, cook them in boiling water for 2 minutes or until done. Sriracha Thai hot chile sauce creates a spicier dressing; omit it for a milder dish. Serve this salad with sauvignon blanc.

DRESSING:

- 2 tablespoons light mayonnaise
- 2 tablespoons water
- 2 tablespoons fresh lemon juice
- 1 teaspoon grated Parmesan cheese
- ¼ teaspoon freshly ground black pepper
- ¼ teaspoon Sriracha Thai hot chile sauce (such as Huy Fong)
- ⅛ teaspoon Worcestershire sauce
- 2 garlic cloves, minced

SALAD:

- ¾ cup fat-free seasoned croutons
- 2 tablespoons grated Parmesan cheese
- 1½ pounds medium shrimp, cooked and peeled
- 1 (10-ounce) package chopped romaine lettuce
- 3 tablespoons pine nuts, toasted

Chopped fresh chives (optional)

1 To prepare dressing, combine first 8 ingredients; stir with a whisk.

2 To prepare salad, combine croutons and next 3 ingredients in a large bowl. Add dressing; toss well to coat. Top with pine nuts. Garnish with chives, if desired. Serve immediately. Yield: 4 servings (serving size: 3 cups salad and 2¼ teaspoons pine nuts).

CALORIES 295 (29% from fat); FAT 9.4g (sat 1.7g, mono 2.1g, poly 4g); PROTEIN 38.6g; CARB 12.2g; FIBER 1.8g; CHOL 261mg; IRON 5.2mg; SODIUM 462mg; CALC 149mg

Quick Tip:
Keep cooked peeled shrimp in the freezer for speedy, no-cook main dish salads. Place the shrimp in a colander, and rinse with cool water to thaw quickly.

MENU *serves 4*

Shrimp Caesar Salad

Sun-dried tomato garlic breadsticks

Preheat oven to 375°. Unroll 1 (11-ounce) can refrigerated soft breadstick dough. Combine 2 tablespoons chopped oil-packed sun-dried tomatoes and 1 teaspoon minced garlic. Spread mixture from center to 1 short end of dough; fold other half of dough over tomato mixture, pinching ends to seal. Cut dough along perforations to form 8 breadsticks. Twist each breadstick; place on a baking sheet coated with cooking spray. Bake at 375° for 15 minutes.

Fresh strawberries with vanilla yogurt

Game Plan

1 Assemble breadsticks.

2 While breadsticks bake:

- •Prepare salad.
- •Slice strawberries.

Greek Salad with Shrimp

Use shredded rotisserie chicken in place of the shrimp, if you'd like.

- 4 quarts water
- 1½ pounds large shrimp, peeled and deveined
- 6 cups torn romaine lettuce
- 1½ cups halved cherry tomatoes
- 1 cup (¼-inch-thick) slices red onion, separated into rings
- 1 cup cucumber, halved lengthwise and cut into ¼-inch slices
- 1 tablespoon chopped fresh flat-leaf parsley
- 3 tablespoons red wine vinegar
- 2 teaspoons Dijon mustard
- 1 teaspoon extra-virgin olive oil
- ¾ teaspoon dried oregano
- ¼ teaspoon salt
- ¼ teaspoon black pepper
- 2 garlic cloves, minced
- ½ cup (2 ounces) crumbled feta cheese
- 8 kalamata olives, pitted and halved
- 4 pepperoncini peppers

1 Bring water to a boil in a large saucepan. Add shrimp; cook 2 minutes or until done. Drain and rinse with cold water; drain. Place shrimp in a bowl; cover and chill.
2 Place lettuce, tomatoes, onion, and cucumber in a large bowl; toss gently to combine. Combine parsley and next 7 ingredients; stir with a whisk. Spoon 1 tablespoon dressing over shrimp; toss to combine. Add shrimp mixture and remaining dressing to lettuce mixture; toss gently to coat. Spoon about 2¾ cups salad onto each of 4 plates. Top each serving with 2 tablespoons cheese, 4 olive halves, and 1 pepperoncini pepper. Yield: 4 servings.

CALORIES 296 (30% from fat); FAT 9.8g (sat 3.2g, mono 3.6g, poly 1.8g); PROTEIN 39.4g; CARB 12.1g; FIBER 3.2g; CHOL 271mg; IRON 6mg; SODIUM 849mg; CALC 219mg

Quick Tip:
Keep a bag of cooked, peeled, and deveined shrimp in the freezer. Place the shrimp in a colander, and rinse with cool water to thaw quickly. Proceed with recipe beginning at step 2.

MENU *serves 4*

Greek Salad with Shrimp

Oregano pita crisps
Preheat oven to 400°. Cut each of 2 (6-inch) pitas into 8 wedges; arrange pita wedges in a single layer on a baking sheet. Lightly coat pita wedges with cooking spray. Combine ½ teaspoon dried oregano, ⅛ teaspoon salt, ⅛ teaspoon garlic powder, and ⅛ teaspoon black pepper; sprinkle evenly over pita wedges. Lightly coat pita wedges again with cooking spray. Bake at 400° for 10 minutes or until golden.

Vanilla low-fat yogurt topped with honey and sliced almonds

Game Plan

1 While oven preheats for pita crisps and water for shrimp comes to a boil:
- Peel and devein shrimp.
- Prepare lettuce.
- Prepare herb mixture for pita crisps.

2 While pita crisps bake:
- Cook shrimp.
- Prepare remaining salad ingredients.

MENU *serves 4*

Shrimp and White Bean Salad with Creamy Lemon-Dill Dressing

Tomato wedges with spiced salt

Combine ¼ teaspoon kosher salt, ⅛ teaspoon chili powder, ⅛ teaspoon ground cumin, and ⅛ teaspoon ground red pepper. Cut each of 4 large plum tomatoes into 4 wedges, and lightly sprinkle with salt mixture.

Pumpernickel bread

Game Plan

1 Prepare shrimp mixture, and refrigerate.

2 While shrimp mixture chills:

- •Prepare watercress mixture.
- •Prepare spiced salt.
- •Cut tomatoes.

3 Just before serving:

- •Spoon shrimp mixture onto watercress.
- •Sprinkle spiced salt on tomato wedges.

Shrimp and White Bean Salad with Creamy Lemon-Dill Dressing

For a flavor variation, try arugula and basil in place of watercress and dill. You can also substitute chopped rotisserie chicken for shrimp.

3	tablespoons reduced-fat mayonnaise
2	tablespoons plain fat-free yogurt
1	tablespoon fresh lemon juice, divided
1½	teaspoons chopped fresh dill
¼	teaspoon salt, divided
¼	teaspoon freshly ground black pepper
¾	cup chopped fennel bulb
⅓	cup julienne-cut carrot
¼	cup thinly vertically sliced red onion
1¼	pounds cooked peeled and deveined large shrimp
1	(15.5-ounce) can Great Northern beans, rinsed and drained
1	teaspoon extra-virgin olive oil
4	ounces trimmed watercress (about 1 bunch)

① Combine mayonnaise, yogurt, 1½ teaspoons lemon juice, dill, ⅛ teaspoon salt, and pepper in a large bowl; stir well with a whisk. Add fennel and next 4 ingredients; toss well. Refrigerate until ready to serve.

② Combine oil, watercress, 1½ teaspoons lemon juice, and ⅛ teaspoon salt in a large bowl; toss gently to coat. Divide watercress mixture evenly among 4 plates; top each serving with 1½ cups shrimp mixture. Yield: 4 servings.

CALORIES 252 (16% from fat); FAT 4.5g (sat 1g, mono 1.4g, poly 1.7g); PROTEIN 35.3g; CARB 16.8g; FIBER 3.9g; CHOL 277mg; IRON 5.7mg; SODIUM 761mg; CALC 144mg

Yucatán Shrimp Cocktail Salad

Anaheim chiles and avocado give this shrimp salad a Mexican spin. They are long and narrow in shape, and have a sweet, simple taste with just a hint of heat.

Cooking spray
- 1½ pounds peeled and deveined medium shrimp
- ⅛ teaspoon ground red pepper
- ¼ cup fresh lime juice
- 2 tablespoons cider vinegar
- 1 tablespoon honey
- ½ teaspoon salt
- 1 cup chopped seeded peeled cucumber
- 1 cup halved cherry tomatoes
- 1 cup chopped seeded Anaheim chile
- ½ cup thinly sliced celery
- ½ cup sliced green onions
- ½ cup chopped fresh cilantro
- ½ cup diced peeled avocado

❶ Heat a large nonstick skillet over medium-high heat; coat with cooking spray. Add shrimp and red pepper; sauté 4 minutes. Remove from heat; set aside.

❷ Combine juice, vinegar, honey, and salt in a large bowl; stir well with a whisk. Add cucumber and remaining 6 ingredients; toss well. Add shrimp mixture; toss well. Yield: 4 servings (serving size: 1¾ cups).

CALORIES 271 (23% from fat); FAT 7g (sat 1.2g, mono 2.9g, poly 1.7g); PROTEIN 35.8g; CARB 12.8g; FIBER 2.7g; CHOL 259mg; IRON 4.7mg; SODIUM 569mg; CALC 117mg

MENU *serves 4*

Yucatán Shrimp Cocktail Salad

Jack cheese tortilla wedges

Preheat broiler. Sprinkle 4 (6-inch) corn tortillas with 1 teaspoon ground cumin and ¼ teaspoon crushed red pepper. Top each tortilla with 2 tablespoons shredded Monterey Jack cheese. Place tortillas on a baking sheet; broil until cheese melts. Cut each tortilla into 4 wedges.

Fresh pineapple chunks

Game Plan

1 Cook shrimp; cool.

2 While broiler heats for tortilla wedges:
   • Prepare salad ingredients.

3 Broil tortilla wedges.

4 Combine salad ingredients; add shrimp mixture.

Mediterranean Potato Salad with Shrimp and Feta

"Baking" the potatoes in the microwave is a simple way to cut the cook time in half.

MENU *serves 4*

Mediterranean Potato Salad with Shrimp and Feta

Garlic toast

Preheat broiler. Rub 4 (1-ounce) French bread slices with cut sides of a halved garlic clove; brush with 1 teaspoon olive oil. Broil 1 minute or until bread is golden.

Orange slices

Game Plan

1 Prepare dressing.

2 Cook potatoes.

3 While potatoes cook:

  •Prepare garlic toast.

  •Slice oranges.

4 Toss salad.

DRESSING:

1½ tablespoons chopped fresh basil

1 tablespoon fresh lemon juice

2 teaspoons extra-virgin olive oil

¾ teaspoon sugar

¼ teaspoon freshly ground black pepper

¼ teaspoon Dijon mustard

SALAD:

5 cups small red potatoes, quartered (about 1½ pounds)

½ teaspoon salt

¼ teaspoon freshly ground black pepper

1 pound medium shrimp, cooked and peeled

3 cups thinly sliced romaine lettuce

1 cup (¼-inch) strips red bell pepper

1 cup (¼-inch) strips yellow bell pepper

1 cup thinly sliced red onion

½ cup (2 ounces) crumbled feta cheese

2 tablespoons chopped pitted kalamata olives

❶ To prepare dressing, combine first 6 ingredients; stir with a whisk.

❷ To prepare salad, arrange potatoes in a single layer on a microwave-safe dish; sprinkle with ½ teaspoon salt and ¼ teaspoon pepper. Microwave at HIGH 15 minutes or until potatoes are tender. Place potatoes in a large bowl.

❸ Add shrimp and 1 tablespoon dressing to potatoes; toss gently. Add remaining dressing, lettuce, bell peppers, onion, and cheese; toss gently to coat. Top each serving with 1½ teaspoons olives. Yield: 4 servings (serving size: 2½ cups).

CALORIES 362 (23% from fat); FAT 9.4g (sat 3.1g, mono 3.8g, poly 1.4g); PROTEIN 30.3g; CARB 39.4g; FIBER 5.5g; CHOL 185mg; IRON 5.1mg; SODIUM 740mg; CALC 183mg

Quick Tip: You can buy precooked shrimp at the seafood counter in large supermarkets.

Warm Sesame Shrimp and Eggplant Salad

To save time, purchase peeled and deveined shrimp at your local supermarket.

1 tablespoon peanut oil, divided
1 teaspoon crushed red pepper, divided
2 teaspoons bottled minced garlic, divided
¼ teaspoon salt
1 pound medium shrimp, peeled
2 red bell peppers, seeded and quartered
1 eggplant, cut into ¾-inch-thick slices (about ¾ pound)
Cooking spray
2 tablespoons rice vinegar
1 tablespoon oyster sauce
2 teaspoons chili garlic sauce (such as Lee Kum Kee)
1 teaspoon bottled ground fresh ginger (such as Spice World)
1 tablespoon sesame seeds
6 cups coarsely chopped bok choy
3 tablespoons water
2 tablespoons chopped green onions
2 tablespoons chopped fresh cilantro

1 Preheat broiler.
2 Combine 2 teaspoons oil, ½ teaspoon crushed red pepper, 1 teaspoon garlic, salt, and shrimp in a bowl. Cover and marinate in refrigerator 10 minutes.

3 Flatten bell pepper pieces with heel of hand. Place bell pepper and eggplant on a baking sheet. Lightly coat with cooking spray. Broil 10 minutes or until tender, turning pieces occasionally. Cut bell pepper and eggplant into 1-inch pieces.
4 Combine 1 teaspoon oil, ½ teaspoon crushed red pepper, 1 teaspoon garlic, rice vinegar, oyster sauce, chili garlic sauce, and ginger in a small bowl.
5 Sprinkle shrimp with sesame seeds. Heat a large nonstick skillet over medium-high heat; coat with cooking spray. Add shrimp, and sauté 2 minutes or until shrimp are done. Place in a large bowl.
6 Add bok choy and water to pan; cover and cook 3 minutes or until bok choy wilts. Add bell pepper, eggplant, bok choy, onions, and cilantro to shrimp. Drizzle shrimp mixture with vinegar mixture; toss. Yield: 4 servings (serving size: 1½ cups).

CALORIES 233 (27% from fat); FAT 7.1g (sat 1.2g, mono 2.3g, poly 2.6g); PROTEIN 26.6g; CARB 16.4g; FIBER 5.1g; CHOL 172mg; IRON 4.5mg; SODIUM 693mg; CALC 207mg

MENU *serves 4*

Warm Sesame Shrimp and Eggplant Salad

Seasoned jasmine rice
Bring 2 cups water to a boil in a medium saucepan. Add 1 cup uncooked jasmine rice and ½ teaspoon salt; cover, reduce heat, and simmer 20 minutes or until liquid is absorbed. Combine 2 tablespoons chopped green onions, 2 tablespoons rice wine vinegar, and 1 teaspoon bottled ground fresh ginger in a small bowl. Pour vinegar mixture over cooked rice, and toss well.

Mango slices with crystallized ginger

Game Plan

1 While water comes to a boil for rice and oven heats for bell peppers and eggplant:
- Peel shrimp, and place in marinade.
- Quarter bell peppers, and slice eggplant.

2 While rice cooks:
- Broil bell peppers and eggplant.
- Cook shrimp and bok choy.
- Combine sauce ingredients for salad.
- Prepare mango.
- Assemble salad.

Thai Beef Salad

MENU *serves 6*

Thai Beef Salad

Coconut rice

Bring ½ cup water, ¼ teaspoon salt, and 1 (14-ounce) can light coconut milk to a simmer in a medium saucepan. Add 1 cup jasmine rice; cover and simmer 20 minutes or until liquid is absorbed.

Strawberry sorbet

Game Plan

1 While water mixture for rice comes to a boil:

- Prepare marinade.
- Marinate steak.
- Slice onion.
- Cut tomatoes into wedges.

2 While rice cooks:

- Cook steak.
- Prepare lettuce, cucumber, and mint for the salad.

The salad gets its heat from 2 tablespoons of chile paste. If you prefer milder food, use half the amount.

½ cup fresh lime juice
¼ cup chopped fresh cilantro
2 tablespoons brown sugar
2 tablespoons Thai fish sauce
2 tablespoons chile paste with garlic
2 garlic cloves, minced
1 (1½-pound) flank steak, trimmed
Cooking spray
1½ cups vertically sliced red onion
4 plum tomatoes, each cut into 6 wedges
6 cups torn romaine lettuce
1¼ cups thinly sliced English cucumber
2 tablespoons chopped fresh mint

1 Prepare grill or broiler.
2 Combine first 6 ingredients, stirring until sugar dissolves; set half of lime mixture aside. Combine remaining half of lime mixture and steak in a large zip-top plastic bag; seal. Marinate in refrigerator 10 minutes, turning once. Remove steak from bag; discard marinade.

3 Place steak on grill rack or broiler pan coated with cooking spray; cook 6 minutes on each side or until desired degree of doneness. Let stand 5 minutes; cut diagonally across the grain into thin slices.
4 Heat a large nonstick skillet over medium-high heat; coat with cooking spray. Add onion; sauté 3 minutes. Add tomatoes; sauté 2 minutes. Place onion mixture, lettuce, cucumber, and mint in a large bowl; toss gently to combine. Divide salad evenly among 6 plates. Top each serving with 3 ounces steak; drizzle each serving with 1 tablespoon reserved lime mixture. Yield: 6 servings.

CALORIES 219 (35% from fat); FAT 8.6g (sat 3.6g, mono 3.3g, poly 0.5g); PROTEIN 24.1g; CARB 12.3g; FIBER 2.2g; CHOL 54mg; IRON 3.1mg; SODIUM 456mg; CALC 44mg

Ingredient Tip:
English cucumbers work well for quick meals because they're virtually seedless.

Grilled Steak Salad with Caper Vinaigrette

This salad is a great use for leftover beef. If you don't like the peppery bite of watercress or just can't find it, use mixed salad greens. Substitute artichoke hearts for the hearts of palm, or just leave them out.

SALAD:

1 pound beef tenderloin, trimmed
Cooking spray
4 cups water
3 cups (1-inch) cut green beans (about ½ pound)
4 cups trimmed watercress (about 1 bunch)
1 cup grape tomatoes, halved
¾ cup thinly sliced red onion
1 (8-ounce) package presliced mushrooms
1 (7.75-ounce) can hearts of palm, rinsed and drained

DRESSING:

¼ cup red wine vinegar
1½ tablespoons fresh lemon juice
1 tablespoon capers
1 tablespoon honey mustard
2 teaspoons extra-virgin olive oil
½ teaspoon sugar
½ teaspoon salt
⅛ teaspoon freshly ground black pepper

❶ Prepare grill.
❷ To prepare salad, place beef on grill rack coated with cooking spray, and grill 7 minutes on each side or until desired degree of doneness. Let stand 10 minutes; cut diagonally across the grain into thin slices. Place in a large bowl.
❸ Bring water to a boil in a saucepan; add beans. Cover; cook 3 minutes or until crisp-tender. Rinse with cold water; drain. Add beans, watercress, and next 4 ingredients to beef; toss gently to combine.
❹ To prepare dressing, combine vinegar and remaining 7 ingredients; stir with a whisk. Drizzle over salad; toss gently to coat. Yield: 4 servings (serving size: 2 cups).

CALORIES 224 (29% from fat); FAT 7.3g (sat 2g, mono 3.3g, poly 0.5g); PROTEIN 27.3g; CARB 16.8g; FIBER 5.2g; CHOL 60mg; IRON 5.7mg; SODIUM 699mg; CALC 114mg

Quick Tip: Using sliced roast beef from the supermarket deli counter can cut your prep time in half.

MENU *serves 4*

Grilled Steak Salad with Caper Vinaigrette

Mozzarella and basil toast

Preheat oven to 425°. Place 2 (4-inch) Italian cheese-flavored pizza crusts (such as Boboli) on a baking sheet; top each with ¼ cup shredded part-skim mozzarella cheese and ¼ cup chopped fresh basil. Bake at 425° for 8 minutes or until cheese melts. Cut each crust into quarters.

Fresh fruit

Game Plan

1 While grill heats:
   • Cook green beans.
   • Prepare dressing.
2 While beef cooks:
   • Prepare toast.
3 Combine salad ingredients, and toss.

Grilled Jamaican Pork Tenderloin Salad

If you can't find papaya, use an extra cup of chopped pineapple.

DRESSING:

- 2 tablespoons fresh or 2 teaspoons dried thyme leaves
- 2 tablespoons fresh lime juice
- 1 tablespoon olive oil
- 1 tablespoon minced peeled fresh ginger
- 2 teaspoons brown sugar
- ½ teaspoon salt
- ½ teaspoon ground allspice
- ½ teaspoon ground cinnamon
- ¼ teaspoon freshly ground black pepper
- ¼ teaspoon ground nutmeg
- 1 garlic clove, minced

SALAD:

- 1 (1-pound) pork tenderloin, trimmed
- Cooking spray
- 4 cups salad greens
- 2 cups chopped peeled fresh pineapple
- 1 cup chopped papaya

1 Prepare grill.

2 To prepare dressing, combine first 11 ingredients in a food processor; process until smooth.

3 To prepare salad, slice pork lengthwise, cutting to, but not through, other side. Open halves, laying pork flat. Rub 2 tablespoons dressing on both sides of pork; reserve remaining dressing. Place pork on grill rack coated with cooking spray; cook 10 minutes on each side or until a meat thermometer registers 155°. Let stand 5 minutes. Cut pork into ¼-inch-thick slices; toss with reserved dressing. Place 1 cup greens on each of 4 plates; top with 3 ounces pork, ½ cup pineapple, and ¼ cup papaya. Yield: 4 servings.

CALORIES 263 (30% from fat); FAT 8.7g (sat 2.3g, mono 4.8g, poly 0.9g); PROTEIN 28.4g; CARB 18.3g; FIBER 3.2g; CHOL 69mg; IRON 2.7mg; SODIUM 371mg; CALC 78mg

Quick Tip: Look for cored fresh pineapple in the produce section of your supermarket. You can also buy bottled sliced papaya.

MENU *serves 4*

Grilled Jamaican Pork Tenderloin Salad

Roasted sweet potato wedges
Preheat oven to 425°. Combine 2 pounds sweet potato wedges, 2 tablespoons vegetable oil, ½ teaspoon salt, and ⅛ teaspoon ground red pepper; toss to coat. Arrange wedges on a baking sheet; bake at 425° for 25 minutes or until tender, turning occasionally.

Hummus with sesame breadsticks

Game Plan

1 While grill heats for pork and oven heats for potatoes:
- •Prepare dressing.
- •Prepare pork.
- •Prepare sweet potatoes.

2 While pork and potatoes cook:
- •Prepare salad.

MENU *serves 4*

Fennel-Grapefruit Salad with Chicken

Peppered fontina breadsticks

Fresh melon

Preheat oven to 375°. Separate dough from 1 (11-ounce) can refrigerated breadstick dough to form 12 breadsticks. Sprinkle dough with ½ cup shredded fontina cheese, gently pressing cheese into dough. Sprinkle with ½ teaspoon freshly ground black pepper. Twist each breadstick, and place on a baking sheet coated with cooking spray. Bake at 375° for 13 minutes or until lightly browned. Refrigerate leftover breadsticks in heavy-duty aluminum foil. Unwrap and place on a baking sheet; reheat at 350° for 5 minutes or until warm.

Game Plan

1 While oven heats for breadsticks:

- Shred cheese for breadsticks.
- Prepare dressing for salad.

2 While breadsticks bake:

- Prepare salad ingredients.
- Prepare melon.

3 Assemble salad.

Fennel-Grapefruit Salad with Chicken

You'll find miso in the refrigerated section of large supermarkets or Asian markets. Look for bottled grapefruit sections in the produce department of your supermarket.

2   cups thinly sliced fennel bulb
2   cups chopped romaine lettuce
2   cups shredded roasted skinless, boneless chicken breast (about 2 breasts)
2   cups bottled red grapefruit sections
¼   cup thinly sliced red onion
2   tablespoons chopped pitted kalamata olives
1   tablespoon thinly sliced fresh mint
1   tablespoon orange juice
1   tablespoon champagne vinegar or white wine vinegar
1   tablespoon miso (soybean paste)
2   teaspoons minced shallots
2   teaspoons extra-virgin olive oil
¼   teaspoon kosher salt
¼   teaspoon freshly ground black pepper

❶ Combine first 6 ingredients in a large bowl; set aside. Combine mint and remaining 7 ingredients in a small bowl; stir with a whisk. Pour dressing over chicken mixture in large bowl; toss well. Serve immediately. Yield: 4 servings (serving size: 1½ cups).

CALORIES 200 (29% from fat); FAT 6.5g (sat 1.3g, mono 3.9g, poly 1.1g); PROTEIN 20.8g; CARB 16.7g; FIBER 3.5g; CHOL 49mg; IRON 0.9mg; SODIUM 888mg; CALC 66mg

Quick Tip: To speed preparation, look for preshredded cooked chicken breast (such as Tyson) in your supermarket.

Chipotle Chicken Taco Salad

The creamy dressing mellows the heat from the chiles, and can be prepared in 30 minutes.

DRESSING:
- ⅔ cup light sour cream
- ⅓ cup chopped fresh cilantro
- 4 teaspoons fresh lime juice
- 1 tablespoon minced chipotle chile, canned in adobo sauce
- 1 teaspoon ground cumin
- 1 teaspoon chili powder
- ¼ teaspoon salt

SALAD:
- 4 cups shredded romaine lettuce
- 2 cups chopped roasted skinless, boneless chicken breast (about 2 breast halves)
- 1 cup cherry tomatoes, halved
- ½ cup diced peeled avocado
- ⅓ cup thinly vertically sliced red onion
- 1 (15-ounce) can black beans, rinsed and drained
- 1 (8¾-ounce) can no-salt-added whole-kernel corn, rinsed and drained

❶ To prepare dressing, combine first 7 ingredients, stirring well.

❷ To prepare salad, combine lettuce and remaining 6 ingredients in a large bowl. Drizzle dressing over salad; toss gently to coat. Serve immediately. Yield: 4 servings (serving size: 2½ cups).

CALORIES 249 (30% from fat); FAT 8.2g (sat 2.8g, mono 2.9g, poly 0.7g); PROTEIN 23.3g; CARB 25.1g; FIBER 7g; CHOL 50mg; IRON 2.2mg; SODIUM 650mg; CALC 106mg

Ingredient Tip:
Avocados are available year-round. To select a ripe one, press lightly on the skin, and feel the flesh yield to pressure. If it feels mushy or is moldy, don't buy it.

MENU *serves 4*

Chipotle Chicken Taco Salad

Watermelon-mango salad
Combine 2 cups cubed seeded watermelon and 1 cup sliced peeled mango in a medium bowl. Combine 1½ tablespoons fresh lime juice, 2 teaspoons honey, and ⅛ teaspoon salt; stir with a whisk. Drizzle juice mixture over fruit; toss gently to coat. Sprinkle with 1 teaspoon chopped fresh mint. Cover and refrigerate until ready to serve.

Baked tortilla chips

Game Plan

1 **Prepare fruit salad; cover and chill.**

2 **While fruit salad chills:**
   - •Prepare taco salad dressing.
   - •Combine taco salad ingredients.

3 **Toss taco salad with dressing just before serving.**

Chicken, Red Potato, and Green Bean Salad

Red potatoes work well and add a nice color to this salad, but you can use any waxy potato, such as fingerling or white. If your potatoes aren't small, cut each into 8 wedges.

DRESSING:
- ⅓ cup coarsely chopped fresh parsley
- 3 tablespoons red wine vinegar
- 1 tablespoon fresh lemon juice
- 1 tablespoon whole-grain Dijon mustard
- 1 tablespoon extra-virgin olive oil
- ½ teaspoon salt
- ¼ teaspoon freshly ground black pepper
- 1 garlic clove, minced

SALAD:
- 1 pound small red potatoes
- 1 teaspoon salt
- ½ pound diagonally cut green beans
- 2 cups cubed cooked chicken (about 8 ounces)
- 2 tablespoons chopped red onion
- 1 (10-ounce) package gourmet salad greens (about 6 cups)

1 To prepare dressing, combine first 8 ingredients; stir well with a whisk.

2 To prepare salad, place potatoes in a saucepan; cover with water. Add 1 teaspoon salt; bring to a boil. Reduce heat, and simmer 10 minutes or until potatoes are almost tender. Add beans, and cook 4 minutes or until beans are crisp-tender. Drain and rinse with cold water; drain.

3 Quarter potatoes. Place potatoes, beans, chicken, onion, and greens in a large bowl. Drizzle with dressing; toss gently to coat. Serve immediately. Yield: 4 servings (serving size: about 1¾ cups).

CALORIES 269 (29% from fat); FAT 8.8g (sat 1.8g, mono 4.4g, poly 1.6g); PROTEIN 22.4g; CARB 26.1g; FIBER 5.8g; CHOL 53mg; IRON 3.8mg; SODIUM 761mg; CALC 96mg

Quick Tip: Use a rotisserie whole chicken purchased at your supermarket's deli section, and you'll have leftovers for another meal.

Greek Salad with Grilled Chicken

Prepare the salad dressing up to a week in advance; cover and store it in the refrigerator. Try making a double or triple batch to have on hand for quick, throw-together salads or to use as a marinade.

¼ cup fat-free, less-sodium chicken broth
2 tablespoons red wine vinegar
2 teaspoons olive oil
1 teaspoon sugar
1 teaspoon dried oregano
½ teaspoon salt
½ teaspoon freshly ground black pepper
1 garlic clove, minced
4 (4-ounce) skinless, boneless chicken breast halves
Cooking spray
8 cups torn romaine lettuce
1 cup sliced cucumber (about 1 small)
8 pitted kalamata olives, halved
4 plum tomatoes, quartered lengthwise
2 (¼-inch-thick) slices red onion, separated into rings
¼ cup (1 ounce) crumbled feta cheese

❶ Prepare grill or broiler.
❷ Combine first 8 ingredients in a small bowl. Brush chicken with 2 tablespoons dressing; set remaining dressing aside.
❸ Place chicken on grill rack or broiler pan coated with cooking spray; cook 5 minutes on each side or until chicken is done. Cut into ¼-inch-thick slices.
❹ Combine romaine lettuce and next 4 ingredients in a large bowl; toss with remaining salad dressing. Divide salad evenly among 4 plates; top each serving with sliced chicken, and sprinkle with feta cheese. Yield: 4 servings (serving size: 2 cups salad, 3 ounces chicken, and 1 tablespoon feta cheese).

CALORIES 231 (30% from fat); FAT 7.7g (sat 2.1g, mono 3.9g, poly 1g); PROTEIN 30.3g; CARB 10.3g; FIBER 3.4g; CHOL 72mg; IRON 2.9mg; SODIUM 613mg; CALC 110mg

---

MENU *serves 4*

Greek Salad with Grilled Chicken

Oregano breadsticks
Preheat oven to 375°. Brush refrigerated breadstick dough with 1 tablespoon olive oil; sprinkle with 1 teaspoon dried oregano. Separate dough into individual breadsticks. Place dough sticks on a baking sheet coated with cooking spray. Bake at 375° for 13 minutes or until lightly browned.

Lime sherbet

Game Plan

1 While grill and oven heat:
   • Prepare dressing for chicken and salad.
   • Prepare vegetables and olives.
   • Prepare breadstick dough.

2 While breadsticks bake:
   • Grill or broil chicken.

3 Assemble salad.

Chicken Souvlaki Salad

The elements of a classic Greek salad and a chicken souvlaki sandwich combine in this piquant dish. You can use lamb in place of the chicken.

MENU *serves 4*

Chicken Souvlaki Salad

Greek pita wedges
Preheat oven to 375°. Cut each of 2 (6-inch) pitas into 6 wedges; arrange on a baking sheet. Coat pita wedges with olive oil–flavored cooking spray; sprinkle with ¼ teaspoon kosher salt and ¼ teaspoon dried oregano. Bake at 375° for 7 minutes or until golden.

Vanilla low-fat ice cream topped with cinnamon and honey

Game Plan

1 While grill or broiler heats:

  • Combine chicken and lemon mixture.

  • Prepare dressing for salad.

2 While chicken cooks:

  • Prepare onion, olives, cucumber, and tomatoes for salad.

  • Bake pita wedges.

2 teaspoons bottled minced garlic, divided
1 teaspoon fresh lemon juice
1 teaspoon extra-virgin olive oil
½ teaspoon dried oregano
¼ teaspoon salt
¼ teaspoon black pepper
1 pound skinless, boneless chicken breast
3 cups cubed peeled cucumber (about 3 cucumbers)
½ cup vertically sliced red onion
½ cup (2 ounces) crumbled feta cheese
2 tablespoons chopped pitted kalamata olives
2 ripe tomatoes, cored and cut into 1-inch pieces (about 1 pound)
½ cup plain fat-free yogurt
¼ cup grated peeled cucumber
1 teaspoon white wine vinegar
½ teaspoon garlic powder
¼ teaspoon salt
¼ teaspoon ground red pepper
¼ teaspoon black pepper

1 Prepare grill or preheat broiler.
2 Combine 1 teaspoon garlic, lemon juice, and next 5 ingredients in a large zip-top plastic bag. Seal bag; shake to coat. Remove chicken from bag. Cook chicken 5 minutes on each side or until done; cut into 1-inch pieces.
3 Combine chicken, cubed cucumber, and next 4 ingredients in a large bowl. Combine 1 teaspoon garlic, yogurt, and remaining 6 ingredients in a small bowl. Pour dressing over chicken mixture; toss well. Yield: 4 servings (serving size: 2 cups).

CALORIES 259 (28% from fat); FAT 8.2g (sat 3g, mono 3.4g, poly 1g); PROTEIN 31.8g; CARB 15.3g; FIBER 2.9g; CHOL 79mg; IRON 2mg; SODIUM 679mg; CALC 161mg

Quick Tip: Place the chicken and seasonings in a zip-top plastic bag. A quick shake will coat the chicken, and there's no bowl to wash.

Asian Turkey Salad

This fresh, bright salad takes Thanksgiving leftovers on a trip East. After the big day, you'll welcome its lightness.

DRESSING:
- ¼ cup rice vinegar
- ¼ cup vegetable broth
- 1 tablespoon low-sodium soy sauce
- 2 teaspoons bottled ground fresh ginger (such as Spice World)
- 2 teaspoons lime juice
- 1 teaspoon bottled minced garlic
- 1 teaspoon peanut oil
- 1 teaspoon sesame oil
- ½ teaspoon salt
- ½ teaspoon sugar
- 1 serrano chile

SALAD:
- 4 cups thinly sliced napa (Chinese) cabbage
- 3 cups shredded cooked turkey
- 1 cup red bell pepper strips (about 1 small pepper)
- ½ cup thinly sliced red onion
- ½ cup chopped fresh cilantro
- ¼ cup sliced green onions
- 1 tablespoon dry-roasted peanuts, chopped

① To prepare salad dressing, place first 11 ingredients in a blender, and process until smooth.
② To prepare salad, combine cabbage and remaining 6 ingredients in a large bowl; pour dressing over salad, tossing to coat. Yield: 4 servings (serving size: 1¾ cups).

CALORIES 250 (30% from fat); FAT 8.3g (sat 2.2g, mono 2.3g, poly 2.6g); PROTEIN 33.2g; CARB 10.3g; FIBER 3.4g; CHOL 80mg; IRON 2.8mg; SODIUM 592mg; CALC 80mg

Quick Tip: To speed preparation, use packaged finely shredded cabbage in place of the napa cabbage.

Meatless Main Dishes

Fontina and Parmesan Mushroom
Bread Pudding, page 131

Whole Wheat Buttermilk Pancakes

Keep cooked pancakes warm in a 200° oven while preparing the remaining pancakes.

¾ cup all-purpose flour
¾ cup whole wheat flour
3 tablespoons sugar
1½ teaspoons baking powder
½ teaspoon baking soda
½ teaspoon salt
1½ cups low-fat buttermilk
1 tablespoon canola oil
1 large egg
1 large egg white
Cooking spray
¾ cup maple syrup
3 tablespoons butter

① Preheat oven to 200°.
② Lightly spoon flours into dry measuring cups, and level with a knife. Combine flours, sugar, baking powder, baking soda, and salt in a large bowl; stir with a whisk. Combine buttermilk, oil, egg, and egg white; stir with a whisk. Add to flour mixture, stirring just until moist.
③ Heat a nonstick griddle or nonstick skillet over medium heat; coat with cooking spray. Spoon about ¼ cup batter for each pancake onto griddle. Turn pancakes when tops are covered with bubbles and edges look cooked. Serve with syrup and butter. Yield: 6 servings (serving size: 2 pancakes, 2 tablespoons syrup, and 1½ teaspoons butter).

CALORIES 351 (26% from fat); FAT 10g (sat 4.6g, mono 2.8g, poly 1.9g); PROTEIN 7.6g; CARB 59.7g; FIBER 2.3g; CHOL 55mg; IRON 2.1mg; SODIUM 570mg; CALC 176mg

MENU *serves 6*

Whole Wheat Buttermilk Pancakes

Fresh fruit salad
Combine 3 cups sliced strawberries, 1 cup blueberries, and 1 cup sliced banana in a large bowl. Sprinkle fruit with 1 tablespoon sugar; toss well to combine. Chill until ready to serve.

Chai tea

Game Plan

1 Prepare fruit salad, and refrigerate.

2 Prepare pancake batter.

3 While pancakes cook:
   •Boil water and steep tea.

MENU *serves 6*

Almond-Buttermilk Hotcakes with Blackberry-Grape Sauce

Meatless sausage links

Minty raspberry sparklers

Combine ¼ cup sugar and ¼ cup water in a small, heavy saucepan; bring to a boil, stirring until sugar dissolves. Add 2 mint sprigs to pan; let stand 5 minutes. Remove mint, and discard. Combine sugar mixture, 3 cups fresh raspberries, and 2 tablespoons fresh lemon juice in a blender, and process until smooth. Strain mixture through a sieve into a bowl, and discard solids. Spoon 3 tablespoons raspberry mixture into each of 6 wine glasses; top each serving with ½ cup chilled Champagne.

Game Plan

1 Prepare sugar mixture for sparklers.

2 While sugar mixture stands:
  - Prepare fruit; measure remaining ingredients for sparklers and blackberry-grape sauce.

3 While blackberry-grape sauce comes to a boil:
  - Blend and strain raspberry mixture.

4 Prepare hotcake batter and cook hotcakes.

5 Assemble sparklers.

Almond-Buttermilk Hotcakes with Blackberry-Grape Sauce

The sauce offers sources of antioxidants that may protect against cancer and improve mental function.

SAUCE:

- 3 tablespoons seedless blackberry jam
- ¼ teaspoon grated lemon rind
- 2 tablespoons fresh lemon juice
- 1 tablespoon water
- 1 teaspoon cornstarch
- 1 cup seedless red grapes, halved lengthwise
- 1½ cups fresh blackberries

HOTCAKES:

- 6¾ ounces all-purpose flour (about 1½ cups)
- ¼ cup sliced almonds, toasted
- 1¼ teaspoons baking powder
- 1 teaspoon baking soda
- ¼ teaspoon freshly ground nutmeg
- ⅛ teaspoon salt
- 1⅓ cups nonfat buttermilk
- ½ cup packed brown sugar
- ⅓ cup water
- 2 tablespoons canola oil
- 1 large egg, lightly beaten

Cooking spray

❶ To prepare sauce, combine first 5 ingredients in a small saucepan over medium heat; stir with a whisk. Add grapes; bring to a boil. Reduce heat, and simmer 1 minute or until slightly thick. Stir in blackberries. Remove from heat.

❷ To prepare hotcakes, lightly spoon flour into dry measuring cups; level with a knife. Combine flour and next 5 ingredients in a large bowl; stir with a whisk. Combine buttermilk and next 4 ingredients; add to flour mixture, stirring until smooth.

❸ Heat a nonstick griddle or nonstick skillet over medium heat; coat with cooking spray. Pour about ¼ cup batter per pancake onto griddle. Cook 2 minutes or until tops are covered with bubbles and edges looked cooked. Carefully turn pancakes over; cook 2 minutes or until bottoms are lightly browned. Repeat procedure with remaining batter. Serve hotcakes with sauce. Yield: 6 servings (serving size: 2 hotcakes and about ¼ cup sauce).

CALORIES 342 (21% from fat); FAT 8.1g (sat 0.8g, mono 4.4g, poly 2.2g); PROTEIN 7.8g; CARB 61.7g; FIBER 3.5g; CHOL 36mg; IRON 2.6mg; SODIUM 435mg; CALC 171mg

Southwestern Omelet

For a variation on this omelet, use kidney beans and Monterey Jack cheese with jalapeños.

2 tablespoons chopped fresh cilantro
¼ teaspoon salt
4 large egg whites
1 large egg
½ cup canned black beans, rinsed and drained
¼ cup chopped green onions
¼ cup (1 ounce) shredded reduced-fat cheddar cheese
¼ cup bottled salsa
Cooking spray

1 Combine first 4 ingredients in a medium bowl, and stir with a whisk. Combine beans, onions, cheese, and salsa.

2 Heat a medium nonstick skillet over medium heat; coat with cooking spray. Pour egg mixture into pan; let egg mixture set slightly. Tilt pan, and carefully lift edges of omelet with a spatula; allow uncooked portion to flow underneath cooked portion. Cook 3 minutes; flip omelet. Spoon bean mixture onto half of omelet. Carefully loosen omelet with a spatula; fold in half. Cook 1 minute or until cheese melts. Slide omelet onto a plate; cut in half. Yield: 2 servings.

CALORIES 181 (27% from fat); FAT 5.5g (sat 2.3g, mono 1g, poly 0.8g); PROTEIN 20.2g; CARB 13.8g; FIBER 6g; CHOL 116mg; IRON 2.1mg; SODIUM 822mg; CALC 184mg

---

MENU *serves 2*

Southwestern Omelet

Quick quesadillas
Preheat broiler. Coat 4 (6-inch) corn tortillas with cooking spray. Place 2 tortillas, coated sides down, on a baking sheet. Top each tortilla with 2 tablespoons shredded reduced-fat cheddar cheese and 2 teaspoons chopped green onions. Top with remaining tortillas, coated sides up. Broil 2 minutes or until golden. Turn quesadillas over; broil 2 minutes or until tops are golden and cheese is melted. Cut each quesadilla into quarters; serve with salsa and fat-free sour cream.

Pineapple juice

Game Plan

1 Preheat broiler for quesadillas.

2 While oven heats:

  • Chop and measure ingredients for quesadillas and omelet.

3 Assemble quesadillas.

4 While quesadillas cook:

  • Prepare omelet.

MENU *serves 4*

Huevos Rancheros with Queso Fresco

Orange, pineapple, and coconut ambrosia
Drain 1 (15¼-ounce) can pineapple chunks in juice and 1 (14-ounce) jar fresh orange sections. Combine pineapple, orange, and 2 tablespoons powdered sugar, tossing to coat. Sprinkle with ⅓ cup flaked sweetened coconut. Cover and refrigerate until ready to serve.

Margaritas

Game Plan

1 Prepare ambrosia; cover and chill until serving time.

2 While tomato mixture cooks:
  • Chop cilantro.
  • Squeeze lime for juice.
  • Heat beans.

3 While eggs cook:
  • Heat tortillas.
  • Prepare margaritas.

Huevos Rancheros with Queso Fresco

Queso fresco is a soft, crumbly, salty Mexican cheese. Look for it in the dairy section of large grocery stores and Hispanic markets. Substitute crumbled feta or goat cheese, if you like.

1 (10-ounce) can diced tomatoes and green chiles, undrained
1 (10-ounce) can red enchilada sauce
⅓ cup chopped fresh cilantro
1 tablespoon fresh lime juice
2 tablespoons water
1 (16-ounce) can pinto beans, rinsed and drained
Cooking spray
4 large eggs
4 (8-inch) fat-free flour tortillas
1 cup (4 ounces) crumbled queso fresco cheese

1 Combine tomatoes and enchilada sauce in a medium saucepan; bring to a boil. Reduce heat; simmer 5 minutes or until slightly thick. Remove from heat; stir in cilantro and juice. Set aside.

2 Place water and beans in a microwave-safe bowl, and partially mash with a fork. Cover and microwave at HIGH 2 minutes or until hot.
3 Heat a large nonstick skillet over medium-high heat; coat with cooking spray. Add eggs, and cook 1 minute on each side or until desired degree of doneness.
4 Warm tortillas according to package directions. Spread about ⅓ cup beans over each tortilla; top each tortilla with 1 egg. Spoon ½ cup sauce around each egg; sprinkle each serving with ¼ cup cheese. Yield: 4 servings (serving size: 1 topped tortilla).

CALORIES 340 (26% from fat); FAT 9.8g (sat 3.2g, mono 2.7g, poly 1g); PROTEIN 15.7g; CARB 37.8g; FIBER 6.1g; CHOL 222mg; IRON 2.1mg; SODIUM 970mg; CALC 153mg

Ingredient Tip: You can substitute corn tortillas for the flour tortillas.

Red Bell Pepper Frittata

Cooked couscous makes this meatless entrée more filling. Substitute 1 cup leftover cooked orzo, spaghetti, or vermicelli.

½   cup water
⅓   cup uncooked couscous
1   tablespoon water
¾   teaspoon salt
¼   teaspoon black pepper
4   large egg whites
3   large eggs
Cooking spray
2   cups red bell pepper strips
1   cup thinly vertically sliced onion
2   garlic cloves, minced
⅓   cup (1½ ounces) shredded Manchego
    or Monterey Jack cheese

❶ Preheat oven to 350°.
❷ Bring ½ cup water to a boil in a small sauce-pan; gradually stir in couscous. Remove from heat; cover and let stand 5 minutes. Fluff with a fork.
❸ Combine 1 tablespoon water, salt, black pepper, egg whites, and eggs in a medium bowl; stir with a whisk.
❹ Heat a 10-inch ovenproof nonstick skillet over medium-high heat; coat with cooking spray. Add bell pepper, onion, and garlic; sauté 5 minutes. Stir in couscous and egg mixture; cook over medium heat 5 minutes or until almost set. Sprinkle with cheese. Bake at 350° for 10 minutes or until set. Let stand 5 minutes before serving. Yield: 4 servings (serving size: 1 wedge).

CALORIES 204 (30% from fat); FAT 6.8g (sat 3g, mono 2.3g, poly 0.7g); PROTEIN 15g; CARB 20.6g; FIBER 2.9g; CHOL 167mg; IRON 1.3mg; SODIUM 716mg; CALC 169mg

---

MENU *serves 4*

Red Bell Pepper Frittata

Toasted English muffins with jam

Roasted vanilla-scented apples
Preheat oven to 400°. Combine 2 cups sliced Granny Smith apples, 1½ tablespoons vanilla syrup, and 1 teaspoon walnut oil or melted butter in an 8-inch square baking dish coated with cooking spray. Bake at 400° for 15 minutes or until tender.

Game Plan

1 While oven heats for apples and water for couscous comes to a boil:

- Slice bell pepper and onion.
- Mince garlic.
- Prepare egg mixture.

2 While apples roast and couscous stands:

- Toast English muffins.
- Cook frittata.

MENU *serves 4*

Onion Bread Pudding

Asparagus salad
Combine 4 cups (½-inch) cooked asparagus pieces, 1 cup chopped plum tomato, ¼ cup chopped red onion, ¼ cup crumbled feta cheese, 2 tablespoons fresh lemon juice, 2 teaspoons chopped fresh dill, 1 teaspoon olive oil, and ¼ teaspoon salt, stirring well.

Fresh fruit

Game Plan

1 Cube bread for pudding.

2 While oven heats:
  • Cook onion slices.
  • Prepare bread and milk mixture.

3 While bread pudding bakes:
  • Prepare asparagus salad.

Onion Bread Pudding

Parmesan, fontina, or Monterey Jack would also work well in place of the Gruyère or Swiss.

1 Vidalia or other sweet onion, cut into ¼-inch slices
2 cups 2% reduced-fat milk
½ teaspoon salt
½ teaspoon dried thyme
⅛ teaspoon freshly ground black pepper
2 large eggs, lightly beaten
8 cups cubed French bread (about 8 ounces)
¾ cup (3 ounces) shredded Gruyère or Swiss cheese, divided
Cooking spray

❶ Preheat oven to 425°.
❷ Heat a large nonstick skillet over medium-high heat. Add onion (keep slices intact); cook 3 minutes on each side or until browned.

❸ Combine milk, salt, thyme, pepper, and eggs in a large bowl; stir with a whisk. Add bread and ½ cup cheese; toss well. Place bread mixture in an 8-inch square baking dish coated with cooking spray. Arrange onion slices on top of bread mixture. Sprinkle with ¼ cup cheese. Bake at 425° for 25 minutes or until set and golden. Yield: 4 servings (serving size: about 1½ cups).

CALORIES 364 (30% from fat); FAT 12.2g (sat 5.7g, mono 3.7g, poly 1.1g); PROTEIN 19.7g; CARB 43.8g; FIBER 3.4g; CHOL 136mg; IRON 2.1mg; SODIUM 806mg; CALC 294mg

Quick Tip: You can assemble the bread pudding ahead of time; cover and refrigerate until you're ready to bake it.

Fontina and Parmesan Mushroom Bread Pudding

This brunch dish is also hearty enough to serve at dinner with a green salad. Choose 100% whole wheat or 100% whole-grain bread (not "made with whole wheat") to ensure you'll reap the benefits of the fiber and phytonutrients found in whole grains. The salad's bright flavor contrasts with the rich, earthy taste of this entrée.

6   cups (1-inch) cubed sturdy 100% whole wheat bread (about 12 ounces)
Cooking spray
1   teaspoon olive oil
⅓   cup chopped shallots
2   (8-ounce) packages presliced cremini mushrooms
2   tablespoons chopped fresh parsley
1   tablespoon chopped fresh thyme
¼   teaspoon salt
¼   teaspoon freshly ground black pepper
1   cup (4 ounces) shredded fontina cheese, divided
2   tablespoons grated fresh Parmesan cheese, divided
1½ cups 1% low-fat milk
½   cup vegetable broth
3   large eggs, lightly beaten

❶ Preheat oven to 350°.
❷ Place bread cubes on a jelly-roll pan; coat with cooking spray. Bake at 350° for 20 minutes or until lightly toasted, turning twice. Remove from oven; cool.
❸ Heat oil in a large nonstick skillet over medium-high heat. Add shallots and mushrooms; sauté 12 minutes or until lightly browned and moisture evaporates. Remove from heat; stir in parsley, thyme, salt, and pepper.
❹ Place half of bread cubes in bottom of an 11 x 7–inch baking dish coated with cooking spray. Arrange mushroom mixture evenly over bread cubes; sprinkle with ½ cup fontina and 1 tablespoon Parmesan. Top with remaining bread cubes. Combine milk, broth, and eggs; stir with a whisk. Pour over bread mixture. Gently press with back of a spoon; let stand 30 minutes. Top with remaining ½ cup fontina and remaining 1 tablespoon Parmesan.
❺ Bake at 350° for 45 minutes or until set. Let stand for 10 minutes before serving. Cut into 6 squares. Yield: 6 servings.

CALORIES 304 (40% from fat); FAT 13.5g (sat 5.2g, mono 3.5g, poly 0.8g); PROTEIN 21.2g; CARB 27.5; FIBER 6.9g; CHOL 132mg; IRON 2.6mg; SODIUM 666mg; CALC 315mg

Yang Chow Fried Rice

Here is a vegetarian version of the classic Chinese dish that traditionally includes shrimp and ham. The fried rice can stand alone as a one-dish meal; however, if you desire a crunchy side, a quick toss of snow peas with soy sauce and sesame oil fills the bill. You can even stir the snow peas into the fried rice.

2 tablespoons canola oil, divided
4 large eggs, lightly beaten and divided
¼ teaspoon freshly ground black pepper, divided
Dash of salt
1¾ cups thinly sliced green onions, divided
2 teaspoons grated peeled fresh ginger
2 garlic cloves, minced
5 cups cooked short-grain rice, chilled
¼ cup low-sodium soy sauce
½ teaspoon salt
1 (10-ounce) package frozen green peas, thawed
3 tablespoons chopped fresh cilantro

❶ Heat 2 teaspoons oil in a large nonstick skillet over medium-high heat. Add half of eggs; swirl to coat bottom of pan evenly. Sprinkle with ⅛ teaspoon pepper and dash of salt; cook 3 minutes or until egg is done. Remove egg from pan; thinly slice, and set aside.

❷ Wipe pan clean with a paper towel. Heat 4 teaspoons oil in pan over medium-high heat. Add 1 cup onions, ginger, and garlic; stir-fry 30 seconds. Add remaining eggs and rice; stir-fry 3 minutes. Stir in half of egg strips, ¾ cup onions, ⅛ teaspoon pepper, soy sauce, ½ teaspoon salt, and peas; cook 30 seconds, stirring well to combine. Top with remaining egg strips and cilantro. Yield: 6 servings (serving size: about 1 cup).

CALORIES 348 (22% from fat); FAT 8.5g (sat 1.5g, mono 4.1g, poly 2g); PROTEIN 11g; CARB 55g; FIBER 4.9g; CHOL 141mg; IRON 3.9mg; SODIUM 683mg; CALC 34mg

Polenta with Tomato-Shiitake Sauce

To make easy work of slicing shiitake mushrooms, slice 3 or 4 stacked caps at a time.

2 teaspoons olive oil
⅓ cup sliced shallots
3 cups thinly sliced shiitake mushroom caps (about ½ pound)
2 teaspoons dried basil
1 teaspoon dried oregano
1 teaspoon bottled minced roasted garlic
¼ teaspoon crushed red pepper
¼ teaspoon sugar
2 (14.5-ounce) cans diced tomatoes, drained
2 cups vegetable broth
1 cup water
¾ cup instant dry polenta
½ cup grated Parmesan cheese

❶ Heat oil in a large skillet over medium-high heat. Add shallots; sauté 2 minutes. Add mushrooms; sauté 3 minutes or until tender. Stir in basil and next 5 ingredients; cook 3 minutes or until thoroughly heated. Keep warm.
❷ Combine vegetable broth and water in a large saucepan, and bring to a boil. Stir in polenta. Reduce heat, and simmer until thick (about 5 minutes), stirring frequently. Stir in cheese. Serve tomato mixture over polenta. Yield: 4 servings (serving size: about ⅔ cup polenta and 1 cup tomato mixture).

CALORIES 221 (29% from fat); FAT 7g (sat 2.7g, mono 2.8g, poly 0.3g); PROTEIN 10.8g; CARB 29.4g; FIBER 3.8g; CHOL 10mg; IRON 2.2mg; SODIUM 876mg; CALC 217mg

MENU *serves 4*

Polenta with Tomato-Shiitake Sauce

Italian broccoli
Steam 1 pound broccoli spears, covered, 5 minutes or until crisp-tender. Toss with 3 tablespoons fat-free Italian dressing; sprinkle with 2 tablespoons grated Parmesan cheese.

Rosemary focaccia

Game Plan

1 Slice shallots and shiitake mushrooms.

2 While tomato mixture cooks:
- Bring broth and water to a boil for polenta.

3 While broccoli steams:
- Cook polenta.

133

MENU *serves 6*

Polenta Lasagna

Salad with lemon, garlic, and Parmesan vinaigrette

Combine 2 tablespoons fresh lemon juice, 1 tablespoon extra-virgin olive oil, ¼ teaspoon salt, ¼ teaspoon sugar, ⅛ teaspoon freshly ground black pepper, and 3 minced garlic cloves; stir with a whisk. Drizzle over 6 cups baby spinach; toss gently to coat. Sprinkle each serving with 1 tablespoon grated fresh Parmesan cheese; top each serving with 2 tablespoons croutons.

Breadsticks

Game Plan

1 While oven heats for the lasagna:

- Chop vegetables and mince garlic.
- Prepare marinara-vegetable mixture.
- Assemble lasagna.

2 While lasagna bakes:

- Prepare salad.

Polenta Lasagna

This meal works well for casual entertaining because all the elements are easy to put together.

1 (26-ounce) jar marinara sauce, divided
1 teaspoon olive oil
1 cup finely chopped onion
½ cup chopped red bell pepper
1 cup meatless fat-free sausage, crumbled (such as Lightlife Gimme Lean)
1 cup chopped mushrooms
½ cup chopped zucchini
2 garlic cloves, minced
1 (16-ounce) tube of polenta, cut into 18 slices
½ cup (2 ounces) preshredded part-skim mozzarella cheese, divided

1 Preheat oven to 350°.

2 Spoon ½ cup marinara sauce into an 8-inch square baking dish to cover bottom, and set aside.

3 Heat oil in a large nonstick skillet over medium-high heat. Add onion and bell pepper; sauté 4 minutes or until tender. Stir in sausage; cook 2 minutes. Add mushrooms, zucchini, and garlic; sauté 2 minutes or until mushrooms are tender, stirring frequently. Add remaining marinara sauce; reduce heat, and simmer 10 minutes.

4 Arrange 9 polenta slices over marinara in baking dish; top evenly with half of vegetable mixture. Sprinkle ¼ cup cheese over vegetable mixture; arrange remaining polenta over cheese. Top polenta with remaining vegetable mixture, and sprinkle with ¼ cup cheese.

5 Cover and bake at 350° for 30 minutes. Uncover and bake an additional 15 minutes or until bubbly. Let stand 5 minutes before serving. Yield: 6 servings (serving size: 1 piece).

CALORIES 221 (20% from fat); FAT 4.9g (sat 1.4g, mono 2.1g, poly 1.1g); PROTEIN 12.3g; CARB 30.9g; FIBER 4.6g; CHOL 5mg; IRON 2.8mg; SODIUM 880mg; CALC 125mg

Bell Pepper and Fresh Mozzarella Couscous

Fast-cooking couscous pairs with bottled roasted bell peppers, canned artichoke hearts, and a simple vinaigrette for a speedy meal. The bottled roasted red peppers and superfast-cooking couscous make this a perfect recipe for your busiest day, and it can be doubled to make 2 meals. Use any leftover artichoke hearts, bell peppers, and mozzarella for a vegetarian pizza.

½ cup water
⅓ cup uncooked couscous
⅛ teaspoon salt
¼ cup chopped bottled roasted red bell peppers
¼ cup canned artichoke hearts, rinsed, drained, and chopped
¼ cup (1 ounce) chopped fresh mozzarella cheese
1 tablespoon chopped fresh basil
1 tablespoon balsamic vinegar
1 teaspoon extra-virgin olive oil
⅛ teaspoon freshly ground black pepper
2 kalamata olives, pitted and sliced

❶ Bring water to a boil in a small saucepan; gradually stir in couscous and salt. Remove from heat; cover and let stand 5 minutes. Fluff with a fork.
❷ Add bell peppers and remaining ingredients; toss gently to combine. Cover and chill. Yield: 1 serving (serving size: 2 cups).

CALORIES 407 (29% from fat); FAT 13.3g (sat 5.1g, mono 4.9g, poly 1g); PROTEIN 14.7g; CARB 54.7g; FIBER 3.5g; CHOL 22mg; IRON 2.2mg; SODIUM 798mg; CALC 197mg

MENU *serves 1*

Bell Pepper and Fresh Mozzarella Couscous

Green salad

Balsamic-brown sugar strawberries
Toss 1 cup halved strawberries with 1 tablespoon brown sugar, 2 teaspoons balsamic vinegar, and 1 teaspoon chopped fresh mint. Let stand at room temperature 20 minutes before serving.

Game Plan

1 While water for couscous comes to a boil:

- Chop roasted red bell peppers and artichokes.

2 While couscous stands:

- Chop mozzarella and basil.

- Slice kalamata olives.

3 While couscous chills:

- Prepare strawberries.

- Assemble salad.

Garlicky Pasta with Fresh Tomatoes and Basil

Seasoned broccoli rabe

Heat a large nonstick skillet over medium-high heat. Add ¼ cup chopped shallots, 1 tablespoon butter, and 2 minced garlic cloves; sauté 4 minutes. Add 1 teaspoon salt, ½ teaspoon crushed red pepper, and 1½ pounds broccoli rabe; sauté 1 minute. Add ¾ cup water; cover and cook 2 minutes or until crisp-tender.

Fresh berries

Game Plan

1 While pasta cooks:

- Mince garlic, and chop shallots, tomatoes, and basil.

- Clean berries.

- Grate cheese.

2 While broccoli rabe cooks:

- Toss pasta.

Garlicky Pasta with Fresh Tomatoes and Basil

Simplicity is a virtue—particularly if you have good tomatoes. The garlic flavor is pronounced here; reduce the amount to 2 cloves, if you prefer. If you can't find campanella, try fusilli, orecchiette, or shells.

- 3 tablespoons extra-virgin olive oil
- 3 garlic cloves, minced
- 5 cups chopped plum tomatoes (about 2 pounds)
- 6 cups hot cooked campanella (about 12 ounces uncooked pasta)
- ⅓ cup chopped fresh basil
- ¼ cup (1 ounce) grated fresh Parmesan cheese
- 1½ teaspoons salt
- ¼ teaspoon freshly ground black pepper

1 Heat oil in a large Dutch oven over medium-high heat. Add garlic; sauté 30 seconds. Add tomatoes; cook 2 minutes or until thoroughly heated, stirring occasionally. Add pasta and remaining ingredients, tossing gently to combine. Yield: 6 servings (serving size: 1⅓ cups).

CALORIES 310 (27% from fat); FAT 9.4g (sat 1.9g, mono 5.5g, poly 1.2g); PROTEIN 9.8g; CARB 47.4g; FIBER 3.6g; CHOL 3mg; IRON 2.8mg; SODIUM 677mg; CALC 81mg

Quick Tip: To remove garlic peels, place the garlic clove on a flat surface, and crush with the blunt side of a chef's knife.

Lasagna Rolls with Roasted Red Pepper Sauce

These rolls require some assembly time, but they provide a nice change of pace from a layered pasta dish.

LASAGNA:

- 8 uncooked lasagna noodles
- 4 teaspoons olive oil
- ½ cup finely chopped onion
- 1 (8-ounce) package presliced mushrooms
- 1 (6-ounce) package fresh baby spinach
- 3 garlic cloves, minced
- ½ cup (2 ounces) shredded mozzarella cheese
- ½ cup part-skim ricotta cheese
- 2 tablespoons minced fresh basil
- ½ teaspoon salt
- ¼ teaspoon crushed red pepper

SAUCE:

- 1 tablespoon red wine vinegar
- ¼ teaspoon salt
- ¼ teaspoon freshly ground black pepper
- 2 garlic cloves, minced
- 1 (14.5-ounce) can diced tomatoes, undrained
- 1 (7-ounce) bottle roasted red bell peppers, undrained
- ⅛ teaspoon crushed red pepper

REMAINING INGREDIENT:

- 2 tablespoons minced fresh basil

❶ To prepare lasagna, cook noodles according to package directions, omitting salt and fat. Drain and rinse with cold water; drain.

❷ Heat oil in a large nonstick skillet over medium-high heat. Add onion, mushrooms, spinach, and 3 garlic cloves; sauté 5 minutes or until onion and mushrooms are tender. Remove from heat, and stir in cheeses and next 3 ingredients.

❸ To prepare sauce, combine vinegar and next 6 ingredients in a blender; process until smooth.

❹ Place cooked noodles on flat surface; spread ¼ cup cheese mixture over each noodle. Roll up noodles, jelly-roll fashion, starting with short side. Place rolls, seam sides down, in a shallow 2-quart microwave-safe dish. Pour ¼ cup sauce over each roll, and cover with heavy-duty plastic wrap. Microwave at HIGH 5 minutes or until thoroughly heated. Sprinkle with 2 tablespoons basil. Yield: 4 servings (serving size: 2 rolls).

CALORIES 393 (27% from fat); FAT 11.7g (sat 4.3g, mono 3.6g, poly 1.5g); PROTEIN 19.3g; CARB 58.3g; FIBER 5.9g; CHOL 20mg; IRON 3.8mg; SODIUM 924mg; CALC 253mg

Game Plan

1 While water for pasta comes to a boil:

- Chop and sauté leek.

2 While pasta cooks:

- Cook pea mixture.
- Mince garlic and chop basil.
- Prepare salad.

3 Blend pea mixture.

4 Cook mushrooms and garlic.

Linguine with Basil-Pea Cream

An easy-to-prepare plum tomato salad provides a pleasantly acidic contrast to the creamy pasta dish. Frozen peas are cooked in a broth mixture, and half are pureed to create a creamy sauce. If the tossed pasta is thick, add a little pasta cooking water to thin the sauce.

- 3 tablespoons butter, divided
- ½ cup chopped leek
- 1½ cups vegetable broth, divided
- 2 (10-ounce) packages frozen green peas
- 1 cup fresh basil leaves
- 1 tablespoon extra-virgin olive oil
- 2 (8-ounce) packages presliced mushrooms
- 2 garlic cloves, minced
- 6 cups hot cooked linguine (about 12 ounces uncooked pasta)
- 1¼ teaspoons salt
- ¼ teaspoon freshly ground black pepper
- ¼ cup chopped fresh basil

❶ Melt 1 tablespoon butter in a large nonstick skillet over medium heat. Add leek; cook 3 minutes, stirring frequently. Stir in ¾ cup broth and peas; bring to a boil. Partially cover, reduce heat, and simmer 5 minutes. Place 1½ cups pea mixture, ¾ cup broth, 1 cup basil leaves, and oil in a blender, and process until smooth. Place pureed pea mixture in a large bowl. Stir in remaining pea mixture.

❷ Melt 2 tablespoons butter in pan over medium-high heat. Add mushrooms and garlic; sauté 6 minutes or until mushrooms are tender. Stir mushroom mixture, pasta, salt, and pepper into pea mixture. Sprinkle 2 teaspoons chopped basil over each serving. Yield: 6 servings (serving size: about 1⅓ cups pasta).

CALORIES 366 (26% from fat); FAT 10.4g (sat 4.8g, mono 3.3g, poly 0.6g); PROTEIN 16.1g; CARB 54.2g; FIBER 6.9g; CHOL 55mg; IRON 3.7mg; SODIUM 805mg; CALC 59mg

Creamy Stove-Top Macaroni and Cheese

Try this dish with any short pasta, such as fusilli, farfalle, or cavatappi. You can also vary the type of cheese; a combination of provolone and Asiago gives this dish an Italian flair.

4 cups uncooked medium elbow macaroni
3 tablespoons all-purpose flour
1 teaspoon salt
¼ teaspoon black pepper
2¼ cups fat-free milk
¼ cup (2 ounces) ⅓-less-fat cream cheese, softened
2 teaspoons Dijon mustard
2 teaspoons Worcestershire sauce
½ teaspoon bottled minced garlic
1¼ cups (5 ounces) shredded reduced-fat cheddar cheese

❶ Cook pasta according to package directions, omitting salt and fat. Drain and set aside.

❷ While pasta cooks, combine flour, salt, and pepper in a large saucepan. Add milk; stir with a whisk. Drop cream cheese by teaspoonfuls into milk mixture; bring to a boil over medium-high heat, stirring constantly. Reduce heat; simmer 2 minutes or until thick and cream cheese melts, stirring occasionally. Stir in mustard, Worcestershire sauce, and garlic; simmer 1 minute. Remove from heat. Add cheddar cheese, stirring until cheese melts. Combine pasta and cheese sauce in a large bowl; toss well. Yield: 6 servings (serving size: 1½ cups).

CALORIES 252 (29% from fat); FAT 8.2g (sat 5.1g, mono 0.1g, poly 0.3g); PROTEIN 14.5g; CARB 30.9g; FIBER 1.1g; CHOL 27mg; IRON 1.4mg; SODIUM 536mg; CALC 312mg

MENU *serves 6*

Creamy Stove-Top Macaroni and Cheese

Seven-layer salad
Layer 6 cups torn iceberg lettuce, 1 (15-ounce) can rinsed and drained kidney beans, 2 cups diced tomatoes, 1 cup diced cucumbers, and 1 cup julienne-cut carrot in a large bowl. Combine ½ cup fat-free sour cream and ½ cup light ranch dressing; spread sour cream mixture over carrot. Top with ½ cup (2 ounces) preshredded reduced-fat sharp cheddar cheese; cover and chill.

Low-fat chocolate-chip ice cream

Game Plan

1 While water for pasta comes to a boil:
 • Assemble salad.

2 While pasta cooks:
 • Prepare cheese sauce.

Orecchiette with Fresh Fava Beans, Ricotta, and Mint

Roasted asparagus with lemon and Parmesan

Preheat oven to 425°. Toss 1 pound trimmed asparagus with 2 teaspoons extra-virgin olive oil; sprinkle with ¼ teaspoon salt and ¼ teaspoon crushed red pepper. Bake at 425° for 5 minutes or until crisp-tender. Toss asparagus with 1½ teaspoons grated lemon rind, and top with 2 tablespoons shredded Parmesan cheese.

Garlic bread

Game Plan

1 While water for fava beans and pasta comes to a boil:

- Shell fava beans.

2 While pasta cooks:

- Cook and remove skins from fava beans.

- Grate and shred Parmesan cheese for orecchiette and asparagus.

- Chop mint.

- Prepare garlic bread.

Orecchiette with Fresh Fava Beans, Ricotta, and Mint

Based on seasonal ingredients, this menu is as refreshing as it is tasty. While fava beans are best, frozen lima beans or green peas can be used in a pinch.

- 2 pounds unshelled fava beans (about 1 cup shelled)
- 1 pound uncooked orecchiette pasta ("little ears" pasta)
- 1 teaspoon extra-virgin olive oil
- ¾ teaspoon salt
- 1 cup part-skim ricotta cheese
- ½ cup (2 ounces) grated fresh Parmesan cheese
- ½ cup coarsely chopped fresh mint
- ½ teaspoon freshly ground black pepper
- Mint sprigs (optional)

1 Remove beans from pods; discard pods. Cook beans in boiling water 1 minute. Remove beans with a slotted spoon. Plunge beans into ice water; drain. Remove tough outer skins from beans; discard skins. Set beans aside.

2 Cook pasta according to package directions, omitting salt and fat. Drain pasta, reserving 1 cup pasta water. Place pasta in a large bowl; add oil and salt. Toss well.

3 Combine 1 cup reserved pasta water, ricotta cheese, Parmesan cheese, chopped mint, and pepper. Add beans and cheese mixture to pasta mixture; toss to combine. Garnish with mint sprigs, if desired. Yield: 6 servings (serving size: about 1 cup).

CALORIES 507 (16% from fat); FAT 8.8g (sat 4.1g, mono 2.5g, poly 1.3g); PROTEIN 29.2g; CARB 85.5g; FIBER 4.7g; CHOL 25mg; IRON 6.2mg; SODIUM 540mg; CALC 255mg

Pasta with Roasted Butternut Squash and Shallots

Use a sharp vegetable peeler to peel the butternut squash. It's easier to handle and less time-consuming than using a knife.

- 3 cups (1-inch) cubed peeled butternut squash
- 1 tablespoon dark brown sugar
- 1½ tablespoons olive oil, divided
- 1 teaspoon salt
- ½ teaspoon black pepper
- 8 shallots, peeled and halved lengthwise (about ½ pound)
- 1 tablespoon chopped fresh or 1 teaspoon dried rubbed sage
- 4 ounces uncooked pappardelle (wide ribbon pasta) or fettuccine
- ¼ cup (1 ounce) grated fresh Parmesan cheese

1 Preheat oven to 475°.

2 Combine squash, sugar, 2½ teaspoons oil, salt, pepper, and shallots in a jelly-roll pan; toss well. Bake at 475° for 20 minutes or until tender, stirring occasionally. Stir in sage.

3 While squash mixture bakes, cook pasta according to package directions, omitting salt and fat. Drain. Place cooked pasta in a bowl. Add 2 teaspoons oil; toss well. Serve squash mixture over pasta. Sprinkle with cheese. Yield: 4 servings (serving size: ¾ cup pasta, ¾ cup squash mixture, and 1 tablespoon cheese).

CALORIES 248 (29% from fat); FAT 7.9g (sat 2g, mono 4.5g, poly 0.8g); PROTEIN 7.1g; CARB 39.4g; FIBER 5.2g; CHOL 5mg; IRON 1.4mg; SODIUM 713mg; CALC 137mg

MENU *serves 4*

Pasta with Roasted Butternut Squash and Shallots

Roasted asparagus
Preheat oven to 475°. Combine 1 pound trimmed asparagus spears, 1 teaspoon bottled minced garlic, 1 teaspoon olive oil, ⅛ teaspoon salt, and ⅛ teaspoon pepper on a baking sheet; toss to coat. Bake at 475° for 10 minutes or until crisp-tender, turning once.

French bread

Game Plan

1 While oven heats:
- •Cube butternut squash.
- •Peel and halve shallots.
- •Trim asparagus.

2 While butternut squash bakes:
- •Cook pasta.
- •Prepare asparagus.
- •Chop sage.
- •Grate Parmesan cheese.

3 Bake asparagus.

Penne with Tomatoes, Olives, and Capers

You can use almost any small pasta, such as macaroni, farfalle, rotelle, or tubetti.

1 tablespoon olive oil
¼ teaspoon crushed red pepper
3 garlic cloves, finely chopped
3 cups chopped plum tomato (about 1¾ pounds)
½ cup chopped pitted kalamata olives
1½ tablespoons capers
¼ teaspoon salt
6 cups hot cooked penne (about 4 cups uncooked tube-shaped pasta)
¾ cup (3 ounces) grated fresh Parmesan cheese
3 tablespoons chopped fresh basil

❶ Heat oil in a large nonstick skillet over medium-high heat. Add pepper and garlic; sauté 30 seconds. Add tomato, olives, capers, and salt. Reduce heat, and simmer 8 minutes; stir occasionally. Add pasta to pan. Toss gently to coat; cook 1 minute or until thoroughly heated. Remove from heat. Sprinkle with cheese and basil. Yield: 4 servings (serving size: about 1¾ cups).

CALORIES 484 (28% from fat); FAT 15.1g (sat 4.7g, mono 7.7g, poly 1.7g); PROTEIN 19.1g; CARB 67.8g; FIBER 4.3g; CHOL 14mg; IRON 3.9mg; SODIUM 870mg; CALC 287mg

Quick Tip: You'll save time in the kitchen if you buy pitted olives.

Penne with Triple-Tomato Sauce

Sun-dried, fresh, and canned tomatoes carry this sauce. You can use reserved oil from the sun-dried tomatoes instead of olive oil to sauté the onion. Crisp purchased breadsticks and a salad dressed with a freshly made Dijon vinaigrette round out this family-friendly pasta dinner.

1   teaspoon olive oil
½   cup finely chopped onion
2   garlic cloves, minced
¼   cup chopped drained oil-packed
    sun-dried tomato halves
1   teaspoon sugar
¼   teaspoon salt
¼   teaspoon freshly ground black pepper
4   plum tomatoes, chopped (about
    ½ pound)
1   (14.5-ounce) can diced tomatoes,
    undrained
12 ounces uncooked penne
½   cup (4 ounces) goat cheese
¼   cup finely chopped fresh flat-leaf parsley
Freshly ground black pepper (optional)
Basil sprigs (optional)

❶ Heat oil in a large nonstick skillet over medium-high heat. Add onion, and sauté 4 minutes or until tender. Add garlic, and sauté 1 minute. Add sun-dried tomatoes and next 5 ingredients. Reduce heat to medium, and cook 20 minutes or until liquid almost evaporates, stirring frequently.
❷ While tomato mixture cooks, prepare pasta according to package directions, omitting salt and fat. Drain; return pasta to pan. Stir in tomato mixture, cheese, and parsley. Garnish with black pepper and basil sprigs, if desired. Yield: 6 servings (serving size: 1⅓ cups).

CALORIES 325 (22% from fat); FAT 8g (sat 4.4g, mono 2.3g, poly 0.4g); PROTEIN 13.2g; CARB 51.6g; FIBER 3.9g; CHOL 15mg; IRON 2.8mg; SODIUM 302mg; CALC 90mg

MENU *serves 6*

Penne with Triple-Tomato Sauce

Tossed salad
Combine 6 cups mixed salad greens, ½ cup thinly sliced radish, ½ cup pre-sliced mushrooms, and 1 seeded and thinly sliced yellow bell pepper in a large bowl. Combine 2 tablespoons extra-virgin olive oil, 1 tablespoon water, 1 tablespoon red wine vinegar, 1 teaspoon Dijon mustard, and ¼ teaspoon freshly ground black pepper in a small bowl; stir with a whisk. Toss dressing with salad. Sprinkle with ⅓ cup shaved fresh Parmesan cheese.

Breadsticks

Game Plan
1 While water for pasta comes to a boil:
   • Chop vegetables and mince garlic.
2 While tomato mixture cooks:
   • Cook pasta.
   • Chop parsley.
   • Prepare salad.

Pasta with Chickpeas and Garlic Sauce

Pureed chickpeas make a hearty and flavorful pasta sauce.

2	teaspoons olive oil
2	garlic cloves, peeled and crushed
¾	teaspoon kosher salt
¼	teaspoon crushed red pepper
1	(15.5-ounce) can chickpeas (garbanzo beans), rinsed and drained
1	(14-ounce) can vegetable broth
1½	cups uncooked medium seashell pasta (about 6 ounces)
½	cup grape tomatoes, halved
2	garlic cloves, minced
1	tablespoon minced fresh parsley
1	tablespoon fresh lemon juice
3	tablespoons shredded Parmigiano-Reggiano cheese

❶ Heat oil in a medium saucepan over medium heat. Add crushed garlic; sauté 1 minute. Add salt and next 3 ingredients; bring to a boil. Cover, reduce heat, and simmer 15 minutes.

❷ While garlic mixture simmers, cook pasta in boiling water 9 minutes, omitting salt and fat; drain well.

❸ Place chickpea mixture in a food processor; process until smooth. Combine chickpea mixture, pasta, tomatoes, minced garlic, parsley, and lemon juice; toss well. Sprinkle with cheese. Serve immediately. Yield: 4 servings (serving size: 1 cup pasta and 2¼ teaspoons cheese).

CALORIES 293 (15% from fat); FAT 4.7g (sat 1.2g, mono 2.2g, poly 0.7g); PROTEIN 11.2g; CARB 52g; FIBER 4.9g; CHOL 3mg; IRON 2.6mg; SODIUM 801mg; CALC 87mg

---

MENU *serves 4*

Pasta with Chickpeas and Garlic Sauce

Broccoli rabe with garlic

Heat 1 tablespoon extra-virgin olive oil in a skillet over medium heat. Add 2 crushed peeled garlic cloves; cook 30 seconds or until garlic is fragrant. Add 1½ pounds cleaned and trimmed broccoli rabe, tossing to coat. Reduce heat to medium-low. Add ¼ cup water; cover and cook 9 minutes or until tender, stirring occasionally. Toss with 2 teaspoons fresh lemon juice, ¼ teaspoon salt, and ⅛ teaspoon black pepper.

Chocolate sorbet

Game Plan

1 While oil heats for garlic:
   - Boil water for pasta.

2 While chickpeas simmer:
   - Cook pasta.
   - Prepare broccoli rabe.
   - Halve tomatoes.
   - Squeeze lemon for juice for broccoli rabe and pasta.

MENU *serves 4*

Garden Tomato and Basil Pesto Pizza

Baby arugula salad with balsamic vinaigrette

Combine 2 tablespoons extra-virgin olive oil, 2 teaspoons balsamic vinegar, 1 teaspoon sugar, ½ teaspoon Dijon mustard, ¼ teaspoon salt, and ¼ teaspoon freshly ground black pepper in a small bowl; stir with a whisk. Combine ¼ cup thinly sliced red onion, ¼ cup toasted sliced almonds, and 1 (5-ounce) package prewashed baby arugula in a serving bowl. Pour vinaigrette over arugula mixture; toss to coat.

Melon slices

Game Plan

1 While oven heats:

- Slice cheese and chop tomato for pizza.
- Prepare vinaigrette for salad.

2 While pizza bakes:

- Combine salad and vinaigrette.
- Slice basil for pizza.

Garden Tomato and Basil Pesto Pizza

Fresh mozzarella is easier to slice when it's very firm. Place mozzarella in the freezer just until firm, and thinly slice. Any brand of prebaked pizza crust will work for this recipe.

    1 (12-ounce) prebaked pizza crust
Cooking spray
    2 tablespoons commercial pesto
    1 cup (4 ounces) thinly sliced fresh
       mozzarella cheese
    2 cups chopped tomato (about
       2 large)
   ¼ teaspoon crushed red pepper
   ¼ cup thinly sliced fresh basil

1 Preheat oven to 450°.

2 Spray crust with cooking spray.

3 Place crust on a baking sheet; bake at 450° for 10 minutes. Spread pesto evenly over crust, leaving a ½-inch border. Top with cheese slices and tomato; sprinkle with pepper. Bake at 450° for 5 minutes or until cheese melts and crust is golden. Sprinkle with basil. Yield: 4 servings (serving size: ¼ pizza).

CALORIES 377 (32% from fat); FAT 13.5g (sat 4.9g, mono 0.1g, poly 0.2g); PROTEIN 14.8g; CARB 48.1g; FIBER 3.1g; CHOL 24mg; IRON 3.2mg; SODIUM 687mg; CALC 209mg

Quick Pizza Margherita

Baking the dough before topping it with tomato keeps the crust crisp. Be sure to use fresh mozzarella, which comes packed in water and can be found with other gourmet cheeses.

1 (10-ounce) can refrigerated pizza crust dough
Cooking spray
1 teaspoon extra-virgin olive oil, divided
1 garlic clove, halved
5 plum tomatoes, thinly sliced (about ¾ pound)
1 cup (4 ounces) shredded fresh mozzarella cheese
1 teaspoon balsamic vinegar
½ cup thinly sliced fresh basil
⅛ teaspoon salt
⅛ teaspoon black pepper

❶ Preheat oven to 400°.
❷ Unroll dough onto a baking sheet coated with cooking spray; pat into a 13 x 11-inch rectangle. Bake at 400° for 8 minutes. Remove crust from oven, and brush with ½ teaspoon oil. Rub crust with cut sides of garlic.
❸ Arrange tomato slices on crust, leaving a ½-inch border; sprinkle evenly with cheese. Bake at 400° for 12 minutes or until cheese melts and crust is golden.
❹ Combine ½ teaspoon oil and vinegar; stir with a whisk.
❺ Sprinkle pizza evenly with sliced basil, salt, and pepper. Drizzle vinegar mixture evenly over pizza. Cut pizza into 8 pieces. Yield: 4 servings (serving size: 2 pieces).

CALORIES 298 (30% from fat); FAT 10g (sat 4.6g, mono 3.5g, poly 1.4g); PROTEIN 12.2g; CARB 38.6g; FIBER 2.1g; CHOL 22mg; IRON 2.6mg; SODIUM 595mg; CALC 175mg

Quick Tip: If you're having trouble shaping the dough, let it rest for 5 minutes, and it will become more elastic.

MENU *serves 4*

Quick Pizza Margherita

Lemon broccoli
Combine 2 teaspoons fresh lemon juice, 1 teaspoon extra-virgin olive oil, ½ teaspoon salt, ⅛ teaspoon black pepper, and 1 minced garlic clove in a large bowl; stir with a whisk. Add 4 cups hot cooked broccoli florets and ¼ cup very thinly sliced red onion; toss broccoli mixture gently to coat.

Chocolate wafer cookies

Game Plan

1 While oven heats:
- Slice tomatoes for pizza.
- Prepare dough.

2 While crust bakes:
- Combine oil and vinegar for pizza.
- Shred cheese.
- Slice basil.

3 While pizza bakes, prepare broccoli.

MENU *serves 6*

Caramelized Onion and Goat Cheese Pizza

Red-pepper pasta

Cook 8 ounces dry spaghetti according to package directions, omitting salt and fat. While pasta cooks, combine 1½ tablespoons olive oil, 2 teaspoons bottled minced garlic, and ¼ teaspoon crushed red pepper in a microwave-safe bowl; cover and microwave at HIGH 1 minute. Toss drained cooked pasta with olive oil mixture and ½ cup vegetable broth. Sprinkle with 3 tablespoons grated Parmesan cheese.

Mixed greens salad with cherry tomatoes and red onion slices

Game Plan

1 While oven heats and water comes to a boil for pasta:

 •Slice and cook onion for pizza and salad.

 •Chop tomatoes for pizza.

 •Prepare pizza.

2 While pasta and pizza cook:

 •Chop basil for pizza.

 •Prepare oil mixture for pasta.

 •Prepare salad.

Caramelized Onion and Goat Cheese Pizza

Microwaving garlic and crushed red pepper in olive oil quickly infuses the oil with flavor.

2 teaspoons olive oil
2 cups thinly sliced onion, separated into rings (about 1 onion)
1 (1-pound) Italian cheese-flavored pizza crust (such as Boboli)
½ cup bottled pizza sauce (such as Contadina)
¼ cup chopped drained oil-packed sun-dried tomato halves
⅔ cup (3 ounces) crumbled goat cheese
¼ cup chopped fresh basil

❶ Preheat oven to 450°.
❷ Heat olive oil in a large nonstick skillet over medium-high heat. Add onion; cover and cook 3 minutes. Uncover and cook 11 minutes or until golden brown, stirring frequently.
❸ Place pizza crust on a baking sheet. Combine sauce and tomatoes; spread over pizza crust. Top with onion and cheese. Bake at 450° for 10 minutes or until crust is golden brown. Sprinkle with basil. Cut into 6 wedges. Yield: 6 servings (serving size: 1 wedge).

CALORIES 285 (29% from fat); FAT 9.2g (sat 3.8g, mono 4g, poly 1g); PROTEIN 11.6g; CARB 38.4g; FIBER 1.4g; CHOL 7mg; IRON 2.6mg; SODIUM 577mg; CALC 238mg

Pizza Olympia

The feta cheese will not melt, so use the crust's golden color as an indicator of doneness.

1 (10-ounce) focaccia, cut in half horizontally
1 tablespoon minced fresh garlic
2 tablespoons tomato paste
2 teaspoons dried oregano
1 (7-ounce) bottle roasted red bell peppers, drained and chopped
½ cup chopped red onion
1 tablespoon drained capers
1 cup (4 ounces) crumbled feta cheese

❶ Preheat oven to 450°.
❷ Place focaccia halves, cut sides up, on a baking sheet. Combine garlic, tomato paste, and oregano in a small bowl; spread evenly over focaccia halves. Top each half evenly with roasted peppers, onion, and capers; sprinkle with feta cheese. Bake at 450° for 12 minutes or until focaccia is golden. Cut each pizza in half. Yield: 4 servings (serving size: ½ pizza).

CALORIES 301 (25% from fat); FAT 8.4g (sat 4.5g, mono 2.7g, poly 0.5g); PROTEIN 11.4g; CARB 45.6g; FIBER 2.6g; CHOL 25mg; IRON 3.2mg; SODIUM 648mg; CALC 160mg

Game Plan

1 While oven heats:

•Prepare tomato paste mixture for pizza.

2 Assemble pizza.

3 While pizza bakes:

•Prepare olives and pepperoncini.

•Prepare yogurt, and chill.

MENU *serves 4*

Spinach and Kale Turnovers

Cream of tomato soup
Heat 2 teaspoons olive oil in a large saucepan over medium-high heat. Add 1 cup chopped onion and 3 minced garlic cloves; sauté 3 minutes or until tender. Add 1 (28-ounce) can crushed tomatoes, 1 tablespoon balsamic vinegar, ½ teaspoon salt, and ¼ teaspoon crushed red pepper; bring to a boil. Reduce heat, and simmer 30 minutes. Place in a blender; process until smooth. Return tomato mixture to pan. Stir in ¾ cup half-and-half; cook until thoroughly heated.

Pound cake

Game Plan

1 While oven heats:
- Chop onion and garlic for turnovers and soup.
- Chop kale.
- Cook kale mixture.

2 While kale mixture cools:
- Cook onion and garlic for soup.

3 While soup cooks:
- Assemble and bake turnovers.

4 While turnovers stand:
- Blend tomato mixture for soup.

Spinach and Kale Turnovers

Enjoy 2 turnovers as a meatless entrée, or serve one as a side dish with steak or roast chicken. They're great made ahead and brown-bagged; reheat in a microwave or toaster oven. You can prepare the turnovers in advance, and freeze them for up to 2 months.

- 2 teaspoons olive oil
- 1 cup chopped onion
- 1 garlic clove, chopped
- 3 cups chopped kale (about 1 small bunch)
- 1 (6-ounce) package fresh baby spinach
- ½ teaspoon freshly ground black pepper
- ¼ teaspoon salt
- ⅛ teaspoon ground nutmeg
- ¾ cup (3 ounces) crumbled feta cheese
- 1 (11.3-ounce) can refrigerated dinner roll dough (such as Pillsbury)
- Cooking spray
- 2½ tablespoons grated fresh Parmesan cheese

1 Preheat oven to 375°.

2 Heat oil in a large skillet over medium-high heat. Add onion; sauté 10 minutes or until tender and lightly browned. Add garlic; sauté 2 minutes. Add kale and spinach; sauté 8 minutes or until kale is tender. Stir in pepper, salt, and nutmeg. Remove from heat; cool slightly. Stir in feta.

3 Separate dough into 8 pieces; roll each piece into a 5-inch circle. Spoon about ⅓ cup kale mixture on half of each circle, leaving ½-inch borders. Fold dough over kale mixture until edges almost meet. Bring bottom edge of dough over top edge; crimp with fingers to form a rim.

4 Place turnovers on a baking sheet coated with cooking spray. Lightly coat turnovers with cooking spray; sprinkle each turnover with about 1 teaspoon Parmesan cheese. Bake at 375° for 18 minutes or until golden brown. Let stand at least 5 minutes before serving; serve warm or at room temperature. Yield: 4 servings (serving size: 2 turnovers).

CALORIES 363 (30% from fat); FAT 12.3g (sat 4.1g, mono 2.9g, poly 0.6g); PROTEIN 15.6g; CARB 47.8g; FIBER 3.7g; CHOL 22mg; IRON 4.5mg; SODIUM 1,028mg; CALC 261mg

Spinach and Feta-Stuffed Focaccia

This calzone-like roll mixes fresh spinach with cheese, raisins, and pine nuts—a flavor combination reminiscent of the Mediterranean.

1 tablespoon olive oil
½ cup chopped onion
3 garlic cloves, minced
2 (6-ounce) packages baby spinach, divided
¾ cup (3 ounces) crumbled feta cheese
⅔ cup golden raisins
3 tablespoons pine nuts, toasted
2 tablespoons fresh lemon juice
1½ teaspoons chopped fresh oregano
¼ teaspoon salt
¼ teaspoon ground red pepper
1 (13.8-ounce) can refrigerated pizza crust dough
Cooking spray
1 tablespoon 2% reduced-fat milk
1 tablespoon water
¼ cup (1 ounce) grated fresh Parmesan cheese

❶ Preheat oven to 450°.

❷ Heat oil in a large nonstick skillet over medium-high heat. Add onion and garlic; sauté 1 minute. Add half of spinach; cook 1 minute or until spinach wilts. Add remaining spinach; cook 2 minutes or until spinach wilts, stirring constantly. Remove from heat; stir in feta and next 6 ingredients.

❸ Place dough on a baking sheet coated with cooking spray; pat dough into a 15 x 12-inch rectangle. Spread spinach mixture lengthwise over half of dough, leaving a 1-inch border. Fold dough over filling; press edges together with a fork. Cut 5 (1-inch) diagonal slits in top of dough.

❹ Combine milk and water; brush evenly over dough. Sprinkle with Parmesan cheese. Bake at 450° for 15 minutes or until golden. Yield: 6 servings (serving size: 1 slice).

CALORIES 334 (29% from fat); FAT 10.6g (sat 3.5g, mono 4.6g, poly 1.3g); PROTEIN 12.6g; CARB 48.7g; FIBER 3.5g; CHOL 16mg; IRON 3.9mg; SODIUM 815mg; CALC 201mg

MENU *serves 6*

Spinach and Feta-Stuffed Focaccia

Romaine, strawberry, and orange salad
Combine 6 cups torn romaine lettuce, 1 cup sliced strawberries, 1 cup drained canned mandarin oranges, and ¾ cup thinly vertically sliced red onion in a large bowl. Combine 2 tablespoons fresh lemon juice, 1 tablespoon honey, 2 teaspoons extra-virgin olive oil, 1 teaspoon Dijon mustard, ¼ teaspoon salt, and ¼ teaspoon black pepper; stir with a whisk. Drizzle dressing over salad; toss gently to coat. Sprinkle with ¼ cup shaved Parmesan cheese.

Vanilla low-fat ice cream with caramel sauce

Game Plan

1 While oven heats for focaccia:
  • Toast pine nuts for focaccia.
  • Prepare filling for focaccia.
  • Prepare dressing for salad.
2 While focaccia bakes:
  • Prepare remaining salad ingredients.

Creamy Spinach-Mushroom Skillet Enchiladas

Flavored cream cheese delivers the taste of green onions and chives without all the chopping.

Game Plan

1 While broiler heats:
  - Cook mushroom mixture.
2 Assemble enchiladas.
3 While enchiladas broil:
  - Prepare salad.

2 teaspoons olive oil
1 teaspoon bottled minced garlic
½ teaspoon chili powder
½ teaspoon ground cumin
1 (8-ounce) package presliced mushrooms
1 (6-ounce) package fresh baby spinach (about 6 cups)
¼ teaspoon salt
2 tablespoons light cream cheese with green onions and chives
1 (16-ounce) bottle green salsa, divided
8 (6-inch) corn tortillas
⅓ cup (1½ ounces) shredded Monterey Jack cheese
¼ cup fat-free sour cream
Cilantro sprigs (optional)

❶ Preheat broiler.
❷ Heat olive oil in a large skillet over medium-high heat. Add garlic, chili powder, cumin, and mushrooms; sauté 5 minutes. Add spinach and salt; cook 1 minute or until spinach wilts, stirring frequently. Drain; return mushroom mixture to pan. Add cream cheese; cook 2 minutes or until cream cheese melts, stirring frequently. Place mushroom mixture in a bowl; set aside.

❸ Heat 1 cup salsa in a saucepan over low heat. Dredge both sides of each tortilla in warm salsa using tongs; stack tortillas on a plate. Spoon 1 heaping tablespoon mushroom mixture into center of each tortilla; fold in half, and arrange in skillet, overlapping slightly. Top with remaining salsa; sprinkle with shredded cheese. Wrap handle of skillet with foil, and broil enchiladas 4 minutes or until cheese melts. Top with sour cream, and garnish with cilantro sprigs, if desired. Yield: 4 servings (serving size: 2 enchiladas and 1 tablespoon sour cream).

CALORIES 273 (29% from fat); FAT 8.7g (sat 3.6g, mono 2.9g, poly 1g); PROTEIN 10.1g; CARB 39.4g; FIBER 6.7g; CHOL 15mg; IRON 2.7mg; SODIUM 806mg; CALC 330mg

Greek-Style Stuffed Eggplant

Leave about ¼-inch eggplant pulp in the shells when you hollow them out. If you're not a fan of eggplant, substitute zucchini; just remember that it will cook a little more quickly.

2 eggplants, cut in half lengthwise (about 3 pounds)
¼ cup water
Cooking spray
1 cup chopped onion
1 cup chopped plum tomato
¼ cup white wine
3 garlic cloves, minced
1 cup (4 ounces) crumbled feta cheese
½ cup chopped fresh parsley, divided
¾ teaspoon salt, divided
¼ teaspoon freshly ground black pepper
2 (1-ounce) slices French bread
2 tablespoons grated fresh Parmesan cheese

❶ Carefully remove pulp from eggplant halves, reserving shells. Coarsely chop pulp to measure 6 cups. Place eggplant shells, cut sides down, in a 10-inch square baking dish. Add ¼ cup water; cover and microwave at HIGH 5 minutes or until shells are tender. Keep warm.
❷ Preheat broiler.
❸ Heat a large nonstick skillet over medium-high heat; coat with cooking spray. Add eggplant pulp; sauté 7 minutes. Add onion; sauté 2 minutes. Stir in tomato, wine, and garlic; cook 3 minutes or until liquid almost evaporates, stirring occasionally. Remove from heat; stir in feta, ¼ cup parsley, ½ teaspoon salt, and pepper. Spoon ¾ cup onion mixture into each eggplant shell.
❹ Place bread slices in food processor; pulse 10 times or until coarse crumbs measure 1 cup. Combine breadcrumbs, ¼ cup parsley, ¼ teaspoon salt, and Parmesan cheese, stirring well. Sprinkle ¼ cup breadcrumb mixture over each stuffed shell. Arrange shells on a baking sheet coated with cooking spray; broil 2 minutes or until lightly browned. Yield: 4 servings (serving size: 1 stuffed eggplant half).

CALORIES 250 (30% from fat); FAT 8.4g (sat 5.1g, mono 1.6g, poly 0.6g); PROTEIN 11.3g; CARB 35.3g; FIBER 10.3g; CHOL 29mg; IRON 2.3mg; SODIUM 906mg; CALC 246mg

Quick Tip: If you don't want to make fresh breadcrumbs, use half the amount called for of canned breadcrumbs instead.

MENU *serves 4*

Greek-Style Stuffed Eggplant

Herbed goat cheese toasts

Preheat broiler. Combine ½ cup crumbled goat cheese, ¾ teaspoon dried oregano, ½ teaspoon garlic powder, ¼ teaspoon paprika, and ⅛ teaspoon salt; sprinkle evenly over 8 (1-ounce) slices French bread. Broil 2 minutes or until lightly browned.

Lemon sorbet with almond biscotti

Game Plan

1 Remove eggplant pulp.

2 While eggplant shells cook:
- Preheat broiler.
- Slice bread for toasts and stuffed eggplant.
- Prepare breadcrumb mixture.

3 While eggplant filling cooks:
- Prepare toasts.

4 Broil stuffed eggplant shells.

153

Stuffed Portobello Mushrooms

Precooked bacon, bottled vinaigrette, and produce department convenience products help this meal come together in a flash. You can substitute freshly made coarse breadcrumbs, if necessary.

4 (6-inch) portobello mushrooms, stems removed
Cooking spray
1 cup chopped red tomato
1 cup chopped yellow tomato
1 cup panko (Japanese) breadcrumbs
1 cup (4 ounces) preshredded part-skim mozzarella cheese
¼ cup chopped fresh chives
¼ teaspoon salt
¼ teaspoon black pepper

❶ Preheat broiler.
❷ Remove brown gills from undersides of mushrooms using a spoon; discard gills. Place mushrooms, gill sides down, on a foil-lined baking sheet coated with cooking spray. Broil mushrooms 5 minutes.
❸ While mushrooms broil, combine tomatoes, breadcrumbs, cheese, and chives.
❹ Turn mushrooms over, and sprinkle evenly with salt and pepper. Divide tomato mixture evenly among mushrooms. Broil 5 minutes or until cheese melts. Yield: 4 servings (serving size: 1 stuffed mushroom).

CALORIES 184 (26% from fat); FAT 5.3g (sat 2.9g, mono 1.3g, poly 0.2g); PROTEIN 12.6g; CARB 21.6g; FIBER 3.5g; CHOL 16mg; IRON 1.3mg; SODIUM 325mg; CALC 209mg

Potato-Zucchini Skillet Pancakes with Cherry Tomato Salad

These potato pancakes make an ideal base for the tangy olive and tomato salad. While the pancakes can stand alone as a meatless main dish, they also make a delightful side for simple sautéed chicken.

PANCAKES:

- 3 cups shredded peeled Yukon gold potato (about 1 pound)
- 2 cups shredded zucchini (about 8 ounces)
- 1 cup shredded onion (about 1 small)
- ½ cup egg substitute
- ¼ cup matzo meal
- ¼ cup freshly grated Parmesan cheese
- ¼ teaspoon salt

Dash of freshly ground black pepper

- 4 teaspoons canola oil, divided

SALAD:

- 3 cups quartered cherry tomatoes
- 2 tablespoons chopped pitted kalamata olives
- 2 tablespoons chopped fresh parsley
- 1 teaspoon extra-virgin olive oil
- ¼ teaspoon salt
- ¼ teaspoon freshly ground black pepper

❶ To prepare pancakes, place first 3 ingredients in a clean towel, and squeeze out excess liquid. Combine potato mixture, egg substitute, and next 4 ingredients in a large bowl, and stir gently to blend.

❷ Heat 1 teaspoon canola oil in a nonstick griddle or large nonstick skillet over medium heat. Spoon about 1 cup potato mixture into hot pan, spreading to a 6-inch diameter. Cook 3 minutes on each side or until lightly browned and cooked through. Transfer to a plate; keep warm. Repeat procedure with 3 teaspoons oil and remaining potato mixture.

❸ To prepare salad, combine tomatoes and remaining 5 ingredients in a medium bowl; toss gently. Serve salad on top of pancakes. Yield: 4 servings (serving size: 1 pancake and about ³⁄₄ cup salad).

CALORIES 271 (35% from fat); FAT 10.4g (sat 1.8g, mono 5.2g, poly 1.9g); PROTEIN 11.3g; CARB 34.4g; FIBER 3.9g; CHOL 5mg; IRON 2.7mg; SODIUM 629mg; CALC 135mg

MENU *serves 4*

Potato-Zucchini Skillet Pancakes with Cherry Tomato Salad

Fresh steamed green beans

Game Plan

1 Shred potato, zucchini, and onion.

2 Prepare potato mixture.

3 While pancakes cook:

- •Prepare salad.
- •Steam green beans.

Rice Noodles with Tofu and Bok Choy

Look for water-packed tofu, which will hold its shape when cooked and tossed with the noodles. If rice noodles are unavailable, substitute angel hair pasta.

- 1 (6-ounce) package rice noodles
- ¼ cup low-sodium soy sauce
- 2 tablespoons rice vinegar
- 1 teaspoon sugar
- 1 teaspoon dark sesame oil
- ½ teaspoon crushed red pepper
- Cooking spray
- 2 cups (¼-inch) red bell pepper strips
- 5 cups sliced bok choy
- ½ pound firm water-packed tofu, drained and cut into ½-inch cubes
- 3 garlic cloves, minced
- ½ cup thinly sliced green onions
- 3 tablespoons chopped fresh cilantro

1 Cook noodles in boiling water 6 minutes; drain. Combine soy sauce and next 4 ingredients; stir with a whisk.

2 Heat a large nonstick skillet over medium-high heat; coat with cooking spray. Add bell pepper strips; sauté 2 minutes. Add bok choy; sauté 1 minute. Add tofu and garlic; sauté 2 minutes. Add noodles and soy sauce mixture; cook 2 minutes or until thoroughly heated, tossing well to coat. Sprinkle with green onions and cilantro. Yield: 4 servings (serving size: 2 cups).

CALORIES 281 (17% from fat); FAT 5.2g (sat 0.8g, mono 0.9g, poly 2.3g); PROTEIN 12.9g; CARB 46.7g; FIBER 4.2g; CHOL 0mg; IRON 3.8mg; SODIUM 575mg; CALC 190mg

Ingredient Tip: If you can't find bok choy, almost any quick-cooking crisp vegetable will work. Try snow peas or shredded napa cabbage.

MENU   *serves 4*

Rice Noodles with Tofu and Bok Choy

Asian spinach salad
Combine 2 cups fresh spinach, 1 cup grated carrot, and 1 cup bean sprouts in a large bowl. Combine 1 tablespoon fresh lime juice, 1 tablespoon rice vinegar, 2 teaspoons low-sodium soy sauce, ½ teaspoon sugar, and ½ teaspoon sesame oil; stir with a whisk. Toss dressing with spinach mixture. Top each serving with 1 teaspoon chopped dry-roasted peanuts.

Iced green tea with mint leaves

Game Plan

1 While water for the noodles comes to a boil:
- Chop vegetables and tofu.

2 While noodles cook:
- Prepare soy sauce mixture.
- Prepare spinach mixture.
- Prepare salad dressing.

3 While tofu mixture cooks:
- Slice green onions.
- Chop cilantro.
- Toss salad with dressing.

Curried Noodles with Tofu

Look for curry paste in the Asian foods section of your supermarket. Use it conservatively, though—a little goes a long way.

MENU *serves 4*

Curried Noodles with Tofu

Sesame-scented snow peas and carrots

Cook 1½ cups snow peas and ½ cup diagonally sliced carrot in boiling water 30 seconds; drain. Toss vegetables with 2 teaspoons low-sodium soy sauce, 1 teaspoon dark sesame oil, 1 teaspoon rice vinegar, and ½ teaspoon sugar.

Green tea

Game Plan

1 While water comes to a boil for snow peas and carrots:

- Prepare tofu, red bell pepper, cabbage, green onions, and cilantro.

- Combine sauce ingredients for noodles.

2 While tofu is sautéing:

- Soak rice sticks in hot water.

3 While noodle mixture cooks in sauce:

- Toss peas and carrots with seasonings.

6 ounces uncooked rice sticks (rice-flour noodles), angel hair pasta, or vermicelli
1 cup light coconut milk
2 tablespoons low-sodium soy sauce
1½ tablespoons bottled ground fresh ginger (such as Spice World)
1 tablespoon sugar
2 teaspoons bottled minced garlic
1 teaspoon green curry paste
½ teaspoon salt
Cooking spray
1 (12.3-ounce) package extra-firm tofu, drained and cut into 1-inch cubes
1 cup red bell pepper strips
4 cups shredded napa (Chinese) cabbage
1 cup chopped green onions
3 tablespoons chopped fresh cilantro

1 Place noodles in a large bowl. Add hot water over noodles to cover, and let stand 5 minutes. Drain.

2 Combine coconut milk and next 6 ingredients in a small bowl.

3 Heat a large nonstick skillet over medium-high heat; coat with cooking spray. Add tofu; sauté 10 minutes or until golden brown. Remove tofu from pan; keep warm.

4 Add bell pepper to pan; sauté 1 minute or until crisp-tender. Add cabbage; sauté 30 seconds. Stir in noodles, coconut milk mixture, and tofu; cook 2 minutes or until noodles are tender. Stir in green onions and cilantro. Yield: 4 servings (serving size: 1¼ cups).

CALORIES 300 (15% from fat); FAT 4.9g (sat 2.3g, mono 0.4g, poly 1.1g); PROTEIN 11.5g; CARB 51.4g; FIBER 4.5g; CHOL 0mg; IRON 3.6mg; SODIUM 678mg; CALC 89mg

Quick Tip: You can use the hot water left over from cooking the snow peas and carrots to soak the rice sticks: Remove the vegetables with a slotted spoon, and pour the cooking water over the noodles.

Spaghetti Squash with Edamame-Cilantro Pesto

Delicate strands of spaghetti squash stand in for pasta in this easy meatless menu. Miniature panini are a welcome accompaniment and offer a nice change from garlic bread or cheese toast. Prepare and chill the pesto up to 2 days ahead, and bring to room temperature before serving; the unique pesto is also good on a pizza with sun-dried tomatoes. Bake and chill the squash halves a day or 2 before; it's actually easier to remove the flesh when the squash is cold. Reheat the cold squash in the microwave.

2   (2½-pound) spaghetti squash
Cooking spray
½   teaspoon salt, divided
1¼   cups chopped fresh cilantro
1   cup vegetable broth
1   tablespoon extra-virgin olive oil
¼   teaspoon freshly ground black pepper
2   garlic cloves, minced
1   pound frozen shelled edamame (fresh soybeans), thawed
¼   cup (1 ounce) grated fresh Parmesan cheese

❶ Preheat oven to 350°.
❷ Cut each squash in half lengthwise; discard seeds. Place squash halves, cut sides down, on a baking sheet coated with cooking spray. Bake at 350° for 1 hour or until tender. Cool slightly. Scrape inside of squash with a fork to remove spaghetti-like strands to measure about 8 cups. Place in a large bowl, and sprinkle with ¼ teaspoon salt; toss gently to combine. Cover squash, and keep warm.
❸ Place ¼ teaspoon salt, cilantro, and next 5 ingredients in a food processor; pulse until coarsely chopped. Serve edamame pesto over squash; sprinkle with cheese. Yield: 6 servings (serving size: 1½ cups squash, ½ cup edamame pesto, and 2 teaspoons cheese).

CALORIES 233 (29% from fat); FAT 7.6g (sat 1.3g, mono 2.8g, poly 2.4g); PROTEIN 12.5g; CARB 31.3g; FIBER 8.8g; CHOL 3mg; IRON 3mg; SODIUM 533mg; CALC 182mg

MENU *serves 6*

Spaghetti Squash with Edamame-Cilantro Pesto

Baguette panini
Top each of 6 diagonally cut French bread baguette slices with 2 tablespoons shredded provolone cheese, 2 thin slices plum tomato, and 3 arugula leaves. Top each with 1 diagonally cut baguette slice. Heat a large nonstick skillet over medium heat. Add panini to pan. Place a cast-iron or heavy skillet on top of panini; press gently to flatten. Cook 3 minutes on each side or until bread is lightly toasted (leave cast-iron skillet on panini while they cook).

Strawberry sorbet with vanilla wafer cookies

Game Plan
1 While spaghetti squash bakes:
•Thaw edamame.
•Prepare pesto.
•Prepare panini.

Fish & Shellfish

Grilled Salmon with Apricot-Mustard Glaze, page 181

Asian Marinated Striped Bass

Although it contains only 4 ingredients, this marinade packs a lot of flavor into each bite.

3 tablespoons fish sauce
2 tablespoons minced fresh cilantro
1 tablespoon sugar
2 garlic cloves, minced
4 (6-ounce) striped bass fillets
Cooking spray

❶ Combine first 4 ingredients in a large zip-top plastic bag; add fish to bag. Seal. Marinate in refrigerator 20 minutes; turn once. Remove fish from bag; reserve marinade.

❷ Heat a large nonstick skillet over medium-high heat; coat with cooking spray. Add fish to pan; cook 4 minutes on each side or until fish flakes easily when tested with a fork. Remove fish from pan. Add marinade to pan; bring to a boil. Cook 30 seconds; serve with fish. Yield: 4 servings (serving size: 1 fillet and about 2 teaspoons sauce).

CALORIES 185 (19% from fat); FAT 4g (sat 0.9g, mono 1.1g, poly 1.3g); PROTEIN 31g; CARB 4.2g; FIBER 0.1g; CHOL 136mg; IRON 1.6mg; SODIUM 1,146mg; CALC 10mg

---

MENU *serves 4*

Asian Marinated Striped Bass

Rice noodles
Soak 4 ounces rice noodles in warm water 20 minutes. Drain; toss with 2 teaspoons peanut oil. Heat 2 teaspoons peanut oil in a large nonstick skillet over medium-high heat; sauté ½ cup thinly sliced shallots 1 minute. Add noodles to pan; cook 3 minutes or until thoroughly heated, tossing well. Stir in ¼ cup chopped green onions, ¼ cup chopped fresh cilantro, 1 tablespoon fish sauce, and 2 teaspoons sugar. Top each serving with 1 teaspoon chopped peanuts.

Steamed baby bok choy

Game Plan

1 While fish marinates:
- Soak noodles.
- Slice shallots.
- Chop green onions, cilantro, and peanuts.
- Steam bok choy, and keep warm.

2 While fish cooks:
- Prepare rice noodles.

Pan-Fried Catfish with Cajun Tartar Sauce

MENU *serves 4*

Pan-Fried Catfish with Cajun Tartar Sauce

Cider-mustard slaw
Combine half of 1 (16-ounce) package cabbage-and-carrot coleslaw, 1 tablespoon brown sugar, 2 tablespoons cider vinegar, 1 tablespoon coarse ground mustard, and ⅛ teaspoon salt.

Corn bread

Vanilla ice cream with caramel sauce

Game Plan

1 Prepare coleslaw.

2 While fish cooks:

•Prepare tartar sauce.

This meal is ready in less than 20 minutes, thanks to such convenience products as Cajun spice blend, packaged coleslaw mix, and bottled caramel sauce. Pick up corn bread or corn muffins from the deli counter at your supermarket to keep things extra easy. The fish is "fried" without the calories or trouble of deep-fat frying. For a spicier sauce, add more hot pepper sauce.

Cooking spray
 4 (6-ounce) farm-raised catfish fillets
 2 teaspoons Cajun seasoning
 ¼ teaspoon salt
 ½ cup fat-free mayonnaise
 1 tablespoon sweet pickle relish
 1 tablespoon minced fresh onion
 1 tablespoon capers, drained
 1 teaspoon hot pepper sauce (such as Tabasco)
 ¼ teaspoon dried oregano

1 Heat a large nonstick skillet over medium-high heat; coat with cooking spray. Sprinkle fish evenly with Cajun seasoning and salt. Add 2 fillets to pan; cook 4 minutes on each side or until fish flakes easily when tested with a fork. Remove fish from pan, and keep warm. Wipe pan clean with paper towels; recoat with cooking spray. Repeat procedure with remaining 2 fillets.

2 While fish cooks, combine mayonnaise and remaining 5 ingredients in a small bowl. Serve mayonnaise mixture with fish. Yield: 4 servings (serving size: 1 fillet and about 3 tablespoons mayonnaise mixture).

CALORIES 262 (48% from fat); FAT 13.9g (sat 3.2g, mono 6.1g, poly 2.7g); PROTEIN 26.7g; CARB 6.3g; FIBER 1g; CHOL 83mg; IRON 1mg; SODIUM 815mg; CALC 20mg

Cornmeal-Crusted Catfish

The bacon drippings used to cook the catfish lend an authentic Southern flavor to this family favorite dish.

    3 slices bacon
    ⅓ cup yellow cornmeal
    2 teaspoons salt-free Cajun seasoning
    ½ teaspoon salt
    4 (6-ounce) farm-raised catfish fillets

❶ Cook bacon in a large nonstick skillet over medium heat until crisp. Remove bacon from pan; reserve 2 teaspoons drippings in pan. Crumble bacon for coleslaw or reserve for another use.

❷ Combine cornmeal, seasoning, and salt in a shallow dish. Dredge fillets in cornmeal mixture, shaking off excess.

❸ Heat reserved drippings in pan over medium-high heat. Add fillets; cook 5 minutes on each side or until fish flakes easily when tested with a fork or until desired degree of doneness. Yield: 4 servings (serving size: 1 fillet).

CALORIES 277 (45% from fat); FAT 13.7g (sat 3.4g, mono 6.9g, poly 2.3g); PROTEIN 27.5g; CARB 8.9g; FIBER 0.9g; CHOL 93mg; IRON 1.6mg; SODIUM 412mg; CALC 13mg

---

MENU *serves 4*

Cornmeal-Crusted Catfish

Steamed green beans with hot pepper vinegar

Creamy coleslaw with bacon

Combine ⅓ cup light mayonnaise, ⅓ cup reduced-fat sour cream, 1 tablespoon minced seeded jalapeño pepper, 1 tablespoon white wine vinegar, 2 teaspoons sugar, ½ teaspoon salt, and 3 cooked and crumbled bacon slices. Add 1 (16-ounce) package coleslaw, tossing well to coat. Cover and chill.

Game Plan

1 Cook bacon.

2 Prepare coleslaw and chill.

3 While catfish cooks:

   •Steam green beans.

Pan-Seared Cod with Basil Sauce

Garlic smashed potatoes

Place 4 cups cubed peeled Yukon gold potatoes in a saucepan; cover with water. Bring to a boil; cook 6 minutes or until tender. Drain. Return potatoes to pan. Add ¼ cup fat-free, less-sodium chicken broth, ¼ cup reduced-fat sour cream, 2 tablespoons butter, ½ teaspoon salt, and 3 minced garlic cloves; mash with a potato masher to desired consistency.

Sautéed spinach

Game Plan

1 While potatoes cook:

- Prepare basil sauce for fish.

2 While fish cooks:

- Finish preparing potatoes.
- Prepare spinach.

Pan-Seared Cod with Basil Sauce

If you have a minichopper, use it to make the basil sauce. Otherwise, take the time to finely chop the herb before stirring in the remaining ingredients.

¼ cup fresh basil, minced
¼ cup fat-free, less-sodium chicken broth
2 tablespoons grated fresh Parmesan cheese
4 teaspoons extra-virgin olive oil
1 teaspoon salt, divided
2 garlic cloves, minced
4 (6-ounce) cod fillets (about 1 inch thick)
¼ teaspoon freshly ground black pepper
Cooking spray

1 Combine basil, broth, cheese, oil, ½ teaspoon salt, and garlic in a small bowl.
2 Sprinkle fish with ½ teaspoon salt and pepper. Heat a large nonstick skillet over medium-high heat; coat with cooking spray. Add fish; sauté 5 minutes on each side or until fish flakes easily when tested with a fork. Serve fish with basil mixture. Yield: 4 servings (serving size: 1 fillet and about 1½ tablespoons basil sauce).

CALORIES 199 (30% from fat); FAT 6.6g (sat 1.3g, mono 3.5g, poly 0.8g); PROTEIN 32g; CARB 1.3g; FIBER 0.6g; CHOL 76mg; IRON 0.7mg; SODIUM 765mg; CALC 85mg

Creole Cod

The mildness of cod takes well to bold flavorings, such as Dijon mustard and Creole seasoning. Lemon juice, added after cooking, brightens the flavor.

  2   teaspoons olive oil
  2   teaspoons Dijon mustard
  ½   teaspoon salt
  ½   teaspoon Creole seasoning blend
        (such as Spice Island)
  4   (6-ounce) cod fillets (about 1 inch thick)
Cooking spray
  1   tablespoon fresh lemon juice
Chopped fresh parsley (optional)

❶ Preheat oven to 400°.
❷ Combine first 4 ingredients; brush over fish.
❸ Place fish on a foil-lined baking sheet coated with cooking spray. Bake at 400° for 17 minutes or until fish flakes easily when tested with a fork. Drizzle juice evenly over fish; garnish with parsley, if desired. Yield: 4 servings (serving size: 1 fillet).

CALORIES 148 (21% from fat); FAT 3.5g (sat 0.4g, mono 1.9g, poly 0.6g); PROTEIN 27.2g; CARB 0.8g; FIBER 0.1g; CHOL 55mg; IRON 0.5mg; SODIUM 523mg; CALC 16mg

Ingredient Tip: If you can't find Creole seasoning in your supermarket, you can make your own: Combine 1 tablespoon paprika with 1 teaspoon each of salt, onion powder, garlic powder, dried oregano, ground red pepper, and black pepper. Store in an airtight container.

MENU   serves 4

Creole Cod

Steamed fingerling potatoes

Warm cabbage slaw
Heat 2 teaspoons olive oil in a large nonstick skillet over medium-high heat. Add 1 (16-ounce) package coleslaw and ½ teaspoon salt; sauté 3 minutes or until coleslaw wilts. Remove from heat. Stir in 2 tablespoons chopped green onions, 1 tablespoon sugar, 3 tablespoons cider vinegar, and 1 tablespoon capers.

Game Plan

1 While water comes to a boil for potatoes and oven heats for fish:
  • Prepare Creole mixture for fish.
  • Squeeze lemon for juice for fish.

2 While fish bakes:
  • Steam potatoes
  • Prepare slaw.

Game Plan

1 While oven heats:

- Prepare vegetable mixture for fish.
- Wash spinach for salad.

2 While vegetable mixture bakes:

- Prepare fish.

3 While fish and vegetables bake:

- Prepare salad.

Pan-Roasted Grouper with Provençale Vegetables

Use a broiler pan for both components of this recipe. The fennel-tomato mixture cooks in the bottom of the pan, helping to steam the fish on the rack above.

2 cups thinly sliced fennel bulb (about 1 medium bulb)
2 tablespoons fresh orange juice
16 picholine olives, pitted and chopped
1 (28-ounce) can whole tomatoes, drained and coarsely chopped
½ teaspoon salt, divided
½ teaspoon black pepper, divided
Cooking spray
2 teaspoons olive oil
1 garlic clove, minced
4 (6-ounce) grouper fillets (about 1 inch thick)

❶ Preheat oven to 450°.
❷ Combine first 4 ingredients. Add ¼ teaspoon salt and ¼ teaspoon pepper; toss well. Spoon mixture into bottom of a broiler pan coated with cooking spray. Bake at 450° for 10 minutes; stir once.
❸ Combine ¼ teaspoon salt, ¼ teaspoon pepper, oil, and garlic; brush evenly over fish. Remove pan from oven. Place fish on broiler pan rack coated with cooking spray; place rack over fennel mixture.
❹ Bake at 450° for 10 minutes or until fish flakes easily when tested with a fork. Yield: 4 servings (serving size: 1 fillet and ¾ cup fennel mixture).

CALORIES 247 (25% from fat); FAT 6.9g (sat 0.7g, mono 3.4g, poly 2.1g); PROTEIN 33.6g; CARB 11.5g; FIBER 2.8g; CHOL 60mg; IRON 2.6mg; SODIUM 898mg; CALC 91mg

Quick Tip:
To make it easier to pit olives, mash each olive with the flat side of a knife; the pit will easily dislodge.

Pan-Seared Grouper with Roasted Tomato Sauce

Most types of fish are high in potassium. Grouper alone provides 822 milligrams in a 6-ounce serving. When it is paired with this potassium-rich sauce of roasted tomatoes, the entire entrée provides more than 1,300 milligrams of potassium per serving. You can prepare the sauce for the fish a day in advance and then reheat it in the microwave shortly before serving.

1 red bell pepper, cut into 1-inch strips
12 plum tomatoes, halved lengthwise and cut into ½-inch slices
Cooking spray
2 tablespoons olive oil, divided
¾ teaspoon salt, divided
½ teaspoon dried Italian seasoning
1 tablespoon red wine vinegar
¼ teaspoon freshly ground black pepper
5 basil leaves
2 tablespoons all-purpose flour
1 tablespoon cornmeal
4 (6-ounce) grouper fillets (about 1 inch thick)
2 tablespoons chopped fresh basil (optional)

❶ Preheat oven to 350°.
❷ Arrange bell pepper and tomato in a single layer on a jelly-roll pan coated with cooking spray; drizzle with 1 tablespoon oil. Sprinkle with ¼ teaspoon salt and Italian seasoning; stir to coat. Bake at 350° for 40 minutes or until edges are lightly browned. Remove from oven.
❸ Increase oven temperature to 400°.
❹ Transfer tomatoes and bell peppers to a food processor. Add ¼ teaspoon salt, vinegar, black pepper, and basil leaves; process until smooth. Spoon tomato mixture into a bowl. Cover and keep warm.
❺ Heat 1 tablespoon oil in a large ovenproof skillet over medium-high heat. Combine flour and cornmeal in a shallow dish. Sprinkle fish with ¼ teaspoon salt; dredge in flour mixture. Add fish to pan; cook 3 minutes. Turn fish over; bake at 400° for 8 minutes or until fish flakes easily when tested with a fork. Serve fish with tomato sauce; garnish with chopped basil, if desired. Yield: 4 servings (serving size: 1 fillet and about ¼ cup tomato sauce).

CALORIES 278 (29% from fat); FAT 9g (sat 1.4g, mono 5.4g, poly 1.5g); PROTEIN 35.4g; CARB 13.4g; FIBER 3g; CHOL 63mg; IRON 2.5mg; SODIUM 543mg; CALC 70mg

MENU *serves 4*

Pan-Seared Grouper with Roasted Tomato Sauce

Couscous pilaf
Heat 2 teaspoons olive oil in a medium saucepan over medium heat. Add 2 minced garlic cloves; cook 1 minute, stirring constantly. Stir in 1 cup uncooked couscous and 1 cup fat-free, less-sodium chicken broth; bring to a boil. Remove from heat; let stand 5 minutes. Fluff couscous with a fork; stir in ⅓ cup grated fresh Parmesan cheese and 2 tablespoons finely chopped fresh parsley.

Sautéed Swiss chard

Game Plan

1 While oven heats:
  • Cut red bell pepper into strips.
  • Slice tomatoes.
2 While red bell pepper and tomatoes cook:
  • Mince garlic, grate Parmesan cheese, and chop parsley for couscous.
  • Chop basil for fish.
3 While fish cooks:
  • Prepare pilaf.
  • Prepare Swiss chard.

"Floribbean" Grouper with Red Pepper–Papaya Jam

MENU *serves 4*

"Floribbean" Grouper with Red Pepper–Papaya Jam

Rice pilaf with green onions

Heat 2 teaspoons olive oil in a small saucepan over medium-high heat. Add ¼ cup chopped green onions and 1 minced garlic clove; sauté 2 minutes. Add 2 tablespoons pinot grigio or other crisp, fruity white wine; cook until liquid evaporates. Add 1 cup water, ½ cup basmati rice, and ¼ teaspoon salt; bring to a boil. Cover, reduce heat, and simmer 20 minutes or until rice is done.

Steamed asparagus

Game Plan

1 While sugar and pepper mixture for jam simmers:

- Chop green onions and mince garlic for pilaf.
- Sauté green onions and garlic.
- Bring water and rice mixture to a boil.

2 While rice simmers and oven heats:

- Prepare panko mixture.
- Dredge fillets in flour, egg whites, and panko mixture.
- Cook fish on the stove top.

3 While fish bakes:

- Steam asparagus.

Flavors and ingredients from Florida and the Caribbean converge in this impressive entrée. The recipe easily doubles if you're serving 4.

JAM:

- 1 cup chopped red bell pepper
- ¾ cup diced peeled papaya
- ½ teaspoon chopped jalapeño pepper
- ¼ cup water
- 3 tablespoons red wine vinegar
- 2 tablespoons sugar

Dash of salt

- ½ teaspoon fresh lime juice

GROUPER:

- ¼ cup panko (Japanese breadcrumbs)
- 2 tablespoons flaked sweetened coconut
- 1½ tablespoons chopped dry-roasted cashews
- 2 tablespoons all-purpose flour
- 2 large egg whites, lightly beaten
- 2 (6-ounce) grouper fillets
- ⅛ teaspoon salt
- ⅛ teaspoon freshly ground black pepper
- 2 teaspoons butter

GARNISH:

Lime wedges (optional)

1 To prepare jam, combine first 3 ingredients in a food processor; process until smooth.

2 Combine water, vinegar, sugar, and dash of salt in a small saucepan over medium-high heat. Cook until sugar dissolves, stirring frequently. Reduce heat to medium. Add puréed pepper mixture; cook 7 minutes or until thickened and reduced to ½ cup, stirring frequently. Remove from heat; stir in lime juice. Cool.

3 Preheat oven to 350°.

4 To prepare grouper, combine panko, coconut, and cashews in food processor; pulse 4 times or until cashews are finely chopped. Place panko mixture in a shallow dish. Place flour in another shallow dish; place egg whites in another shallow dish. Sprinkle fillets with ⅛ teaspoon salt and black pepper. Dredge 1 fillet in flour. Dip fillet into egg whites; dredge in panko mixture, gently pressing coating onto fillet to adhere. Repeat procedure with remaining fillet, flour, egg whites, and panko mixture.

5 Melt butter in a large nonstick ovenproof skillet over medium-high heat. Add fillets; cook 2 minutes or until lightly browned on bottom. Turn fillets over; wrap handle of pan with foil. Place pan in oven; bake at 350° for 8 minutes or until fish flakes easily when tested with a fork. Serve immediately with jam. Garnish with lime wedges, if desired. Yield: 2 servings (serving size: 1 fillet and ¼ cup jam).

CALORIES 411 (23% from fat); FAT 10.6g (sat 4.3g, mono 3.8g, poly 1.4g); PROTEIN 40.5g; CARB 38.5g; FIBER 1.8g; CHOL 73mg; IRON 3mg; SODIUM 466mg; CALC 75mg

Halibut with Charmoula

Charmoula is a flavorful Moroccan herb sauce traditionally used to season or marinate fish.

SAUCE:
- 1 tablespoon olive oil
- 1 teaspoon paprika
- ½ teaspoon salt
- ½ teaspoon ground cumin
- ½ teaspoon black pepper
- 2 garlic cloves
- 1 cup loosely packed fresh flat-leaf parsley leaves
- 1 cup loosely packed fresh cilantro leaves
- 2 tablespoons capers
- 2 teaspoons grated lemon rind
- ¼ cup fresh lemon juice

FISH:
- 4 (6-ounce) halibut fillets (about 1 inch thick)
- ¼ teaspoon salt
- ¼ teaspoon black pepper
- Cooking spray

GARNISH:
- Parsley sprigs (optional)

❶ Preheat oven to 350°.

❷ To prepare sauce, combine first 6 ingredients in a food processor; process until garlic is finely chopped. Add parsley leaves, cilantro, capers, rind, and juice; pulse until herbs are coarsely chopped.

❸ To prepare fish, sprinkle fish with ¼ teaspoon salt and ¼ teaspoon pepper. Place fish on a foil-lined baking sheet coated with cooking spray.

❹ Bake at 350° for 15 minutes or until fish flakes easily when tested with a fork. Serve fish with sauce. Garnish with parsley sprigs, if desired. Yield: 4 servings (serving size: 1 fillet and 1 tablespoon sauce).

CALORIES 234 (29% from fat); FAT 7.6g (sat 1.1g, mono 3.8g, poly 1.6g); PROTEIN 36.6g; CARB 3.8g; FIBER 1.3g; CHOL 54mg; IRON 2.9mg; SODIUM 701mg; CALC 118mg

---

MENU *serves 4*

Halibut with Charmoula

Couscous tossed with golden raisins

Frozen yogurt with spiced honey and walnuts
Place ½ cup honey and ¼ teaspoon pumpkin-pie spice in a microwave-safe bowl. Microwave at HIGH 30 seconds or until warm. Spoon ½ cup vanilla fat-free frozen yogurt into each of 4 bowls, and top each serving with 2 tablespoons spiced honey and 1½ teaspoons chopped toasted walnuts.

Game Plan

1 While oven heats for fish:
- •Prepare sauce.

2 While fish bakes:
- •Prepare couscous.
- •Scoop frozen yogurt into bowls, and place in freezer.
- •Toast walnuts.
- •Combine honey and pumpkin-pie spice (microwave after dinner).

169

MENU *serves 4*

Cornflake-Crusted Halibut with Chile-Cilantro Aïoli

Oven fries
Preheat oven to 450°. Cut 2 large Yukon gold potatoes into ½ x 1-inch sticks; toss with 2 teaspoons olive oil, and spread in a single layer on a baking sheet lightly coated with cooking spray. Bake at 450° for 30 minutes or until golden, turning after 15 minutes. Toss with ½ teaspoon salt; serve immediately.

Cabbage salad

Game Plan

1 While oven heats:
- •Prepare aïoli.
- •Cut potatoes.
- •Combine milk and egg white.
- •Prepare cornflake mixture.

2 While potatoes cook:
- •Prepare fish.
- •Toss salad.

Cornflake-Crusted Halibut with Chile-Cilantro Aïoli

We gave this recipe our highest rating. Make the mayonnaise-based aïoli ahead, if you like. To crush the cornflakes, place them in a zip-top plastic bag, seal, and press with a rolling pin.

AÏOLI:
- 3 tablespoons fat-free mayonnaise
- 2 tablespoons minced fresh cilantro
- 1 serrano chile, seeded and minced
- 1 garlic clove, minced

FISH:
- 1 cup fat-free milk
- 1 large egg white, lightly beaten
- 2 cups cornflakes, finely crushed
- ¼ cup all-purpose flour
- ½ teaspoon salt
- ¼ teaspoon black pepper
- 2 tablespoons olive oil
- 4 (6-ounce) halibut fillets (about 1 inch thick)
- 4 lemon wedges

1 To prepare aïoli, combine first 4 ingredients.

2 To prepare fish, combine milk and egg white in a shallow dish; stir with a whisk. Combine cornflakes, flour, salt, and black pepper in a shallow dish.

3 Heat oil in a large nonstick skillet over medium-high heat. Dip fish in milk mixture; dredge in cornflake mixture. Add fish to pan; cook 4 minutes on each side or until fish flakes easily when tested with a fork. Serve with mayonnaise mixture and lemon wedges. Yield: 4 servings (serving size: 1 fillet, about 1 tablespoon mayonnaise mixture, and 1 lemon wedge).

CALORIES 367 (27% from fat); FAT 11.2g (sat 1.6g, mono 6.3g, poly 1.9g); PROTEIN 40.8g; CARB 25.1g; FIBER 2.2g; CHOL 56mg; IRON 2.4mg; SODIUM 645mg; CALC 166mg

Garlic-and-Herb Oven-Fried Halibut

Coat fillets with crumbs and bake at a high temperature for a crisp texture similar to fried fish. Fresh herbs and other seasonings heighten the flavor.

1 cup panko (Japanese breadcrumbs)
1 tablespoon chopped fresh basil
1 tablespoon chopped fresh flat-leaf parsley
½ teaspoon onion powder
1 large garlic clove, minced
2 large egg whites, lightly beaten
1 large egg, lightly beaten
2 tablespoons all-purpose flour
6 (6-ounce) halibut fillets
¾ teaspoon salt
¼ teaspoon black pepper
2 tablespoons olive oil, divided
Cooking spray

❶ Preheat oven to 450°.
❷ Combine first 5 ingredients in a shallow dish. Combine egg whites and egg in a shallow dish. Place flour in a shallow dish. Sprinkle fish with salt and pepper. Dredge fish in flour. Dip in egg mixture; dredge in panko mixture.
❸ Heat 1 tablespoon oil in a large nonstick skillet over medium-high heat. Add 3 fish fillets; cook 2½ minutes on each side or until browned. Place fish on a broiler pan coated with cooking spray. Repeat procedure with 1 tablespoon oil and remaining fish. Bake at 450° for 6 minutes or until fish flakes easily when tested with a fork or until desired degree of doneness. Yield: 6 servings (serving size: 1 fillet).

CALORIES 293 (29% from fat); FAT 9.6g (sat 1.4g, mono 4.9g, poly 1.8g); PROTEIN 39.4g; CARB 9.2g; FIBER 0.5g; CHOL 90mg; IRON 1.8mg; SODIUM 446mg; CALC 89mg

MENU *serves 6*

Garlic-and-Herb Oven-Fried Halibut

Red potatoes with herbed vinaigrette
Place 1½ pounds quartered red potatoes in a medium saucepan. Cover with cold water; bring to a boil. Cook 8 minutes or until tender; drain. Cool. Combine 2 tablespoons white wine vinegar, 1 tablespoon extra-virgin olive oil, ¼ teaspoon salt, and ¼ teaspoon black pepper in a large bowl. Add potatoes, ¼ cup sliced green onions, and 2 teaspoons chopped fresh parsley to vinegar mixture; toss.

Steamed broccoli

Game Plan
1 While oven heats:
  • Cook potatoes.
  • Prepare fish.
2 While fish cooks:
  • Finish preparing potatoes.
  • Steam broccoli.

Halibut with White Beans in Tomato-Rosemary Broth

Arugula-Asiago salad
Place 6 cups arugula in a large bowl. Combine 1 tablespoon fresh lemon juice, 2 teaspoons extra-virgin olive oil, ¼ teaspoon salt, and ¼ teaspoon freshly ground black pepper, stirring well. Drizzle dressing over arugula; toss gently to coat. Top salad with ¼ cup shaved fresh Asiago cheese.

French bread baguette slices

Game Plan

1 While fish cooks:
- Mince garlic.
- Chop tomato.
- Rinse and drain beans.

2 While tomato-broth mixture cooks:
- Chop rosemary.
- Prepare salad.

Halibut with White Beans in Tomato-Rosemary Broth

Beans absorb some of the delicious broth. For a special dinner, serve in shallow rimmed bowls and top each serving with a fresh rosemary sprig.

- 1 tablespoon olive oil
- 4 (6-ounce) halibut fillets (about 1 inch thick)
- ¼ teaspoon salt
- ¼ teaspoon freshly ground black pepper
- 2 garlic cloves, minced
- 2 cups chopped plum tomato (about 4)
- 1½ cups fat-free, less-sodium chicken broth
- ½ cup dry white wine
- 1 (16-ounce) can cannellini beans or other white beans, rinsed and drained
- ½ teaspoon chopped fresh rosemary

❶ Heat oil in a large nonstick skillet over medium-high heat. Sprinkle fish evenly with salt and pepper. Add fish; cook 5 minutes on each side or until fish flakes easily when tested with a fork or until desired degree of doneness. Remove fish; keep warm. Add garlic; cook 30 seconds, stirring constantly. Stir in tomato, broth, wine, and beans; bring to a boil. Reduce heat, and simmer 5 minutes. Remove from heat; stir in rosemary. Serve immediately with fish. Yield: 4 servings (serving size: 1 fillet and about ¾ cup bean mixture).

CALORIES 299 (24% from fat); FAT 7.9g (sat 1.1g, mono 3.8g, poly 2g); PROTEIN 39.8g; CARB 14.9g; FIBER 4g; CHOL 54mg; IRON 3.2mg; SODIUM 535mg; CALC 117mg

Flavor Tip: If the fresh tomatoes at your market aren't at their best, substitute 1 (14.5-ounce) can diced tomatoes, drained.

Salmon with Orange-Fennel Sauce

Be careful not to marinate the fish longer than 20 minutes; as in ceviche, the citrus marinade can "cook" the fish. Crush the fennel seeds with a mortar and pestle, or place them in a zip-top plastic bag on a cutting board and crush with a heavy pan.

2   teaspoons grated orange rind
½   cup fresh orange juice
1   teaspoon chopped fresh rosemary
1   teaspoon fennel seeds, crushed
4   (6-ounce) salmon fillets (about
      1 inch thick)
Cooking spray
¼   teaspoon salt
⅛   teaspoon black pepper

1 Combine first 4 ingredients in a large zip-top plastic bag; add fish. Seal and marinate in refrigerator 20 minutes, turning once.
2 Preheat broiler.
3 Remove fish from bag, reserving marinade.

Place fish, skin sides down, on a broiler pan coated with cooking spray; sprinkle with salt and pepper. Broil 10 minutes or until fish flakes easily when tested with a fork.
4 Bring reserved marinade to a boil in a small saucepan. Reduce heat, and simmer 3 minutes. Serve sauce with fish. Yield: 4 servings (serving size: 1 fillet and about 1 tablespoon sauce).

CALORIES 244 (39% from fat); FAT 10.7g (sat 2.5g, mono 4.7g, poly 2.5g); PROTEIN 31.3g; CARB 3.8g; FIBER 0.4g; CHOL 80mg; IRON 0.7mg; SODIUM 214mg; CALC 28mg

Quick Tip: Prepare the marinade for the fish up to a day in advance; refrigerate in an airtight container until ready to use.

MENU   *serves 4*

Salmon with Orange-Fennel Sauce

Rice pilaf
Heat 2 teaspoons olive oil over medium-high heat in a large nonstick skillet. Add 1 cup chopped onion; sauté 5 minutes or until tender. Stir in 1 cup uncooked long-grain rice; sauté 1 minute. Add 2 cups water, ½ teaspoon salt, ¼ teaspoon dried thyme, and ⅛ teaspoon black pepper; bring to a boil. Cover, reduce heat, and simmer 20 minutes or until water is absorbed. Sprinkle with 1 tablespoon chopped fresh parsley.

Sautéed snow peas

Game Plan
1 Prepare marinade.
2 While fish marinates:
  - Preheat broiler for fish.
  - Cook rice pilaf.
3 While fish cooks:
  - Cook reserved marinade.
  - Sauté snow peas.
  - Chop parsley for rice pilaf.

MENU *serves 4*

Miso-Glazed Salmon

Wasabi mashed potatoes

Place 2 pounds cubed red potato in a large saucepan; cover with water. Bring to a boil; cook 15 minutes or until tender. Drain. Combine potato; ¼ cup fat-free, less-sodium chicken broth; ¼ cup reduced-fat sour cream; 2 tablespoons butter; 1 teaspoon wasabi paste; ½ teaspoon salt; and ¼ teaspoon black pepper in a large bowl. Mash to desired consistency.

Steamed bok choy

Game Plan

1 While water comes to a boil for potato and the broiler heats for fish:

- Prepare miso mixture for fish.

- Combine flavorings for mashed potatoes in a large bowl.

2 While potato and fish cook:

- Steam bok choy.

- Chop chives.

Miso-Glazed Salmon

A sweet-salty miso, brown sugar, and soy sauce glaze caramelizes in about 10 minutes as it cooks atop this rich, meaty salmon.

¼ cup packed brown sugar
2 tablespoons low-sodium soy sauce
2 tablespoons hot water
2 tablespoons miso (soybean paste)
4 (6-ounce) salmon fillets (about 1 inch thick)
Cooking spray
1 tablespoon chopped fresh chives

❶ Preheat broiler.
❷ Combine first 4 ingredients; stir with a whisk. Arrange fish in a shallow baking pan coated with cooking spray. Spoon miso mixture evenly over fish.
❸ Broil 10 minutes or until fish flakes easily when tested with a fork, basting twice with miso mixture. Sprinkle with chives. Yield: 4 servings (serving size: 1 fillet).

CALORIES 297 (33% from fat); FAT 10.9g (sat 2.5g, mono 4.7g, poly 2.8g); PROTEIN 32.4g; CARB 15.7g; FIBER 0.3g; CHOL 80mg; IRON 1mg; SODIUM 742mg; CALC 29mg

Sweet-Spicy Glazed Salmon

Chinese-style hot mustard has a sharp bite similar to that of wasabi. If you can't find it, use Dijon mustard or 1 teaspoon dry mustard such as Coleman's.

3 tablespoons dark brown sugar
4 teaspoons Chinese-style hot mustard
1 tablespoon low-sodium soy sauce
1 teaspoon rice vinegar
4 (6-ounce) salmon fillets (about 1 inch thick)
Cooking spray
¼ teaspoon salt
¼ teaspoon freshly ground black pepper

1 Preheat oven to 425°.
2 Combine first 4 ingredients in a saucepan; bring to a boil. Remove from heat.
3 Place fillets on a foil-lined jelly-roll pan coated with cooking spray. Sprinkle fillets evenly with salt and pepper. Bake at 425° for 12 minutes. Remove from oven.
4 Preheat broiler.
5 Brush sugar mixture evenly over fillets; broil 3 inches from heat 3 minutes or until fish flakes easily when tested with a fork. Yield: 4 servings (serving size: 1 fillet).

CALORIES 252 (37% from fat); FAT 10.3g (sat 2.3g, mono 4.4g, poly 2.5g); PROTEIN 27.7g; CARB 11g; FIBER 0.1g; CHOL 65mg; IRON 0.9mg; SODIUM 470mg; CALC 33mg

MENU *serves 4*

Sweet-Spicy Glazed Salmon

Baked sweet potatoes with brown sugar-pecan butter

Pierce 4 (8-ounce) sweet potatoes with a fork. Microwave at HIGH 12 minutes or until done. Combine 2 tablespoons softened butter, 2 tablespoons brown sugar, and 1½ tablespoons finely chopped toasted pecans. Top each potato with about 1 tablespoon butter mixture.

Steamed broccoli spears

Game Plan

1 While oven heats for salmon:
- Prepare glaze.
- Scrub sweet potatoes.
- Prepare butter mixture for sweet potatoes.

2 While salmon cooks:
- Cook sweet potatoes.
- Prepare broccoli.

Salmon Saté with Dill Mustard Glaze

To prevent fish from falling off the skewers, resist turning them more than once while the fish cooks.

- 2 tablespoons chopped fresh dill
- 2 tablespoons whole-grain Dijon mustard
- 1 teaspoon grated lemon rind
- 2 tablespoons fresh lemon juice
- ¼ teaspoon salt
- ¼ teaspoon ground red pepper
- 2 garlic cloves, minced
- 1 (1-pound) salmon fillet, skinned and cut crosswise into 16 pieces

Cooking spray
Dill sprigs (optional)

1 Prepare grill.

2 Combine first 7 ingredients in a bowl; stir with a whisk. Add salmon pieces; toss gently to coat. Thread 4 salmon pieces onto each of 4 (8-inch) skewers. Place salmon on grill rack coated with cooking spray, and grill 3 minutes on each side or until fish flakes easily when tested with a fork or until desired degree of doneness. Garnish with dill sprigs, if desired. Yield: 4 servings (serving size: 1 skewer).

CALORIES 223 (49% from fat); FAT 12.1g (sat 3.5g, mono 5g, poly 3.2g); PROTEIN 23.2g; CARB 3g; FIBER 1.1g; CHOL 57mg; IRON 0.5mg; SODIUM 321mg; CALC 43mg

---

MENU *serves 4*

Salmon Saté with Dill Mustard Glaze

Asparagus with tarragon vinaigrette
Combine 1 pound trimmed fresh asparagus and 1 tablespoon water in a shallow microwave-safe dish; cover with plastic wrap. Microwave at HIGH 3 minutes or until asparagus is crisp-tender; drain. Rinse with cold water, and drain; cool. Combine 2 tablespoons tarragon vinegar, 1½ teaspoons Dijon mustard, 1 teaspoon olive oil, ⅛ teaspoon freshly ground black pepper, 1 minced garlic clove, and a dash of salt in a small bowl; stir with a whisk. Drizzle over asparagus; toss to combine. Sprinkle with 2 tablespoons Parmesan cheese.

Angel hair pasta

Game Plan

1 While grill heats:
- Microwave asparagus.
- Prepare vinaigrette for asparagus.

2 While water comes to a boil and pasta cooks:
- Prepare glaze for salmon.
- Thread salmon on skewers.

3 Grill salmon.

Smoked Salmon with Mustard and Dill

MENU *serves 4*

Smoked Salmon with Mustard and Dill

Creamy cucumber salad

Combine 3 cups (2-inch) julienne-cut English cucumber, ⅓ cup plain low-fat yogurt, 1 tablespoon prepared horseradish, 2 teaspoons fresh lemon juice, and ½ teaspoon salt; toss well.

Roasted potato wedges

Game Plan

1 While wood chips soak:

- Prepare mustard mixture and brush over salmon.
- Refrigerate salmon.
- Prepare grill.

2 While fish cooks:

- Prepare potatoes.
- Prepare salad.

Smoked salmon and dill are a classic Nordic pairing. You can easily double the recipe and menu if you're cooking for more than 4.

- 2 cups wood chips
- 1 tablespoon minced fresh dill
- 1 tablespoon fresh lemon juice
- 3 tablespoons sweet-hot mustard (such as Inglehoffer)
- ½ teaspoon salt
- 1 (1½-pound) salmon fillet
- Cooking spray

1 Soak wood chips in water 30 minutes; drain.
2 Combine dill, juice, mustard, and salt; stir well. Place salmon, skin side down, in a shallow baking dish; brush mustard mixture over salmon. Cover and refrigerate 20 minutes.
3 Prepare grill for indirect grilling, heating 1 side to low and leaving 1 side with no heat. Maintain temperature at 200° to 225°.
4 Place wood chips on hot coals. Place a disposable aluminum foil pan on unheated side of grill; pour 2 cups water into pan. Coat grill rack with cooking spray, and place on grill. Place salmon, skin side down, on grill rack over foil pan on unheated side. Close lid; cook 35 minutes or until fish flakes easily when tested with a fork or until desired degree of doneness. Yield: 4 servings (serving size: about 4½ ounces).

CALORIES 262 (40% from fat); FAT 11.6g (sat 2.5g, mono 4.6g, poly 2.5g); PROTEIN 31g; CARB 4.8g; FIBER 0g; CHOL 80mg; IRON 0.5mg; SODIUM 429mg; CALC 16mg

Honey-Ginger Glazed Salmon with Arugula Salad

Honey and ginger bookend this delicious meal: They both flavor the entrée and enhance the dessert. You can substitute basil or parsley for the cilantro in the side dish, if you prefer. If sage honey isn't available, substitute alfalfa or another light-colored, mild honey. For bolder flavor, try a dark honey, such as gallberry.

²/₃ cup sage honey
¼ cup fresh lemon juice, divided
2 tablespoons warm water (100° to 110°)
1½ teaspoons grated peeled fresh ginger
1 garlic clove, minced
4 (6-ounce) skinless salmon fillets (about 1 inch thick)
½ teaspoon salt, divided
1 tablespoon olive oil
¼ teaspoon freshly ground black pepper
4 cups trimmed arugula

❶ Preheat oven to 350°.
❷ Combine honey, 2 tablespoons juice, water, ginger, and garlic in a small bowl; stir with a whisk. Pour honey mixture into a 13 x 9-inch baking pan. Arrange fish on top of honey mixture in pan, skinned sides up. Refrigerate 20 minutes. Turn fish over; sprinkle with

¼ teaspoon salt. Bake at 350° for 7 minutes. Remove from oven.
❸ Preheat broiler.
❹ Brush fish with honey mixture; broil 7 minutes or until fish is browned and flakes easily when tested with a fork or until desired degree of doneness.
❺ Combine 2 tablespoons juice, ¼ teaspoon salt, oil, and pepper in a medium bowl; stir with a whisk. Add arugula; toss gently to coat. Serve salad with fish. Yield: 4 servings (serving size: 1 fillet and about ½ cup salad).

CALORIES 396 (38% from fat); FAT 16.6g (sat 3.6g, mono 8.2g, poly 3.6g); PROTEIN 36.9g; CARB 25g; FIBER 0.5g; CHOL 87mg; IRON 1.1mg; SODIUM 378mg; CALC 56mg

Wine Note: Honey intensifies the rich meatiness of the salmon in this dish, which requires a clean, crisp wine.

MENU *serves 4*

Honey-Ginger Glazed Salmon with Arugula Salad

Cilantro orzo pilaf
Cook 1½ cups orzo according to package directions, omitting salt and fat. Drain; place in a medium bowl. Add 1 tablespoon finely chopped cilantro, 1 tablespoon extra-virgin olive oil, 1 teaspoon grated lemon rind, and ¼ teaspoon salt. Toss well.

Vanilla yogurt with honey and gingersnap cookies

Game Plan

1 Prepare honey mixture and marinate fish.

2 While fish bakes:
• Bring water for pasta to a boil.

3 While fish broils:
• Cook pasta.
• Chop cilantro and grate lemon rind for pilaf.
• Prepare salad.

4 Combine ingredients for pilaf.

Five-Spice Salmon with Leeks in Parchment

Cooking this fish in a parchment pouch uses both the radiant heat of the oven and steam inside the packet to produce moist, succulent results. Toasting and grinding the spices takes a little extra time but pays off with vivid flavor.

1¼ teaspoons whole fennel seeds
6 whole black peppercorns
2 whole cloves
1 whole star anise
1 (1½-inch) cinnamon stick
4 (6-ounce) skinless salmon fillets (about 1 inch thick)
½ teaspoon salt
1 leek, halved lengthwise and thinly sliced (about 1 cup)

❶ Preheat oven to 425°.

❷ Combine first 5 ingredients in a small skillet over medium heat; cook 1 minute or until spices are fragrant. Transfer spices to a spice grinder or coffee grinder; grind until fine.

❸ Cut 4 (12-inch) squares of parchment paper. Place 1 fillet in center of each square. Sprinkle evenly with salt and spice mixture; top fillets evenly with leeks. Fold paper; seal edges with narrow folds. Place packets on a baking sheet. Bake at 425° for 20 minutes or until puffy and lightly browned. Place on serving plates; cut open. Serve immediately. Yield: 4 servings (serving size: 1 fillet and ¼ cup leeks).

CALORIES 295 (41% from fat); FAT 13.5g (sat 3.1g, mono 5.8g, poly 3.3g); PROTEIN 36.8g; CARB 5g; FIBER 1.5g; CHOL 87mg; IRON 1.8mg; SODIUM 382mg; CALC 60mg

Ingredient Tip: Substitute 1 tablespoon five-spice powder for the freshly ground spice mixture, if desired.

Grilled Salmon with Apricot-Mustard Glaze

Friends and family will beg for the recipe when you serve this sophisticated take on salmon. Brush the fruit reduction on the fish at the last minute to prevent sugars from burning on the grill.

SALMON:

- 4 (6-ounce) salmon fillets (about 1 inch thick)
- 1½ teaspoons minced garlic
- ½ teaspoon kosher salt
- ¼ teaspoon freshly ground black pepper

GLAZE:

- ¼ cup apricot nectar
- ¼ cup apricot preserves
- 1 tablespoon Dijon mustard
- 1½ teaspoons white wine vinegar
- 1½ teaspoons honey
- ¼ teaspoon kosher salt
- ¼ teaspoon freshly ground black pepper

REMAINING INGREDIENT:

Cooking spray

1 Prepare grill.

2 To prepare fish, sprinkle fillets with garlic, ½ teaspoon salt, and ¼ teaspoon pepper. Cover and refrigerate 15 minutes.

3 To prepare glaze, combine nectar and next 6 ingredients in a small saucepan; bring to a boil. Reduce heat, and simmer until reduced to ¼ cup (about 10 minutes). Remove from heat; set aside.

4 Place fillets, skin sides up, on grill rack coated with cooking spray. Grill 2 minutes; carefully turn over, and grill 4 minutes or until fish flakes easily when tested with a fork or until desired degree of doneness. Brush each fillet with 1 tablespoon glaze; grill 30 seconds. Yield: 4 servings (serving size: 1 fillet).

CALORIES 342 (34% from fat); FAT 13.1g (sat 3.1g, mono 5.7g, poly 3.2g); PROTEIN 36.4g; CARB 18.1g; FIBER 0.2g; CHOL 87mg; IRON 0.7mg; SODIUM 482mg; CALC 25mg

---

MENU *serves 4*

Grilled Salmon with Apricot-Mustard Glaze

Parmesan-spinach orzo pilaf
Prepare 8 ounces orzo according to package directions, omitting salt and fat. Add 3 ounces fresh baby spinach and 1½ teaspoons bottled minced garlic; stir well. Cover and let stand 4 minutes, stirring twice to slightly wilt spinach. Add ½ teaspoon kosher salt and ½ teaspoon freshly ground black pepper. Just before serving, stir in ¼ cup grated fresh Parmesan cheese.

Pineapple chunks with chopped fresh mint

Game Plan

1 Season salmon fillets.

2 While salmon refrigerates:
- Prepare glaze.

3 While glaze simmers:
- Boil water for orzo.
- Grate cheese for orzo.

4 Prepare grill.

5 While salmon grills:
- Cook orzo.

6 Combine orzo and remaining pilaf ingredients.

MENU *serves 4*

Spiced Salmon with Mustard Sauce

Sautéed spinach
Melt 1 tablespoon butter in a large nonstick skillet over medium-high heat. Add 2 minced garlic cloves to pan; sauté 1 minute. Add 12 cups fresh trimmed spinach to pan; sauté 3 minutes or until spinach begins to wilt. Sprinkle with ½ teaspoon salt and ¼ teaspoon freshly ground black pepper.

Couscous

Game Plan

1 While broiler heats:
- Bring water to a boil for couscous.
- Prepare salmon.

2 While salmon broils:
- Prepare couscous.
- Prepare spinach.

Spiced Salmon with Mustard Sauce

Butter-sautéed spinach makes a nice side dish accompaniment, but any wilted greens will do.

2 teaspoons whole-grain mustard
1 teaspoon honey
¼ teaspoon ground turmeric
¼ teaspoon ground red pepper
⅛ teaspoon garlic powder
¼ teaspoon salt
4 (6-ounce) salmon fillets (about 1 inch thick)
Cooking spray

❶ Preheat broiler.
❷ Combine first 6 ingredients in a small bowl; stir with a fork. Rub mustard mixture evenly over fillets. Place fillets, skin sides down, on a jelly-roll pan coated with cooking spray. Broil 8 minutes or until fish flakes easily when tested with a fork or until desired degree of doneness. Yield: 4 servings (serving size: 1 fillet).

CALORIES 324 (53% from fat); FAT 18.9g (sat 3.7g, mono 6.6g, poly 6.7g); PROTEIN 34g; CARB 2.9g; FIBER 0.1g; CHOL 100mg; IRON 0.8mg; SODIUM 268mg; CALC 22mg

Quick-Cured Sake Salmon with Quinoa

Sake's nutty flavor nicely complements the quinoa and helps to tenderize the salmon.

- 1 (1-pound) salmon fillet
- 1 teaspoon kosher salt
- 2 teaspoons sugar, divided
- 1½ cups sake, divided
- ½ teaspoon chili paste
- 2 garlic cloves, minced
- 1 cup quinoa
- 1 teaspoon butter
- 1½ teaspoons olive oil, divided
- ½ cup finely chopped red bell pepper
- ½ cup finely chopped carrot
- ¼ cup finely chopped onion
- 1 cup water
- ½ cup orange juice
- ¼ teaspoon salt
- 1 tablespoon chopped fresh parsley

1 Place salmon, skin side down, on a plate. Combine kosher salt and 1 teaspoon sugar; rub salt mixture evenly over skinned sides of salmon. Cover with plastic wrap; chill 2 hours.

2 Remove plastic wrap from salmon; rinse salmon with cold water, and pat dry with paper towel. Combine 1 cup sake, 1 teaspoon sugar, chili paste, and garlic in a zip-top plastic bag. Add salmon; seal and marinate in refrigerator 1 hour, turning occasionally.

3 Place quinoa in a fine sieve; place sieve in a large bowl. Cover quinoa with water. Using your hands, rub grains together for 30 seconds; rinse and drain. Repeat procedure twice. Drain.

4 Heat butter and 1 teaspoon oil in a medium saucepan over medium-high heat until butter melts. Add pepper, carrot, and onion; sauté 2 minutes or until onion is tender. Add quinoa; cook 1 minute, stirring constantly. Stir in 1 cup water, ½ cup sake, juice, and ¼ teaspoon salt; bring to a boil. Cover, reduce heat, and simmer 20 minutes or until liquid is absorbed and quinoa is tender. Remove from heat; fluff with a fork. Stir in parsley. Keep warm.

5 Preheat oven to 450°.

6 Remove salmon from bag, reserving marinade. Place marinade in a small saucepan over medium-high heat, and cook until reduced to 2 tablespoons (about 7 minutes).

7 Brush skinned sides of salmon with ½ teaspoon oil. Heat an oven-proof skillet over medium-high heat. Add salmon to pan, skin side up; cook 3 minutes or until golden brown. Turn salmon over, and baste with reduced marinade. Place pan in oven, and bake at 450° for 5 minutes or until fish flakes easily when tested with a fork or until desired degree of doneness. Serve immediately with quinoa. Yield: 4 servings (serving size: 3 ounces salmon and about ¾ cup quinoa).

CALORIES 519 (23% from fat); FAT 13.5g (sat 2.9g, mono 6.3g, poly 3.4g); PROTEIN 30.3g; CARB 41.7g; FIBER 4g; CHOL 60mg; IRON 3.4mg; SODIUM 717mg; CALC 53mg

MENU serves 4

Quick-Cured Sake Salmon with Quinoa

Sesame green beans
Heat 2 teaspoons canola oil in a large nonstick skillet over medium-high heat. Add ½ cup vertically sliced red onion and 1 pound trimmed green beans; sauté 5 minutes or until beans are crisp-tender. Remove from heat; stir in 2 tablespoons low-sodium soy sauce, 1 teaspoon toasted sesame seeds, and 2 teaspoons dark sesame oil.

Lime sorbet

Game Plan

1. Rub salt mixture over salmon, and chill.

2. While salmon marinates in sake mixture:
   - Chop red bell pepper, carrot, and onion.

3. While quinoa simmers:
   - Cook marinade.
   - Cook salmon.
   - Chop parsley.
   - Prepare green beans.

MENU *serves 4*

Lemon-Dill Salmon Croquettes with Horseradish Sauce

Green bean-mushroom sauté

Cook 1 pound trimmed green beans in boiling water 4 minutes or until crisp-tender. Drain and plunge into ice water; drain. Melt 1 tablespoon butter in a large skillet. Add ¼ cup thinly sliced shallot rings; sauté 2 minutes. Add 2 cups quartered cremini mushrooms, ¼ teaspoon salt, and ¼ teaspoon freshly ground black pepper; sauté 4 minutes or until liquid evaporates. Add cooked beans, ¼ teaspoon salt, and ¼ teaspoon freshly ground black pepper to pan; sauté 1 minute or until thoroughly heated.

Long-grain rice with parsley

Game Plan

1 While horseradish sauce chills:

- Prepare salmon mixture and shape into patties.

2 While rice cooks:

- Cook patties.
- Prepare green beans and mushrooms.
- Chop parsley for rice.

Lemon-Dill Salmon Croquettes with Horseradish Sauce

Salmon is a great source of omega-3 fatty acids. A serving of croquettes supplies about a day's worth of the fat. The green bean side dish is a quick, fresh take on the flavors of classic green bean casserole. It makes a homey accompaniment for the croquettes.

SAUCE:

- 2 tablespoons light mayonnaise
- 2 tablespoons fat-free sour cream
- 1 teaspoon prepared horseradish
- ⅛ teaspoon ground red pepper
- ⅛ teaspoon black pepper

Dash of salt

CROQUETTES:

- 1 tablespoon all-purpose flour
- 1 tablespoon chopped fresh dill
- 3 tablespoons light mayonnaise
- ½ teaspoon grated lemon rind
- ½ teaspoon black pepper
- 1 (15-ounce) can salmon
- 1 egg white
- 5 tablespoons dry breadcrumbs, divided

Cooking spray

❶ To prepare sauce, combine first 6 ingredients in a small bowl; stir with a whisk. Cover and refrigerate.

❷ To prepare croquettes, combine flour and next 6 ingredients and 3 tablespoons breadcrumbs. Divide mixture into 4 equal portions, shaping each into a ½-inch-thick patty; refrigerate 1 hour. Place remaining 2 tablespoons breadcrumbs on a plate; dredge patties in breadcrumbs.

❸ Heat a large nonstick skillet over medium-high heat; coat with cooking spray. Add patties to pan; cook 9 minutes on each side or until golden. Serve with sauce. Yield: 4 servings (serving size: 1 croquette and about 1 tablespoon sauce).

CALORIES 193 (48% from fat); FAT 10.3g (sat 1.9g, mono 3.2g, poly 4.4g); PROTEIN 13.6g; CARB 11.1g; FIBER 0.6g; CHOL 30mg; IRON 1.2mg; SODIUM 537mg; CALC 157mg

Veracruz-Style Red Snapper

Adding fresh cilantro and olives to bottled salsa and canned beans gives you fresh-from-the-garden taste without much chopping. Feel free to use your favorite canned beans for variety. The salsa is also great with grilled chicken.

 4   (6-ounce) red snapper or tilapia fillets
Cooking spray
 ½   teaspoon ground cumin
 ¼   teaspoon salt
 ¼   teaspoon ground red pepper
 ¼   cup chopped fresh cilantro
 ¼   cup chopped pitted green olives
 ¼   cup bottled salsa
 1   (16-ounce) can pinto beans, drained
 1   (14.5-ounce) can diced tomatoes, drained
 4   lime wedges (optional)

1 Prepare grill or preheat broiler.
2 Coat both sides of fillets with cooking spray; sprinkle with cumin, salt, and pepper. Place fillets on grill rack or broiler pan coated with cooking spray; cook 5 minutes on each side or until fish flakes easily when tested with a fork.
3 Combine cilantro and next 4 ingredients. Serve fillets with salsa mixture and, if desired, lime wedges. Yield: 4 servings (serving size: 1 fillet, ½ cup salsa, and 1 lime wedge).

CALORIES 202 (14% from fat); FAT 3.2g (sat 0.5g, mono 1g, poly 1.2g); PROTEIN 28.2g; CARB 14.6g; FIBER 5.2g; CHOL 42mg; IRON 1.9mg; SODIUM 571mg; CALC 94mg

Quick Tip: To chop cilantro quickly, wash and dry the entire bunch while it's still bound together. Starting at the top of the bunch, chop only the amount of cilantro leaves you need. (Don't worry about including the stems; they won't affect the flavor.) This method also works for parsley.

MENU *serves 4*

Veracruz-Style Red Snapper

Steamed green beans

Fruit tea
Combine 4 cups unsweetened tea with ½ cup raspberry or fruit-flavored syrup (such as Torani) in a pitcher. Fill 4 tall glasses ¾ full of ice; pour tea mixture over ice just before serving. Garnish with lime wedges.

Game Plan

1 While grill or broiler heats:

  • Sprinkle fish with cumin, salt, and pepper.

  • Prepare cilantro salsa.

2 While fish cooks:

  • Steam green beans.

3 Prepare tea.

Sole with Tarragon-Butter Sauce

Quick enough for a weeknight but special enough for company, this menu works well with Chablis or white Burgundy. Both are made from chardonnay grapes.

- 4 (6-ounce) sole fillets
- ½ teaspoon salt, divided
- ¼ teaspoon freshly ground black pepper
- Cooking spray
- ¾ cup dry white wine
- ¾ cup fat-free, less-sodium chicken broth
- ⅓ cup finely chopped shallots
- 1 tablespoon minced fresh garlic
- 5 teaspoons butter, cut into small pieces
- 1 tablespoon chopped fresh chives
- 1½ teaspoons chopped fresh tarragon

1 Sprinkle fish with ¼ teaspoon salt and pepper. Heat a large nonstick skillet over medium-high heat; coat with cooking spray. Add 2 fish fillets to pan; cook 2 minutes on each side or until fish flakes easily when tested with a fork or until desired degree of doneness. Remove from pan; cover and keep warm. Repeat with remaining fish.
2 Add wine, broth, shallots, and garlic to pan; bring to a boil. Reduce heat, and simmer until reduced to about ½ cup (about 10 minutes). Remove from heat; stir in ¼ teaspoon salt, butter, chives, and tarragon. Spoon sauce over fish; serve immediately. Yield: 4 servings (serving size: 1 fillet and 3 tablespoons sauce).

CALORIES 197 (30% from fat); FAT 6.6g (sat 3.4g, mono 1.6g, poly 1g); PROTEIN 29.4g; CARB 3.4g; FIBER 0.4g; CHOL 92mg; IRON 0.8mg; SODIUM 528mg; CALC 38mg

MENU *serves 4*

Sole with Tarragon-Butter Sauce

Rice amandine
Melt 2 teaspoons butter in a medium saucepan over medium-high heat. Add 1 cup long-grain rice; sauté 1 minute. Add 2 cups fat-free, less-sodium chicken broth. Cover, reduce heat, and simmer 15 minutes or until rice is tender. Stir in ¼ cup chopped parsley and 2 tablespoons sliced toasted almonds.

Sautéed haricots verts

Game Plan

1 Sauté rice.

2 While rice mixture simmers:
   - Chop shallots and mince garlic for wine mixture.
   - Cook fish.
   - Bring wine mixture to a boil.

3 While wine mixture simmers:
   - Chop herbs for fish and rice.
   - Toast almonds for rice.
   - Cut butter into small pieces.
   - Sauté haricot verts.

Aromatic Swordfish Steaks

The Caribbean spices on the fish go surprisingly well with the Indian-accented rice pilaf.

MENU *serves 4*

Aromatic Swordfish Steaks

Basmati rice pilaf

Heat 1 tablespoon canola oil in a large saucepan over medium-high heat. Add 1 cup basmati rice to pan; sauté 2 minutes. Add 1 (14-ounce) can light coconut milk and ¾ cup fat-free, less-sodium chicken broth; bring to a boil. Cover, reduce heat, and simmer 20 minutes or until tender. Transfer rice to a bowl. Add 3 tablespoons chopped pistachios, 3 tablespoons golden raisins, 3 tablespoons chopped fresh parsley, ¼ teaspoon garam masala, and ¼ teaspoon salt; toss well.

Sautéed spinach

Game Plan

1 Marinate fish.

2 While rice simmers:
- Chop pistachios and parsley for rice.
- Grill fish.
- Sauté spinach.

3 Toss together ingredients for rice.

¾ cup plain yogurt
1 tablespoon Jamaican jerk seasoning (such as Spice Islands)
1 tablespoon fresh lemon juice
1 teaspoon garlic powder
1 teaspoon ground cumin
1 teaspoon chili powder
½ teaspoon ground cinnamon
½ teaspoon ground ginger
4 (6-ounce) swordfish steaks (about ¾ inch thick)
Cooking spray

① Combine first 8 ingredients in a large zip-top plastic bag. Add fish, turning to coat. Cover and refrigerate 1 hour, turning bag occasionally.
② Prepare grill.
③ Remove fish from bag. Discard marinade. Place fish on grill rack coated with cooking spray; grill 4 minutes on each side or until fish flakes easily when tested with a fork or until desired degree of doneness. Yield: 4 servings (serving size: 1 steak).

CALORIES 241 (30% from fat); FAT 8.5g (sat 2.8g, mono 3g, poly 1.7g); PROTEIN 35.5g; CARB 3.8g; FIBER 0.7g; CHOL 72mg; IRON 1.8mg; SODIUM 406mg; CALC 69mg

Spiced Tilapia with Roasted Pepper–Tomatillo Sauce

Latin flavors infuse this menu. The sauce, which offers a great way to use fresh tomatillos, supplies vitamin C, vitamin E, and a little lycopene.

SAUCE:

- 1 large red bell pepper
- 2 teaspoons canola oil
- 1 cup finely chopped tomatillo
- ¼ teaspoon salt
- 1 garlic clove, minced
- 2 tablespoons chopped fresh cilantro
- 1 teaspoon rice vinegar
- 1 teaspoon honey

FISH:

- 2 tablespoons flour
- 2 teaspoons chili powder
- ½ teaspoon dried oregano
- ¼ teaspoon ground cumin
- 4 (6-ounce) tilapia fillets
- ¼ teaspoon salt
- ¼ teaspoon freshly ground black pepper
- 2 teaspoons canola oil

Cilantro sprigs (optional)

1 Preheat broiler.
2 To prepare sauce, cut bell pepper in half lengthwise; discard seeds and membranes. Place pepper halves, skin sides up, on a foil-lined baking sheet; flatten with hand. Broil 15 minutes or until blackened. Place in a zip-top plastic bag; seal. Let stand 10 minutes. Peel and cut into chunks.

3 Heat 2 teaspoons oil in a large nonstick skillet over medium heat. Add tomatillo to pan; cook 6 minutes or until tender. Add ¼ teaspoon salt and garlic; cook 1 minute. Transfer mixture to a blender or food processor. Add bell pepper, chopped cilantro, vinegar, and honey to blender. Remove center piece of blender lid (to allow steam to escape); secure blender lid on blender. Place a clean towel over opening in blender lid (to avoid splatters). Blend until smooth; set aside. Wipe pan with a paper towel.
4 To prepare fish, combine flour, chili powder, oregano, and cumin in a shallow dish; stir flour and spices with a whisk. Sprinkle fish evenly with ¼ teaspoon salt and pepper; dredge in flour mixture.
5 Heat 2 teaspoons oil in pan over medium-high heat. Add fish to pan; cook 2 minutes or until lightly browned. Carefully turn fish over; cook 4 minutes or until fish flakes easily when tested with a fork or until desired degree of doneness. Serve fish with sauce. Garnish with cilantro sprigs, if desired. Yield: 4 servings (serving size: 1 fillet and about ¼ cup sauce).

CALORIES 239 (32% from fat); FAT 8.5g (sat 1.6g, mono 4g, poly 2.4g); PROTEIN 34.3g; CARB 7.4g; FIBER 1.6g; CHOL 73mg; IRON 1.4mg; SODIUM 382mg; CALC 27mg

---

MENU *serves 4*

Spiced Tilapia with Roasted Pepper–Tomatillo Sauce

Saffron and cilantro rice

Heat 1 tablespoon olive oil in a large saucepan over medium-high heat. Add ½ cup chopped onion and 2 minced garlic cloves; sauté 2 minutes. Add 1 cup long-grain white rice; sauté 1 minute. Stir in 2 cups fat-free, less-sodium chicken broth and ⅛ teaspoon crushed saffron threads; bring to a boil. Cover, reduce heat, and simmer 20 minutes or until liquid is absorbed. Stir in ⅓ cup chopped fresh cilantro, 1 tablespoon fresh lime juice, and ¼ teaspoon salt.

Steamed green beans

Game Plan

1 While broiler heats:

- Chop onion and mince garlic for rice and sauce.
- Prepare red bell pepper for fish.

2 While red bell pepper broils and stands:

- Sauté onion and garlic for rice.
- Bring rice mixture to a boil.
- Chop tomatillo and cilantro for sauce.

3 While rice simmers:

- Blend roasted red pepper and tomatillo.
- Cook fish.
- Steam green beans.

MENU *serves 4*

Roasted Tilapia with Tomatoes and Olives

Arugula salad

Combine 6 cups trimmed arugula, ¼ cup (1 ounce) shaved fresh pecorino Romano cheese, and 2 tablespoons toasted chopped slivered almonds in a large bowl. Combine 2 tablespoons sherry vinegar and 2 teaspoons extra-virgin olive oil in a small bowl. Drizzle vinegar mixture over arugula mixture, and toss gently.

Brown rice

Game Plan

1 While rice cooks:
- •Prepare fish.

2 While fish bakes:
- •Prepare salad.

Roasted Tilapia with Tomatoes and Olives

Juicy tomatoes, briny olives, and fresh parsley add a savory bite to this mild white fish. For speedy cleanup, line your jelly-roll pan with aluminum foil. Be sure to coat it with cooking spray before adding the fish and other ingredients.

4 (6-ounce) tilapia fillets
¼ teaspoon salt
¼ teaspoon freshly ground black pepper
Cooking spray
1 cup cherry tomatoes, halved
¾ cup pitted green olives, coarsely chopped
3 tablespoons chopped fresh flat-leaf parsley
3 garlic cloves, minced

1 Preheat oven to 375°.
2 Sprinkle fish with salt and pepper. Arrange fish in a single layer in center of a jelly-roll pan lightly coated with cooking spray. Combine tomatoes and remaining ingredients; toss gently. Arrange tomato mixture around fish on baking sheet.
3 Bake at 375° for 20 minutes or until fish flakes easily when tested with a fork or until desired degree of doneness. Place 1 fillet on each of 4 plates; top each serving with about ¼ cup tomato mixture. Yield: 4 servings (serving size: 1 fillet).

CALORIES 207 (27% from fat); FAT 6.3g (sat 1.4g, mono 3.3g, poly 1g); PROTEIN 34.9g; CARB 3.6g; FIBER 1.3g; CHOL 85mg; IRON 1.5mg; SODIUM 572mg; CALC 38mg

Quick Tip: Boil-in-bag brown rice cooks in about half the time as cooking regular white rice.

Pan-Seared Tilapia with Citrus Vinaigrette

Sherry vinegar is mildly acidic. If you can't find it, substitute white wine vinegar.

Cooking spray
- 4 (6-ounce) tilapia fillets
- ½ teaspoon salt, divided
- ½ teaspoon freshly ground black pepper, divided
- ½ cup white wine
- 2 tablespoons finely chopped shallots
- 2 tablespoons fresh lemon juice
- 2 tablespoons fresh orange juice
- 4 teaspoons extra-virgin olive oil
- 2 teaspoons sherry vinegar

1 Heat a large nonstick skillet over medium-high heat; coat with cooking spray. Sprinkle fish evenly with ¼ teaspoon salt and ¼ teaspoon pepper. Add 2 fillets to pan; cook 4 minutes on each side or until fish flakes easily when tested with a fork or until desired degree of doneness. Remove from pan; keep warm. Repeat procedure with remaining fillets.

2 Add white wine to pan; cook 30 seconds or until liquid almost evaporates. Combine shallots and remaining ingredients; stir with a whisk. Stir in remaining ¼ teaspoon salt and remaining ¼ teaspoon pepper. Add shallot mixture to pan; sauté 1 minute or until thoroughly heated, stirring frequently. Place 1 fillet on each of 4 plates; top each serving with about 3 tablespoons pan sauce. Yield: 4 servings.

CALORIES 215 (31% from fat); FAT 7.4g (sat 1.6g, mono 4.1g, poly 1.1g); PROTEIN 34.5g; CARB 2.9g; FIBER 0.2g; CHOL 85mg; IRON 1.2mg; SODIUM 357mg; CALC 24mg

Quick Tip: Cut Brussels sprouts into halves so that they will cook quickly and evenly.

MENU *serves 4*

Pan-Seared Tilapia with Citrus Vinaigrette

Couscous pilaf
Bring 1½ cups fat-free, less-sodium chicken broth to a boil in a medium saucepan over medium-high heat. Add 1 cup uncooked couscous; cover and remove from heat. Let couscous stand 5 minutes; uncover and fluff with a fork. Stir in ⅓ cup dried cherries, ¼ cup toasted slivered almonds, 3 tablespoons chopped fresh flat-leaf parsley, 1 tablespoon extra-virgin olive oil, ½ teaspoon grated fresh lemon rind, ¼ teaspoon salt, and ¼ teaspoon freshly ground black pepper; stir well.

Roasted Brussels sprouts

Game Plan

1 While oven heats:
- •Trim Brussels sprouts.

2 While Brussels sprouts roast:
- •Prepare couscous.

3 While couscous stands:
- •Prepare fish.

4 Finish pilaf.

Grilled Tilapia with Smoked Paprika and Parmesan Polenta

Smoked paprika, a staple spice in Spanish cuisine, adds a heady flavor to this simple dish. Creamy polenta complements the full-flavored fish.

POLENTA:
- 4 cups fat-free milk
- 1 cup quick-cooking polenta
- ¼ teaspoon salt
- ⅓ cup (1½ ounces) grated Parmesan cheese

FISH:
- Cooking spray
- 1½ tablespoons olive oil
- 1 teaspoon smoked paprika
- ½ teaspoon garlic powder
- ½ teaspoon salt
- ¼ teaspoon freshly ground black pepper
- 4 (6-ounce) tilapia fillets

❶ To prepare polenta, bring milk to a boil in a medium saucepan; gradually add polenta, stirring constantly with a whisk. Reduce heat, and cook 5 minutes or until thick, stirring constantly; stir in ¼ teaspoon salt. Remove from heat. Stir in cheese; cover and keep warm.

❷ To prepare fish, heat a large nonstick grill pan over medium-high heat; coat with cooking spray. Combine oil and next 4 ingredients in a bowl, stirring well. Rub fish evenly with oil mixture. Add fish to pan; cook 4 minutes on each side or until fish flakes easily when tested with a fork or until desired degree of doneness. Yield: 4 servings (serving size: 1 fillet and 1 cup polenta).

CALORIES 422 (21% from fat); FAT 9.7g (sat 3g, mono 5.1g, poly 1.1g); PROTEIN 39.9g; CARB 34.2g; FIBER 4.1g; CHOL 73mg; IRON 1mg; SODIUM 751mg; CALC 414mg

Quick Tip: Purchase pregrated Parmesan cheese for the polenta.

Tilapia Tacos with Peach Salsa

You'll probably have leftover bean dip; try using it as filling for burritos or quesadillas with shredded rotisserie chicken. You can substitute other seafood, such as salmon or shrimp, for the tilapia.

SALSA:
- 2 cups finely chopped peeled peach (about 2 medium)
- ½ cup finely chopped red onion
- 2 tablespoons chopped cilantro
- 1 tablespoon fresh lime juice
- ½ teaspoon kosher salt
- ⅛ teaspoon ground red pepper
- 1 jalapeño pepper, seeded and finely chopped
- 1 garlic clove, minced

REMAINING INGREDIENTS:
- ½ cup panko (Japanese breadcrumbs)
- ½ teaspoon kosher salt
- ¼ teaspoon ground red pepper
- 1 pound tilapia, cut into 2-inch strips
- Cooking spray
- 8 (6-inch) corn tortillas

❶ To prepare salsa, combine first 8 ingredients in a medium bowl. Let stand 30 minutes at room temperature.

❷ Preheat oven to 375°.

❸ Combine panko, ½ teaspoon salt, and ¼ teaspoon pepper in a medium bowl. Add fish to panko mixture, tossing to coat. Place fish in a single layer on a baking sheet coated with cooking spray. Bake at 375° for 10 minutes or until desired degree of doneness, turning once halfway through baking.

❹ Heat tortillas according to package directions. Divide fish evenly among tortillas. Top fish evenly with salsa. Yield: 4 servings (serving size: 2 tacos).

CALORIES 250 (15% from fat); FAT 4.1g (sat 1g, mono 0.5g, poly 0.9g); PROTEIN 25.8g; CARB 30.6g; FIBER 3.5g; CHOL 75mg; IRON 0.6mg; SODIUM 533mg; CALC 30mg

MENU *serves 4*

Tilapia Tacos with Peach Salsa

Chipotle bean dip with chips
Drain 1 (16-ounce) can pinto beans in a colander over a bowl. Place beans and 2 tablespoons drained liquid in a medium bowl; mash until smooth or desired consistency. Stir in ¼ cup finely chopped red bell pepper and 1 teaspoon chopped chipotle chile, canned in adobo sauce. Sprinkle with ¼ cup finely chopped green onions. Serve with baked tortilla chips.

Mexican beer

Game Plan
1 Prepare salsa.
2 While salsa stands:
   • Prepare bean dip.
   • Preheat oven.
   • Coat fillets in panko mixture.
3 While fish bakes:
   • Warm corn tortillas.

MENU *serves 4*

Trout with Lentils

Mixed greens salad with goat cheese croutons

Spread 2 teaspoons goat cheese onto each of 8 (1-ounce) French bread baguette slices; broil 1 minute. Combine 2 teaspoons extra-virgin olive oil, 2 teaspoons sherry vinegar, 1 teaspoon honey, ¼ teaspoon salt, and ⅛ teaspoon freshly ground black pepper; stir with a whisk. Toss 4 cups mixed salad greens with vinegar mixture; serve with cheese croutons.

Angel food cake with lemon curd

Game Plan

1 While lentils cook:
- Chop celery and parsley.
- Preheat broiler.

2 Broil trout.

3 While cheese croutons broil:
- Stir trout into lentil mixture.
- Toss salad.

Trout with Lentils

Serve this dish warm or as a chilled salad over a bed of greens. If you purchase smoked trout, the recipe will come together even faster.

- 1 teaspoon olive oil
- ¼ cup chopped leek
- ¼ cup finely chopped carrot
- 2 garlic cloves, minced
- 1 cup dried lentils
- ½ cup water
- 1 (14-ounce) can fat-free, less-sodium chicken broth
- ¼ cup chopped celery
- 1 tablespoon finely chopped fresh parsley
- 1 tablespoon sherry vinegar
- ¾ teaspoon salt, divided
- ½ teaspoon freshly ground black pepper, divided
- 2 (6-ounce) trout fillets

Cooking spray

❶ Heat oil in a medium saucepan over medium-high heat. Add leek, carrot, and garlic; sauté 2 minutes. Stir in lentils, water, and broth; bring to a boil. Cover and reduce heat. Simmer 25 minutes or until lentils are tender and liquid is nearly absorbed. Remove from heat. Add celery, parsley, vinegar, ½ teaspoon salt, and ¼ teaspoon pepper to lentil mixture; stir well.

❷ Preheat broiler.

❸ Sprinkle fillets with ¼ teaspoon salt and ¼ teaspoon pepper. Place fish on a baking sheet coated with cooking spray; broil 5 minutes or until fish flakes easily when tested with a fork. Break fish into chunks; add to lentil mixture, tossing gently to combine. Yield: 4 servings (serving size: 1 cup).

CALORIES 311 (18% from fat); FAT 6.2g (sat 1.6g, mono 2.2g, poly 1.9g); PROTEIN 32.8g; CARB 31.3g; FIBER 15.2g; CHOL 50mg; IRON 5mg; SODIUM 668mg; CALC 96mg

Tuna with Avocado Green Goddess Aïoli

The aïoli features heart-healthy avocado, which contributes vitamin E to this dish. However, the real nutritional standout is the tuna, which is rich in niacin.

AÏOLI:
- 6 tablespoons chopped ripe peeled avocado
- ¼ cup fat-free sour cream
- 2 tablespoons fat-free mayonnaise
- 2 tablespoons chopped fresh cilantro
- 1 tablespoon chopped fresh basil leaves
- 1 tablespoon chopped fresh flat-leaf parsley
- 1 teaspoon fresh lemon juice
- ¼ teaspoon salt
- 1 garlic clove, chopped

TUNA:
- ¾ teaspoon ground coriander
- ½ teaspoon salt
- ½ teaspoon ground cumin
- ½ teaspoon garlic powder
- ¼ teaspoon chili powder
- ⅛ teaspoon freshly ground black pepper
- 4 (6-ounce) tuna steaks (about 1 inch thick)

Cooking spray

❶ To prepare aïoli, place first 9 ingredients in a blender; process until smooth.

❷ To prepare tuna, combine coriander and next 5 ingredients in a small bowl; sprinkle spice mixture evenly over tuna.

❸ Heat a grill pan over medium-high heat; coat with cooking spray. Add tuna; cook 2 minutes on each side or until medium-rare or desired degree of doneness. Serve with aïoli. Yield: 4 servings (serving size: 1 steak and about 2½ tablespoons aïoli).

CALORIES 234 (24% from fat); FAT 6.1g (sat 1.8g, mono 2.6g, poly 1.2g); PROTEIN 39g; CARB 6.1g; FIBER 1.3g; CHOL 82mg; IRON 2.4mg; SODIUM 581mg; CALC 82mg

Wine Note:
Like salmon, tuna is capable of handling lighter red wines, especially when the fish is grilled.

MENU *serves 4*

Tuna with Avocado Green Goddess Aïoli

Garlic-roasted red potatoes
Preheat oven to 425°. Combine 2 tablespoons olive oil, 1 tablespoon minced fresh garlic, ¾ teaspoon salt, ½ teaspoon freshly ground black pepper, and 1 (24-ounce) package refrigerated red potato wedges (such as Simply Potatoes) on a jelly-roll pan; toss well. Bake at 425° for 20 minutes or until golden.

Steamed green beans

Game Plan

1 While oven heats for the potatoes:
  - Mince garlic.
2 While potatoes bake:
  - Prepare aïoli.
  - Cook fillets.
  - Steam green beans.

MENU *serves 6*

Linguine with
Clam Sauce

Cold cucumber soup

Combine 1 large coarsely
chopped seeded peeled
cucumber, 5 coarsely
chopped green onions,
2 garlic cloves, and ¼ cup
coarsely chopped fresh dill
in a food processor; process
until finely chopped. Add
2 (6-ounce) cartons plain
low-fat yogurt; 1 (14-ounce)
can fat-free, less-sodium
chicken broth; and ½ tea-
spoon salt; process until
combined.

Sautéed asparagus
spears

Game Plan

1 While water for linguine
   comes to a boil:

   • Mince garlic for
     linguine and soup.

   • Chop parsley for
     linguine.

   • Peel, seed, and chop
     cucumber for soup.

   • Chop onions and dill
     for soup and parsley
     for linguine.

2 While linguine cooks:

   • Prepare clam sauce.

   • Sauté asparagus.

   • Process soup.

3 Combine linguine and
   clam sauce.

Linguine with Clam Sauce

Store live clams in your refrigerator up to 2 days. Clams are a good source of iron, and this dish provides almost half of the recommended daily allowance (18 milligrams) for women ages 25 to 50.

1 (12-ounce) package linguine
3 tablespoons butter
5 garlic cloves, minced
½ cup dry white wine
½ teaspoon salt
1 (8-ounce) bottle clam juice
2 (6½-ounce) cans minced clams, undrained
24 littleneck clams, scrubbed
1 cup finely chopped parsley
2 tablespoons fresh lemon juice
⅛ teaspoon freshly ground black pepper
Lemon wedges (optional)

❶ Cook linguine according to package directions, omitting salt and fat. Set aside.

❷ Melt butter in a large skillet over medium heat. Add garlic; cook 3 minutes or until golden. ❸ Stir in wine, salt, and clam juice. Drain minced clams; add juice to pan (reserve minced clams). Simmer 5 minutes. Add little-neck clams; cover and cook 3 to 4 minutes or until shells open. Remove from heat, and discard any unopened shells. Add reserved minced clams, parsley, lemon juice, and pepper. ❹ Place pasta in a large bowl. Add clam mixture to pasta, and toss well. Serve with lemon wedges, if desired. Yield: 6 servings (serving size: about 1 cup).

CALORIES 332 (19% from fat); FAT 7g (sat 3.8g, mono 1.7g, poly 0.3g); PROTEIN 17.1g; CARB 47.5g; FIBER 2.2g; CHOL 39mg; IRON 8.5mg; SODIUM 627mg; CALC 54mg

Steamed Clams with Basil and Chiles

Look for oyster sauce—a concentrated sauce made of oysters, brine, and soy sauce—in the Asian foods section of your supermarket.

- 1 tablespoon canola oil
- 4 garlic cloves, chopped
- 2 teaspoons minced serrano chile
- ⅓ cup dry white wine
- 1 tablespoon fish sauce
- 2 teaspoons oyster sauce
- 1 teaspoon sugar
- ½ teaspoon freshly ground black pepper
- 3 pounds littleneck clams in shells, scrubbed
- 1 cup chopped fresh basil

1 Heat oil in a large nonstick skillet over medium-high heat. Add garlic; sauté 1 minute or until golden. Add chile; sauté 10 seconds.

Stir in wine and next 4 ingredients. Bring wine mixture to a boil. Add clams; cover and cook 7 minutes or until shells open. Add basil; cover and cook 1 additional minute. Discard any unopened shells, and remove clams from pan with a slotted spoon. Serve with sauce. Yield: 4 servings (serving size: about 13 clams and about ⅓ cup sauce).

CALORIES 298 (21% from fat); FAT 6.9g (sat 0.6g, mono 2.3g, poly 2.1g); PROTEIN 44.2g; CARB 12g; FIBER 0.6g; CHOL 116mg; IRON 48.1mg; SODIUM 559mg; CALC 183mg

Flavor Tip: For even spicier and more traditional flavor, use 2 teaspoons Thai bird chile instead of serrano. Look for bird chiles at an Asian market.

MENU *serves 4*

Steamed Clams with Basil and Chiles

Rice noodles with cilantro

Cardamom-spiced iced coffee

Combine 4 cups strong brewed coffee, ¼ cup sweetened condensed milk, and ⅛ teaspoon cardamom in a medium bowl; stir until blended. Chill. Serve over ice.

Game Plan

1 Prepare iced coffee.

2 While noodles soak:
- •Chop cilantro.
- •Prepare ingredients for clams.

3 While clams cook:
- •Toss noodles with cilantro.

Mussels Ravigote

Mussels and fries are a classic pairing in Belgium and France. Ravigote is a traditional French vinegar-herb sauce that is often served with seafood.

¼ cup finely chopped red onion
3 tablespoons sliced cornichons
2 tablespoons chopped fresh parsley
1 tablespoon minced fresh tarragon
1 tablespoon white wine vinegar
2 teaspoons capers
1½ teaspoons extra-virgin olive oil
1 teaspoon Dijon mustard
1 garlic clove, minced
1 cup dry white wine
1 (8-ounce) bottle clam juice
48 mussels (about 2 pounds), scrubbed and debearded

❶ Combine first 9 ingredients in a small bowl; set aside.

❷ Combine wine and clam juice in a Dutch oven, and bring to a boil. Add mussels; cover and cook 2 minutes or until shells open. Remove mussels from pan with a slotted spoon; discard any unopened shells. Keep warm.

❸ Bring wine mixture to a boil over high heat; cook until reduced to $\frac{1}{3}$ cup (about 15 minutes). Pour over mussels. Add cornichon mixture; toss. Yield: 2 servings (serving size: 24 mussels and about 3 tablespoons wine mixture).

CALORIES 244 (30% from fat); FAT 8.1g (sat 1.3g, mono 3.6g, poly 1.6g); PROTEIN 24.4g; CARB 18.2g; FIBER 0.9g; CHOL 57mg; IRON 9mg; SODIUM 1,141mg; CALC 96mg

Angel Hair Pasta with Mussels and Red Pepper Sauce

Sweet red peppers help balance the flavors of the naturally salty mussels and the slightly acidic tomatoes.

8 ounces uncooked angel hair pasta
2 teaspoons olive oil
⅓ cup diced onion
1 garlic clove, minced
2 cups diced red bell pepper (about 2 medium)
½ teaspoon salt
Dash of ground red pepper
1 (14.5-ounce) can whole tomatoes, undrained and chopped
½ cup white wine
36 mussels (about 3 pounds), scrubbed and debearded
3 tablespoons chopped fresh parsley

❶ Cook pasta according to package directions, omitting salt and fat. Drain; keep warm.
❷ Heat oil in a large saucepan over medium-high heat. Add onion and garlic; sauté 5 minutes or until tender. Add bell pepper, salt, and ground red pepper; sauté 2 minutes. Add tomatoes and wine; bring to a boil. Reduce heat to low, and simmer 10 minutes. Add mussels, and increase heat to medium; cover and simmer 7 minutes or until shells open. Discard any unopened shells. Serve mussel mixture over pasta; sprinkle with parsley. Yield: 4 servings (serving size: 9 mussels, about 1 cup pasta, and about 2 teaspoons parsley).

CALORIES 372 (18% from fat); FAT 7.4g (sat 1g, mono 2.6g, poly 1.3g); PROTEIN 24.9g; CARB 46.9g; FIBER 4.5g; CHOL 40mg; IRON 8.7mg; SODIUM 809mg; CALC 85mg

MENU *serves 4*

Angel Hair Pasta with Mussels and Red Pepper Sauce

Toasted French bread

Pound cake with strawberry-pepper sauce

Combine 3 tablespoons brown sugar, 1½ teaspoons balsamic vinegar, ⅛ teaspoon freshly ground black pepper, and 6 ounces frozen strawberries in a small saucepan; bring to a boil. Combine 1 tablespoon cornstarch and 1 tablespoon water; stir with a whisk. Add to pan; boil 1 minute, stirring constantly. Serve over sliced reduced-fat pound cake.

Game Plan

1 While water for pasta comes to a boil:
   • Prep ingredients for mussels.

2 While tomato mixture simmers:
   • Prepare strawberry-pepper sauce.

3 While mussels cook:
   • Cook pasta.
   • Slice pound cake.

MENU *serves 4*

Scallops with Chipotle-Orange Sauce

Yellow pepper rice
Prepare 1 (3½-ounce) bag boil-in-bag white rice according to package directions. Heat 1 tablespoon olive oil in a large nonstick skillet coated with cooking spray over medium heat. Add 2 cups thinly sliced yellow bell pepper; cook 10 minutes or until golden brown, stirring frequently. Add cooked rice and ¼ teaspoon salt; cook 2 minutes, stirring constantly.

Steamed broccoli spears

Game Plan

1 While rice cooks in boiling water:
- Slice yellow bell peppers for rice.
- Chop chipotle and green onions for scallops.

2 While yellow bell pepper cooks:
- Heat skillet to cook scallops.
- Boil water to cook broccoli.

3 While scallops cook:
- Steam broccoli spears.
- Finish preparing rice.

Scallops with Chipotle-Orange Sauce

Chipotle peppers are smoked jalapeños that are often canned in sauce. Use more or less than we call for here, depending on your tolerance for heat.

2 tablespoons butter, divided
Cooking spray
1½ pounds large sea scallops
½ teaspoon paprika
¼ teaspoon salt, divided
½ cup fresh orange juice
1 tablespoon finely chopped canned chipotle chile in adobo sauce
¼ cup chopped green onions

1 Melt 1 tablespoon butter in a large skillet coated with cooking spray over medium-high heat. Sprinkle scallops with paprika and ⅛ teaspoon salt; add to pan, and cook 3 minutes on each side or until browned. Remove from pan; keep warm.

2 Add juice and chile to pan, scraping pan to loosen browned bits. Bring liquid to a boil; cook until reduced to ¼ cup (about 1 minute). Add 1 tablespoon butter and ⅛ teaspoon salt to pan; stir with a whisk. Serve sauce over scallops; garnish with green onions. Yield: 4 servings (serving size: about 4½ ounces scallops, about 1 tablespoon sauce, and 1 tablespoon green onions).

CALORIES 218 (29% from fat); FAT 7.1g (sat 3.7g, mono 1.7g, poly 0.7g); PROTEIN 28.9g; CARB 8.1g; FIBER 0.4g; CHOL 72mg; IRON 0.6mg; SODIUM 488mg; CALC 47mg

Quick Tip: Heat the pan while you prep the ingredients.

Seared Sea Scallops on Asian Slaw

Noodle and vegetable toss

Cook 8 ounces vermicelli according to package directions, omitting salt and fat. Drain; place in a large bowl. Combine 2 tablespoons fresh orange juice, 1 tablespoon low-sodium soy sauce, 1 tablespoon dark sesame oil, and 1 teaspoon bottled ground fresh ginger; stir with a whisk. Drizzle dressing over pasta; toss to coat. Stir in ½ cup red bell pepper strips and ½ cup green bell pepper strips.

Jasmine tea

Game Plan

1 Brew tea.

2 While water for pasta comes to a boil:

  • Prepare dressing for pasta.

  • Cut red bell pepper and green bell pepper into strips.

  • Slice cabbage and radishes for scallops.

3 While pasta cooks:

  • Prepare vinegar mixture for scallops.

  • Cook scallops.

  • Assemble scallops and slaw on serving plates.

4 Toss ingredients together for pasta.

Seared Sea Scallops on Asian Slaw

From start to finish, this entire meal takes about 30 minutes to prepare. Look for pretoasted sesame seeds in Asian markets.

- 4 cups thinly sliced napa (Chinese) cabbage (about 1 small head)
- ½ cup thinly sliced radishes (about 6 small)
- 2 tablespoons rice vinegar
- 2 tablespoons low-sodium soy sauce
- 2 teaspoons dark sesame oil, divided
- ⅛ teaspoon crushed red pepper
- 16 large sea scallops (about 1½ pounds)
- ¼ teaspoon salt
- ¼ teaspoon freshly ground black pepper
- 2 teaspoons sesame seeds, toasted

1 Combine cabbage and radishes in a large bowl; set aside.

2 Combine rice vinegar, soy sauce, 1 teaspoon oil, and red pepper; stir with a whisk.

3 Heat 1 teaspoon oil in a large nonstick skillet over medium-high heat. Sprinkle scallops with salt and black pepper. Add scallops to pan; cook 3 minutes on each side or until done. Arrange 1 cup cabbage mixture on each of 4 plates; top each serving with 4 scallops. Drizzle each serving with 1 tablespoon vinegar mixture; sprinkle each serving with ½ teaspoon sesame seeds. Serve immediately. Yield: 4 servings.

CALORIES 135 (25% from fat); FAT 3.8g (sat 0.5g, mono 1.2g, poly 1.3g); PROTEIN 16.4g; CARB 7g; FIBER 1.3g; CHOL 37mg; IRON 0.6mg; SODIUM 597mg; CALC 78mg

MENU *serves 6*

Southern Shrimp and Grits

Green salad with avocado and tomatoes
Combine 4 cups chopped romaine lettuce, 1 cup halved cherry tomatoes, ½ cup thinly vertically sliced red onion, and 1 sliced ripe avocado. Combine 2 tablespoons fresh lime juice, 2 teaspoons extra-virgin olive oil, 1 teaspoon bottled minced garlic, ¼ teaspoon salt, and ¼ teaspoon black pepper; stir with a whisk. Drizzle dressing over salad; toss gently to coat. Cover and refrigerate until ready to serve.

Orange sorbet

Game Plan

1 Prepare salad; cover and chill until serving time.

2 While water for grits comes to a boil:
- Combine lemon juice, hot sauce, and shrimp.
- Chop bacon and green onions.
- Shred cheese.

3 While shrimp mixture cooks:
- Cook grits.

Southern Shrimp and Grits

This shellfish specialty of the Carolina low country, sometimes called "breakfast shrimp," tastes great anytime. To minimize prep time, start with frozen bell pepper and onion, as well as peeled and deveined shrimp.

- 3 tablespoons fresh lemon juice
- ½ teaspoon hot sauce (such as Tabasco)
- 1½ pounds peeled and deveined large shrimp
- 2 bacon slices, chopped
- 1 cup frozen chopped onion
- ¼ cup frozen chopped green bell pepper
- 1½ teaspoons bottled minced garlic
- 1 cup fat-free, less-sodium chicken broth
- ½ cup chopped green onions, divided
- 5 cups water
- 1½ cups uncooked quick-cooking grits
- 1 tablespoon butter
- 1 teaspoon salt
- ¾ cup (3 ounces) shredded sharp cheddar cheese

❶ Combine first 3 ingredients in a large bowl; set aside.

❷ Cook bacon in a large nonstick skillet over medium heat until crisp. Add onion, bell pepper, and garlic to drippings in pan. Cook 5 minutes or until tender, stirring occasionally. Stir in shrimp mixture, broth, and ¼ cup green onions; cook 5 minutes or until shrimp are done, stirring frequently.

❸ Bring water to a boil in a medium saucepan; gradually add grits, stirring constantly. Reduce heat to low; simmer, covered, 5 minutes or until thick, stirring occasionally. Stir in butter and salt. Serve shrimp mixture over grits; sprinkle with cheese and remaining green onions. Yield: 6 servings (serving size: ⅔ cup shrimp mixture, ⅔ cup grits, 2 tablespoons cheese, and 2 teaspoons green onions).

CALORIES 408 (28% from fat); FAT 12.5g (sat 5.6g, mono 4.1g, poly 1.3g); PROTEIN 32.8g; CARB 39.9g; FIBER 2g; CHOL 246mg; IRON 5.1mg; SODIUM 890mg; CALC 154mg

Quick Tip:
Quick-cooking grits are a welcome weeknight alternative to stone-ground versions, which can take up to 45 minutes to cook.

Shrimp and Grits Casserole

A few spoonfuls of cream cheese give this casserole a velvety texture. Garnish with a sprig of fresh parsley, if you like.

- 2 cups 2% reduced-fat milk
- ¾ cup fat-free, less-sodium chicken broth
- 1 cup uncooked quick-cooking grits
- ¼ teaspoon salt
- ½ cup (2 ounces) shredded Parmesan cheese
- 2 tablespoons butter
- 1 (3-ounce) package ⅓-less-fat cream cheese
- 3 tablespoons chopped fresh flat-leaf parsley
- 1 tablespoon chopped fresh chives
- 1 tablespoon fresh lemon juice
- 2 large egg whites
- 1 pound peeled and deveined medium shrimp, coarsely chopped
- Cooking spray
- Hot pepper sauce (optional)

❶ Preheat oven to 375°.
❷ Combine milk and broth in a medium-heavy saucepan; bring to a boil. Gradually add grits and salt to pan, stirring constantly with a whisk. Cook 5 minutes or until grits are thick, stirring constantly; remove pan from heat. Add Parmesan cheese, butter, and cream cheese to pan; stir until smooth. Add parsley and next 4 ingredients to pan; stir just until blended throughout. Spoon grits mixture into an 11 x 7-inch baking dish coated with cooking spray. Bake at 375° for 25 minutes or until set. Serve with hot pepper sauce, if desired. Yield: 6 servings (serving size: about 1 cup).

CALORIES 341 (34% from fat); FAT 13g (sat 7.5g, mono 3.5g, poly 1g); PROTEIN 27.5g; CARB 27.2g; FIBER 0.6g; CHOL 149mg; IRON 3.2mg; SODIUM 571mg; CALC 293mg

MENU *serves 6*

Shrimp and Grits Casserole

Cherry tomato salad
Combine 3 cups halved cherry tomatoes, ½ cup thinly sliced green onions, and ¼ cup chopped fresh flat-leaf parsley. Sprinkle with ½ teaspoon salt and ¼ teaspoon fresh ground black pepper. Combine 3 tablespoons red wine vinegar, 1½ tablespoons extra-virgin olive oil, and 1 tablespoon Dijon mustard; stir well. Drizzle vinegar mixture over tomato mixture; toss gently.

Lima beans

Game Plan

1 Preheat oven.

2 While milk mixture comes to a boil:
- Prepare ingredients for casserole.

3 While casserole bakes:
- Prepare salad.
- Cook lima beans.

MENU *serves 4*

Asian Rice with Shrimp and Snow Peas

Spicy-sweet cantaloupe salad
Combine 3 cups cubed cantaloupe, 2 teaspoons chopped seeded jalapeño, and 2 teaspoons chopped fresh mint in a medium bowl. Combine 2 tablespoons fresh orange juice, 1 teaspoon sugar, and 1 teaspoon fresh lime juice; stir until sugar dissolves. Pour juice mixture over cantaloupe mixture; toss. Chill 30 minutes.

Iced green tea

Game Plan

1 Prepare salad.

2 While salad chills:

•Cook rice.

3 While rice cooks:

•Boil water to cook snow peas and shrimp.

•Trim snow peas, and cut green onions.

•Toast almonds.

Asian Rice with Shrimp and Snow Peas

Leftovers of this dish reheat well to make a terrific lunch or dinner for the next day.

1 cup uncooked long-grain rice
1 cup water
1 cup fat-free, less-sodium chicken broth
3 tablespoons low-sodium soy sauce
3 tablespoons rice vinegar
1 tablespoon dark sesame oil
2 teaspoons bottled chopped garlic
1 teaspoon hot sauce
2 cups snow peas, trimmed (about 6 ounces)
1½ pounds large peeled and deveined shrimp
½ cup diagonally cut green onions
4 teaspoons slivered almonds, toasted

❶ Combine first 3 ingredients in a medium saucepan; bring to a boil. Cover, reduce heat, and simmer 20 minutes or until liquid is absorbed. Keep warm.

❷ Combine soy sauce and next 4 ingredients in a large bowl; stir with a whisk. Set aside.
❸ Cook snow peas and shrimp in boiling water 2 minutes or until shrimp are done. Drain. Add snow peas, shrimp, green onions, and rice to soy mixture; toss well to combine. Top with almonds. Serve immediately. Yield: 4 servings (serving size: 2 cups rice mixture and 1 teaspoon almonds).

CALORIES 334 (20% from fat); FAT 7.6g (sat 1.2g, mono 1.9g, poly 3.5g); PROTEIN 38.9g; CARB 25.4g; FIBER 2.3g; CHOL 259mg; IRON 5.7mg; SODIUM 776mg; CALC 129mg

Ingredient Tip: "Easy peel" deveined raw shrimp costs half as much as peeled and deveined shrimp. Peeling the shrimp yourself will add a few extra minutes when preparing this recipe, but the price difference will make it worth your time. Look for it in your local supermarket.

Shrimp and Sausage Paella

Saffron is expensive; fortunately, just a pinch goes a long way. Dulce de leche is caramelized sweetened condensed milk, and it's available on the ethnic aisle in most supermarkets.

2 links Spanish chorizo sausage (about 6½ ounces) or turkey kielbasa, cut into ½-inch-thick slices
1 cup chopped onion
1 cup chopped green bell pepper (about 1 medium)
2 teaspoons bottled minced garlic
¼ teaspoon black pepper
¼ teaspoon crushed saffron threads
1½ cups instant rice
¾ cup water
½ teaspoon dried marjoram
1 (14.5-ounce) can no-salt-added diced tomatoes, undrained
1 (8-ounce) bottle clam juice
8 ounces medium shrimp, peeled and deveined

❶ Heat a large nonstick skillet over medium-high heat. Add sausage to pan; sauté 1 minute. Add onion and bell pepper to pan; sauté 4 minutes. Stir in garlic, black pepper, and saffron; sauté 1 minute. Stir in rice and next 4 ingredients; bring to a boil. Cover, reduce heat, and simmer 4 minutes or until rice is almost tender. Stir in shrimp. Cover and simmer 3 minutes or until shrimp are done. Yield: 4 servings (serving size: about 1½ cups).

CALORIES 390 (30% from fat); FAT 13.2g (sat 4.6g, mono 5.8g, poly 1.5g); PROTEIN 23.3g; CARB 41.8g; FIBER 2.7g; CHOL 114mg; IRON 5.1mg; SODIUM 626mg; CALC 66mg

MENU s

Shrimp and Sausage Paella

Tossed green salad

Dulce de leche parfait
Place ¼ cup fat-free vanilla ice cream in each of 4 footed glasses. Combine 6 tablespoons dulce de leche and 2 tablespoons hot water; stir well; top each serving with 1 tablespoon dulce de leche mixture and 2 teaspoons chopped toasted almonds. Repeat layers.

Game Plan

1 Peel and devein shrimp.

2 Slice sausage, and chop onion and bell pepper for paella.

3 Prepare rice mixture.

4 While rice mixture cooks:
   •Prepare tossed salad.

5 Add shrimp to rice mixture.

6 Assemble dessert.

Shrimp in Yellow Sauce

MENU *serves 4*

Shrimp in Yellow Sauce

Coconut rice

Combine 1 cup long-grain rice; 1¼ cups fat-free, less-sodium chicken broth; 1 teaspoon salt; and 2 teaspoons canola oil in a medium saucepan over high heat; bring to a boil. Reduce heat, and add ½ cup light coconut milk and ½ stalk fresh lemongrass, crushed. Cover and simmer 15 minutes or until liquid is absorbed. Let stand 10 minutes; fluff with a fork.

Shrimp crackers

Game Plan

1 Peel and devein shrimp.

2 While rice cooks:

   • Process and cook spice paste.

3 While rice stands:

   • Cook shrimp.

Garnish with chopped fresh cilantro and lime wedges. Use more sambal oelek for extra heat. Shrimp crackers come in a variety of shapes and are available in Asian markets.

SPICE PASTE:
- ½ teaspoon grated lime rind
- 2 tablespoons lime juice
- 1 to 2 teaspoons sambal oelek (chile paste with garlic)
- 1 teaspoon fish sauce
- ½ teaspoon coriander seeds
- ½ teaspoon turmeric
- 3 garlic cloves
- 2 shallots, chopped
- 1 (1-inch) piece fresh ginger, peeled

REMAINING INGREDIENTS:
Cooking spray
- 1 cup light coconut milk
- 1 pound large shrimp, peeled and deveined
Chopped cilantro (optional)

❶ To prepare spice paste, place first 9 ingredients in a food processor; process until smooth. ❷ Heat a large nonstick skillet over medium-high heat; coat with cooking spray. Add spice paste to pan; sauté 1 minute or until fragrant. Add coconut milk and shrimp; simmer 4 minutes or until shrimp are done. Garnish with cilantro, if desired. Yield: 4 servings (serving size: about ¾ cup).

CALORIES 175 (26% from fat); FAT 5.1g (sat 3.2g, mono 0.3g, poly 0.8g); PROTEIN 24.4g; CARB 8.1g; FIBER 0.4g; CHOL 172mg; IRON 3.4mg; SODIUM 302mg; CALC 72mg

Flavor Tip: For an authentic Asian flavor, use shrimp paste (such as Lee Kum Kee) in place of the fish sauce.

Jambalaya with Shrimp and Andouille Sausage

To speed up preparation, pick up peeled and deveined frozen shrimp from the frozen foods section of your supermarket. Thaw shrimp in the refrigerator or under cold, running water.

1 tablespoon olive oil
1 cup chopped onion
1 cup chopped red bell pepper
1 tablespoon minced garlic
6 ounces andouille sausage, sliced
1 cup uncooked long-grain white rice
1 teaspoon paprika
1 teaspoon freshly ground black pepper
1 teaspoon dried oregano
½ teaspoon onion powder
½ teaspoon dried thyme
¼ teaspoon garlic salt
1 bay leaf
2 cups fat-free, less-sodium chicken broth
¾ cup water
1 tablespoon tomato paste
½ teaspoon hot pepper sauce
1 (14.5-ounce) can no-salt-added diced tomatoes, undrained
½ pound peeled and deveined medium shrimp
2 tablespoons chopped fresh parsley

❶ Heat oil in a large Dutch oven over medium-high heat. Add onion, bell pepper, garlic, and sausage; sauté 5 minutes or until vegetables are tender.
❷ Add rice and next 7 ingredients; cook 2 minutes. Add broth and next 4 ingredients; bring to a boil. Cover, reduce heat, and simmer 20 minutes. Add shrimp; cook 5 minutes. Let stand 5 minutes. Discard bay leaf. Stir in parsley. Yield: 4 servings (serving size: 1½ cups).

CALORIES 426 (27% from fat); FAT 12.7g (sat 3.9g, mono 2.8g, poly 1g); PROTEIN 25g; CARB 52.7g; FIBER 4.9g; CHOL 117mg; IRON 5.1mg; SODIUM 763mg; CALC 99mg

Garden Shrimp Pasta

You can make this dish vegetarian by substituting tofu for the shrimp.

- 2 tablespoons olive oil
- 1 teaspoon chopped fresh oregano
- 1 teaspoon grated lemon rind
- 1 teaspoon grated orange rind
- ¼ teaspoon crushed red pepper
- ¼ teaspoon salt
- 2 pounds medium peeled and deveined shrimp
- 8 ounces uncooked angel hair pasta
- 5 cups chopped seeded tomato (about 1½ pounds)
- ¼ cup thinly sliced fresh basil
- ¼ cup thinly sliced fresh mint
- 2 tablespoons red wine vinegar
- 1 tablespoon olive oil
- 2 teaspoons spicy brown mustard
- 1 teaspoon sugar
- ½ teaspoon grated lemon rind
- 1 teaspoon fresh lemon juice
- ⅛ teaspoon salt
- ⅛ teaspoon freshly ground black pepper
- ¾ cup (3 ounces) crumbled feta cheese

1 Combine first 7 ingredients in a large bowl; toss well. Heat a large nonstick skillet over medium-high heat. Add shrimp mixture to pan; sauté 6 minutes or until done. Remove from heat; set aside.

2 Cook pasta according to package directions, omitting salt and fat. Place pasta in a large bowl; add tomato, basil, and mint.

3 Combine vinegar and next 7 ingredients in a small bowl. Pour over pasta mixture, and toss to coat. Place about 1¾ cups pasta mixture on each of 6 plates. Top each serving with about 3 ounces shrimp mixture and 2 tablespoons cheese. Yield: 6 servings.

CALORIES 420 (29% from fat); FAT 13.6g (sat 3.8g, mono 6.2g, poly 2.5g); PROTEIN 39g; CARB 35.4g; FIBER 3.1g; CHOL 242mg; IRON 5.7mg; SODIUM 560mg; CALC 181mg

MENU *serves 6*

Garden Shrimp Pasta

Tossed salad with avocado and cashews
Combine 4 cups red leaf lettuce, 2 cups torn Bibb lettuce, 2 cups julienne-cut yellow bell pepper, 1½ cups chopped peeled avocado, ⅓ cup coarsely chopped cashews, and ⅓ cup chopped green onions in a large bowl; toss gently. Combine 2 tablespoons white wine vinegar, 1½ tablespoons fresh lime juice, 1 tablespoon extra-virgin olive oil, ½ teaspoon salt, and ¼ teaspoon freshly ground black pepper; stir with a whisk. Drizzle vinegar mixture over lettuce mixture; toss gently.

Crusty French bread

Game Plan

1 While water for pasta comes to a boil:
- Prepare salad.
- Chop oregano.
- Grate lemon and orange rind.

2 While pasta cooks:
- Sauté shrimp mixture.
- Chop and seed tomato.
- Chop basil and mint.

3 Assemble pasta mixture and shrimp on serving plates.

MENU *serves 4*

Sun-Dried Tomato Spiced Shrimp

Coconut-almond couscous

Bring 1½ cups light coconut milk to a boil in a medium saucepan. Gradually stir in 1 cup uncooked couscous, ¼ cup chopped green onions, ¾ teaspoon salt, and ¼ teaspoon ground red pepper. Remove from heat; cover and let stand 5 minutes. Fluff with a fork. Sprinkle with ¼ cup toasted slivered almonds.

Steamed broccoli spears with lemon rind

Game Plan

1 Peel and devein shrimp.

2 Marinate shrimp.

3 While grill heats:

•Prepare couscous.

4 While shrimp grills:

•Steam broccoli.

Sun-Dried Tomato Spiced Shrimp

Start marinating the shrimp as soon as you get home from work. The rest of the meal comes together in no time at all. To get the most flavor from the marinade, press the sides of the bag when you turn it during the marinating process.

1 (8-ounce) jar oil-packed sun-dried tomato halves
1 cup chopped fresh cilantro
½ teaspoon lemon rind
2 tablespoons fresh lemon juice
1¼ teaspoons curry paste
1½ pounds large shrimp, peeled and deveined
Cooking spray

❶ Drain sun-dried tomatoes in a sieve over a bowl, reserving oil. Place 1 tablespoon oil in a food processor. Coarsely chop 1 cup tomatoes; add to food processor. Place remaining oil and sun-dried tomatoes in sun-dried tomato jar; refrigerate and reserve for another use. Add cilantro, rind, juice, and curry to food processor; process until smooth. Combine tomato mixture and shrimp in a large zip-top plastic bag. Seal and marinate in refrigerator 1 hour, turning bag occasionally. Remove shrimp from bag; discard marinade.
❷ Prepare grill to medium-high heat.
❸ Place shrimp on grill rack coated with cooking spray; grill 3 minutes on each side or until done. Yield: 4 servings (serving size: about 6 ounces).

CALORIES 224 (25% from fat); FAT 6.1g (sat 1g, mono 2.5g, poly 1.5g); PROTEIN 35.5g; CARB 5.7g; FIBER 1.2g; CHOL 259mg; IRON 4.8mg; SODIUM 292mg; CALC 102mg

Fettuccine with Shrimp and Portobellos

Serve this entrée in a bowl with toasted bread to soak up every drop of the flavorful broth.

8 ounces uncooked fettuccine
1 (4-inch) portobello mushroom cap (about 5 ounces)
1 tablespoon olive oil
1 cup finely chopped onion
¼ cup chopped fresh flat-leaf parsley
¼ teaspoon salt
1 garlic clove, minced
1 cup fat-free, less-sodium chicken broth
¼ cup dry white wine
¾ pound large shrimp, peeled and deveined
½ cup (2 ounces) shredded Asiago cheese
1 tablespoon chopped fresh chives

1 Cook pasta according to package directions, omitting salt and fat. Drain and rinse with cold water; drain.

2 Remove brown gills from underside of mushroom cap using a spoon; discard gills. Cut cap into thin slices. Cut slices in half crosswise.

3 Heat oil in a large saucepan over medium-high heat. Add mushroom, onion, parsley, salt, and garlic; sauté 4 minutes or until mushroom releases moisture, stirring frequently. Stir in broth, wine, and shrimp; bring to a boil. Add pasta, and cook 3 minutes or until shrimp are done, tossing to combine. Sprinkle with cheese and chives. Yield: 4 servings (serving size: 1¾ cups shrimp mixture, 2 tablespoons cheese, and about 1 teaspoon chives).

CALORIES 384 (21% from fat); FAT 9.1g (sat 3.3g, mono 2.7g, poly 0.9g); PROTEIN 23.8g; CARB 48.9g; FIBER 2.8g; CHOL 114mg; IRON 4.5mg; SODIUM 540mg; CALC 156mg

MENU *serves 4*

Fettuccine with Shrimp and Portobellos

Arugula salad

Combine 1 tablespoon fresh lemon juice, 2 teaspoons extra-virgin olive oil, ¼ teaspoon kosher salt, ⅛ teaspoon cracked black pepper, and 1 minced garlic clove. Place 1½ cups arugula on each of 4 salad plates. Drizzle dressing evenly over salads. Shave 1 ounce fresh Parmesan cheese; divide evenly among salads.

Garlic bread

Game Plan

1 While water boils:
 • Peel and devein shrimp.
 • Clean and slice mushroom.
 • Chop onion and parsley.
 • Mince garlic for fettuccine and salad.
2 While pasta cooks:
 • Cook mushroom mixture.
 • Prepare salad.
 • Shred cheese.

Shrimp Pad Thai

Pad Thai is the most popular noodle dish in Thailand. Pungent fish sauce (also called nam pla) is an important flavoring for this dish; you can find it in the Asian foods section of most large supermarkets or Asian markets. Substitute 4 cups hot cooked linguine for the rice stick noodles if you have trouble finding them.

MENU *serves 6*

Shrimp Pad Thai

Spicy cucumber salad
Combine 2 cups thinly sliced seeded peeled cucumber, 1 cup julienne-cut red bell pepper, and ¼ cup thinly sliced red onion in a large bowl. Combine 1 tablespoon sugar, 2 tablespoons fresh lime juice, 1 tablespoon fish sauce, and ½ teaspoon crushed red pepper in a small bowl. Pour dressing over vegetables; toss to combine.

Lemon sorbet

Game Plan

1 While water for noodles heats:

- Prepare cucumber salad.

2 While noodles soak:

- Peel and devein shrimp.

- Combine sauce ingredients.

- Beat eggs.

- Slice green onions.

8 ounces wide rice stick noodles (Banh Pho)
¼ cup ketchup
3 tablespoons fish sauce
2 tablespoons sugar
½ teaspoon crushed red pepper
2 tablespoons vegetable oil, divided
1 pound medium shrimp, peeled and deveined
2 large eggs, lightly beaten
1 cup fresh bean sprouts
¾ cup (1-inch) sliced green onions
1 teaspoon bottled minced garlic
2 tablespoons chopped unsalted, dry-roasted peanuts

❶ Place noodles in a large bowl. Add hot water to cover; let stand 12 minutes or until tender. Drain, and set aside.
❷ Combine ketchup, fish sauce, sugar, and pepper in a small bowl.

❸ Heat 2 teaspoons oil in a large nonstick skillet over medium-high heat. Add shrimp; sauté 2 minutes or until shrimp are done. Remove shrimp from pan; keep warm.
❹ Heat 4 teaspoons oil in pan over medium-high heat. Add eggs to pan; cook 30 seconds or until soft-scrambled, stirring constantly. Add sprouts, green onions, and garlic to pan; cook 1 minute. Add noodles, ketchup mixture, and shrimp to pan; cook 3 minutes or until heated. Sprinkle shrimp and noodle mixture evenly with peanuts. Yield: 6 servings (serving size: 1½ cups).

CALORIES 343 (24% from fat); FAT 9.2g (sat 1.6g, mono 2.6g, poly 3.9g); PROTEIN 21.3g; CARB 42.4g; FIBER 1.4g; CHOL 186mg; IRON 3mg; SODIUM 912mg; CALC 60mg

Quick Tip:
Ask the folks in the seafood department of your supermarket to peel and devein the shrimp to help you save time when preparing this recipe.

Grilled Teriyaki Shrimp Kebabs

You can also brush this versatile sauce over cubed skinless, boneless chicken breasts or thighs. Or use it as a dipping sauce with spring rolls.

SAUCE:
- ¼ cup low-sodium teriyaki sauce
- 1 tablespoon sesame seeds, toasted

KEBABS:
- 48 large peeled and deveined shrimp (about 1½ pounds)
- 32 (1-inch) pieces cubed fresh pineapple (about ¾ pound)
- 1 red onion, cut into 8 wedges
- Cooking spray

❶ Prepare grill.
❷ To prepare sauce, combine teriyaki sauce and sesame seeds in a small bowl.

❸ To prepare kebabs, thread 6 shrimp, 4 pineapple cubes, and 1 onion wedge alternately onto each of 8 (10-inch) skewers. Brush kebabs with teriyaki mixture. Place kebabs on a grill rack coated with cooking spray; grill 8 minutes or until shrimp are done, turning once. Yield: 4 servings (serving size: 2 kebabs).

CALORIES 254 (14% from fat); FAT 4g (sat 0.7g, mono 0.8g, poly 1.6g); PROTEIN 35.6g; CARB 17.6g; FIBER 1.9g; CHOL 259mg; IRON 4.6mg; SODIUM 514mg; CALC 110mg

Quick Tip:
Use cubed pineapple from the supermarket produce section. It costs a bit more, but using it will be worth the time you'll save putting this supper together.

MENU *serves 4*

Grilled Teriyaki Shrimp Kebabs

Mashed sweet potatoes
Microwave 1 (24-ounce) package refrigerated mashed sweet potatoes according to package directions. Stir in 1 teaspoon butter, 1 teaspoon maple syrup, and ¼ teaspoon salt. Sprinkle with ½ teaspoon toasted sesame seeds. Keep warm until ready to serve.

Grilled asparagus

Game Plan

1 While skewers soak:
 - •Preheat grill.
 - •Trim asparagus.
 - •Prepare mashed sweet potatoes; keep warm.

2 Prepare kebabs.

3 Grill kebabs and asparagus.

Shrimp Saté with Pineapple Salsa

Buy peeled, cored fresh pineapple for the salsa. Enjoy the rest of it in a fresh fruit salad.

SALSA:

- ¾ cup finely chopped pineapple
- ¼ cup finely chopped red onion
- 1 tablespoon minced seeded jalapeño pepper
- 1 tablespoon chopped fresh cilantro
- 1 tablespoon cider vinegar
- 1 teaspoon honey

SATÉ:

- 2 tablespoons chopped fresh mint
- 2 tablespoons fresh lime juice
- ¼ teaspoon salt
- ¼ teaspoon chili powder
- 24 large shrimp, peeled and deveined (about 1½ pounds)

Cooking spray

- 4 cilantro sprigs (optional)

1 Prepare grill.

2 To prepare salsa, combine first 6 ingredients in a medium bowl.

3 To prepare saté, combine mint, juice, salt, and chili powder in a large bowl; add shrimp, tossing gently to coat. Thread 3 shrimp onto each of 8 (6-inch) skewers. Place shrimp on grill rack coated with cooking spray; grill 1½ minutes on each side or until shrimp turn pink. Serve with salsa. Garnish with cilantro sprigs, if desired. Yield: 4 servings (serving size: 2 skewers and ¼ cup salsa).

CALORIES 208 (13% from fat); FAT 3g (sat 0.6g, mono 0.4g, poly 1.2g); PROTEIN 34.9g; CARB 8.7g; FIBER 0.7g; CHOL 259mg; IRON 4.3mg; SODIUM 403mg; CALC 98mg

Shrimp with Lemon, Mint, and Goat Cheese

You can also serve this saucy shrimp mixture over a thin pasta in place of the garlic bread.

1 tablespoon olive oil

6 small garlic cloves, minced

2¼ pounds peeled and deveined large shrimp

1 cup frozen green peas, thawed

¾ cup thinly sliced green onions

¼ cup mirin (sweet rice wine)

1 teaspoon grated lemon rind

2 tablespoons fresh lemon juice

½ teaspoon salt

4 plum tomatoes, diced (about 1 pound)

½ cup chopped fresh mint

½ cup (2 ounces) crumbled goat cheese

❶ Heat oil in a large nonstick skillet over medium-high heat. Add garlic to pan; sauté 1 minute or until browned. Add shrimp to pan; cook 1 to 2 minutes, stirring constantly. Add peas and next 6 ingredients to pan; cook 8 minutes or until shrimp are done. Top each serving evenly with mint and goat cheese. Yield: 6 servings (serving size: 1 cup shrimp mixture, 4 teaspoons mint, and 4 teaspoons goat cheese).

CALORIES 286 (22% from fat); FAT 7.1g (sat 2.7g, mono 2.6g, poly 1.2g); PROTEIN 40.3g; CARB 11.8g; FIBER 2.6g; CHOL 337mg; IRON 7.3mg; SODIUM 660mg; CALC 125mg

MENU *serves 6*

Shrimp with Lemon, Mint, and Goat Cheese

Marinated mushrooms

Combine 1 teaspoon grated orange rind, ½ cup fresh orange juice, 2 tablespoons white wine vinegar, 2 tablespoons honey, 1 tablespoon olive oil, 1 tablespoon chopped fresh tarragon, and 2 (8-ounce) packages quartered button mushrooms. Add ½ teaspoon salt and ¼ teaspoon pepper. Let stand 20 minutes before serving, stirring occasionally.

Garlic bread

Game Plan

1 While mushrooms marinate:

- Prepare vegetables for shrimp dish.
- Grate lemon rind and squeeze juice.

2 While shrimp mixture cooks:

- Chop mint.

MENU *serves 4*

Spicy Passion Fruit-Glazed Shrimp

Jasmine rice pilaf with pistachios

Heat 1 tablespoon olive oil in a medium saucepan over medium-high heat. Add ⅓ cup chopped shallots and 2 minced garlic cloves; sauté 2 minutes. Add 1 cup jasmine rice; sauté 1 minute. Stir in 2 cups fat-free, less-sodium chicken broth and ½ teaspoon salt; bring to a boil. Cover, reduce heat, and simmer 20 minutes or until rice is done. Stir in ¼ cup chopped toasted pistachios and 2 tablespoons chopped cilantro.

Sautéed yellow squash and red bell peppers

Game Plan

1 Prepare fruit mixture.

2 While passion fruit mixture cools:

  • Soak skewers.

  • Peel and devein shrimp.

3 While shrimp marinates:

  • Preheat grill.

  • Prepare shallots, garlic, cilantro, and pistachios for rice.

  • Sauté rice mixture.

4 While rice simmers:

  • Prepare yellow squash and red bell peppers.

  • Thread shrimp on skewers.

5 Grill shrimp.

Spicy Passion Fruit-Glazed Shrimp

Passion fruit gives the glaze a sweet-and-sour taste. It's not necessary to strain the pulp initially; the seeds will be strained when preparing the glaze. When straining the glaze, press with the back of a spoon to extract as much passion fruit pulp as possible. Serve these kebabs over a bed of basmati or jasmine rice.

½ cup water
½ cup sugar
½ cup passion fruit pulp (about 4 passion fruit)
2 tablespoons fresh lime juice
1 teaspoon low-sodium soy sauce
½ teaspoon crushed red pepper
¼ teaspoon salt
32 large shrimp, peeled and deveined (about 1½ pounds)
Cooking spray
8 lime wedges

❶ Bring water and sugar to a boil in a small saucepan, stirring frequently until sugar dissolves. Add passion fruit pulp, stirring well; cook 1 minute. Remove from heat, and cool 15 minutes.

❷ Strain passion fruit mixture through a sieve into a large bowl; discard seeds. Add lime juice, soy sauce, red pepper, and salt, stirring well. Set ½ cup fruit mixture aside. Add shrimp to remaining passion fruit mixture, and toss well to coat. Cover and refrigerate 15 minutes.

❸ Prepare grill.

❹ Thread 4 shrimp on each of 8 (10-inch) skewers. Place skewers on grill rack coated with cooking spray. Grill 2 minutes on each side or until done, basting with reserved ½ cup passion fruit mixture. Serve with lime wedges. Yield: 4 servings (serving size: 2 skewers and 2 lime wedges).

CALORIES 277 (10% from fat); FAT 3.1g (sat 0.6g, mono 0.5g, poly 1.2g); PROTEIN 35.2g; CARB 26.2g; FIBER 0.7g; CHOL 259mg; IRON 4.5mg; SODIUM 403mg; CALC 92mg

Shrimp Potpies with Oyster Cracker Topping

These individual servings make a special entrée, whether you're serving them at a week-night dinner for your family or entertaining a small group.

1 tablespoon butter
1 cup chopped onion
½ cup chopped celery
½ cup chopped carrot
2 garlic cloves, minced
2 tablespoons brandy
½ cup half-and-half
3 tablespoons tomato paste
2 (8-ounce) bottles clam juice
1½ tablespoons cornstarch
1 tablespoon water
2 tablespoons chopped fresh parsley
¼ teaspoon salt
¼ teaspoon freshly ground black pepper
¾ pound cooked shrimp, chopped (about 1½ cups)
Cooking spray
1 cup oyster crackers, coarsely crushed

❶ Preheat oven to 400°.
❷ Melt butter in a large nonstick skillet over medium-high heat. Add onion, celery, carrot, and garlic; sauté 5 minutes or until tender. Add brandy; cook 30 seconds. Stir in half-and-half, tomato paste, and clam juice; bring to a boil. Cook 4 minutes, stirring occasionally. Combine cornstarch and 1 tablespoon water. Add cornstarch mixture, parsley, salt, pepper, and shrimp to pan; cook 1 minute, stirring constantly.
❸ Divide shrimp mixture evenly among 4 (10-ounce) ramekins coated with cooking spray. Top each serving with ¼ cup cracker crumbs. Arrange ramekins on a baking sheet. Bake at 400° for 10 minutes or until bubbly and lightly browned. Yield: 4 servings (serving size: 1 potpie).

CALORIES 267 (30% from fat); FAT 8.8g (sat 4.4g, mono 2.8g, poly 0.8g); PROTEIN 21.5g; CARB 19.9g; FIBER 1.8g; CHOL 188mg; IRON 4.5mg; SODIUM 875mg; CALC 111mg

MENU *serves 4*

Shrimp Potpies with Oyster Cracker Topping

Fruit salad with lemon-ginger dressing
Combine 2 cups halved strawberries, 1 cup cubed cantaloupe, and 1 cup cubed pineapple in a medium bowl. Combine 1½ tablespoons honey, 1 tablespoon fresh lemon juice, 1 teaspoon olive oil, and ¼ teaspoon minced peeled fresh ginger in a small bowl; stir with a whisk. Drizzle over fruit; toss to coat.

Garlic bread

Game Plan

1 While oven heats:
• Prepare potpies.

2 While potpies bake:
• Prepare fruit salad.
• Prepare garlic bread.

MENU *serves 4*

Shrimp Tacos

Corn and avocado salsa

Combine 2 cups fresh corn kernels, ⅓ cup peeled and diced avocado, ¼ cup finely chopped red onion, 2 tablespoons chopped fresh cilantro, 1 tablespoon fresh lime juice, and ½ teaspoon salt.

Lemon sorbet

Game Plan

1 Peel and devein shrimp.

2 Cut limes into quarters.

3 Bring cooking water for shrimp to a boil.

4 While cooking water comes to a boil:

• Chop cilantro, avocado, jalapeño, and red onion.

• Cut kernels off corn cobs.

• Squeeze lime for juice for salsa and tacos.

5 While shrimp cooks:

• Chop tomato and green onions.

Shrimp Tacos

Shredded rotisserie chicken or flaked, cooked fish also works well in these tasty tacos.

    3 tablespoons black peppercorns
    3 quarts water
    1 tablespoon salt
    1 teaspoon ground red pepper
    2 limes, quartered
    1 pound medium shrimp, peeled
       and deveined
    ½ cup coarsely chopped fresh
       cilantro
    ¼ cup fresh lime juice
    1 tablespoon minced seeded
       jalapeño pepper
   12 (6-inch) corn tortillas
    ¾ cup chopped peeled tomato
    ½ cup reduced-fat sour cream
    ½ cup chopped green onions

❶ Place peppercorns on a double layer of cheesecloth. Gather edges of cheesecloth together, and tie securely. Combine cheesecloth bag, water, salt, red pepper, and lime quarters in a Dutch oven. Bring to a boil; cook 2 minutes. Add shrimp; cook 2 minutes or until done. Drain. Discard cheesecloth bag and lime quarters.

❷ Combine shrimp, cilantro, lime juice, and jalapeño pepper, tossing well to coat. Heat tortillas according to package directions. Spoon ⅓ cup shrimp mixture into each tortilla; top each taco with 1 tablespoon tomato, 2 teaspoons sour cream, and 2 teaspoons onions. Yield: 4 servings (serving size: 3 tacos).

CALORIES 358 (20% from fat); FAT 7.8g (sat 3g, mono 0.8g, poly 1.7g); PROTEIN 29.3g; CARB 43.6g; FIBER 5.1g; CHOL 188mg; IRON 4.1mg; SODIUM 612mg; CALC 250mg

Quick Tip: The corn and avocado salsa and these tacos call for chopped cilantro and fresh lime juice, so measure for both recipes at the same time if you're preparing the entire menu.

Chipotle-Spiced Shrimp

A fresh green salad rounds out this weeknight meal. Follow our recipe for a quick home-made vinaigrette, or use a light bottled dressing in a pinch. Chipotle chile powder adds smoky, slightly sweet spiciness to the dish. Hot paprika makes a good substitute, or use sweet paprika for a milder heat.

1	(3½-ounce) bag boil-in-bag long-grain rice
2½	tablespoons butter, divided
1	teaspoon bottled minced garlic
¼	teaspoon salt
¼	teaspoon chipotle chile powder
36	large shrimp, peeled and deveined (about 1 pound)
2	tablespoons dry vermouth
1	tablespoon fresh lime juice
¼	teaspoon sugar
2	tablespoons chopped fresh cilantro

❶ Cook rice according to package directions, omitting salt and fat.

❷ Melt 1½ tablespoons butter in a large non-stick skillet over medium-high heat. Add garlic to pan; sauté 30 seconds. Add salt, chile powder, and shrimp to pan; sauté 2 minutes. Stir in vermouth, juice, and sugar; cook 2 minutes or until shrimp are done. Remove from heat; stir in 1 tablespoon butter and cilantro. Serve over rice. Yield: 4 servings (serving size: 9 shrimp and about ½ cup rice).

CALORIES 290 (29% from fat); FAT 9.3g (sat 4.9g, mono 2.2g, poly 1.1g); PROTEIN 25.4g; CARB 24.3g; FIBER 0.4g; CHOL 191mg; IRON 3.8mg; SODIUM 317mg; CALC 73mg

MENU *serves 4*

Chipotle-Spiced Shrimp

Green salad
Combine 6 cups mixed salad greens, 2 cups halved cherry tomatoes, 1 cup thinly sliced radish, and ½ cup thinly sliced red onion in a large bowl. Combine 2 table-spoons sherry vinegar, 1 tablespoon extra-virgin olive oil, 1 teaspoon Dijon mustard, ½ teaspoon salt, and ¼ teaspoon freshly ground black pepper in a small bowl; stir with a whisk. Drizzle dressing over salad mixture.

Angel food cake with fresh strawberries

Game Plan

1. Peel and devein shrimp.
2. While water for rice comes to a boil:
   - Prepare vegetables for salad.
3. While rice cooks:
   - Assemble salad.
   - Squeeze lime for juice for shrimp, and chop cilantro.
   - Sauté shrimp.
4. Prepare dessert.

Border-Style Shrimp

Potatoes bravas

Heat 1 tablespoon olive oil in a large nonstick skillet over medium-high heat. Add 1 (20-ounce) package refrigerated prepared potato wedges (such as Simply Potatoes); cook 5 minutes or until lightly browned, stirring occasionally. Add ½ teaspoon ground cumin, ½ teaspoon crushed red pepper, and 1 (14.5-ounce) can diced tomatoes, drained; cook 5 minutes, stirring frequently. Stir in 2 teaspoons lime juice and ½ teaspoon coarse salt.

Bagged coleslaw mix with bottled vinaigrette

Game Plan

1 Peel and devein shrimp.

2 While skillets heat for potatoes and shrimp:

  • Chop onion, mince garlic, and squeeze lime for juice for potatoes and shrimp.

  • Measure spices for potatoes and shrimp.

3 While shrimp and potatoes cook:

  • Prepare coleslaw.

Border-Style Shrimp

Ready in just 15 minutes, this colorful Tex-Mex dish is a festive and flavorful weeknight meal.

Cooking spray
1½ cups chopped white onion
1 teaspoon ground cumin
1 teaspoon chili powder
1½ pounds medium shrimp, peeled and deveined
2 garlic cloves, minced
2 tablespoons butter
½ teaspoon salt
⅛ teaspoon hot pepper sauce
¼ cup fresh lime juice
¼ cup finely chopped green onions
Lime wedges (optional)

❶ Heat a large nonstick skillet over medium-high heat; coat with cooking spray. Add onion to pan, and sauté 3 minutes. Add cumin, chili powder, shrimp, and garlic to pan; sauté 4 minutes. Remove pan from heat; add butter, salt, and hot sauce to pan. Stir just until butter melts. Stir in lime juice and green onions. Garnish with lime wedges, if desired. Yield: 4 servings (serving size: about 1 cup shrimp).

CALORIES 266 (30% from fat); FAT 9g (sat 4.1g, mono 2.1g, poly 1.4g); PROTEIN 35.6g; CARB 9.7g; FIBER 1.8g; CHOL 274mg; IRON 4.5mg; SODIUM 618mg; CALC 113mg

Quick Tip: Have the seafood counter at your supermarket peel and devein the shrimp for you while you finish shopping.

Seafood Lasagna

This shrimp- and scallop-filled lasagna is refined enough for a dinner party. Assemble the lasagna up to a day ahead, and bake just before serving. The refrigerated dish may require an extra 5 to 10 minutes in the oven.

1½ ounces all-purpose flour (about ⅓ cup)
3 cups 2% reduced-fat milk
1 tablespoon butter
1 tablespoon chopped fresh thyme
¼ teaspoon salt
¼ teaspoon freshly ground black pepper
2 cups (8 ounces) grated Parmigiano-Reggiano cheese, divided
⅛ teaspoon grated whole nutmeg
Cooking spray
2 cups thinly sliced onion
6 garlic cloves, minced
⅓ cup (3 ounces) block-style ⅓-less-fat cream cheese, softened
½ cup half-and-half
½ cup chopped fresh parsley, divided
¾ pound medium shrimp, peeled, deveined, and coarsely chopped
¾ pound scallops, coarsely chopped
3 large eggs
1 (15-ounce) carton fat-free ricotta cheese
12 no-cook lasagna noodles

1 Preheat oven to 350°.

2 Lightly spoon flour into a dry measuring cup; level with a knife. Place a large saucepan over medium heat; add flour to pan. Gradually add milk to pan, stirring constantly with a whisk until smooth; cook 1 minute. Stir in butter, thyme, salt, and pepper; bring to a boil. Cook 5 minutes or until thick, stirring constantly. Remove pan from heat; stir in 1¼ cups Parmigiano and nutmeg. Set cheese sauce aside.

3 Heat a large nonstick skillet over medium-high heat; coat with cooking spray. Add onion; sauté 4 minutes. Add garlic; sauté 1 minute. Remove from heat. Add cream cheese; stir until cheese melts. Stir in half-and-half, ¼ cup parsley, shrimp, and scallops. Place eggs and ricotta in a food processor; process until smooth. Stir ricotta mixture into seafood mixture.

4 Spoon 1 cup cheese sauce into bottom of a 13 x 9–inch baking dish coated with cooking spray. Arrange 4 noodles over sauce; top with half of ricotta mixture. Repeat layers with 4 noodles, remaining ricotta mixture, and 4 noodles. Pour remaining cheese sauce over noodles; sprinkle with ¾ cup Parmigiano. Bake at 350° for 45 minutes or until lightly browned. Sprinkle lasagna with ¼ cup parsley. Let stand 10 minutes before serving.
Yield: 12 servings (serving size: 1 piece).

CALORIES 383 (30% from fat); FAT 12.9g (sat 7g, mono 3.6g, poly 0.9g); PROTEIN 31.5g; CARB 33.1g; FIBER 1.4g; CHOL 150mg; IRON 3.3mg; SODIUM 583mg; CALC 428mg

MENU *serves 12*

Seafood Lasagna

Garlic breadsticks
Preheat oven to 375°. Unroll 1 (11-ounce) can refrigerated breadstick dough; separate it into 12 pieces. Combine 3 tablespoons grated Parmesan cheese and 1½ teaspoons minced garlic. Brush 1 tablespoon butter evenly over dough pieces. Sprinkle cheese mixture evenly over dough pieces; press lightly. Twist each piece several times, forming spirals. Bake at 375° for 13 minutes or until lightly browned.

Tossed salad

Game Plan

1 Peel, devein, and coarsely chop shrimp.

2 Coarsely chop scallops.

3 Prepare and measure ingredients for lasagna.

4 Prepare cheese sauce and seafood mixture.

5 While lasagna bakes:
  • Prepare breadstick dough.

6 While lasagna stands:
  • Increase oven temperature to 375°.
  • Bake breadsticks.
  • Prepare salad.

Meats

Spicy Pork Tenderloins with Uniq Fruit Salsa,
page 275

Barbecue Meat Loaf

Use your family's favorite barbecue sauce to top this easy-to-prepare meat loaf.

1½ pounds ground beef, extra lean
½ cup dry breadcrumbs
½ cup chopped onion
1 tablespoon barbecue sauce
1 tablespoon prepared mustard
1½ teaspoons chili powder
1 teaspoon garlic powder
½ teaspoon salt
½ teaspoon freshly ground black
   pepper
2 large egg whites, lightly beaten
Cooking spray
¼ cup plus 1 teaspoon barbecue sauce

❶ Preheat oven to 350°.
❷ Combine first 10 ingredients in a large bowl.
❸ Shape meat mixture into a 9 x 5-inch loaf on a broiler pan coated with cooking spray. Spread ¼ cup plus 1 teaspoon barbecue sauce over top of meat loaf. Bake at 350° for 1 hour or until a thermometer registers 160°. Let stand 10 minutes. Cut loaf into 12 slices. Yield: 6 servings (serving size: 2 slices).

CALORIES 203 (24% from fat); FAT 5.4g (sat 2.2g, mono 2.2g, poly 0.5g); PROTEIN 27.3g; CARB 10.5g; FIBER 1.1g; CHOL 61mg; IRON 3.2mg; SODIUM 517mg; CALC 26mg

MENU *serves 6*

Barbecue Meat Loaf

Creamy coleslaw
Combine ⅓ cup reduced-fat mayonnaise, 2 tablespoons cider vinegar, ¼ teaspoon salt, and ¼ teaspoon ground red pepper in a small bowl; stir with a whisk to blend. Combine 1 (12-ounce) bag coleslaw, ½ cup diced red bell pepper, and ½ cup diced yellow bell pepper in a large bowl. Add dressing, stirring well to combine.

Dinner rolls

Game Plan

1 While oven heats:
   • Prepare meatloaf.
2 Bake meatloaf.
3 While meatloaf stands:
   • Heat dinner rolls.
   • Prepare coleslaw.

Stuffed Peppers

Spiced beef and rice fill these tender, flavorful peppers. Bringing the sauce to a boil before adding it to the dish cuts down on the overall cook time of this 45-minute recipe.

1 (3½-ounce) bag boil-in-bag long-grain rice
4 red bell peppers
¾ pound ground sirloin
1 cup chopped onion
½ cup chopped fresh parsley
1 teaspoon paprika
½ teaspoon salt
⅛ teaspoon ground allspice
2 cups bottled tomato-and-basil pasta sauce (such as Classico), divided
½ cup (2 ounces) grated fresh Parmesan cheese
½ cup dry red wine
Cooking spray

1 Preheat oven to 450°.
2 Cook rice according to package directions, omitting salt and fat. Set aside.
3 While rice cooks, cut tops off bell peppers; reserve tops. Discard seeds and membranes. Place peppers, cut sides down, in an 8-inch square baking dish; cover with plastic wrap. Microwave at HIGH 2 minutes or until peppers are crisp-tender. Cool.
4 Heat a large nonstick skillet over medium-high heat. Add beef and next 5 ingredients; cook 4 minutes or until beef is lightly browned, stirring to crumble. Remove from heat. Add rice, ½ cup pasta sauce, and cheese to beef mixture, stirring to combine.
5 While beef cooks, combine 1½ cups pasta sauce and wine in a small saucepan; bring to a boil.
6 Spoon about ¾ cup beef mixture into each pepper. Place peppers in a 2-quart baking dish coated with cooking spray; add wine mixture to dish. Cover with foil.
7 Bake at 450° for 20 minutes. Uncover; bake an additional 5 minutes or until lightly browned. Serve peppers with sauce. Garnish with pepper tops. Yield: 4 servings (serving size: 1 stuffed pepper and ⅓ cup sauce).

CALORIES 347 (20% from fat); FAT 7.9g (sat 3.9g, mono 2.6g, poly 0.7g); PROTEIN 26.6g; CARB 39.9g; FIBER 4.6g; CHOL 55mg; IRON 4.1mg; SODIUM 747mg; CALC 284mg

Mini Meat Loaves

Cooking meat loaf in single-serving portions cuts cooking time in half and keeps the meat juicy. The tangy ketchup-mustard glaze helps these loaves brown nicely, too.

½ cup ketchup
1½ tablespoons Dijon mustard
1 pound ground sirloin
¾ cup finely chopped onion
¼ cup seasoned breadcrumbs
½ teaspoon salt
½ teaspoon dried oregano
⅛ teaspoon black pepper
1 large egg, lightly beaten
Cooking spray

❶ Preheat oven to 400°.
❷ Combine ketchup and mustard; stir with a whisk. Reserve 2½ tablespoons ketchup mixture. Combine remaining ketchup mixture, beef, and next 6 ingredients in a large bowl, stirring to combine.

❸ Divide beef mixture into 4 equal portions. Shape each portion into a 4 x 2½-inch loaf; place loaves on a jelly-roll pan coated with cooking spray.
❹ Spread about 2 teaspoons reserved ketchup mixture evenly over each loaf. Bake at 400° for 25 minutes or until done. Yield: 4 servings (serving size: 1 loaf).

CALORIES 255 (28% from fat); FAT 7.9g (sat 2.8g, mono 3.2g, poly 0.4g); PROTEIN 27.4g; CARB 15.7g; FIBER 0.9g; CHOL 120mg; IRON 2.7mg; SODIUM 944mg; CALC 31mg

Quick Tip: Using seasoned breadcrumbs rather than the plain variety reduces the need for extra spices in the ingredients list.

MENU *serves 4*

Mini Meat Loaves

Steak house-style lettuce wedges

Combine 2 tablespoons crumbled blue cheese, 1 tablespoon fat-free buttermilk, 2 tablespoons fat-free sour cream, 1 tablespoon light mayonnaise, ¾ teaspoon white vinegar, and ¼ teaspoon salt; stir with a whisk. Cut a small head of iceberg lettuce into 4 wedges; place 1 wedge on each of 4 plates. Drizzle each wedge with about 1½ tablespoons dressing.

Mashed potatoes

Game Plan

1 While oven heats for meat loaves:

• Combine ketchup and mustard.

• Chop onion.

2 While meat loaves bake:

• Prepare lettuce wedges.

• Prepare mashed potatoes.

Beef and Vegetable Potpie

The beef filling is first cooked in a large skillet on the stove top and then spooned into a baking dish. Finish the casserole in the oven to brown the breadstick dough topping.

    1   tablespoon olive oil, divided
    1   pound ground sirloin
    2   cups chopped zucchini
    1   cup prechopped onion
    1   cup chopped carrot
    1   teaspoon dried basil
    ½   teaspoon dried thyme
    1   (8-ounce) package presliced mushrooms
    3   garlic cloves, minced
    ½   cup dry red wine
    ¼   cup tomato paste
    1½ teaspoons Worcestershire sauce
    ½   teaspoon freshly ground black pepper
    1   (14-ounce) can fat-free, less-sodium beef broth
    2   tablespoons cornstarch
    2   tablespoons water
Cooking spray
    1   (11-ounce) can refrigerated soft breadstick dough

1 Preheat oven to 400°.

2 Heat 1½ teaspoons oil in a large nonstick skillet over medium-high heat. Add beef; cook 3 minutes or until browned, stirring to crumble. Drain. Wipe drippings from pan with a paper towel. Heat 1½ teaspoons oil in pan. Add zucchini and next 6 ingredients; sauté 7 minutes or until vegetables are tender. Return beef to pan. Stir in wine and next 4 ingredients. Bring to a boil; cook 3 minutes. Combine cornstarch and 2 tablespoons water in a small bowl; stir with a whisk. Add cornstarch mixture to pan; cook 1 minute, stirring constantly.

3 Spoon beef mixture into an 11 x 7–inch baking dish coated with cooking spray. Separate breadstick dough into strips. Arrange strips in a lattice fashion over beef mixture. Bake at 400° for 12 minutes or until browned. Yield: 6 servings (serving size: 1⅓ cups).

CALORIES 313 (24% from fat); FAT 8.5g (sat 1.7g, mono 3g, poly 0.7g); PROTEIN 22g; CARB 37.6g; FIBER 2.7g; CHOL 40mg; IRON 3.9mg; SODIUM 679mg; CALC 41mg

Quick Tip: Remove the can of breadsticks from the refrigerator before you prepare the filling. The dough will be more pliable and easier to handle if it is at room temperature.

Steak, Shiitake, and Bok Choy Stir-Fry

Pick up sliced onions, bell peppers, and mushrooms at your supermarket deli salad bar. You can use Asian stir-fry greens (usually a mix of bok choy and mustard greens) from the produce aisle in place of bok choy.

2 tablespoons grated peeled fresh ginger
1 tablespoon minced fresh garlic
3 tablespoons low-sodium soy sauce
4 teaspoons cornstarch, divided
1 teaspoon toasted sesame oil
½ teaspoon crushed red pepper
1 pound flank steak, trimmed and thinly sliced
Cooking spray
2 cups thinly sliced shiitake mushrooms (about ½ pound)
1 cup thinly vertically sliced onion
1 cup red bell pepper strips
4 cups sliced bok choy (about 1 medium head)
1 cup less-sodium beef broth

❶ Combine ginger, garlic, soy sauce, 2 teaspoons cornstarch, oil, and crushed red pepper in a large zip-top bag; add steak to bag. Seal and marinate in refrigerator 20 minutes.
❷ Heat a large nonstick skillet over medium-high heat; coat with cooking spray. Add mushrooms, onion, and bell pepper to pan. Cook 3 minutes or until crisp-tender; transfer to a large bowl. Add bok choy to pan; sauté 2 minutes or until slightly wilted; add to bowl; keep warm.
❸ Recoat pan with cooking spray. Add half of steak mixture to pan; cook 3 minutes or until browned, stirring occasionally. Transfer to a large bowl; keep warm. Recoat pan with cooking spray. Add remaining steak mixture to pan; cook 3 minutes or until browned, stirring occasionally. Add to bowl; keep warm.
❹ Combine broth and remaining 2 teaspoons cornstarch; stir with a whisk. Add mixture to pan, scraping pan to loosen browned bits. Bring to a boil, and cook 1 minute or until mixture thickens, stirring constantly. Return steak and vegetables to pan; toss gently to coat. Yield: 4 servings (serving size: about 1½ cups).

CALORIES 270 (30% from fat); FAT 9g (sat 3.1g, mono 3.2g, poly 1g); PROTEIN 28.6g; CARB 16.9g; FIBER 3.4g; CHOL 45mg; IRON 4.5mg; SODIUM 706mg; CALC 244mg

---

MENU *serves 4*

Steak, Shiitake, and Bok Choy Stir-Fry

Jasmine rice
Bring 2 cups water, 1 tablespoon unsalted butter, and ½ teaspoon salt to a boil in a medium saucepan; add 2 cups jasmine rice. Cover, reduce heat, and simmer 20 minutes or until liquid is absorbed. Fluff with a fork. Stir in ⅓ cup sliced green onions.

Coconut sorbet with fresh mangoes

Game Plan

1 While steak marinates:
   • Slice vegetables for stir-fry.
   • Boil water for rice.

2 While rice simmers:
   • Cook vegetables and steak.

3 Prepare sorbet following dinner or just before serving.

Rice Noodles with Sesame-Ginger Flank Steak

Have all the vegetables ready to go—once you start, the cooking goes quickly. If you can't find fresh sugar snap peas, use thawed frozen peas, and add them to the dish when you return the steak to the pan. You can also save time by purchasing toasted sesame seeds at Asian markets. Look for bags of shredded carrots in the produce section of your supermarket.

⅓ cup rice vinegar
3 tablespoons low-sodium soy sauce
1 tablespoon hoisin sauce
2 teaspoons cornstarch
2 teaspoons grated peeled fresh ginger
1½ teaspoons sugar
¼ teaspoon salt
3 garlic cloves, minced
2 teaspoons dark sesame oil, divided
1 (1-pound) flank steak, trimmed and cut into ¼-inch strips
1½ cups shredded carrot
1½ cups sugar snap peas, trimmed
1 cup (¼-inch) red bell pepper strips
½ cup fresh bean sprouts
4 cups hot cooked rice noodles (about 8 ounces uncooked noodles)
½ cup chopped green onions
1 tablespoon sesame seeds, toasted

❶ Combine first 8 ingredients, stirring until sugar dissolves.

❷ Heat a large nonstick skillet over medium-high heat. Add 1 teaspoon oil. Add half of steak; sauté 4 minutes or until browned. Remove steak from pan. Repeat procedure with 1 teaspoon oil and remaining steak. Add vinegar mixture, carrot, peas, bell pepper, and sprouts to pan; cook 3 minutes, stirring frequently. Return steak to pan. Add noodles; cook 1 minute, stirring constantly. Sprinkle with onions and sesame seeds. Yield: 6 servings (serving size: 1⅓ cups).

CALORIES 369 (25% from fat); FAT 10.4g (sat 3.7g, mono 4g, poly 1.4g); PROTEIN 24.3g; CARB 42.9g; FIBER 4.4g; CHOL 51mg; IRON 3.1mg; SODIUM 542mg; CALC 63mg

Quick Tip: To grate ginger easily, place a small piece in a garlic press and squeeze as you would for garlic.

MENU serves 6

Rice Noodles with Sesame-Ginger Flank Steak

Orange sections tossed with chopped fresh mint

Herbed green tea
Place 6 large mint leaves, 5 (¼-inch) slices lemon, 5 (¼-inch) slices lime, 3 (⅛-inch) slices peeled fresh ginger, and 3 green tea bags in a medium bowl. Pour 6 cups boiling water over mint mixture; cover and steep 5 minutes. Remove tea bags; stir in ¼ cup honey. Strain mixture through a sieve into a small pitcher.

Game Plan

1 While water for noodles comes to a boil:

- Prepare and refrigerate orange sections.

2 While noodles cook:

- Prepare vinegar mixture.
- Chop vegetables.

3 While beef mixture cooks:

- Steep tea.

Tacos al Carbón

Substitute chicken breast or thighs, lamb, or shrimp for the steak. Serve with lime wedges.

Cooking spray
- 1½ cups thinly sliced red bell pepper (about 1 medium)
- 1½ cups thinly sliced onion (about 1 medium)
- 1 (1-pound) flank steak, trimmed and thinly sliced
- 1 tablespoon chili powder
- 1 tablespoon fresh lime juice
- 2½ teaspoons olive oil
- ¾ teaspoon salt
- 8 garlic cloves, minced
- 8 (6-inch) corn tortillas
- 3 tablespoons chopped fresh cilantro
- 6 tablespoons fat-free sour cream

1 Heat a grill pan over medium-high heat; coat with cooking spray. Add bell pepper to pan; cook 4 minutes. Add onion; sauté 10 minutes or until vegetables are tender. Place pepper mixture in a large bowl; cover and keep warm.

2 Add beef to pan; cook 7 minutes or until desired degree of doneness. Add beef to pepper mixture in a large bowl. Add chili powder, juice, oil, salt, and garlic to bowl; toss to coat.

3 Heat tortillas according to package directions. Spoon steak mixture evenly over tortillas. Top each taco with about 1 teaspoon cilantro and 2¼ teaspoons sour cream. Yield: 4 servings (serving size: 2 tacos).

CALORIES 371 (32% from fat); FAT 13.1g (sat 3.8g, mono 5.7g, poly 1.7g); PROTEIN 29g; CARB 36g; FIBER 4g; CHOL 49mg; IRON 2.9mg; SODIUM 608mg; CALC 164mg

---

MENU *serves 4*

Tacos al Carbón

Spicy cabbage salad
Combine 6 cups thinly sliced cabbage, ½ cup thinly sliced green onions, 2 tablespoons fresh lime juice, 1 tablespoon extra-virgin olive oil, 1 teaspoon salt, and 1 seeded and minced jalapeño pepper; toss well.

Salsa and baked tortilla chips

Game Plan

1 Slice pepper and onion for tacos.

2 While peppers and onion cook:
- Trim and slice beef.

3 While beef cooks:
- Squeeze lime for juice for salad and tacos.
- Mince garlic and chop cilantro for tacos.
- Prepare salad.
- Heat tortillas.
- Assemble tacos.

MENU *serves 4*

**Rosemary-Merlot
Flank Steak**

**Garlic-roasted new
potatoes**

Preheat oven to 500°. Combine 1 tablespoon olive oil, ½ teaspoon salt, ¼ teaspoon dried Italian seasoning, ¼ teaspoon paprika, ¼ teaspoon black pepper, 4 minced garlic cloves, and 1½ pounds quartered small red potatoes on a jelly-roll pan coated with cooking spray. Bake at 500° for 25 minutes or until tender, stirring every 10 minutes.

Tossed salad

Game Plan

1 While oven heats for potatoes:

- Prepare marinade.

- Marinate steak.

- Toss potatoes with seasonings.

2 While potatoes bake:

- Prepare salad.

- Prepare grill or preheat broiler.

3 While steak cooks:

- Prepare sauce.

Rosemary-Merlot Flank Steak

If you don't have dried Italian seasoning on hand for both the potatoes and steak, use ⅛ teaspoon dried basil and ⅛ teaspoon dried oregano. You can also substitute 1 teaspoon dried rosemary for the fresh.

- 1 cup finely chopped onion
- ¾ cup low-sodium beef broth
- ¾ cup merlot or other dry red wine
- 1 tablespoon chopped fresh rosemary
- ½ teaspoon salt
- ¼ teaspoon dried Italian seasoning
- 2 garlic cloves, minced
- 1 (1-pound) flank steak, trimmed

Cooking spray

- 1 tablespoon tomato paste
- 2 teaspoons Dijon mustard

1 Prepare grill or preheat broiler.

2 Combine first 7 ingredients in a large zip-top plastic bag. Add steak; seal bag. Marinate in refrigerator 20 minutes, turning once. Remove steak from bag, reserving marinade.

3 Place steak on grill rack or broiler pan coated with cooking spray; cook 6 minutes on each side or until desired degree of doneness. Let stand 5 minutes. Cut steak diagonally across the grain into thin slices; keep warm.

4 While steak cooks, combine reserved marinade, tomato paste, and mustard in a medium saucepan over medium-high heat; stir with a whisk. Bring to a boil, and cook until reduced to 1 cup (about 7 minutes). Serve sauce with steak. Yield: 4 servings (serving size: 3 ounces steak and ¼ cup sauce).

CALORIES 203 (39% from fat); FAT 8.8g (sat 3.6g, mono 3.5g, poly 0.5g); PROTEIN 23.8g; CARB 6.1g; FIBER 1.1g; CHOL 54mg; IRON 2.7mg; SODIUM 445mg; CALC 32mg

Quick Tip: Prepare marinade up to a day in advance, and store in an airtight container in the refrigerator.

Flank Steak with Chunky Mojo Relish

Mojo is a garlicky, citrusy Caribbean sauce. Garnish this dish with lime wedges and mint.

¼ cup fresh orange juice
2 tablespoons fresh lime juice
1 teaspoon minced garlic
1 teaspoon ground cumin
¾ teaspoon salt
½ teaspoon freshly ground black pepper
1 (1½-pound) flank steak, trimmed
2 cups diced, peeled orange (about 2 oranges)
3 tablespoons chopped fresh mint
¼ teaspoon hot pepper sauce (such as Tabasco)
6 pimiento-stuffed olives, minced
Cooking spray

❶ Combine first 3 ingredients in a small bowl. Reserve 2 tablespoons juice mixture in a medium bowl; set aside. Add cumin, salt, and pepper to remaining juice mixture. Place steak in a shallow dish; brush evenly with spice mixture. Cover and chill 20 minutes.
❷ Preheat broiler.
❸ Add orange and next 3 ingredients to reserved juice mixture; toss gently.
❹ Place steak on a broiler pan coated with cooking spray; brush remaining spice mixture over steak. Broil 6 minutes on each side or until desired degree of doneness. Let stand 5 minutes; cut into thin slices. Serve with orange mixture. Yield: 6 servings (serving size: 3 ounces steak and 3 tablespoons orange mixture).

CALORIES 188 (30% from fat); FAT 6.2g (sat 2.4g, mono 2.5g, poly 0.3g); PROTEIN 24.6g; CARB 7.8g; FIBER 1.4g; CHOL 37mg; IRON 2mg; SODIUM 431mg; CALC 49mg

Ingredient Tip: Purchase bottled citrus salad to use as a substitute for the oranges. You can find it in the produce section of your local supermarket.

MENU *serves 6*

Flank Steak with Chunky Mojo Relish

Cuban black beans
Heat 2 teaspoons olive oil in a medium skillet over medium heat. Add ½ cup chopped onion and ½ teaspoon minced garlic to pan; cook 5 minutes, stirring occasionally. Stir in 2 (15-ounce) cans rinsed and drained black beans, ½ teaspoon hot sauce, and ¼ teaspoon salt; cook 2 minutes or until thoroughly heated, stirring frequently. Stir in ½ cup chopped plum tomato and 2 tablespoons chopped fresh cilantro.

Pineapple sherbet

Game Plan

1 While steak marinates:
  • Prepare orange and olive mixture.
  • Prepare black beans.
2 Preheat broiler.
3 Cook steak.

MENU *serves 4*

Flank Steak Marinated with Shallots and Pepper

Corn and sugar snap pea salad

Combine 1½ cups fresh or thawed frozen corn kernels, 1½ cups chopped fresh sugar snap peas, ¼ cup chopped green onions, 2 tablespoons chopped fresh cilantro, and 2 teaspoons chopped seeded jalapeño pepper in a large bowl. Combine 1 tablespoon fresh lime juice, 1 teaspoon vegetable oil, ¼ teaspoon salt, and ¼ teaspoon black pepper in a small bowl; stir with a whisk. Drizzle dressing over salad; toss to combine.

Mashed sweet potatoes

Game Plan

1 Prepare marinade, and marinate steak 8 hours or overnight.

2 While grill or broiler heats for steak:
- Bring water to a boil for potatoes.
- Prepare corn salad.

3 While steak cooks:
- Cook and mash potatoes.

Flank Steak Marinated with Shallots and Pepper

Balsamic and red wine vinegars give this steak a tangy kick. You may substitute green onions for the shallots, if you like.

¼   cup chopped shallots
¼   cup red wine vinegar
2   tablespoons balsamic vinegar
1   teaspoon coarsely ground black pepper, divided
1   (1-pound) flank steak, trimmed
¼   teaspoon salt
Cooking spray

❶ Combine first 3 ingredients in a large zip-top plastic bag; add ½ teaspoon pepper and steak. Seal and marinate in refrigerator 8 hours or overnight, turning occasionally.

❷ Prepare grill or preheat broiler.

❸ Remove steak from bag; discard marinade. Sprinkle steak with ½ teaspoon pepper and salt. Place steak on grill rack or broiler pan coated with cooking spray; cook 6 minutes on each side or until desired degree of doneness. Cut steak diagonally across grain into thin slices. Yield: 4 servings (serving size: 3 ounces).

CALORIES 184 (42% from fat); FAT 8.6g (sat 3.7g, mono 3.5g, poly 0.4g); PROTEIN 23.2g; CARB 1.8g; FIBER 0.2g; CHOL 57mg; IRON 2.5mg; SODIUM 220mg; CALC 12mg

Quick Tip: If the corn you have for the salad is less than the freshest, grill it alongside the steak for the same amount of time, turning occasionally.

Tex-Mex Flank Steak and Vegetables

Chipotle salsa—used as a key ingredient in the marinade and a condiment for the meat and vegetables—has a smokier, more full-bodied flavor than regular tomato salsa.

½ cup bottled chipotle salsa (such as Pace)
2 tablespoons fresh lime juice
4 (¼-inch-thick) slices red onion (about 1 large)
2 garlic cloves, minced
1 red bell pepper, quartered and seeded
1 yellow bell pepper, quartered and seeded
1 (1-pound) flank steak, trimmed
Cooking spray
8 (7-inch) flour tortillas
¼ cup bottled chipotle salsa
2 tablespoons minced fresh cilantro

1 Combine first 7 ingredients in a large zip-top plastic bag. Seal and marinate in refrigerator 4 hours or overnight, turning occasionally.
2 Prepare grill or preheat broiler.
3 Remove steak and vegetables from bag; discard marinade. Place steak and vegetables on grill rack or broiler pan coated with cooking spray; cook 7 minutes on each side or until desired degree of doneness. Cut steak diagonally across grain into thin slices. Cut peppers into thin strips. Cut onion slices in half.
4 Warm tortillas according to package directions. Divide steak, bell peppers, and onion evenly among tortillas; roll up. Top each tortilla with 1 tablespoon chipotle salsa and 1½ teaspoons cilantro. Serve immediately. Yield: 4 servings.

CALORIES 547 (26% from fat); FAT 16.1g (sat 5.6g, mono 7.3g, poly 1.5g); PROTEIN 33.9g; CARB 65.5g; FIBER 5.5g; CHOL 59mg; IRON 6.3mg; SODIUM 685mg; CALC 73mg

Quick Tip: Because the steak has to marinate at least 4 hours, you'll need to start this recipe ahead of time. Marinating in a zip-top plastic bag eliminates cleanup—just throw the bag away.

MENU *serves 4*

Tex-Mex Flank Steak and Vegetables

Chipotle refried beans
Combine 1 (16-ounce) can fat-free refried beans, 2 tablespoons chipotle salsa, and 2 tablespoons chopped fresh cilantro. Microwave at HIGH 1½ minutes or until thoroughly heated.

Sliced ripe papaya and fresh lime wedges

Game Plan

1 Marinate steak and vegetables 4 hours or overnight.

2 Prepare grill or preheat broiler.

3 While steak and vegetables grill:
- Cook beans.
- Chop cilantro for beans and steak.
- Prepare papaya.

4 While tortillas warm:
- Slice grilled steak and vegetables.

MENU *serves 4*

Flank Steak with Creamy Mushroom Sauce

Egg noodles

Sautéed buttered asparagus

Steam 1 pound trimmed asparagus, covered, 3 minutes or until crisp-tender; drain. Melt 1 tablespoon butter in a large skillet over medium-high heat. Add asparagus, ½ teaspoon salt, and ¼ teaspoon black pepper; toss well. Sauté 2 minutes or until thoroughly heated.

Game Plan

1 While broiler heats:

- Bring water for noodles to a boil.
- Trim asparagus.
- Steam asparagus.
- Season steak.

2 While steak broils:

- Cook noodles.
- Prepare sauce.
- Sauté asparagus.

Flank Steak with Creamy Mushroom Sauce

This recipe calls for a gourmet mushroom mix, but most mushrooms will work equally well.

1 (1-pound) flank steak, trimmed
½ teaspoon salt
½ teaspoon freshly ground black pepper
Cooking spray
½ cup chopped shallots
1 (4-ounce) package gourmet mushroom mix
⅓ cup water
2 teaspoons Dijon mustard
1 tablespoon Worcestershire sauce
½ teaspoon chopped fresh thyme
¼ cup fat-free sour cream

❶ Preheat broiler.

❷ Sprinkle steak evenly with salt and pepper. Place steak on a broiler pan coated with cooking spray. Broil 6 minutes on each side or until desired degree of doneness; let steak stand 10 minutes.

❸ Heat a large nonstick skillet over medium heat; coat with cooking spray. Add shallots to pan; cook 3 minutes, stirring occasionally. Add mushrooms; cover and cook 4 minutes or until mushrooms are tender, stirring occasionally. Stir in ⅓ cup water, mustard, Worcestershire, and thyme. Cover and cook 2 minutes. Remove from heat, and stir in sour cream.

❹ Cut steak diagonally across grain into thin slices. Serve with mushroom sauce. Yield: 4 servings (serving size: 3 ounces steak and about ⅓ cup sauce).

CALORIES 186 (27% from fat); FAT 5.6g (sat 2.3g, mono 2.2g, poly 0.3g); PROTEIN 25.6g; CARB 7.5g; FIBER 0.5g; CHOL 38mg; IRON 2.1mg; SODIUM 443mg; CALC 49mg

MENU *serves 4*

Italian Ribeye Steak

Roasted red potatoes with parsley

Preheat oven to 400°. Place 6 cups quartered red potatoes in a large bowl. Drizzle potatoes with 1 tablespoon olive oil, and sprinkle with ½ teaspoon kosher salt; toss to coat. Arrange potato mixture in an even layer on a baking sheet. Bake at 400° for 40 minutes or until tender, turning once. Toss potatoes with ¼ cup chopped fresh flat-leaf parsley.

Steamed green beans

Game Plan

1 While oven heats:
- Prepare ingredients for potatoes.

2 While potatoes cook:
- Prepare steaks.

3 While steaks stand:
- Toss potatoes with parsley.
- Prepare green beans.

Italian Ribeye Steak

Marbled ribeye steaks require very little embellishment to deliver a big satisfying flavor.

1 teaspoon chopped fresh rosemary
½ teaspoon kosher salt
½ teaspoon freshly ground black pepper
2 garlic cloves, minced
2 (8-ounce) ribeye steaks, trimmed and cut in half crosswise
Cooking spray
4 lemon wedges

❶ Combine first 4 ingredients in a bowl, stirring well. Rub rosemary mixture evenly over both sides of steaks. Heat a grill pan over medium-high heat; coat with cooking spray. Add steaks to pan; cook 2½ minutes. Turn steaks over; cook 2 minutes or until desired degree of doneness. Let steaks stand 10 minutes. Serve with lemon wedges. Yield: 4 servings (serving size: 3 ounces steak and 1 lemon wedge).

CALORIES 238 (39% from fat); FAT 10.3g (sat 3.9g, mono 4.1g, poly 0.4g); PROTEIN 33g; CARB 1.4g; FIBER 0.3g; CHOL 103mg; IRON 2.4mg; SODIUM 304mg; CALC 24mg

MENU serves 4

Sirloin Steak with Tarragon-Garlic Sour Cream

Roasted baby carrots
Preheat oven to 450°. Combine 1 pound baby carrots, 2 teaspoons olive oil, ½ teaspoon salt, ¼ teaspoon black pepper, and ⅛ teaspoon dried tarragon on a jelly-roll pan; toss gently to coat. Bake at 450° for 15 minutes or until carrots are lightly browned, stirring once.

Low-fat vanilla ice cream with chocolate syrup

Game Plan

1 While oven heats:
- •Prep carrots.

2 While carrots roast:
- •Cook steak and potatoes.

3 Scoop ice cream into individual dishes and top with chocolate syrup; freeze until time to serve.

Sirloin Steak with Tarragon-Garlic Sour Cream

The tangy steak sauce dresses up this steak-house favorite. Packaged potato wedges round out the dish.

- ⅓ cup sour cream
- ¼ cup low-fat mayonnaise
- 2 tablespoons whole-grain Dijon mustard
- 1 teaspoon dried tarragon
- 1 teaspoon bottled minced garlic
- ½ teaspoon salt, divided
- ¼ teaspoon black pepper, divided
Cooking spray
- 1 (1-pound) boneless sirloin steak, trimmed
- 1 (20-ounce) package refrigerated red potato wedges (such as Simply Potatoes)

① Combine first 5 ingredients in a small bowl; stir in ¼ teaspoon salt and ⅛ teaspoon pepper. Set aside.

② Heat a large nonstick skillet over medium-high heat; coat with cooking spray. Sprinkle both sides of steak with ¼ teaspoon salt and ⅛ teaspoon pepper; add steak to pan. Cook 5 minutes on each side or until desired degree of doneness. Remove from pan; let steak stand 5 minutes. Cut into ¼-inch-thick slices. Keep warm.

③ Wipe pan with a paper towel; recoat pan with cooking spray, and return to heat. Add potatoes; sauté 15 minutes or until browned and thoroughly heated, stirring occasionally. Serve with steak and sauce. Yield: 4 servings (serving size: 3 ounces steak, ⅔ cup potatoes, and 3 tablespoons sauce).

CALORIES 307 (32% from fat); FAT 11g (sat 4.8g, mono 3.6g, poly 0.4g); PROTEIN 26.4g; CARB 22.9g; FIBER 3.7g; CHOL 53mg; IRON 2.1mg; SODIUM 732mg; CALC 44mg

Quick Tip: Have the steak trimmed at the meat counter of your supermarket.

Cumin-Coriander Sirloin Steak

The combination of cumin, coriander, and ground red pepper creates a tasty rub for the beef while brown sugar aids with the caramelization of its juices.

Cooking spray
- 1 tablespoon brown sugar
- ½ teaspoon salt
- ½ teaspoon ground cumin
- ½ teaspoon ground coriander seeds
- ¼ teaspoon ground red pepper
- 1 pound boneless sirloin steak (about 1¼ inches thick), trimmed

❶ Preheat oven to 450°.
❷ Place an 8-inch cast-iron skillet in oven for 5 minutes; remove from oven and coat pan with cooking spray.
❸ Combine brown sugar and next 4 ingredients in a small bowl; rub brown sugar mixture evenly over both sides of steak. Place steak in preheated pan.
❹ Bake at 450° for 7 minutes on each side or until desired degree of doneness. Let steak stand 5 minutes; cut steak diagonally across grain into thin slices. Yield: 4 servings (serving size: 3 ounces).

CALORIES 198 (39% from fat); FAT 8.6g (sat 3.4g, mono 3.6g, poly 0.3g); PROTEIN 25.1g; CARB 3.7g; FIBER 0.3g; CHOL 76mg; IRON 2.9mg; SODIUM 350mg; CALC 17mg

Quick Tip: Cooking the steak in a preheated cast-iron skillet seasons the steak without having to first brown it on the stove top.

MENU *serves 6*

Steak and Blue Cheese Pizza

Romaine salad with garlic-balsamic vinaigrette

Combine 1 tablespoon balsamic vinegar, 2 teaspoons extra-virgin olive oil, $\frac{1}{2}$ teaspoon Dijon mustard, $\frac{1}{4}$ teaspoon salt, $\frac{1}{8}$ teaspoon black pepper, and 1 minced garlic clove; stir with a whisk. Drizzle vinaigrette over 6 cups torn romaine lettuce; toss gently to coat.

Raspberry sorbet

Game Plan

1 Slice onions for pizza.

- Cook onion and mushroom mixture.

- Cook steak.

2 While oven heats:

- Prepare mayonnaise mixture.

3 While pizza crusts bake:

- Prepare salad.

4 Prepare pizza and bake.

Steak and Blue Cheese Pizza

Bake the topping for the pizza in stages to prevent the steak from becoming overcooked.

Cooking spray
2   cups vertically sliced onion
1   (8-ounce) package presliced mushrooms
$\frac{3}{4}$ teaspoon salt, divided
1   (8-ounce) boneless sirloin steak, trimmed
$\frac{1}{4}$ teaspoon coarsely ground black pepper
3   (7-inch) refrigerated individual pizza crusts (such as Mama Mary's)
2   tablespoons low-fat mayonnaise
$1\frac{1}{2}$ teaspoons prepared horseradish
$\frac{1}{3}$ cup (about $1\frac{1}{2}$ ounces) crumbled blue cheese

1 Preheat oven to 450°.
2 Heat a large nonstick skillet over medium-high heat; coat with cooking spray. Add onion and mushrooms; cover and cook 3 minutes. Uncover and cook 5 minutes, stirring occasionally. Stir in $\frac{1}{4}$ teaspoon salt; remove onion mixture from pan.
3 Sprinkle steak with $\frac{1}{2}$ teaspoon salt and pepper. Add seasoned steak to pan; cook over medium-high heat 3 minutes on each side or until desired degree of doneness. Let steak stand 5 minutes; cut diagonally across grain into thin slices.
4 Place crusts on a baking sheet. Bake at 450° for 3 minutes. Remove cooked crusts from oven.
5 Combine mayonnaise and horseradish in a small bowl; spread each crust with about 2 teaspoons mayonnaise mixture. Arrange onion mixture evenly over mayonnaise mixture in each crust; bake at 450° for 2 minutes. Divide steak and cheese evenly among crusts; bake an additional 2 minutes or until cheese melts. Cut each pizza in half. Yield: 6 servings (serving size: 1 pizza half).

CALORIES 323 (30% from fat); FAT 10.8g (sat 3.7g, mono 3.3g, poly 3.3g); PROTEIN 12.4g; CARB 38.6g; FIBER 4.2g; CHOL 31mg; IRON 2.3mg; SODIUM 599mg; CALC 91mg

Quick Tip: Covering the onion-mushroom mixture for the first few minutes in the skillet helps it cook faster.

Citrus-Rubbed Skirt Steak

Flavorful skirt steak is a favorite cut in Mexican cuisine. Because of its oblong shape, it may be difficult to fit the entire steak in your grill pan. If so, simply cut it in half across the grain and cook both halves at the same time.

2 teaspoons grated lemon rind
2 teaspoons grated orange rind
¼ teaspoon kosher salt
⅛ teaspoon ground red pepper
1 garlic clove, minced
1 (1-pound) skirt steak, trimmed
Cooking spray

1 Combine first 5 ingredients in a bowl, stirring well. Lightly coat steak with cooking spray. Rub rind mixture evenly over steak. Heat a grill pan over medium-high heat; coat with cooking spray. Add steak to pan; cook 5 minutes on each side or until desired degree of doneness. Let steak stand 5 minutes; cut diagonally across grain into thin slices. Yield: 4 servings (serving size: 3 ounces steak).

CALORIES 177 (44% from fat); FAT 8.6g (sat 3.3g, mono 4.4g, poly 0.3g); PROTEIN 22.8g; CARB 0.7g; FIBER 0.2g; CHOL 50mg; IRON 2.4mg; SODIUM 653mg; CALC 14mg

MENU *serves 4*

Citrus-Rubbed Skirt Steak

Orange and red onion salad
Combine 4 cups torn Boston lettuce, 1 cup orange sections, and ¼ cup thinly sliced red onion in a large bowl. Combine ¼ cup fresh orange juice, 2 tablespoons white wine vinegar, 1 table-spoon extra-virgin olive oil, ¼ teaspoon freshly ground black pepper, and ⅛ teaspoon salt in a small bowl; stir with a whisk. Drizzle lettuce mixture with juice mixture; toss gently to coat.

Couscous

Game Plan

1 While steak cooks:
   • Prepare couscous.
   • Prepare ingredients for orange and red onion salad.

2 While steak stands:
   • Toss salad.
   • Fluff couscous.

MENU *serves 4*

Filet Mignon with Cabernet Sauce

Sautéed mushrooms with prosciutto

Heat 1½ teaspoons olive oil in a medium nonstick skillet. Add 3 cups quartered cremini mushrooms, ¼ teaspoon kosher salt, and 2 minced garlic cloves to pan; sauté 4 minutes or until moisture evaporates. Remove from heat; stir in ¼ cup chopped prosciutto and 1 tablespoon chopped fresh flat-leaf parsley.

Mashed potatoes with chives

Game Plan

1 While potatoes cook:
- Prepare ingredients for steak.
- Prepare ingredients for mushrooms.

2 Prepare steak and sauce.

3 Prepare mushrooms.

4 Mash potatoes.

Filet Mignon with Cabernet Sauce

Just a touch of soy sauce adds depth and balances the wine reduction sauce. Butter renders a supple finish. Use a fresh parsley sprig as a simple garnish.

Cooking spray
- 4 (4-ounce) filet mignon steaks
- ½ teaspoon salt, divided
- ½ teaspoon freshly ground black pepper, divided
- ¼ cup minced shallots
- 1 tablespoon red wine vinegar
- 2 teaspoons low-sodium soy sauce
- 1 cup cabernet sauvignon
- 1 cup fat-free, less-sodium beef broth
- 2 teaspoons butter

1 Heat a large nonstick skillet over medium-high heat; coat with cooking spray. Sprinkle both sides of steaks evenly with ¼ teaspoon salt and ¼ teaspoon pepper. Add steaks to pan; cook 3 minutes on each side or until desired degree of doneness. Remove from pan; cover and keep warm. Add shallots to pan; sauté 1 minute. Stir in vinegar and soy sauce, scraping pan to loosen browned bits; cook 1 minute or until liquid evaporates, stirring constantly. Add ¼ teaspoon salt, ¼ teaspoon pepper, wine, and broth; bring to a boil. Cook until reduced to ½ cup (about 11 minutes). Remove from heat; stir in butter. Serve with steaks. Yield: 4 servings (serving size: 1 steak and about 2 tablespoons sauce).

CALORIES 358 (57% from fat); FAT 22.5g (sat 9.5g, mono 9.3g, poly 0.9g); PROTEIN 23.2g; CARB 3.6g; FIBER 0.2g; CHOL 80mg; IRON 1.8mg; SODIUM 565mg; CALC 32mg

MENU *serves 4*

Classic Steak House Rubbed Filet Mignon

Grilled asparagus with lemon

Prepare grill. Combine 1 pound trimmed asparagus spears, 1 teaspoon olive oil, ¼ teaspoon kosher salt, and ¼ teaspoon black pepper in a large zip-top plastic bag. Seal bag; shake well to coat. Place asparagus on a grill rack or in a grilling basket coated with cooking spray; grill 3 minutes or until lightly browned, turning frequently. Garnish with lemon slices, if desired. Serve immediately.

Baked potatoes with chives and reduced-fat sour cream

Game Plan

1 While grill heats:

- •Prepare rub for beef.
- •Combine asparagus with seasonings.
- •Wash potatoes.
- •Begin cooking potatoes in microwave.

2 While beef cooks on grill:

- •Chop chives for potatoes.
- •Place asparagus on grill during last 3 minutes of beef's cooking time.

Classic Steak House Rubbed Filet Mignon

Dry mustard powder has a pleasant bitterness and mild heat that pair well with the tender beef. Peppercorns and rosemary add even more flavor.

2 teaspoons black peppercorns
¼ teaspoon dried rosemary
1 teaspoon dry mustard
¾ teaspoon kosher salt
½ teaspoon garlic powder
4 (4-ounce) beef tenderloin steaks, trimmed (1 inch thick)
Cooking spray

❶ Prepare grill.
❷ Place peppercorns and rosemary in a spice or coffee grinder; pulse until pepper is coarsely ground. Combine pepper mixture, dry mustard, salt, and garlic powder in a small bowl; rub evenly over both sides of steaks. Place steaks on a grill rack coated with cooking spray; grill 3 minutes on each side or until desired degree of doneness. Yield: 4 servings (serving size: 1 steak).

CALORIES 188 (43% from fat); FAT 8.9g (sat 3.2g, mono 3.3g, poly 0.3g); PROTEIN 24.5g; CARB 0.8g; FIBER 0.2g; CHOL 72mg; IRON 3.3mg; SODIUM 407mg; CALC 11mg

Grilled Tenderloin with Warm Vegetable Salad

Bottled minced garlic is a smart time-saver. For each garlic clove in a recipe, substitute ½ teaspoon bottled minced garlic.

- 4 (4-ounce) beef tenderloin steaks, trimmed (about 1 inch thick)
- ½ teaspoon salt, divided
- ½ teaspoon black pepper, divided
- 2 tablespoons red wine vinegar
- 2 teaspoons bottled minced garlic
- 2 small zucchini, halved lengthwise
- 2 small yellow squash, halved lengthwise
- 2 plum tomatoes, halved lengthwise
- 2 green onions

Cooking spray
- 1 tablespoon commercial pesto

Oregano sprigs (optional)

❶ Prepare grill or preheat broiler.

❷ Sprinkle steaks with ¼ teaspoon salt and ¼ teaspoon pepper.

❸ Combine ¼ teaspoon salt, ¼ teaspoon pepper, vinegar, and next 5 ingredients in a large zip-top plastic bag. Seal bag, and shake to coat.

❹ Place steaks on grill rack or broiler pan coated with cooking spray; cook 4 minutes on each side or until desired degree of doneness. Place zucchini and yellow squash on grill rack or broiler pan coated with cooking spray; cook 3 minutes on each side or until tender. Place tomato and onions on grill rack or broiler pan; cook 2 minutes or just until tender.

❺ Coarsely chop vegetables, and place in a bowl. Add pesto; stir gently. Serve with steaks. Garnish with oregano, if desired. Yield: 4 servings (serving size: 1 steak and ½ cup vegetable mixture).

CALORIES 245 (39% from fat); FAT 10.5g (sat 3.7g, mono 4.3g, poly 0.6g); PROTEIN 27.2g; CARB 10.4g; FIBER 4.1g; CHOL 72mg; IRON 4.4mg; SODIUM 385mg; CALC 85mg

MENU *serves 4*

Grilled Tenderloin with Warm Vegetable Salad

Steamed new potato wedges

Garlic-herb French bread
Preheat oven to 350°. Cut a French bread baguette into ½-inch-thick slices. Place bread slices on a baking sheet. Coat bread with olive oil–flavored cooking spray; sprinkle with garlic powder and Italian seasoning. Bake at 350° for 5 minutes or until crisp.

Game Plan

1 While water comes to a boil for potatoes:
- Cut potatoes into wedges.
- Halve zucchini, yellow squash, and tomatoes for warm salad.
- Preheat grill or preheat broiler.

2 While potatoes steam:
- Cook steak and vegetables.
- Prepare baguette slices for baking.

3 While baguette slices bake:
- Chop grilled vegetables.

Chile-Spiced Tenderloin Steaks

Toasted corn and tomato salad

Combine 2 tablespoons lime juice, 1 tablespoon olive oil, 1 teaspoon bottled minced garlic, ¼ teaspoon salt, and ¼ teaspoon hot sauce in a small bowl; stir with a whisk. Toast 1 cup fresh corn in dry skillet 2 minutes or until golden, stirring frequently. Combine corn with 1 cup halved cherry tomatoes, ½ cup diced red bell pepper, ½ cup diced red onion, and 1 tea- spoon fresh oregano in a medium bowl; toss. Stir in juice mixture; cover and let stand 15 minutes. Toss gently before serving.

Flour tortillas

Game Plan

1 Combine marinade ingredients and steaks, and let stand.

2 While steak marinates:
- Roast corn for salad.
- Halve tomatoes; dice pepper and onion for salad.
- Prepare grill.

3 Prepare toasted corn and tomato salad; cover and let stand.

4 While salad stands:
- Grill steaks.

5 While steaks stand:
- Toss salad gently.
- Warm tortillas.

Chile-Spiced Tenderloin Steaks

You can find ancho chile powder in the spice aisle of most supermarkets. Use bottled minced garlic to save a little prep time.

3 tablespoons fresh lime juice
2 teaspoons minced garlic
1 teaspoon ancho chile powder
1 teaspoon dried oregano
¾ teaspoon kosher salt
½ teaspoon ground cumin
½ teaspoon ground coriander
½ teaspoon freshly ground black pepper
¼ teaspoon ground red pepper
4 (4-ounce) beef tenderloin steaks (about 1 inch thick)
Cooking spray
Lime wedges (optional)

❶ Prepare grill.
❷ Combine first 9 ingredients in a small bowl, and rub marinade mixture evenly over both sides of steaks. Let steaks stand at room tem- perature 15 minutes. Remove steaks from marinade; discard marinade. Place steaks on a grill rack coated with cooking spray; grill 5 minutes on each side or until desired degree of doneness. Remove from grill, and let stand 5 minutes. Serve with lime wedges, if desired. Yield: 4 servings (serving size: 1 steak).

CALORIES 173 (35% from fat); FAT 6.8g (sat 2.6g, mono 2.7g, poly 0.3g); PROTEIN 24.5g; CARB 2g; FIBER 0.4g; CHOL 67mg; IRON 1.9mg; SODIUM 424mg; CALC 29mg

Fresh Herb-Coated Beef Tenderloin Steaks with Mushroom Gravy

A lean cut of beef and cornstarch-thickened gravy keep this dinner deliciously low calorie.

BEEF:

- 1 teaspoon salt
- 1 teaspoon chopped fresh thyme
- 1 teaspoon chopped fresh rosemary
- ½ teaspoon freshly ground black pepper
- 4 garlic cloves, minced
- 4 (4-ounce) beef tenderloin steaks

Cooking spray

GRAVY:

- 1 teaspoon olive oil
- ½ teaspoon chopped fresh thyme
- 1 (8-ounce) package presliced cremini mushrooms
- 4 garlic cloves, minced
- ½ cup fat-free, less-sodium chicken broth
- ½ cup white wine
- 1 tablespoon water
- 1 teaspoon cornstarch

❶ Preheat oven to 450°.

❷ To prepare beef, combine first 5 ingredients.

Coat both sides of steaks with cooking spray, and rub steaks evenly with thyme mixture. Place steaks on rack of a broiler or roasting pan coated with cooking spray; bake at 450° for 8 minutes on each side or until desired degree of doneness. Remove from oven, and keep warm.

❸ To prepare gravy, heat oil in a large nonstick skillet over medium-high heat. Add ½ teaspoon thyme, mushrooms, and 4 garlic cloves; cook 5 minutes or until mushrooms are tender. Add broth and wine; bring to a boil. Cook until reduced to 1 cup (about 4 minutes).

❹ Combine water and cornstarch in a small bowl; stir with a whisk. Add cornstarch mixture to pan; bring to a boil. Cook 1 minute or until slightly thick, stirring constantly. Serve sauce with steaks. Yield: 4 servings (serving size: 1 steak and ¼ cup gravy).

CALORIES 202 (29% from fat); FAT 6.5g (sat 2.2g, mono 2.9g, poly 0.4g); PROTEIN 24.5g; CARB 6.3g; FIBER 0.7g; CHOL 52mg; IRON 2mg; SODIUM 692mg; CALC 44mg

---

MENU *serves 4*

Fresh Herb-Coated Beef Tenderloin Steaks with Mushroom Gravy

Green peas and leeks

Melt 2 teaspoons butter in a medium nonstick skillet over medium heat. Add ½ cup thinly sliced leek (white part only); cover and cook 5 minutes or until tender. Add ¼ cup fat-free, less-sodium chicken broth and 1 (10-ounce) package frozen green peas. Cover and cook 10 minutes or until thoroughly heated. Stir in ¼ teaspoon salt and ¼ teaspoon black pepper.

Baked potatoes

Game Plan

1 While oven heats:
- Microwave potatoes at HIGH 6 minutes.
- Rub spices on steaks.
- Wash and slice leeks.

2 While steaks cook:
- Cook leeks.
- Sauté mushrooms and garlic for gravy.

3 While steaks stand:
- Add cornstarch mixture to thicken gravy.
- Add peas to leeks.

Combine ⅓ cup fat-free milk, 3 tablespoons sugar, and 3 tablespoons heavy cream in a microwave-safe bowl. Microwave at HIGH 3 minutes or until sugar dissolves, stirring after every minute. Stir in 1 teaspoon vanilla extract. Pour mixture over 3 ounces semisweet chocolate and 3 ounces bittersweet chocolate; stir with a whisk until chocolate melts. Stir in 2 tablespoons finely chopped hazelnuts. Pour over cake.

Game Plan

1 Chop onion, garlic, and parsley.

2 Trim and cube beef; dice bacon.

3 Cook bacon.

4 While beef mixture simmers:

- Cook egg noodles.

- Chop parsley.

- Prepare hazelnut chocolate sauce.

Carbonnade à la Flamande

A classic Belgian dish, this stew features beef and onions in a beer-laced broth. We used Newcastle Brown Ale; for more authentic flavor, try dark Trappist beers from Chimay or Orval.

3⅓ ounces all-purpose flour (about ¾ cup)
 ½ teaspoon salt
 ½ teaspoon black pepper
 ⅛ teaspoon ground nutmeg
2½ pounds boneless chuck roast, trimmed and cut into 1½-inch cubes
 2 strips bacon, diced (uncooked)
 2 cups chopped onion (about 2 large onions)
 1 tablespoon chopped garlic
 1 (14-ounce) can less-sodium beef broth
 1 cup water
 2 tablespoons brown sugar
 2 tablespoons red wine vinegar
 2 tablespoons tomato paste
 2 tablespoons Dijon mustard
 1 teaspoon fresh thyme
 2 bay leaves
 1 (12-ounce) bottle dark beer
 2 tablespoons chopped fresh parsley

❶ Combine first 5 ingredients in a large zip-top plastic bag. Seal; shake to coat.
❷ Heat a large Dutch oven over medium-high heat. Add bacon to pan; cook 1 minute. Add beef mixture to pan; cook 3 minutes or until browned. Remove beef mixture from pan; keep warm.
❸ Add onion and garlic to pan; sauté 5 minutes or until tender.
❹ Return beef mixture to pan. Stir in broth, scraping pan to loosen browned bits. Add water and next 7 ingredients; bring to boil. Cover, reduce heat, and simmer 30 minutes. Uncover and cook 30 minutes or until beef is tender. Discard bay leaves. Sprinkle with parsley. Yield: 8 servings (serving size: 1 cup).

CALORIES 328 (24% from fat); FAT 8.8g (sat 3.9g, mono 3.2g, poly 0.5g); PROTEIN 41.1g; CARB 19.1g; FIBER 1.2g; CHOL 67mg; IRON 4.2mg; SODIUM 448mg; CALC 46mg

Pork and Fennel Ragù

The flavor of the meat sauce in this recipe is reminiscent of traditional Italian sausage.

Cooking spray
1 cup finely chopped onion
1 cup finely chopped fennel bulb
2 garlic cloves, minced
1 tablespoon fennel seeds
2 teaspoons sugar
1 teaspoon dried oregano
½ teaspoon salt
½ teaspoon crushed red pepper
¼ teaspoon ground red pepper
¼ teaspoon freshly ground black pepper
8 ounces lean ground pork
2 cups chopped tomato
½ cup fat-free, less-sodium chicken broth
4 cups hot cooked rigatoni (about 8 ounces uncooked pasta)
Fennel fronds (optional)

1 Heat a large nonstick skillet over medium-high heat; coat with cooking spray. Add onion, chopped fennel, and garlic; sauté 5 minutes. Add fennel seeds and next 7 ingredients, stirring to combine; sauté 3 minutes.

2 Add tomato and broth; bring to a boil. Reduce heat, and simmer 15 minutes, stirring occasionally. Serve over pasta. Garnish with fennel fronds, if desired. Yield: 4 servings (serving size: 1 cup ragù and 1 cup pasta).

CALORIES 408 (30% from fat); FAT 13.7g (sat 4.7g, mono 5.7g, poly 1.6g); PROTEIN 18.6g; CARB 52.8g; FIBER 5g; CHOL 41mg; IRON 3.5mg; SODIUM 405mg; CALC 64mg

MENU *serves 4*

Pork and Fennel Ragù

Romaine salad
Combine 2 tablespoons light mayonnaise, 1 tablespoon Dijon mustard, 2 teaspoons fresh lemon juice, 1 teaspoon red wine vinegar, ½ teaspoon Worcestershire sauce, and 2 minced garlic cloves in a large bowl; stir with a whisk. Add 8 cups torn romaine lettuce, tossing gently to coat.

Focaccia

Game Plan

1 While ragù cooks:
- Bring water for pasta to a boil.
- Prepare salad dressing.

2 While pasta cooks:
- Toss salad.
- Warm focaccia.

MENU *serves 4*

Mustard and Tarragon Braised Lamb

Spinach salad with heirloom tomatoes and basil vinaigrette
Combine 4 cups baby spinach and ½ cup sliced mushrooms in a large bowl. Cut 2 large heirloom tomatoes into 8 wedges each, and add to spinach mixture. Combine 1 tablespoon balsamic vinegar, 2 teaspoons thinly sliced fresh basil, 2 teaspoons extra-virgin olive oil, ½ teaspoon salt, and ¼ teaspoon black pepper in a small bowl, stir with a whisk. Drizzle vinaigrette over spinach mixture, tossing to coat.

Mashed potatoes

Game Plan

1 Trim and cube lamb.

2 Trim carrots.

3 While lamb mixture simmers:

  •Prepare salad.

  •Prepare mashed potatoes.

Mustard and Tarragon Braised Lamb

Braise your way to goodness in this one-pan dish seasoned with 2 types of mustard and fresh tarragon. The lamb emerges richly flavored and tender after only 30 minutes on the stove top.

1 tablespoon all-purpose flour
½ teaspoon dry mustard
½ teaspoon black pepper
1 pound boneless leg of lamb, trimmed and cubed
1 tablespoon olive oil
2 cups frozen pearl onions, thawed
2 cups baby carrots with tops (about ¾ pound), trimmed
1⅓ cups less-sodium beef broth
⅔ cup white wine
2 tablespoons Dijon mustard
1 tablespoon minced fresh tarragon

❶ Combine first 3 ingredients in a medium bowl; add lamb, tossing to coat.
❷ Heat oil in a large nonstick skillet over medium-high heat. Add lamb mixture, and sauté 4 minutes or until browned. Add onions and carrots; sauté 4 minutes. Stir in broth and wine. Cover, reduce heat, and simmer 7 minutes or until carrots are crisp-tender. Stir in mustard and tarragon. Increase heat to medium-high; cook, uncovered, 2 minutes or until slightly thickened. Yield: 4 servings (serving size: 1 cup).

CALORIES 332 (27% from fat); FAT 10g (sat 2.7g, mono 5g, poly 1.1g); PROTEIN 28.7g; CARB 25.3g; FIBER 1.9g; CHOL 75mg; IRON 3mg; SODIUM 341mg; CALC 67mg

Herbes de Provence–Crusted Lamb Chops

The Dijon mustard and dried herbs rub also tastes great on chicken thighs or beef fillets. Herbes de Provence is a combination of several dried herbs—including lavender, thyme, rosemary, and basil—that evokes flavors from the south of France.

2   tablespoons Dijon mustard
1   tablespoon dried herbes de Provence
½   teaspoon kosher salt
¼   teaspoon freshly ground black pepper
1   garlic clove, minced
8   (4-ounce) lamb loin chops, trimmed
Cooking spray

❶ Prepare grill.
❷ Combine first 5 ingredients; rub evenly over both sides of lamb.
❸ Place lamb on a grill rack coated with cooking spray; grill 4 minutes on each side or until desired degree of doneness. Yield: 4 servings (serving size: 2 lamb chops).

CALORIES 220 (41% from fat); FAT 10g (sat 3.4g, mono 4.3g, poly 0.8g); PROTEIN 29.2g; CARB 1.7g; FIBER 0.6g; CHOL 90mg; IRON 2.6mg; SODIUM 505mg; CALC 44mg

Quick Tip: Use half the grill to cook the potatoes and the other half for the lamb. Make sure to allow an extra 5 minutes before serving the meal so the potatoes can cool slightly. This also gives the lamb time to stand.

MENU   *serves 4*

Herbes de Provence–Crusted Lamb Chops

Grilled red potatoes with mint

Prepare grill. Toss 1½ pounds small red potatoes with 1 teaspoon kosher salt and 2 teaspoons olive oil. Place potatoes ¼ inch apart on a grill rack coated with cooking spray. Grill 15 minutes; turn over with tongs. Grill 15 minutes or until done. Cool slightly. Cut potatoes in half; toss with ⅓ cup thinly sliced mint leaves.

Steamed green beans

Game Plan

1 While grill heats:
- Combine potatoes with salt and oil.
- Prepare rub for lamb.
- Wash and trim green beans.

2 While potatoes cook on grill:
- Slice mint for potatoes.
- Steam green beans.
- Place lamb on grill during last 8 minutes of potatoes' cooking time.

Lamb Chops in Fennel-Tomato-Caper Sauce

Game Plan

1 While rice cooks:

- Cook chops.
- Chop parsley and olives for rice.
- Steam broccoli.

2 Toss together ingredients for olive and feta rice.

Ready in about 20 minutes, these lamb chops make an easy weeknight meal, but they're impressive enough to serve guests. Serve this dish with rice to soak up the flavorful sauce.

8   (4-ounce) lamb loin chops, trimmed
¼   teaspoon salt, divided
¼   teaspoon black pepper, divided
Cooking spray
½   cup prechopped onion
1   teaspoon bottled minced garlic
½   teaspoon fennel seeds
1   tablespoon capers
1   (14.5-ounce) can diced tomatoes, undrained

❶ Sprinkle lamb chops with ⅛ teaspoon salt and ⅛ teaspoon pepper. Heat a large nonstick skillet over medium-high heat; coat with cooking spray. Add lamb to pan, and cook 2 minutes on each side or until lightly browned. Remove lamb from pan. Add ⅛ teaspoon salt, ⅛ teaspoon pepper, onion, and garlic to pan; sauté 2 minutes.

❷ Place fennel seeds in a heavy-duty zip-top plastic bag; seal bag. Crush seeds with a rolling pin. Add seeds, capers, and tomatoes to pan; bring to a boil. Return lamb to pan. Cover, reduce heat, and cook 6 minutes or until desired degree of doneness. Yield: 4 servings (serving size: 2 lamb chops and ½ cup sauce).

CALORIES 228 (31% from fat); FAT 7.8g (sat 2.8g, mono 3.1g, poly 0.7g); PROTEIN 28.3g; CARB 9.6g; FIBER 1.1g; CHOL 86mg; IRON 3.3mg; SODIUM 551mg; CALC 75mg

Barbecue-Rubbed Pork Chops

This bold, zesty rub is made up of 7 spices. Turn up the heat by using hot paprika or ¼ teaspoon ground red pepper.

- 1 tablespoon light brown sugar
- 1 teaspoon salt
- 1 teaspoon paprika
- 1 teaspoon chili powder
- ¾ teaspoon garlic powder
- ¾ teaspoon ground cumin
- ¼ teaspoon dry mustard
- ⅛ teaspoon ground allspice
- ⅛ teaspoon ground red pepper
- 4 (6-ounce) bone-in center-cut loin pork chops, trimmed (about ½ inch thick)

Cooking spray

1 Combine first 9 ingredients in a small bowl; rub spice mixture over both sides of pork. Heat a grill pan over medium-high heat; coat with cooking spray. Add pork, and cook 2 minutes on each side. Reduce heat to medium; cook 8 minutes or until done, turning occasionally. Remove pork from pan, and let stand 5 minutes. Yield: 4 servings (serving size: 1 pork chop).

CALORIES 277 (34% from fat); FAT 10.5g (sat 3.8g, mono 4.7g, poly 0.8g); PROTEIN 38.8g; CARB 4.3g; FIBER 0.5g; CHOL 105mg; IRON 1.4mg; SODIUM 669mg; CALC 48mg

MENU   *serves 4*

Barbecue-Rubbed Pork Chops

Cheddar grits

Bring 2 cups fat-free milk and 1¼ cups water to a boil in a medium saucepan over medium-high heat. Slowly add ¾ cup quick-cooking grits, stirring with a whisk. Cover, reduce heat, and simmer 5 minutes or until thick, stirring occasionally. Remove from heat. Add 1 cup reduced-fat shredded sharp cheddar cheese, 1 tablespoon butter, ½ teaspoon salt, and ⅛ teaspoon freshly ground black pepper; stir until cheese melts.

Cucumber–red onion salad

Game Plan

1 While milk mixture comes to a boil:

- Prepare pork chop rub.

2 Grill pork chops.

3 While grits simmer:

- Assemble salad.

MENU *serves 4*

Pan-Seared Pork Chops with Red Currant Sauce

Mushroom-barley pilaf

Cook 1 cup quick-cooking barley according to package directions, omitting salt and fat. Heat 1 tablespoon olive oil in a large saucepan over medium-high heat. Add 1 cup chopped onion and 1 (8-ounce) package presliced mushrooms; sauté 4 minutes. Stir in 2 minced garlic cloves; sauté 1 minute. Add ¼ cup dry sherry; cook until liquid almost evaporates. Stir in barley, and cook 2 minutes or until thoroughly heated. Season with ½ teaspoon salt and ¼ teaspoon freshly ground black pepper.

Arugula salad with balsamic vinaigrette

Game Plan

1 While barley cooks:

- Prepare mushroom mixture for pilaf, and keep warm.

2 Prep ingredients for pork chops.

3 Cook pork chops.

4 Assemble and dress salad.

Pan-Seared Pork Chops with Red Currant Sauce

Tart cider vinegar balances the sweet currant jelly in the full-bodied, glossy sauce.

    2   teaspoons olive oil
    4   (6-ounce) bone-in center-cut loin
        pork chops, trimmed (about
        ½ inch thick)
    1   teaspoon ground coriander
    ¾   teaspoon salt, divided
    ¼   cup chopped shallots
    ¼   teaspoon dried thyme
    2   garlic cloves, minced
    2   tablespoons cider vinegar
    1   cup fat-free, less-sodium beef broth
    ⅓   cup red currant jelly
    ¼   teaspoon freshly ground black pepper
    1   teaspoon cornstarch
    1   teaspoon water
    Chopped fresh chives (optional)

❶ Heat oil in a large nonstick skillet over medium-high heat. Sprinkle pork with coriander and ½ teaspoon salt. Add pork to pan; cook 3 minutes on each side. Remove from pan. Add shallots, thyme, garlic, and ¼ teaspoon salt to pan; sauté 1 minute. Stir in vinegar; cook 15 seconds or until liquid almost evaporates. Stir in broth; bring to a boil. Cook until reduced to ⅔ cup (about 3 minutes). Add jelly and pepper; cook 2 minutes or until jelly melts. ❷ Combine cornstarch and 1 teaspoon water in a small bowl. Add cornstarch mixture to pan; bring to a boil. Cook 1 minute, stirring constantly. Add pork to pan; cook 1 minute or until thoroughly heated. Garnish pork with chives, if desired. Yield: 4 servings (serving size: 1 pork chop and about 3 tablespoons sauce).

CALORIES 361 (32% from fat); FAT 12.6g (sat 4.1g, mono 6.3g, poly 1g); PROTEIN 39.4g; CARB 20.4g; FIBER 0.2g; CHOL 105mg; IRON 1.3mg; SODIUM 631mg; CALC 48mg

Flavor Tip: For brighter taste, substitute ½ teaspoon chopped fresh thyme for the dried herb used on the chops.

Buttermilk-Brined Pork Chops

Brine these chops up to 2 days ahead. After an overnight soak, cover in plastic wrap and refrigerate until ready to cook.

  2 cups fat-free buttermilk
  2 tablespoons kosher salt
  2 tablespoons sugar
  1 tablespoon grated lemon rind
  1 teaspoon chopped fresh rosemary
  1 teaspoon chopped fresh sage
  4 (6-ounce) bone-in center-cut pork chops
     (about ½ inch thick)
  2 teaspoons freshly ground black pepper
Cooking spray

❶ Combine first 6 ingredients in a large zip-top plastic bag; shake well to dissolve salt and sugar. Add pork to bag; seal and refrigerate overnight, turning bag occasionally. Remove pork from bag, and discard brine. Pat pork dry with a paper towel. Sprinkle pork with pepper.

❷ Heat a large nonstick grill pan over medium-high heat; coat with cooking spray. Add pork to pan; cook 3½ minutes on each side or until desired degree of doneness. Yield: 4 servings (serving size: 1 chop).

CALORIES 183 (35% from fat); FAT 7.2g (sat 2.5g, mono 3.2g, poly 0.6g); PROTEIN 26g; CARB 2g; FIBER 0.3g; CHOL 69mg; IRON 0.8mg; SODIUM 345mg; CALC 43mg

MENU *serves 4*

Buttermilk-Brined Pork Chops

Roasted butternut squash

Preheat oven to 400°. Coat a nonstick baking sheet with cooking spray. Arrange 4 cups (½-inch) diced butternut squash in a single layer on pan; sprinkle with ½ teaspoon salt, ¼ teaspoon ground cinnamon, and ¼ teaspoon ground nutmeg. Coat squash with cooking spray. Bake at 400° for 10 minutes; turn with a spatula. Bake an additional 10 minutes or until squash is soft and begins to brown.

Steamed green beans

Game Plan

1 Brine pork chops overnight.

2 While oven heats:
   • Dice squash.

3 While squash bakes:
   • Cook pork chops.
   • Steam green beans.

Teriyaki Pork and Vegetables with Noodles

serves 4

Teriyaki Pork and Vegetables with Noodles

Sautéed bok choy

Toast 1 tablespoon sesame seeds in a large skillet over medium-high heat 1 minute or until golden brown. Remove seeds from pan; set aside. Heat 1 teaspoon dark sesame oil in pan. Add 3 cups sliced bok choy to pan; cook 3 minutes or until browned. Add 1 teaspoon low-sodium soy sauce and ⅛ teaspoon salt to pan; cover and cook 3 minutes. Sprinkle with sesame seeds.

Fresh orange sections and fortune cookies

Game Plan

1 While water boils for pasta:
- Prepare green onions.
- Slice red bell pepper and pork.
- Slice bok choy.

2 While pasta cooks:
- Section oranges.
- Cook pork mixture.

3 Toss pasta with pork mixture.

4 Cook bok choy.

The sweet-savory flavor of teriyaki sauce is a centuries-old mixture of soy sauce and mirin (sweet cooking wine). Over time, Japanese-Americans added ginger, brown sugar, pineapple juice, and green onions—elements of the bottled teriyaki sauce Americans know today.

8   ounces uncooked spaghetti
4   green onions
1   tablespoon dark sesame oil
1   cup thinly sliced red bell pepper
3   (4-ounce) boneless center-cut loin pork chops (about ½ inch thick), cut into ¼-inch strips
1   (3½-ounce) package shiitake mushrooms, sliced
⅓   cup low-sodium teriyaki sauce
4   teaspoons chili garlic sauce (such as Lee Kum Kee)

❶ Cook pasta according to package directions, omitting salt and fat. Drain, reserving ¼ cup cooking liquid; keep pasta warm.

❷ Remove green tops from green onions; thinly slice, and set aside. Mince white portions of green onions; set aside.

❸ Heat oil in a large nonstick skillet over medium-high heat. Add minced green onions, bell pepper, pork, and mushrooms; sauté 3 minutes or until pork is browned. Combine reserved ¼ cup cooking liquid, teriyaki sauce, and chili garlic sauce in a small bowl; stir with a whisk. Add pasta and teriyaki sauce mixture to pan; toss well to coat. Stir in sliced green onion tops. Yield: 4 servings (serving size: about 1¾ cups).

CALORIES 444 (27% from fat); FAT 13.5g (sat 4.1g, mono 4.6g, poly 2.7g); PROTEIN 26.3g; CARB 51.9g; FIBER 3.1g; CHOL 55mg; IRON 3.4mg; SODIUM 633mg; CALC 40mg

Pork Chops with Country Gravy

This recipe makes enough gravy to smother the pork chops, or you can spoon half over the chops and half over the mashed potatoes. Substitute dried basil if you don't have marjoram.

1   ounce all-purpose flour (about
     ¼ cup)
¾   teaspoon salt
¼   teaspoon dried marjoram
¼   teaspoon dried thyme
¼   teaspoon dried rubbed sage
4   (4-ounce) boneless center-cut
     loin pork chops (about ¾ inch thick)
1   tablespoon butter
Cooking spray
1½   cups 1% low-fat milk

❶ Lightly spoon flour into a dry measuring cup; level with a knife. Place flour, salt, and next 3 ingredients in a shallow dish. Dredge pork in flour mixture, turning to coat; shake off excess. Reserve remaining flour mixture.

❷ Melt butter in a large nonstick skillet coated with cooking spray over medium-high heat. Add pork to pan; cook 2 minutes on each side or until browned. Reduce heat, and cook 10 minutes or until done, turning pork once. Remove pork from pan; keep warm.
❸ Combine reserved flour mixture and milk in a small bowl; stir with a whisk. Add milk mixture to pan; place over medium-high heat. Bring to a boil, scraping pan to loosen browned bits. Reduce heat, and simmer 2 minutes or until slightly thick, stirring constantly. Serve with chops. Yield: 4 servings (serving size: 1 chop and ½ cup gravy).

CALORIES 252 (34% from fat); FAT 9.6g (sat 4.4g, mono 3.6g, poly 0.8g); PROTEIN 28.9g; CARB 10.6g; FIBER 0.3g; CHOL 83mg; IRON 1.5mg; SODIUM 584mg; CALC 142mg

Pork Chops with Carolina Rub

Season the pork chops and let them stand about 10 minutes before grilling to allow the meat time to absorb the flavorful spice rub. For a nice side dish to accompany these pork chops, consider purchasing preshredded coleslaw mix and low-fat bottled dressing at the supermarket.

    1   teaspoon garlic powder
    1   teaspoon onion powder
    1   teaspoon sugar
    1   teaspoon paprika
    1   teaspoon chili powder
    1   teaspoon freshly ground black pepper
    ½   teaspoon salt
    4   (4-ounce) boneless center-cut pork loin chops
Cooking spray
    ¼   cup barbecue sauce

1 Prepare grill.
2 Combine first 7 ingredients in a small bowl. Rub pork with spice mixture; let pork stand 10 minutes.
3 Place pork on grill rack coated with cooking spray. Grill 4 minutes. Turn pork, and grill 2 minutes. Brush each chop with 1 tablespoon sauce, and grill 2 minutes or until desired degree of doneness. Yield: 4 servings (serving size: 1 pork chop).

CALORIES 185 (34% from fat); FAT 6.9g (sat 2.4g, mono 3g, poly 0.7g); PROTEIN 24.6g; CARB 5g; FIBER 0.8g; CHOL 65mg; IRON 1.1mg; SODIUM 477mg; CALC 35mg

MENU

Pork Chops with Carolina Rub

Stove-top barbecue beans

Melt 1 tablespoon butter in a saucepan over medium-high heat. Add ½ cup chopped onion and 1 minced garlic clove; sauté 3 minutes. Stir in ⅓ cup ketchup, 2 tablespoons brown sugar, 2 tablespoons prepared mustard, 2 tablespoons fresh lemon juice, 2 tablespoons low-sodium soy sauce, 1 teaspoon chili powder, and 2 (15.5-ounce) cans rinsed and drained Great Northern beans. Cook 10 minutes, stirring occasionally.

Coleslaw

Game Plan

1 While grill heats:

- Prepare seasoning mixture for pork.

- Season pork.

2 While pork stands:

- Chop and measure ingredients for beans.

- Prepare beans.

- Toss slaw.

MENU *serves 4*

Pork with Curried Orange Sauce

Herbed basmati pilaf
Heat 2 teaspoons olive oil in a medium saucepan over medium heat. Add 1 teaspoon bottled minced garlic; sauté 1 minute. Add 1 cup basmati rice; sauté 2 minutes. Stir in 2 cups fat-free, less-sodium chicken broth; bring to a boil. Cover, reduce heat, and simmer 20 minutes or until liquid is absorbed. Remove from heat; stir in ¼ cup chopped green onions and ½ teaspoon dried thyme.

Steamed broccoli spears

Game Plan

1 While rice cooks:
- Chop green onions.
- Cook pork chops.
- Steam broccoli.

2 Toss together ingredients for pilaf.

Pork with Curried Orange Sauce

Herbed basmati pilaf and steamed broccoli spears make great accompaniments for these pork chops.

¾ teaspoon curry powder, divided
¼ teaspoon paprika
¼ teaspoon salt
4 (4-ounce) boneless center-cut loin pork chops, trimmed (about ½ inch thick)
⅓ cup orange marmalade
1½ teaspoons prepared horseradish
1½ teaspoons balsamic vinegar
⅛ teaspoon crushed red pepper
Cooking spray

❶ Combine ¼ teaspoon curry, paprika, and salt. Sprinkle pork with mixture.

❷ Combine ½ teaspoon curry, marmalade, horseradish, vinegar, and pepper.

❸ Heat a large nonstick skillet over medium-high heat; coat with cooking spray. Add pork; cook 3 minutes on each side or until pork loses its pink color. Remove from pan. Add marmalade mixture to pan; cook 15 seconds, scraping pan to loosen browned bits. Spoon sauce over pork chops. Yield: 4 servings (serving size: 1 pork chop and 1 tablespoon sauce).

CALORIES 254 (31% from fat); FAT 8.7g (sat 3.1g, mono 3.9g, poly 0.6g); PROTEIN 25.3g; CARB 18.5g; FIBER 0.3g; CHOL 69mg; IRON 0.9mg; SODIUM 224mg; CALC 41mg

Spiced Chops with Mango-Mint Salsa

Allspice and mango bring Caribbean flair to this dish. The salsa, redolent of mint, also packs a bit of heat, thanks to a dusting of crushed red pepper. A Jamaican beer, such as Red Stripe, would complement this meal.

¾   teaspoon chili powder
¼   teaspoon salt
⅛   teaspoon ground allspice
4   (4-ounce) boneless center-cut loin pork chops, trimmed
Cooking spray
1½ cups finely chopped peeled mango
2   tablespoons chopped fresh mint
½   teaspoon grated lemon rind
1   tablespoon fresh lemon juice
2   teaspoons sugar
¼   teaspoon crushed red pepper

1 Combine first 3 ingredients in a small bowl; sprinkle evenly over pork.

2 Heat a large nonstick skillet over medium-high heat; coat with cooking spray. Add pork; cook 4 minutes on each side or until done.

3 Combine mango and remaining 5 ingredients in a medium bowl. Serve with pork. Yield: 4 servings (serving size: 1 pork chop and about ⅓ cup salsa).

CALORIES 222 (29% from fat); FAT 7.1g (sat 2.6g, mono 3.2g, poly 0.5g); PROTEIN 26.1g; CARB 13.2g; FIBER 1.3g; CHOL 70mg; IRON 0.9mg; SODIUM 201mg; CALC 36mg

Flavor Tip: To tweak the taste of the salsa, use lime juice and rind instead of lemon. Or substitute chopped papaya for the mango, if you prefer; look for ripe, golden-yellow papaya that yields slightly to finger pressure.

MENU *serves 4*

Spiced Chops with Mango-Mint Salsa

Roasted sweet potatoes

Preheat oven to 425°. Cut 2 (8-ounce) peeled sweet potatoes in half lengthwise; cut each half lengthwise into 6 wedges. Combine sweet potatoes, 1 tablespoon olive oil, ½ teaspoon salt, ½ teaspoon ground cumin, and ⅛ teaspoon ground red pepper in a bowl; toss gently to coat. Place wedges on a baking sheet; bake at 425° for 25 minutes or until tender.

Sautéed baby spinach

Game Plan

1 While oven heats for sweet potatoes:

- Cut potatoes, and coat with spice mixture.

2 While potatoes bake:

- Prepare salsa.
- Cook pork.
- Sauté spinach.

MENU serves 4

Sautéed Boneless Pork Chops with Tomato-Sage Pan Sauce

Penne with butter and Parmesan cheese

Cook 8 ounces penne pasta according to package directions, omitting salt and fat. Drain; toss with 1 tablespoon butter and ¼ cup grated fresh Parmesan cheese. Sprinkle with chopped fresh parsley.

Lettuce salad with marinated artichoke hearts and tomatoes

Game Plan

1 While water for pasta comes to a boil:

- Grate Parmesan cheese for pasta.
- Chop sage for pork.
- Chop and seed tomatoes for pork.
- Season chops.

2 While pasta cooks:

- Make salad.
- Cook chops and sauce.

Sautéed Boneless Pork Chops with Tomato-Sage Pan Sauce

The black pepper bite of this pan sauce pairs nicely with the mild flavor of buttered penne.

2 teaspoons chopped fresh sage, divided
½ teaspoon kosher salt
½ teaspoon freshly ground black pepper
4 (4-ounce) boneless center-cut loin pork chops (about 3/4 inch thick)
Cooking spray
½ cup dry white wine
2 garlic cloves, minced
1 cup chopped seeded tomato
¼ cup fat-free, less-sodium chicken broth
¼ teaspoon kosher salt
⅛ teaspoon freshly ground black pepper

① Combine 1 teaspoon sage, ½ teaspoon salt, and ½ teaspoon pepper in a small bowl. Sprinkle both sides of pork with sage mixture.
② Heat a large nonstick skillet over medium-high heat; coat with cooking spray. Add pork; cook 3 minutes on each side or until browned. Remove from pan; set aside.
③ Add 1 teaspoon sage, wine, and garlic to pan, scraping to loosen browned bits. Cook 1½ minutes or until reduced to about ¼ cup. Stir in tomato and broth, and cook 4 minutes or until slightly thick. Return pork and accumulated juices to pan. Cover and cook 1 minute or until heated. Sprinkle with ¼ teaspoon salt and ⅛ teaspoon pepper. Yield: 4 servings (serving size: 1 chop and about 1 tablespoon sauce).

CALORIES 175 (34% from fat); FAT 6.6g (sat 2.4g, mono 2.9g, poly 0.5g); PROTEIN 24.6g; CARB 3.3g; FIBER 0.6g; CHOL 65mg; IRON 1.1mg; SODIUM 435mg; CALC 35mg

Quick Tip: Use drained canned Italian-style diced tomatoes as a substitute for chopped and seeded fresh tomatoes.

Pork Loin Chops with Cinnamon Apples

Pork and apples are simply meant for each other. Tart Granny Smiths balance the caramel sweetness of brown sugar.

1   teaspoon dried rubbed sage
½   teaspoon salt
¼   teaspoon freshly ground black
     pepper
4   (4-ounce) boneless center-cut
     loin pork chops (about ½ inch thick)
½   teaspoon canola oil
Cooking spray
1   teaspoon butter
4   cups (½-inch) slices peeled
     Granny Smith apples (about
     4 medium)
1   tablespoon brown sugar
1   teaspoon fresh lemon juice
½   teaspoon ground cinnamon
Dash of salt

1 Combine first 3 ingredients, and sprinkle over pork. Heat oil in a large nonstick skillet coated with cooking spray over medium heat. Add pork; cook 3 minutes on each side or until done. Remove pork from pan. Cover and keep warm.

2 Melt butter in pan over medium heat. Add apple and remaining 4 ingredients, and cook 5 minutes or until tender, stirring frequently. Serve with pork. Yield: 4 servings (serving size: 1 pork chop and ¾ cup apple mixture).

CALORIES 251 (30% from fat); FAT 8.3g (sat 3.1g, mono 3.3g, poly 0.9g); PROTEIN 24.1g; CARB 20.2g; FIBER 2.3g; CHOL 67mg; IRON 0.9mg; SODIUM 388mg; CALC 38mg

Quick Tip: To quickly peel the apples, use a vegetable peeler instead of a paring knife.

MENU *serves 4*

Pork Loin Chops with Cinnamon Apples

Buttered poppy seed noodles

Cook 8 ounces wide egg noodles according to package directions, omitting salt and fat; drain. Place noodles in a large bowl. Add 2 tablespoons chopped fresh parsley, 1½ tablespoons butter, 2 teaspoons poppy seeds, ¼ teaspoon salt, and ¼ teaspoon pepper; toss to combine.

Green peas

Game Plan

1 While water for noodles comes to a boil:

•Peel and slice apples.

•Sprinkle pork with sage mixture.

2 While noodles cook:

•Cook pork and apples.

•Prepare peas.

•Chop parsley for noodles.

MENU *serves 4*

Pork Chops Stuffed with Feta and Spinach

Herbed pita
Preheat oven to 425°. Cut 2 (6-inch) pitas into 8 wedges. Lightly coat pita wedges with cooking spray. Sprinkle with ¼ teaspoon dried basil, ¼ teaspoon dried coriander, ⅛ teaspoon salt, and ⅛ teaspoon dried thyme. Place pita wedges on a baking sheet; bake at 425° for 8 minutes or until toasted.

Yogurt drizzled with honey and cinnamon

Game Plan

1 Preheat oven.

2 Bake pita wedges.

3 While broiler preheats:

  •Prepare feta stuffing.

4 Stuff and broil pork chops.

Pork Chops Stuffed with Feta and Spinach

The combination of lemon juice and rind add a citrusy tang to this Greek-inspired filling.

Cooking spray
  4 garlic cloves, minced and divided
  ½ teaspoon salt, divided
  ¼ teaspoon freshly ground black pepper, divided
  5 sun-dried tomatoes, packed without oil, diced
  1 (10-ounce) package frozen chopped spinach, thawed, drained, and squeezed dry
  ¼ cup (1 ounce) crumbled reduced-fat feta cheese
  3 tablespoons (1½ ounces) block-style fat-free cream cheese
  ½ teaspoon grated lemon rind
  4 (4-ounce) boneless center-cut loin pork chops (about ½ inch thick), trimmed
  2 tablespoons fresh lemon juice
  2 teaspoons Dijon mustard
  ¼ teaspoon dried oregano

❶ Preheat broiler.
❷ Heat a large nonstick skillet over medium-high heat, and coat with cooking spray. Add 2 minced garlic cloves; sauté 1 minute. Add ¼ teaspoon salt, ⅛ teaspoon pepper, tomatoes, and spinach; sauté until moisture evaporates. Remove from heat; stir in cheeses and rind.
❸ Cut a horizontal slit through thickest portion of each pork chop to form a pocket. Stuff about ¼ cup spinach mixture into each pocket. Sprinkle ¼ teaspoon salt and ⅛ teaspoon pepper over pork. Arrange pork on rack of a broiler pan or roasting pan coated with cooking spray; place rack in pan. Combine 2 minced garlic cloves, juice, mustard, and oregano in a bowl; stir well. Brush half of mustard mixture over pork. Broil 6 minutes; turn chops. Brush remaining mixture over pork; broil 2 minutes or until done. Yield: 4 servings (serving size: 1 pork chop).

CALORIES 232 (33% from fat); FAT 8.6g (sat 3.4g, mono 3.1g, poly 0.7g); PROTEIN 32.1g; CARB 7.2g; FIBER 2.8g; CHOL 73mg; IRON 2.5mg; SODIUM 640mg; CALC 186mg

Grilled Plum and Prosciutto-Stuffed Pork Chops

The balsamic vinegar and sweet molasses glaze balances out the spicy flavor of the rub on the pork.

    4   pitted dried plums, halved
    2   very thin slices prosciutto (about
        ¾ ounce), halved
    ½   teaspoon crushed fennel seeds
    ½   teaspoon paprika
    ½   teaspoon chopped fresh sage
    ½   teaspoon chopped fresh rosemary
    ¼   teaspoon kosher salt
    ¼   teaspoon crushed red pepper
    ¼   teaspoon freshly ground black pepper
    4   (4-ounce) boneless center-cut loin
        pork chops (about ¾ inch thick)
Cooking spray
    2   teaspoons balsamic vinegar
    2   teaspoons molasses

1 Prepare grill.
2 Soak plum halves in boiling water 5 minutes. Drain well.

3 Wrap 2 plum halves in each prosciutto piece.
4 Combine fennel seeds and next 6 ingredients in a small bowl.
5 Cut a horizontal slit through thickest portion of each pork chop to form a pocket. Stuff 1 prosciutto wrap into each pocket. Sprinkle pork chops with fennel mixture. Place pork chops on grill rack coated with cooking spray; grill 5 minutes on each side or until desired degree of doneness. Combine vinegar and molasses; brush over pork chops. Yield: 4 servings (serving size: 1 chop).

CALORIES 205 (32% from fat); FAT 7.2g (sat 2.6g, mono 2.9g, poly 0.5g); PROTEIN 25.7g; CARB 8.5g; FIBER 0.9g; CHOL 70mg; IRON 1.3mg; SODIUM 270mg; CALC 42mg

Quick Tip: Get a head start by assembling the stuffed pork chops the night before. Sprinkle them with the fennel mixture just before grilling.

MENU *serves 4*

Grilled Plum and Prosciutto-Stuffed Pork Chops

Hominy sauté
Melt 2 teaspoons butter in a large nonstick skillet. Add ½ cup chopped onion and 2 minced garlic cloves; sauté 2 minutes or until tender. Add 1 (15.5-ounce) can drained white hominy, ¼ cup chopped green onions, ¼ teaspoon salt, and ¼ teaspoon freshly ground black pepper. Cook 2 minutes or until thoroughly heated.

Strawberry sorbet

Game Plan

1 While grill heats:
- Chop sage and rosemary for pork chops.
- Chop onion and green onions for hominy.
- Mince garlic for hominy.
- Soak dried plums in boiling water.

2 While pork grills:
- Sauté hominy.

MENU *serves 6*

Indian-Spiced Pork in Tomato Sauce

Pineapple salad
Combine 4 cups cubed fresh pineapple, ½ cup very thinly vertically sliced red onion, 1 tablespoon thinly sliced fresh mint, 1 tablespoon fresh lime juice, 1 tablespoon honey, and ⅛ teaspoon salt.

Basmati rice

Game Plan

1 Marinate pork.

2 While pork simmers:
  • Cook basmati rice.
  • Prepare pineapple salad.

Indian-Spiced Pork in Tomato Sauce

The sweetness of pineapple balances the spiciness of the pork. Pita bread or basmati rice would be good with this saucy dish. Toasting the whole spices before adding them to the other ingredients intensifies their flavors.

  1 teaspoon ground red pepper
  1 teaspoon cumin seeds
  1 teaspoon mustard seeds
  ½ teaspoon ground coriander
  ½ teaspoon ground cardamom
  ½ teaspoon ground cinnamon
  ¼ teaspoon black peppercorns
  2 cups chopped onion (1 medium)
  3 tablespoons white vinegar
  1 tablespoon finely chopped fresh ginger
  2 teaspoons sugar
  6 garlic cloves, crushed
  2 pounds boneless pork loin, trimmed and cut into ½-inch cubes
Cooking spray
  1 cup fat-free, less-sodium chicken broth
  4 cups (1½ pounds) baking potato, cut into ½-inch cubes
  ¾ teaspoon salt
  1 (28-ounce) can diced tomatoes, undrained
Chopped fresh cilantro (optional)

❶ Heat first 7 ingredients in a dry skillet over medium heat about 3 minutes or until fragrant, stirring frequently. Place in a blender or food processor. Add onion and next 4 ingredients; process 2 minutes or until well blended.
❷ Combine pork and spice mixture in a large glass bowl, tossing to coat. Cover and chill 30 minutes.
❸ Heat a Dutch oven over medium heat; coat with cooking spray. Add half of pork mixture; cook 5 minutes or until pork begins to brown, stirring frequently. Transfer pork mixture to a bowl. Repeat procedure with cooking spray and remaining pork mixture. Add broth to pan, scraping pan to loosen browned bits. Add pork mixture to pan. Stir in potato, salt, and tomatoes; bring to a boil. Cover, reduce heat, and simmer 1 hour or until potato is cooked and pork is tender, stirring occasionally. Garnish with cilantro, if desired. Yield: 6 servings (serving size: about 1½ cups).

CALORIES 383 (26% from fat); FAT 10.7g (sat 3.9g, mono 4.6g, poly 0.9g); PROTEIN 36.1g; CARB 35.8g; FIBER 5g; CHOL 90mg; IRON 3.2mg; SODIUM 611mg; CALC 93mg

Caribbean Pork and Plantain Hash

Use semiripe plantains—not green or soft, but ripe black ones. The plantains brown better if not stirred too much as they cook. Serve leftovers with poached eggs for breakfast.

1 tablespoon low-sodium soy sauce
¾ teaspoon salt, divided
¾ teaspoon dried thyme
¼ teaspoon ground ginger
¼ teaspoon ground red pepper
⅛ teaspoon ground allspice
1 pound pork tenderloin, trimmed and cut into ½-inch pieces
1½ tablespoons canola oil, divided
1 tablespoon butter
1½ cups coarsely chopped onion
1 cup chopped green bell pepper
2 large yellow plantains, chopped (about 3 cups)
½ teaspoon black pepper
4 garlic cloves, minced
1 teaspoon habanero hot pepper sauce
2 tablespoons chopped fresh cilantro

❶ Combine soy sauce, ¼ teaspoon salt, thyme, and next 4 ingredients in a large bowl; toss well to coat. Heat 1½ teaspoons oil in a large nonstick skillet over medium-high heat. Add pork mixture to pan; sauté 4 minutes or until done. Remove pork from pan; keep warm. Add remaining 1 tablespoon oil and butter to pan. Add onion, bell pepper, plantains, ½ teaspoon salt, and black pepper to pan; cook 6 minutes, stirring occasionally. Stir in garlic; sauté 2 minutes or until plantains are tender. Return pork mixture to pan. Drizzle with hot sauce, and stir well. Sprinkle with cilantro. Yield: 4 servings (serving size: about 1½ cups).

CALORIES 384 (29% from fat); FAT 12.5g (sat 4g, mono 3.8g, poly 3.7g); PROTEIN 26.8g; CARB 44.9g; FIBER 4.7g; CHOL 81mg; IRON 2.8mg; SODIUM 674mg; CALC 38mg

MENU *serves 4*

Caribbean Pork and Plantain Hash

Tomato and hearts of palm salad
Cut each of 4 plum tomatoes lengthwise into 8 wedges; place in a medium bowl. Drain 1 (14-ounce) can hearts of palm; cut each heart of palm lengthwise into quarters. Cut each heart of palm quarter in half crosswise; add to tomato wedges. Add ½ cup thinly vertically sliced red onion, 1 tablespoon chopped cilantro, 1½ tablespoons fresh lime juice, 1 teaspoon olive oil, ¼ teaspoon salt, and ¼ teaspoon black pepper. Toss well.

Mango slices drizzled with lime juice

Game Plan

1 While pork cooks:
- Chop onion, bell pepper, and plantains for hash.

2 While plantain mixture cooks:
- Mince garlic.
- Prepare salad.
- Prepare mango.

MENU *serves 4*

Tangy Pork with Tomatillos, Tomatoes, and Cilantro

Mango salad

Combine ¼ cup white wine vinegar, 2 tablespoons honey, and 1 tablespoon olive oil. Toss with 1 (10-ounce) bag gourmet mixed salad greens and 2 cups cubed mango.

Game Plan

1 While rice cooks:

- Cube pork.
- Chop onion and tomatillos.
- Sauté pork and vegetables.

2 While pork and vegetables cook:

- Halve tomatoes, and chop cilantro.
- Prepare mango salad.

Tangy Pork with Tomatillos, Tomatoes, and Cilantro

If you're looking for a great way to serve tomatillos in a main dish, this is it. The tomatillos and tomatoes are a perfect complement to the pork.

- 1½ teaspoons ground cumin
- 1 teaspoon chili powder
- ½ teaspoon salt
- ¼ teaspoon ground red pepper
- 1 pound pork tenderloin, trimmed and cut into 1-inch cubes
- 1 tablespoon olive oil, divided
- Cooking spray
- 1 cup chopped Vidalia or other sweet onion
- 1 teaspoon bottled minced garlic
- 2 cups chopped fresh tomatillos (about 8 ounces)
- 2 cups halved cherry tomatoes (about 8 ounces)
- ½ cup chopped fresh cilantro
- 4 cups hot cooked instant rice

1 Combine first 4 ingredients in a medium bowl. Add pork; toss well. Heat 1½ teaspoons oil in a large nonstick skillet coated with cooking spray over medium-high heat. Add pork; sauté 3 minutes. Remove pork from pan; keep warm.

2 Heat 1½ teaspoons oil in pan over medium-high heat. Add onion and garlic; sauté 30 seconds. Add tomatillos; sauté 1 minute. Add pork, and cover and cook 10 minutes or until pork is done. Add tomatoes and cilantro; cover and cook 1 minute. Serve with rice. Yield: 4 servings (serving size: 1 cup pork mixture and 1 cup rice).

CALORIES 375 (18% from fat); FAT 7.7g (sat 1.6g, mono 4.1g, poly 0.9g); PROTEIN 29.4g; CARB 46g; FIBER 4g; CHOL 74mg; IRON 4.3mg; SODIUM 379mg; CALC 62mg

Lime-Cilantro Pork Tacos

Browning the pork improves its color, and the browned bits enrich the sauce's flavor.
Increase the amount of jalapeño pepper if you enjoy your food spicy.

2 teaspoons olive oil
1 pound pork tenderloin, trimmed and cut into thin strips
¼ teaspoon salt
⅛ teaspoon freshly ground black pepper
1½ cups thinly sliced onion
1 small jalapeño pepper, seeded and chopped
½ cup fat-free, less-sodium chicken broth
½ cup chopped plum tomato
3 tablespoons chopped cilantro
2½ tablespoons fresh lime juice
8 (6-inch) flour tortillas
Lime wedges (optional)

❶ Heat oil in a large nonstick skillet over medium-high heat. Sprinkle pork with salt and black pepper. Add pork to pan, and sauté 4 minutes or until browned. Remove pork from pan; place in a bowl. Add onion and jalapeño to pan; sauté 5 minutes or until tender. Add broth; reduce heat, and simmer 1 minute, scraping pan to loosen browned bits. Stir in tomato; simmer 2 minutes.

❷ Return pork and accumulated juices to pan. Stir in cilantro and lime juice; cook 1 minute or until pork is done.

❸ Heat tortillas according to package directions. Spoon ½ cup pork mixture into each tortilla, and roll up. Serve with lime wedges, if desired. Yield: 4 servings (serving size: 2 tacos).

CALORIES 416 (28% from fat); FAT 13.1g (sat 3.6g, mono 6.8g, poly 1.6g); PROTEIN 30.2g; CARB 43.1g; FIBER 3.6g; CHOL 75mg; IRON 3.8mg; SODIUM 569mg; CALC 101mg

Quick Tip: Partially freeze the pork tenderloin to make it easier to cut into thin strips.

MENU *serves 4*

Lime-Cilantro Pork Tacos

Black bean salad with bell peppers and onions
Combine 1 (15-ounce) can rinsed and drained black beans, 1 cup chopped red bell pepper, ½ cup chopped red onion, ¼ cup chopped fresh parsley, 1½ tablespoons red wine vinegar, 1 tablespoon olive oil, ¼ teaspoon black pepper, ⅛ teaspoon salt, and 1 minced garlic clove. Serve at room temperature.

Lemon sorbet

Game Plan

1 While skillet heats:
 •Prepare black bean salad.
 •Chop jalapeño pepper, tomato, and cilantro for tacos.
 •Slice onion and squeeze lime for juice.

2 While tomatoes simmer in sauce, warm tortillas.

Dilled Pork Stroganoff

This version of a classic Russian dish uses pork instead of the traditional beef and gives the sour cream sauce a touch of dill flavor.

- 3 cups uncooked medium egg noodles (about 6 ounces)
- 1 (1-pound) pork tenderloin, trimmed and cut into ½-inch strips
- ½ teaspoon salt, divided
- ¼ teaspoon black pepper
- 2½ teaspoons butter, divided
- Cooking spray
- ½ cup fat-free, less-sodium chicken broth
- 2 cups chopped Walla Walla or other sweet onion
- 1 (8-ounce) package presliced mushrooms
- 1 cup low-fat sour cream
- 1 tablespoon chopped fresh dill
- 1 tablespoon Dijon mustard
- 1 teaspoon all-purpose flour
- Dill sprigs (optional)

1 Cook pasta according to package directions, omitting salt and fat.

2 Sprinkle pork with ¼ teaspoon salt and pepper. Melt 1½ teaspoons butter in a large nonstick skillet coated with cooking spray over medium-high heat. Add pork; sauté 4 minutes or until pork loses pink color. Remove pork from pan; keep warm.

3 Add broth to pan; cook 30 seconds. Add 1 teaspoon butter, ¼ teaspoon salt, onion, and mushrooms; cook 8 minutes or until vegetables are lightly browned. Remove pan from heat.

4 Combine sour cream, chopped dill, mustard, and flour in a small bowl. Add pork and sour cream mixture to pan; stir well. Serve pork mixture immediately over noodles. Garnish with dill sprigs, if desired. Yield: 4 servings (serving size: 1 cup pork mixture and 1 cup noodles).

CALORIES 384 (30% from fat); FAT 13g (sat 7.1g, mono 2.9g, poly 1g); PROTEIN 34.4g; CARB 31.6g; FIBER 3g; CHOL 123mg; IRON 3.5mg; SODIUM 585mg; CALC 120mg

Spicy Pork-and-Bell Pepper Tacos

To save time, use preshredded cheese and a thawed 16-ounce package of frozen pepper stir-fry with yellow, green, and red bell peppers and onions.

1½ pounds pork tenderloin, trimmed and cut into ½-inch strips
1½ teaspoons dried Italian seasoning
½ teaspoon ground red pepper
¼ teaspoon salt
4 teaspoons canola oil, divided
Cooking spray
1½ cups red bell pepper strips (about 1 large)
1½ cups green bell pepper strips (about 1 large)
1½ cups yellow bell pepper strips (about 1 large)
1½ teaspoons bottled minced garlic
¼ teaspoon salt
6 (8-inch) fat-free flour tortillas
¾ cup (3 ounces) shredded reduced-fat cheddar cheese
¾ cup bottled salsa
Lime wedges (optional)

❶ Combine first 4 ingredients in a medium bowl. Heat 2 teaspoons oil in a large nonstick skillet coated with cooking spray over medium-high heat. Add pork, and cook 8 minutes or until pork loses its pink color. Remove from pan; keep warm.
❷ Heat 2 teaspoons oil in pan coated with cooking spray over medium-high heat. Add bell peppers, garlic, and ¼ teaspoon salt, and sauté 5 minutes or until tender. Warm the tortillas according to package directions. Divide pork evenly among tortillas; top each serving with ½ cup pepper mixture, 2 tablespoons cheese, and 2 tablespoons salsa, and fold. Serve with lime wedges, if desired. Yield: 6 servings.

CALORIES 341 (25% from fat); FAT 9.3g (sat 3.2g, mono 2.2g, poly 2.1g); PROTEIN 32.2g; CARB 31.2g; FIBER 2.9g; CHOL 83mg; IRON 4.3mg; SODIUM 839mg; CALC 148mg

MENU *serves 6*

Spicy Pork-and-Bell Pepper Tacos

Black bean salad
Combine 1 (15-ounce) can black beans, drained and rinsed; 2 chopped green onions; 1 chopped plum tomato; and 1 tablespoon each of chopped fresh cilantro, fresh lime juice, and olive oil.

Game Plan

1 Prepare black bean salad.

2 Cut pork and bell peppers into strips for tacos.

3 While pork and bell peppers cook:
   ▪ Shred cheese.
   ▪ Warm tortillas.

MENU *serves 4*

Pork Medallions with Double-Apple Sauce

Lemon Broccolini
Steam 1 pound Broccolini, covered, 5 minutes or until crisp-tender; drain. Combine 1 tablespoon extra-virgin olive oil, 1 teaspoon grated lemon rind, 1 tablespoon fresh lemon juice, ¼ teaspoon salt, ¼ teaspoon crushed red pepper, and 1 minced garlic clove. Drizzle dressing over Broccolini, and toss well to coat.

Egg noodles

Game Plan

1 While water for noodles comes to a boil:

   • Prepare Broccolini, and set aside at room temperature.

   • Cut apples into wedges.

   • Slice pork into medallions.

2 While noodles cook:

   • Prepare pork dish.

Pork Medallions with Double-Apple Sauce

Half-and-half finishes the sauce of tart green Granny Smith apples and sweet cider, richly mellowing the flavors. If you are serving wine, chardonnay is a good match for this menu.

    1   cup apple cider
    2   large Granny Smith apples, peeled and
        each cut into 8 wedges (about 14 ounces)
    1   (1-pound) pork tenderloin, trimmed
        and cut crosswise into 8 (½-inch-thick)
        slices
    ½   teaspoon salt
    ¼   teaspoon black pepper
    Cooking spray
    ½   cup half-and-half
    ½   teaspoon dried rosemary, crushed
    Chopped fresh parsley (optional)

❶ Pour cider into a large nonstick skillet; bring to a boil. Add apples. Reduce heat, and simmer 5 minutes or until apples are barely tender. Remove apples from pan with a slotted spoon, and place in a medium bowl. Cook cider until reduced to ½ cup (about 3 minutes). Pour reduced cider over apples; set aside.
❷ Sprinkle pork evenly with salt and pepper. Wipe pan clean with a damp paper towel. Heat pan over medium-high heat; coat with cooking spray. Add pork to pan; cook 3 minutes on each side or until browned. Remove from heat. Add apple mixture, half-and-half, and rosemary, tossing gently to combine. Garnish with parsley, if desired. Serve immediately. Yield: 4 servings (2 pork medallions, 4 apple wedges, and about ¼ cup sauce).

CALORIES 259 (26% from fat); FAT 7.5g (sat 3.5g, mono 2.8g, poly 0.6g); PROTEIN 25.2g; CARB 22.9g; FIBER 1.4g; CHOL 85mg; IRON 1.5mg; SODIUM 360mg; CALC 45mg

Flavor Tip: Crush dried herbs by hand to release extra aroma and flavor.

Pork Medallions with Olive-Caper Sauce

Easy enough for a weeknight meal, this dish is also elegant enough for entertaining guests.

1 pound pork tenderloin, trimmed
½ teaspoon salt
½ teaspoon black pepper
¼ cup all-purpose flour
1 tablespoon olive oil, divided
½ cup dry white wine
½ cup fat-free, less-sodium chicken broth
½ cup coarsely chopped pitted kalamata olives
2 tablespoons capers
2 tablespoons chopped fresh flat-leaf parsley

1 Cut pork crosswise into 8 pieces. Place each pork piece between 2 sheets of heavy-duty plastic wrap, and pound to ¼-inch thickness using a meat mallet or rolling pin. Sprinkle both sides of pork with salt and pepper. Place flour in a shallow bowl. Dredge pork in flour; shake off excess flour. Heat 1½ teaspoons olive oil in a nonstick skillet over medium-high heat. Add half of pork, and cook 2 minutes on each side or until done. Remove pork from pan, and keep warm. Repeat procedure with remaining 1½ teaspoons oil and pork. Return pork to pan. Add wine and broth; bring to a boil. Stir in olives and capers; cook 4 minutes. Sprinkle with parsley. Yield: 4 servings (serving size: 2 medallions and 2 tablespoons sauce).

CALORIES 212 (34% from fat); FAT 8.1g (sat 1.8g, mono 5.1g, poly 0.9g); PROTEIN 25.5g; CARB 8.1g; FIBER 0.9g; CHOL 74mg; IRON 2.7mg; SODIUM 894mg; CALC 30mg

MENU *serves 4*

Pork Medallions with Olive-Caper Sauce

Steamed fresh (or frozen whole) green beans

Vermicelli with garlic and herbs

Cook 8 ounces vermicelli according to package directions, omitting salt and fat. Drain and toss with 2 tablespoons each of extra-virgin olive oil, lemon juice, and chopped fresh parsley; 2 teaspoons bottled minced garlic; and 1 teaspoon each of dried basil, salt, and black pepper.

Game Plan

1 While water for pasta comes to a boil:

   • Cut, pound, and dredge pork.

2 While pasta cooks:

   • Cook pork.

   • Steam green beans.

3 Toss ingredients together for pasta.

Spice-Rubbed Pork Skewers with Tomatoes

MENU *serves 4*

Spice-Rubbed Pork Skewers with Tomatoes

Peanutty couscous

Place 1½ cups fat-free, less-sodium chicken broth in a 1½-quart casserole dish. Cover and microwave at HIGH 3 minutes. Stir in 1 (5.7-ounce) box couscous; cover and let stand 5 minutes. Combine 3 tablespoons low-sodium soy sauce, 1 tablespoon peanut oil, ½ teaspoon crushed red pepper, and ¼ teaspoon garlic powder in a small bowl. Fluff couscous with a fork; stir in soy mixture, 2 tablespoons chopped roasted peanuts, and 2 sliced green onions.

Limeade

Game Plan

1 While grill heats:

- Prepare seasoning mixture for pork.
- Slice pork.
- Season pork.
- Let pork stand.

2 While pork stands:

- Prepare couscous.

3 While couscous stands:

- Grill pork skewers.

If you are using wooden skewers, soak them in about 2 inches of water for approximately 15 minutes while the grill heats, and pat them dry before adding the meat and tomatoes. This prevents the skewers from burning on the grill.

1 tablespoon brown sugar
1 teaspoon ground coriander
½ teaspoon garlic powder
½ teaspoon freshly ground black pepper
¼ teaspoon salt
¼ teaspoon ground cumin
⅛ teaspoon ground ginger
1 (1-pound) pork tenderloin, trimmed
1 teaspoon chile paste
16 cherry tomatoes
Cooking spray
2 tablespoons low-sodium soy sauce
1 teaspoon dark sesame oil

❶ Prepare grill.

❷ Combine first 7 ingredients. Cut pork in half crosswise; cut each half into 8 lengthwise strips. Combine pork strips and chile paste in a shallow dish; toss to coat. Sprinkle brown sugar mixture evenly over pork; toss to coat. Let pork stand 10 minutes.

❸ Thread 1 pork strip and 1 tomato onto each of 16 (10-inch) wooden skewers. Place skewers on a grill rack coated with cooking spray. Grill 3 minutes on each side or until desired degree of doneness. Combine soy sauce and oil in a small bowl. Drizzle soy sauce mixture evenly over pork. Yield: 4 servings (serving size: 4 skewers).

CALORIES 196 (30% from fat); FAT 6.6g (sat 2g, mono 2.6g, poly 1g); PROTEIN 25.5g; CARB 8.2g; FIBER 1.2g; CHOL 75mg; IRON 1.8mg; SODIUM 507mg; CALC 18mg

Pork au Poivre

Not only is this recipe easy to prepare, but it also contains a short ingredients list and is loaded with flavor. It's perfect for just about any occasion.

- 1 pound pork tenderloin, trimmed
- 1 tablespoon coarsely ground black pepper, divided
- 2 teaspoons olive oil

Cooking spray

- ½ cup fat-free, less-sodium chicken broth
- ½ cup dry red wine
- 1 teaspoon Dijon mustard
- 1 teaspoon tomato paste
- ¼ teaspoon salt

❶ Preheat oven to 425°.

❷ Cut pork lengthwise, cutting to, but not through, other side. Open halves, laying pork flat. Sprinkle each side of open pork halves with 1½ teaspoons pepper. Heat oil in a large ovenproof skillet coated with cooking spray over medium-high heat. Add pork; cook 2 minutes on each side. Place pan in oven, and bake at 425° for 12 minutes or until meat thermometer registers 160° (slightly pink). Remove pork from pan; keep warm.

❸ Add broth and remaining 4 ingredients to pan; stir well with a whisk. Bring to a boil over medium heat; cook until reduced to ½ cup (about 3 minutes). Yield: 4 servings (serving size: 3 ounces pork and 2 tablespoons sauce).

CALORIES 162 (32% from fat); FAT 5.7g (sat 1.3g, mono 2.9g, poly 0.5g); PROTEIN 24.5g; CARB 1.9g; FIBER 0.5g; CHOL 74mg; IRON 2.1mg; SODIUM 303mg; CALC 18mg

---

MENU *serves 4*

Pork au Poivre

Boiled new potatoes tossed with parsley

Creamed spinach
Heat a large nonstick skillet over medium-high heat; coat with cooking spray. Add ½ cup chopped onion, and sauté 5 minutes or until tender. Stir in 2 (10-ounce) packages thawed frozen chopped spinach; cook 1 minute. Stir in ½ cup spreadable cheese with garlic and herbs (such as Alouette); sprinkle with 2 tablespoons grated fresh Parmesan cheese.

Game Plan

1 While potatoes cook:
- •Cook pork.
- •Prepare spinach.

2 While broth mixture for pork reduces:
- •Chop parsley.
- •Toss potatoes with parsley.

Pork Tenderloin with Onions and Dried Cranberries

Parmesan spinach
Heat 2 teaspoons olive oil in a large nonstick skillet over medium-high heat. Add 3 minced garlic cloves; sauté 2 minutes. Add 2 (10-ounce) packages thawed frozen chopped spinach; cook 5 minutes or until thoroughly heated. Stir in ½ cup shredded fresh Parmesan cheese, ½ teaspoon salt, and ¼ teaspoon freshly ground black pepper.

Couscous

Game Plan

1 While pork browns:
- •Slice onion.

2 While pork simmers:
- •Prepare Parmesan spinach.
- •Prepare couscous.

Pork Tenderloin with Onions and Dried Cranberries

For a casual get-together, this easy meal accommodates a crowd. Plain couscous soaks up all the tasty sauce from the pork.

  2 (1-pound) pork tenderloins, trimmed
  1 teaspoon salt, divided
  ¼ teaspoon freshly ground black pepper
  1 tablespoon olive oil
  3 cups (¼-inch-thick) slices onion (about 3 medium)
  1 cup light beer
  1 cup fat-free, less-sodium chicken broth
  ½ cup dried cranberries

1 Sprinkle pork with ¾ teaspoon salt and pepper. Heat oil in a large nonstick skillet over medium-high heat. Add pork; cook 6 minutes, browning on all sides. Remove pork from pan. Add onion to pan; reduce heat, and cook 8 minutes or until browned. Remove onion from pan; sprinkle with ¼ teaspoon salt, and set aside. Add beer to pan; cook 1 minute over high heat or until reduced to ½ cup.

2 Return pork and onion to pan; add broth, and bring to a boil. Cover, reduce heat, and simmer 30 minutes. Stir in cranberries; cover and cook 30 minutes or until pork is tender. Remove pan from heat. Place pork on a cutting board; cover and let stand 5 minutes. Cut each tenderloin into 12 slices. Serve pork with onion mixture. Yield: 8 servings (serving size: 3 pork slices and ¼ cup onion mixture).

CALORIES 178 (27% from fat); FAT 5.4g (sat 1.5g, mono 2.9g, poly 0.6g); PROTEIN 22.5g; CARB 9.4g; FIBER 0.8g; CHOL 68mg; IRON 1.5mg; SODIUM 394mg; CALC 14mg

Spicy Pork Tenderloins with Uniq Fruit Salsa

The spice mixture easily doubles; store in an airtight container, and use to season chicken or shrimp for a quick, flavorful entrée. Garnish with lime wedges.

PORK:
- 1 tablespoon salt-free Mexican seasoning blend
- 1 teaspoon ground cinnamon
- 1 teaspoon ground cumin
- ¾ teaspoon kosher salt
- ¼ teaspoon ground red pepper
- ⅛ teaspoon ground nutmeg
- 2 teaspoons minced garlic
- 2 (1-pound) pork tenderloins, trimmed

Cooking spray

SALSA:
- 2 cups chopped peeled Uniq fruit (about 1)
- ½ cup diced red onion
- ½ cup diced red bell pepper
- ½ cup diced avocado
- ¼ cup chopped fresh cilantro
- 1 tablespoon honey
- 1 tablespoon fresh lime juice
- ¼ teaspoon kosher salt

① To prepare pork, combine first 6 ingredients in a small bowl. Rub garlic over pork. Rub spice mixture over pork. Cover and chill 1 hour.

② Preheat oven to 400°.

③ Heat a cast-iron or ovenproof grill pan over medium-high heat; coat with cooking spray. Add pork to pan; cook 4 minutes or until just browned on all sides. Transfer pork to oven. Bake at 400° for 20 minutes or until a thermometer registers 160° (slightly pink). Let pork stand 10 minutes before slicing. Cut into ¼-inch-thick slices.

④ To prepare salsa, combine Uniq fruit and remaining ingredients in a bowl. Cover and chill until ready to serve. Serve pork with salsa. Yield: 8 servings (serving size: 3 ounces pork and ⅓ cup salsa).

CALORIES 211 (30% from fat); FAT 7g (sat 2.2g, mono 3.1g, poly 0.7g); PROTEIN 26.8g; CARB 9.9g; FIBER 1.7g; CHOL 80mg; IRON 1.7mg; SODIUM 323mg; CALCmg

---

MENU *serves 8*

Spicy Pork Tenderloins with Uniq Fruit Salsa

Black beans and rice
Bring 1¼ cups fat-free, less-sodium chicken broth to a boil in a medium saucepan. Add ¾ cup long-grain rice; cover, reduce heat, and simmer 18 minutes or until liquid is absorbed. Stir in 1 cup rinsed and drained canned black beans and ¼ cup chopped fresh cilantro; cook until heated. Stir in ¼ teaspoon salt.

Game Plan

1 Rub spice mixture over pork; cover and chill.

2 While oven heats:
- Boil broth for rice.

3 While pork and rice cook:
- Prepare salsa; cover and chill.

4 While pork stands:
- Add remaining ingredients to rice.

Pork Tenderloin Studded with Rosemary and Garlic

MENU *serves 4*

Pork Tenderloin Studded with Rosemary and Garlic

Caramelized carrots
Preheat oven to 475°. Combine 1 pound baby carrots, 1 tablespoon low-sodium soy sauce, 2 teaspoons brown sugar, 2 teaspoons olive oil, ¼ teaspoon salt, and ¼ teaspoon black pepper. Arrange in a single layer on a baking sheet coated with cooking spray; if preparing entire menu, place in oven on rack below pork. Bake at 475° for 15 minutes or until tender, turning once.

Boiled red potatoes

Game Plan

1 While oven heats:
- Trim and make slits in pork.
- Rub pork with rosemary mixture.
- Bring water to a boil for potatoes.

2 While pork roasts:
- Prepare carrots.
- Place carrots in oven during final 15 minutes of pork's cooking time.
- Boil potatoes.

Tender, moist, and fragrant, this hearty main dish is a breeze to prepare. Strip rosemary leaves by running your fingertips along the stem in the opposite direction from which the leaves grow.

- 2 tablespoons finely chopped fresh rosemary
- 4 garlic cloves, minced
- 1 (1-pound) pork tenderloin, trimmed
- ½ teaspoon salt
- ¼ teaspoon black pepper

Cooking spray

1 Preheat oven to 475°.
2 Combine rosemary and garlic. Make several ½-inch-deep slits in pork; place about half of rosemary mixture in slits. Rub pork with remaining rosemary mixture; sprinkle with salt and pepper. Place pork on a jelly-roll pan coated with cooking spray. Insert a meat thermometer into thickest portion of pork.
3 Bake at 475° for 20 minutes or until thermometer registers 160° (slightly pink) or to desired degree of doneness. Let stand 5 minutes, and cut into ¼-inch-thick slices. Yield: 4 servings (serving size: 3 ounces).

CALORIES 147 (26% from fat); FAT 4.2g (sat 1.4g, mono 1.6g, poly 0.4g); PROTEIN 24.2g; CARB 1.5g; FIBER 0.1g; CHOL 67mg; IRON 1.6mg; SODIUM 342mg; CALC 23mg

Korean-Style Pork Tenderloin

Nutty, slightly sweetened spaghetti squash and tender, sweet Broccolini nicely complement this pork and its zesty marinade.

⅓ cup low-sodium soy sauce
3 tablespoons rice vinegar
2 tablespoons sugar
1 tablespoon minced peeled fresh ginger
1 tablespoon dark sesame oil
¼ teaspoon crushed red pepper
4 garlic cloves, minced
1½ pounds pork tenderloin, trimmed
Cooking spray

❶ Combine first 7 ingredients in a large zip-top plastic bag; add pork. Seal and marinate in refrigerator 8 hours or overnight, turning occasionally.
❷ Preheat oven to 425°.
❸ Heat a large ovenproof skillet over medium-high heat; coat with cooking spray. Remove pork from bag, reserving marinade. Add pork to pan; cook 6 minutes, browning on all sides.
❹ Place pan in oven; bake at 425° for 15 minutes or until meat thermometer registers 160° (slightly pink) or until desired degree of doneness. Let stand 5 minutes before slicing.
❺ Bring reserved marinade to a boil in a small saucepan. Reduce heat, and simmer 5 minutes.
❻ Cut pork into ¼-inch-thick slices; serve with sauce. Yield: 6 servings (serving size: 3 ounces pork and about 1 tablespoon sauce).

CALORIES 184 (30% from fat); FAT 6.2g (sat 1.7g, mono 2.7g, poly 1.4g); PROTEIN 24.7g; CARB 6.2g; FIBER 0.2g; CHOL 74mg; IRON 1.7mg; SODIUM 531mg; CALC 12mg

Quick Tip: To mince ginger easily, place a small, peeled piece in a garlic press and squeeze.

MENU *serves 6*

Korean-Style Pork Tenderloin

Buttered spaghetti squash

Cut 1 (3-pound) spaghetti squash in half lengthwise; discard seeds. Place squash halves, cut sides down, in a baking dish; add ¼ cup water to dish. Cover with heavy-duty plastic wrap; vent. Microwave at HIGH 15 minutes or until squash is tender when pierced with a fork. Scrape inside of squash with a fork to remove the spaghetti-like strands. Toss squash strands with 1 tablespoon butter, 2 teaspoons sugar, 1 teaspoon grated lemon rind, ¼ teaspoon salt, and ¼ teaspoon black pepper.

Sautéed Broccolini

Game Plan

1 **Prepare marinade, and marinate pork 8 hours or overnight.**

2 **While oven heats for pork:**
   • Microwave spaghetti squash.

3 **While pork cooks:**
   • Cook reserved marinade.
   • Scrape squash, and toss with seasonings.
   • Sauté Broccolini.

MENU *serves 8*

Peppercorn-Crusted Pork Tenderloin with Soy-Caramel Sauce

Asian vegetable stir-fry

Heat 1 tablespoon canola oil in a large skillet over medium-high heat. Add 2 teaspoons minced garlic; sauté 30 seconds. Add 2 cups matchstick-cut carrots and 2 cups blanched broccoli florets; sauté 3 minutes or until beginning to soften. Add 1 cup red bell pepper strips, 1 cup sliced shiitake mushrooms, ½ teaspoon salt, and ¼ teaspoon crushed red pepper; sauté 5 minutes or until liquid almost evaporates and vegetables are crisp-tender. Stir in 1½ teaspoons sesame oil.

Jasmine rice with green onions

Game Plan

1 While pork cooks:

- Cook rice.

- Prepare Asian vegetable stir-fry.

2 While pork stands:

- Chop green onions for rice.

- Prepare sauce.

3 Toss together rice and green onions.

Peppercorn-Crusted Pork Tenderloin with Soy-Caramel Sauce

Impress your guests with this Asian-inspired menu. Cook the no-fuss rice and prepare the stir-fry as the tenderloin roasts.

Cooking spray
- ¼ cup minced white onion
- 1 teaspoon grated peeled fresh ginger
- 2 garlic cloves, minced
- 1 cup water
- ½ cup sugar
- ¼ cup low-sodium soy sauce
- 2 tablespoons red wine vinegar
- 1½ teaspoons Dijon mustard
- 2 tablespoons butter
- 2 (1-pound) pork tenderloins, trimmed
- 1 tablespoon black peppercorns, crushed
- 1½ teaspoons chopped fresh thyme
- ¼ teaspoon salt

1 Heat a small saucepan over medium heat; coat with cooking spray. Add onion, ginger, and garlic; sauté 2 minutes. Add water and sugar; bring to a boil. Cook until reduced to ½ cup (about 5 minutes). Remove from heat; carefully stir in soy sauce, vinegar, and mustard. Add butter, stirring with a whisk. Set aside; keep warm.

2 Preheat oven to 350°.

3 Rub tenderloins evenly with pepper, thyme, and salt. Heat a large ovenproof non-stick skillet over medium-high heat; coat with cooking spray. Add tenderloins, browning on all sides (about 5 minutes). Bake at 350° for 23 minutes or until a thermometer registers 160° (slightly pink); let stand 10 minutes. Cut each tenderloin into 12 slices; serve with sauce. Yield: 8 servings (serving size: 3 slices pork and 2 tablespoons sauce).

CALORIES 227 (28% from fat); FAT 7g (sat 2.8g, mono 3g, poly 0.6g); PROTEIN 24.5g; CARB 15.3g; FIBER 0.4g; CHOL 81mg; IRON 1.7mg; SODIUM 441mg; CALC 16mg

Hoisin Pork Tenderloin

To prepare 2 servings of this dish, replace the pork tenderloin with 2 (4-ounce) boneless pork chops, and reduce the marinade ingredients by half. Sprinkle each pork chop with 1 teaspoon sesame seeds for the last 5 to 10 minutes of cooking. Substitute soba or lo mein noodles for udon, if you prefer.

¼ cup hoisin sauce
2 tablespoons sliced green onions
2 tablespoons low-sodium soy sauce
1 tablespoon rice wine vinegar
2 garlic cloves, minced
1 (1-pound) pork tenderloin, trimmed
Cooking spray
1 tablespoon sesame seeds

❶ Combine first 5 ingredients in a large zip-top plastic bag; add pork to bag. Seal and marinate in refrigerator 2 hours, turning bag once.
❷ Preheat oven to 425°.
❸ Remove pork from bag, reserving marinade. Place pork on rack of a broiler pan or roasting pan coated with cooking spray; place rack in pan. Bake at 425° for 15 minutes. Sprinkle pork with sesame seeds; bake an additional 5 minutes or until a thermometer registers 160° (slightly pink). Place pork on a cutting board; let stand 10 minutes. Cut into ½-inch-thick slices.
❹ Pour reserved marinade into a small saucepan; bring to a boil. Cook until reduced to ⅓ cup (about 2 minutes); serve with pork. Yield: 4 servings (serving size: 3 ounces pork and about 4 teaspoons sauce).

CALORIES 194 (27% from fat); FAT 5.8g (sat 1.7g, mono 2.2g, poly 1.1g); PROTEIN 25.4g; CARB 8.7g; FIBER 0.9g; CHOL 68mg; IRON 2mg; SODIUM 574mg; CALC 37mg

MENU   *serves 4*

Hoisin Pork Tenderloin

Udon noodle toss
Heat 1 tablespoon canola oil in a large nonstick skillet over medium-high heat. Add 1 cup red bell pepper strips, ½ cup matchstick-cut carrots, and 2 minced garlic cloves; sauté 3 minutes. Add 4 cups hot cooked udon noodles, 2 tablespoons chopped fresh cilantro, 2 tablespoons low-sodium soy sauce, 2 tablespoons fresh lime juice, and 2 teaspoons dark sesame oil; toss to coat.

Steamed sugar snap peas

Game Plan

1 Marinate pork.

2 While pork bakes:
- Cook pasta.
- Cut red bell pepper into strips, mince garlic, and chop cilantro.
- Squeeze lime for juice for noodle toss.

3 While pork stands:
- Steam sugar snap peas.
- Sauté red pepper mixture, and toss pasta ingredients.

Pork Tenderloin with Pomegranate Glaze

Wild rice pilaf

Melt 1 tablespoon butter in a large saucepan over medium-high heat. Add ¼ cup diced shallots; sauté 2 minutes. Stir in 1 cup long-grain and wild rice blend; sauté 1 minute. Stir in 2 cups fat-free, less-sodium chicken broth; 1 cup water; ¼ teaspoon salt; and ¼ teaspoon freshly ground black pepper. Bring to a boil; cover, reduce heat, and simmer 30 minutes. Stir in ½ cup dried cherries; cover and cook 10 minutes or until liquid is absorbed. Remove from heat; stir in ⅓ cup chopped fresh parsley and ⅓ cup toasted chopped pecans.

Steamed green beans

Game Plan

1 While rice cooks:
- •Prepare glaze for pork.

2 Preheat oven.

3 Cook pork.

4 While pork stands:
- •Steam green beans.

Pork Tenderloin with Pomegranate Glaze

For food safety reasons, a portion of the glaze is kept separate to baste the pork with while raw and during cooking; the remainder is served with the cooked roasts. The glaze will thicken significantly if made ahead; microwave at HIGH for a few seconds at a time, stirring after each heating, until the glaze is thinned.

- 2 cups pomegranate juice
- ¼ cup sugar
- 2 (¾-pound) pork tenderloins, trimmed
- ½ teaspoon salt
- ¼ teaspoon freshly ground black pepper
- Cooking spray

1 Preheat oven to 450°.

2 Combine juice and sugar in a medium saucepan over medium heat, and bring to a boil. Cook until reduced to ½ cup (about 8 minutes). Pour half of glaze into a small bowl, and set aside.

3 Sprinkle pork evenly with salt and pepper. Place pork on rack of a broiler pan coated with cooking spray; place rack in pan. Brush pork with half of glaze in saucepan. Bake at 450° for 15 minutes or until a thermometer registers 145°. Baste pork with remaining glaze in saucepan; bake an additional 5 minutes or until thermometer registers 160° (slightly pink).

4 Remove pork from oven; baste with half of glaze in bowl. Let pork stand 10 minutes; cut across grain into thin slices. Serve pork with remaining glaze mixture. Yield: 6 servings (serving size: 3 ounces pork and 2 teaspoons glaze mixture).

CALORIES 215 (16% from fat); FAT 3.9g (sat 1.3g, mono 1.8g, poly 0.4g); PROTEIN 24.2g; CARB 20.1g; FIBER 0g; CHOL 74mg; IRON 1.5mg; SODIUM 263mg; CALC 19mg

MENU *serves 8*

Jerk Pork Tenderloin with Pineapple-Plum Relish

Coconut rice

Heat 2 tablespoons olive oil in a large saucepan over medium-high heat. Add 2 cups uncooked basmati rice; sauté 1 minute. Stir in 2 cups fat-free, less-sodium chicken broth, 1 (14-ounce) can coconut milk, and 1 teaspoon salt; bring to a boil. Cover, reduce heat, and simmer 20 minutes or until liquid is absorbed. Stir in ½ cup chopped green onions.

Stewed turnip greens

Game Plan

1 Marinate pork.

2 While turnip greens cook:
   - Grill pork.
   - Prepare rice.

3 While pork stands:
   - Prepare relish for pork.

4 Slice pork.

Jerk Pork Tenderloin with Pineapple-Plum Relish

Jerk seasoning is characteristically sweet and spicy. Habanero peppers crank up the heat; if you prefer your food with less heat, use a milder pepper, such as jalapeño. The sweet-tartness of the relish complements the spicy flavors.

PORK:

- 1½ cups chopped green onions
- ¼ cup red wine vinegar
- 3 tablespoons brown sugar
- 2 tablespoons olive oil
- 2 tablespoons fresh lime juice
- 2 tablespoons low-sodium soy sauce
- 1 teaspoon salt
- 1 teaspoon ground allspice
- ¾ teaspoon dried thyme
- ¼ teaspoon ground cinnamon
- ¼ teaspoon freshly ground black pepper
- 2 garlic cloves, peeled
- 1 habanero pepper
- 2 (1-pound) pork tenderloins, trimmed

Cooking spray

RELISH:

- 2 cups finely chopped pineapple
- ¾ cup finely chopped ripe plum (about 3 medium)
- 2 tablespoons chopped fresh mint
- 1 tablespoon cider vinegar
- 1 tablespoon honey
- 2 teaspoons grated peeled fresh ginger
- 1 teaspoon low-sodium soy sauce

❶ To prepare pork, combine first 13 ingredients in a blender; process until smooth. Place green onion mixture in a large zip-top bag. Add pork to bag; seal. Marinate in refrigerator 8 hours or overnight, turning occasionally.

❷ Prepare grill.

❸ Remove pork from bag; discard marinade. Place pork on a grill rack coated with cooking spray; grill 23 minutes or until a thermometer registers 160° (slightly pink) or until desired degree of doneness. Let pork stand 10 minutes. Cut pork into ½-inch-thick slices.

❹ To prepare relish, combine pineapple and remaining 6 ingredients in a bowl, stirring well. Serve with pork. Yield: 8 servings (serving size: 3 ounces pork and about ⅓ cup relish).

CALORIES 154 (24% from fat); FAT 4.1g (sat 1.4g, mono 1.8g, poly 0.4g); PROTEIN 17.5g; CARB 11.7g; FIBER 0.5g; CHOL 48mg; IRON 1.1mg; SODIUM 101mg; CALC 13mg

Cumin-Spiced Pork with Avocado-Tomatillo Salsa

The lemon juice in the salsa keeps the avocado green. Pile the sliced pork and salsa on warm flour tortillas, and roll up for soft tacos.

PORK:
- 1 teaspoon ground cumin
- 1 teaspoon chili powder
- ½ teaspoon paprika
- ½ teaspoon lemon pepper
- ⅛ teaspoon salt
- 1 (1-pound) pork tenderloin, trimmed

SALSA:
- 2 tomatillos
- ½ cup diced peeled avocado
- ½ cup chopped peeled cucumber
- ¼ cup chopped fresh cilantro
- 1 teaspoon lemon rind
- 2 tablespoons fresh lemon juice
- ¼ teaspoon salt
- 1 minced seeded jalapeño pepper

❶ Preheat oven to 425°.

❷ To prepare pork, combine first 5 ingredients; rub over pork. Place pork on a jelly-roll pan. Bake at 425° for 25 minutes or until a thermometer registers 160° (slightly pink). Let stand 5 minutes before slicing.

❸ To prepare salsa, discard husks and stems from tomatillos. Finely chop tomatillos; place in a bowl. Add avocado and remaining 6 ingredients; toss well. Yield: 4 servings (serving size: 3 ounces pork and about ⅓ cup salsa).

CALORIES 182 (36% from fat); FAT 7.2g (sat 1.9g, mono 3.6g, poly 1g); PROTEIN 24.7g; CARB 4.5g; FIBER 2g; CHOL 74mg; IRON 2.1mg; SODIUM 343mg; CALC 20mg

Quick Tip: You can substitute ½ cup chopped drained canned tomatillos or ½ cup chopped green tomatoes for fresh tomatillos.

MENU *serves 4*

Cumin-Spiced Pork with Avocado-Tomatillo Salsa

Seasoned black beans
Heat 1 tablespoon olive oil in a saucepan over medium heat. Add ¾ cup chopped onion, 1 tablespoon chopped jalapeño, and 2 teaspoons minced garlic; cook 5 minutes or until tender, stirring frequently. Add 1 tablespoon red wine vinegar, ¼ teaspoon dried oregano, and 1 (15-ounce) can black beans, rinsed and drained; cook 5 minutes or until thoroughly heated, stirring frequently.

Warm flour tortillas

Game Plan

1 While oven heats:
- Combine spice mixture for pork.
- Chop ingredients for salsa and black beans.

2 While pork bakes:
- Prepare black beans.
- Combine salsa ingredients.

3 While pork stands:
- Warm tortillas according to package directions.

MENU *serves 4*

Red Chile-Pork Tacos with Caramelized Onions

Fruit salsa

Combine 2 cups sliced banana, ½ cup diced pineapple, ¼ cup chopped fresh cilantro, 1 teaspoon brown sugar, ¼ teaspoon salt, and 2 diced seeded jalapeño peppers.

Green salad

Game Plan

1 Prepare pork.

2 While pork cooks:

- Slice onion.
- Chop tomato and green onions.
- Prepare salad.

3 While onion cooks:

- Prepare salsa.

Red Chile-Pork Tacos with Caramelized Onions

Sweet, succulent onions are the perfect foil for this savory pork taco filling. Ancho chile powder gives the meat a mild, slightly fruity chile flavor.

> 1 tablespoon ancho chile powder
> 1 teaspoon brown sugar
> ½ teaspoon salt
> 1 pound pork tenderloin, trimmed
> Cooking spray
> 1 teaspoon canola oil
> 3 cups thinly sliced onion
> 8 hard taco shells
> ½ cup chopped tomato
> 8 teaspoons chopped green onions

❶ Preheat oven to 425°.

❷ Combine first 3 ingredients; rub evenly over pork. Place pork on a broiler pan coated with cooking spray. Bake at 425° for 20 minutes or until a thermometer registers 160° (slightly pink). Remove pork from oven; let stand 5 minutes before slicing.

❸ While pork cooks, heat oil in a large nonstick skillet coated with cooking spray over medium heat. Add onion; cover and cook 10 minutes or until golden brown, stirring frequently. Uncover and sauté 1 minute.

❹ Fill each taco shell with about 2 ounces pork, 3 tablespoons sautéed onion, 1 tablespoon tomato, and 1 teaspoon green onions. Yield: 4 servings (serving size: 2 tacos).

CALORIES 304 (30% from fat); FAT 10.2g (sat 2.2g, mono 5.4g, poly 1.8g); PROTEIN 26.9g; CARB 25g; FIBER 4.5g; CHOL 74mg; IRON 2.1mg; SODIUM 444mg; CALC 46mg

Quick Tip: Covering the onions while they cook helps them caramelize more quickly and requires less oil.

Sunny Frittata

A combination of egg substitute, cheddar cheese, and yellow bell pepper lends the frittata a cheerful hue. Substitute red or green bell pepper, if you prefer. Stir the egg mixture while it cooks for the first 2 minutes to keep it from browning too much.

2 cups egg substitute
½ cup fat-free milk
¼ teaspoon salt
¼ teaspoon black pepper
Cooking spray
⅔ cup (4 ounces) diced ham
½ cup diced yellow bell pepper
½ cup thinly sliced green onions
¼ cup (1 ounce) reduced-fat shredded cheddar cheese

1 Preheat oven to 375°.
2 Combine first 4 ingredients in a small bowl; stir with a whisk.

3 Heat a medium nonstick skillet over medium-high heat; coat with cooking spray. Add ham, bell pepper, and onions to pan; sauté 2 minutes. Stir in egg mixture. Reduce heat to medium, and cook 5 minutes, stirring occasionally during first 2 minutes. Top with cheese. Wrap handle of pan with foil; bake at 375° for 12 minutes or until center is set. Cut frittata into 4 wedges. Yield: 4 servings (serving size: 1 wedge).

CALORIES 194 (37% from fat); FAT 8g (sat 2.7g, mono 2.1g, poly 2.2g); PROTEIN 24.8g; CARB 4.6g; FIBER 0.9g; CHOL 28mg; IRON 3.1mg; SODIUM 401mg; CALC 153mg

MENU *serves 4*

Sunny Frittata

Pineapple salad
Combine 4 cups cubed fresh pineapple and 1 cup halved red grapes in a medium bowl. Combine 2 tablespoons orange juice, 1 tablespoon honey, ⅛ teaspoon ground red pepper, and a dash of salt in a small bowl. Drizzle juice mixture over pineapple mixture; sprinkle evenly with 2 tablespoons toasted sweetened coconut and 2 tablespoons chopped macadamia nuts.

Mango sorbet

Game Plan

1 While oven heats:
- Dice ham and bell pepper, slice green onions, and shred cheese.
- Mix egg substitute, milk, and seasonings.
- Sauté frittata ingredients.

2 While frittata bakes:
- Prepare pineapple salad.

Lumberjack Hash

MENU *serves 4*

Lumberjack Hash

Honeyed citrus salad
Place 2 cups grapefruit sections and 2 cups orange sections in a large bowl. Combine 1 tablespoon chopped fresh mint, 1 tablespoon fresh lime juice, and 2 tablespoons honey in a small bowl; stir with a whisk. Pour dressing over fruit; toss gently to coat. Refrigerate until ready to serve.

Corn bread twists (such as Pillsbury)

Game Plan

1 Preheat oven for corn bread twists.

2 While oven heats:
  •Prepare citrus salad; refrigerate until serving time.

3 While twists bake:
  •Prepare hash

Frozen hash browns make this version of the popular diner dish quick and easy to prepare.

2 teaspoons canola oil
2 teaspoons butter
1 cup chopped onion
1 cup chopped green bell pepper
2 garlic cloves, minced
8 cups frozen shredded hash brown potatoes, thawed (about 1 pound)
½ teaspoon salt
½ teaspoon black pepper
4 ounces 33%-less-sodium ham, diced
¾ cup (3 ounces) shredded reduced-fat cheddar cheese

1 Heat oil and butter in a large nonstick skillet over medium heat. Add onion; cook 5 minutes. Add bell pepper and garlic; cook 3 minutes. Add potatoes, salt, pepper, and ham; cook 16 minutes or until potatoes are golden brown, stirring occasionally. Top with cheese; cook 2 minutes or until cheese melts. Yield: 4 servings (serving size: 1¼ cups).

CALORIES 276 (30% from fat); FAT 9.1g (sat 4.2g, mono 1.6g, poly 1.6g); PROTEIN 16.5g; CARB 33.7g; FIBER 3.5g; CHOL 33mg; IRON 0.8mg; SODIUM 738mg; CALC 208mg

Smoked Ham Hash

Vary the taste of this recipe by using smoked turkey or rotisserie chicken in place of the ham.

1 tablespoon butter
2 cups frozen hash brown potatoes with onions and peppers
1 cup chopped onion
¾ cup chopped red bell pepper
1½ cups fat-free, less-sodium chicken broth
2 tablespoons half-and-half
2 teaspoons Worcestershire sauce
2 teaspoons ketchup
1½ cups chopped smoked ham
¼ teaspoon freshly ground black pepper
2 tablespoons thinly sliced green onions
2 tablespoons chopped fresh parsley

❶ Heat butter in a large nonstick skillet over medium-high heat. Add potatoes, onion, and bell pepper to pan; sauté 5 minutes or until lightly browned. Stir in broth and next 3 ingredients; bring to a boil. Cook 5 minutes or until liquid almost evaporates. Stir in ham and black pepper; cook 1½ minutes or until thoroughly heated. Sprinkle with onions and parsley. Yield: 4 servings (serving size: about 1 cup).

CALORIES 206 (29% from fat); FAT 6.6g (sat 3.4g, mono 1.1g, poly 0.3g); PROTEIN 13.8g; CARB 25g; FIBER 3.6g; CHOL 41mg; IRON 2.1mg; SODIUM 847mg; CALC 47mg

Quick Tip: Purchase prechopped ham from the fresh pork or luncheon meat section of your supermarket.

MENU *serves 4*

Smoked Ham Hash

Peppery wilted spinach

Heat 1 tablespoon olive oil in a large nonstick skillet over medium-high heat. Add 1 minced garlic clove; sauté 30 seconds. Gradually add 2 (10-ounce) packages fresh spinach; cook 3 minutes or until spinach wilts. Stir in 1 tablespoon pepper vinegar, ¼ teaspoon salt, and ⅛ teaspoon freshly ground black pepper.

Orange wedges

Game Plan

1 **While potatoes cook:**
   • Chop ham and parsley.
   • Slice green onions.

2 **While broth mixture cooks:**
   • Mince garlic for spinach.
   • Cut oranges into wedges.

3 **Remove hash from skillet; cook spinach in same pan.**

MENU *serves 4*

Ham and Gruyère–Stuffed Potatoes

Green bean salad
Cook 1 pound (1-inch) cut green beans in boiling water 5 minutes or until crisp-tender; drain and rinse with cold water. Drain green beans thoroughly, and place in a large bowl; add 2 cups halved cherry tomatoes to green beans. Combine 2 tablespoons fresh lemon juice, 2 teaspoons olive oil, 1 teaspoon bottled minced garlic, ½ teaspoon dried basil, ¼ teaspoon salt, and ¼ teaspoon pepper in a small bowl; stir with a whisk. Pour vinaigrette over green bean mixture; toss to coat.

Garlic bread

Game Plan

1 While microwaving potatoes:

- Shred cheese.
- Chop ham and parsley.
- Measure ingredients for potatoes.
- Halve cherry tomatoes for salad.

2 While potatoes bake:

- Warm garlic bread.
- Prepare green bean salad.

Ham and Gruyère-Stuffed Potatoes

Microwaving cooks the potatoes in a flash; briefly baking them at a high temperature once they're stuffed toasts the cheese topping.

4 (8-ounce) baking potatoes
2 teaspoons butter
1 teaspoon bottled minced garlic
½ cup fat-free milk
½ cup (2 ounces) shredded Gruyère cheese, divided
½ cup chopped cooked ham
1 tablespoon chopped fresh parsley
¼ teaspoon salt
¼ teaspoon black pepper

1 Preheat oven to 500°.

2 Pierce potatoes with a fork, and arrange in a circle on paper towels in microwave oven. Cover potatoes with damp paper towels. Microwave potatoes at HIGH 12 minutes or until done, rearranging after 6 minutes. Let stand 2 minutes. Split open potatoes; scoop out pulp, leaving ¼-inch-thick shells. Reserve shells; set pulp aside.

3 Heat butter in a small skillet over medium-high heat. Add garlic; sauté 30 seconds. Add milk; bring to a simmer. Pour milk mixture over potato pulp. Add ¼ cup cheese, ham, and remaining 3 ingredients, mixing well. Stuff shells with potato mixture. Sprinkle evenly with ¼ cup cheese. Bake at 500° for 8 minutes or until cheese begins to brown. Yield: 4 servings.

CALORIES 358 (19% from fat); FAT 7.5g (sat 4.2g, mono 2.4g, poly 0.5g); PROTEIN 14.1g; CARB 59.8g; FIBER 5.5g; CHOL 30mg; IRON 3.5mg; SODIUM 425mg; CALC 209mg

Quick Tip: Keeping potatoes covered with damp paper towels helps them cook faster and stay moist as they microwave.

Spaghetti Carbonara

Chopped ham replaces the bacon for a meatier texture in this version of a classic Italian dish.

8 ounces uncooked spaghetti
1 cup chopped cooked ham
⅓ cup (1½ ounces) grated Parmigiano-Reggiano or Parmesan cheese
¼ cup reduced-fat sour cream
½ teaspoon salt
2 large eggs, lightly beaten
1 garlic clove, minced
¼ teaspoon coarsely ground black pepper

1 Cook pasta according to package directions, omitting salt and fat. Drain pasta in a colander over a bowl, reserving ½ cup cooking liquid.
2 Heat a large nonstick skillet over medium heat. Add ham, and cook 2 minutes or until thoroughly heated. Add pasta, and stir well. Combine cheese and next 4 ingredients; stir with a whisk. Add reserved cooking liquid to egg mixture, stirring with a whisk. Pour egg mixture over pasta mixture; stir well. Cook over low heat 5 minutes or until sauce thickens, stirring constantly (do not boil). Sprinkle with pepper. Yield: 4 servings (serving size: 1 cup).

CALORIES 352 (25% from fat); FAT 9.6g (sat 4.6g, mono 2.2g, poly 0.9g); PROTEIN 21g; CARB 45g; FIBER 1.4g; CHOL 139mg; IRON 1.7mg; SODIUM 748mg; CALC 179mg

Quick Tip: The water for the pasta will come to a boil faster if the pot is covered.

MENU *serves 4*

Spaghetti Carbonara

Steamed broccoli tossed with grated lemon rind

Mini ice-cream sandwiches
Spoon about 1 tablespoon strawberry low-fat ice cream onto each of 12 vanilla wafers; top each with 1 vanilla wafer. Freeze until ready to serve.

Game Plan

1 Prepare ice-cream sandwiches.

2 While pasta cooks:
  •Mince garlic.
  •Lightly beat eggs.
  •Measure ingredients for sauce.

3 While pasta mixture cooks:
  •Prepare broccoli.

MENU *serves 8*

Ham and Cheese Macaroni Bake with Peas

Spinach salad with poppy seed dressing

Combine ¼ cup low-fat evaporated milk, 3 tablespoons sugar, 1½ tablespoons poppy seeds, 2 tablespoons light sour cream, and 2 tablespoons white vinegar in a small bowl; stir with a whisk until smooth. Refrigerate until ready to toss salad. Combine 1½ cups quartered strawberries, ¼ cup thinly sliced red onion, and 1 (6-ounce) package baby spinach in a large bowl; toss gently. Drizzle dressing mixture over spinach mixture; toss gently. Serve immediately.

Orange sections over low-fat vanilla ice cream

Game Plan

1 Preheat oven.

2 While water for pasta comes to a boil:

  • Prepare ingredients for casserole.

3 While pasta cooks:

  • Prepare salad dressing; chill.

  • Prepare orange sections; chill.

4 While casserole bakes:

  • Toss salad.

Ham and Cheese Macaroni Bake with Peas

The heat of the red pepper gives this mac and cheese an added punch of flavor.

1 pound uncooked medium elbow macaroni
1½ cups chopped lean ham
1½ cups frozen peas
Cooking spray
½ cup finely chopped onion
3 cups 2% reduced-fat milk
1 cup (4 ounces) shredded reduced-fat extrasharp cheddar cheese
1 cup (4 ounces) shredded Swiss cheese
¾ teaspoon salt
¼ teaspoon freshly ground black pepper
⅛ teaspoon ground red pepper
2 (1-ounce) slices white bread
2 tablespoons butter, melted

1 Preheat oven to 400°.

2 Cook pasta in boiling water 6 minutes. Drain pasta and rinse with cold water; drain again. Combine pasta, ham, and peas in a large bowl; set aside.

3 Heat a medium saucepan over medium heat; coat with cooking spray. Add onion to pan; cook 4 minutes, stirring frequently. Add milk; bring to simmer. Remove from heat; stir in cheeses, salt, and peppers. Pour cheese mixture over pasta mixture; stir to coat. Spoon pasta mixture into a 13 x 9-inch baking dish coated with cooking spray.

4 Place bread in a food processor; pulse 10 times or until coarse crumbs measure 1¼ cups. Combine breadcrumbs and butter in a bowl. Arrange breadcrumb mixture evenly over pasta mixture. Bake at 400° for 20 minutes or until lightly browned. Yield: 8 servings (serving size: 1¼ cups).

CALORIES 470 (29% from fat); FAT 15.1g (sat 8.5g, mono 4.4g, poly 1.1g); PROTEIN 27g; CARB 56.1g; FIBER 3.1g; CHOL 54mg; IRON 2.8mg; SODIUM 771mg; CALC 393mg

Quick Tip: Look for preshredded cheese in the dairy section of your supermarket.

MENU *serves 4*

Prosciutto and Gruyère Strombolis

Tomato-basil soup
Heat 2 teaspoons olive oil in a medium saucepan. Add ½ cup chopped onion and 3 chopped garlic cloves; sauté 4 minutes or until onion is tender. Add 1 (28-ounce) can whole tomatoes, drained; bring to a boil. Cover, reduce heat, and simmer 10 minutes. Pour tomato mixture into a blender; add ½ cup packed fresh basil leaves, 2 tablespoons whipping cream, and ½ teaspoon salt. Process until smooth.

Cantaloupe cubes tossed with fresh mint

Game Plan

1 While oven heats for strombolis:

   • Bring tomato mixture to a boil.

   • Arrange stromboli fillings on dough.

   • Cut cantaloupe.

2 While soup simmers:

   • Bake strombolis.

   • Wash basil for soup.

   • Chop mint for cantaloupe.

Prosciutto and Gruyère Strombolis

These 5 ingredients come together quickly to deliver bold Italian flavor to these sandwiches.

1 (11-ounce) can refrigerated French bread dough
2 ounces thinly sliced prosciutto
1 cup trimmed arugula
½ cup (2 ounces) shredded Gruyère cheese
¼ cup chopped fresh parsley

1 Preheat oven to 425°.

2 Unroll dough onto a baking sheet; pat into a 14 x 11-inch rectangle. Cut dough into quarters to form 4 (7 x 5½-inch) rectangles. Top each rectangle with ½ ounce prosciutto, ¼ cup arugula, 2 tablespoons cheese, and 1 tablespoon parsley. Beginning at short side of each rectangle, roll up dough, jelly-roll fashion; pinch seam to seal (do not seal ends of rolls). Arrange rolls 4 inches apart on baking sheet. Bake at 425° for 10 minutes or until rolls are lightly browned. Serve warm. Yield: 4 servings (serving size: 1 roll).

CALORIES 275 (28% from fat); FAT 8.5g (sat 4.4g, mono 2.1g, poly 0.5g); PROTEIN 14g; CARB 34.4g; FIBER 1.5g; CHOL 24mg; IRON 2.3mg; SODIUM 754mg; CALC 158mg

MENU *serves 4*

Mushroom-Prosciutto Pizza

Arugula salad with garlic-sherry vinaigrette

Combine 1½ teaspoons sherry vinegar, 1 teaspoon extra-virgin olive oil, ¼ teaspoon salt, ⅛ teaspoon freshly ground black pepper, and 1 crushed garlic clove in a large bowl; stir with a whisk. Add 6 cups arugula, ½ cup halved grape tomatoes, and ½ cup chopped yellow bell pepper; toss to coat.

Angel food cake topped with fresh berries

Game Plan

1 While oven heats:

- Slice mushrooms and prosciutto.
- Chop shallots, garlic, and thyme.

2 While pizza toppings cook:

- Bake untopped pizza crust.

3 While untopped pizza crust bakes:

- Shred cheese.
- Prepare salad.

Mushroom-Prosciutto Pizza

For a crisp crust, bake the pizza dough on the lowest rack for a few minutes before adding the toppings. Substitute presliced button mushrooms for the creminis, if you prefer.

Cooking spray
8 ounces sliced cremini mushrooms
¼ cup finely chopped shallots
1 garlic clove, minced
1 teaspoon chopped fresh thyme
2 teaspoons sherry vinegar
1 (10-ounce) Italian cheese-flavored thin pizza crust (such as Boboli)
2 ounces prosciutto, cut into thin strips
⅓ cup (about 1½ ounces) shredded fontina cheese

1 Preheat oven to 450°.
2 Heat a 12-inch nonstick skillet over medium-high heat; coat with cooking spray. Add mushrooms and shallots; sauté 7 minutes or until mushrooms are tender. Add garlic and thyme; sauté 1 minute. Stir in vinegar, and remove from heat.
3 Place crust on bottom rack of oven. Bake at 450° for 4 minutes.
4 Place crust on a baking sheet. Spread mushroom mixture evenly over crust; sprinkle evenly with prosciutto and fontina cheese. Bake at 450° for 6 minutes or until cheese melts. Yield: 4 servings.

CALORIES 273 (28% from fat); FAT 8.4g (sat 3.7g, mono 2.4g, poly 0.8g); PROTEIN 15.3g; CARB 34.5g; FIBER 0.4g; CHOL 23mg; IRON 2.3mg; SODIUM 723mg; CALC 254mg

Quick Tip:
Use a fresh thyme sprig that has small leaves so you don't have to chop them; just strip them off the stem.

McKerr Muffins

This recipe offers a whole new twist on breakfast. Lemon- and dill-flavored mushrooms enliven the egg-topped English muffins to create a filling meal that's great for lazy weekend mornings.

Cooking spray
- 4 (2½-inch) mushrooms
- 2 teaspoons fresh lemon juice
- ½ teaspoon chopped fresh dill
- ⅛ teaspoon ground red pepper
- 1 teaspoon butter
- 1½ cups egg substitute
- 2 whole wheat English muffins, split and toasted
- 4 (1-ounce) slices Canadian bacon
- 4 (1-ounce) slices part-skim mozzarella cheese
- 1 tablespoon finely chopped green onions

❶ Heat a medium nonstick skillet over medium heat; coat with cooking spray. Remove stems from mushrooms; discard stems. Add mushroom caps to pan, under sides up. Pour ½ teaspoon lemon juice into each cap. Sprinkle evenly with dill and pepper. Cook 6 minutes or until mushroom tops are browned. Turn mushrooms over; cook 1 minute. Remove from pan; cover and keep warm.

❷ Wipe pan with a paper towel. Melt butter in pan over medium heat. Add egg substitute; allow to set about 30 seconds. Gently scrape cooked part of egg substitute to center of pan with a rubber spatula; continue gently scraping occasionally until egg substitute is set (about 3 minutes). Remove from heat.

❸ Preheat broiler.

❹ Arrange muffin halves, cut sides up, on a baking sheet. Top each muffin half with 1 Canadian bacon slice, about ⅓ cup scrambled egg substitute, and 1 mushroom cap, stem side down; gently press mushroom cap down. Top each mushroom cap with 1 cheese slice. Broil 1½ minutes or until cheese melts. Sprinkle with green onions, and serve immediately. Yield: 4 servings (serving size: 1 mushroom-topped muffin half).

CALORIES 241 (30% from fat); FAT 8g (sat 4.2g, mono 2.6g, poly 0.7g); PROTEIN 25.2g; CARB 17.4g; FIBER 2.6g; CHOL 32mg; IRON 2.9mg; SODIUM 843mg; CALC 328mg

MENU *serves 4*

McKerr Muffins

Spicy hash browns
Heat 1 tablespoon canola oil in a large nonstick skillet over medium-high heat. Add ⅔ cup chopped onion; sauté 3 minutes. Add 3 minced garlic cloves; sauté 1 minute. Add 1 (1-pound, 4 ounce) package refrigerated shredded hash browns (such as Simply Potatoes); cook 20 minutes or until lightly browned, stirring occasionally. Sprinkle with ½ teaspoon salt, ½ teaspoon chipotle chile powder, and ¼ teaspoon ground red pepper; toss to combine.

Orange juice and coffee

Game Plan

1 Sauté onion and garlic for hash browns.

2 While hash browns cook:
- Brew coffee.
- Cook mushrooms and egg substitute.

3 Assemble sandwiches.

4 While sandwiches broil:
- Toss potatoes with seasonings.
- Chop green onions for sandwiches.

Penne with Sausage, Eggplant, and Feta

Meaty breakfast sausage, earthy eggplant, and zesty feta complement each other in this hearty pasta dish. Buy precrumbled feta cheese to save prep time.

4½ cups cubed peeled eggplant (about 1 pound)
½ pound bulk pork breakfast sausage
4 garlic cloves, minced
2 tablespoons tomato paste
1 teaspoon dried oregano
¼ teaspoon freshly ground black pepper
1 (14.5-ounce) can diced tomatoes, undrained
6 cups hot cooked penne (about 10 ounces uncooked tube-shaped pasta)
½ cup (2 ounces) crumbled feta cheese
¼ cup chopped fresh parsley

❶ Cook eggplant, sausage, and garlic in a large nonstick skillet over medium-high heat 5 minutes or until sausage is browned and eggplant is tender. Add tomato paste and next 3 ingredients; cook over medium heat 5 minutes, stirring occasionally.

❷ Place pasta in a large bowl. Add tomato mixture, cheese, and parsley; toss well. Yield: 4 servings (serving size: 2 cups).

CALORIES 535 (31% from fat); FAT 18.9g (sat 7.6g, mono 7.5g, poly 2.1g); PROTEIN 25.5g; CARB 67.5g; FIBER 4.6g; CHOL 57mg; IRON 4.5mg; SODIUM 884mg; CALC 141mg

Quick Tip: Reduce chopping time by substituting 2 teaspoons bottled minced garlic for 4 garlic cloves.

Cajun Quiche in a Rice Crust

If you don't have cooked rice, use boil-in-a-bag rice and follow the microwave directions on the package. Cool the rice slightly before adding the egg.

CRUST:

- 2 cups cooked long-grain white rice, cooled
- 1 teaspoon garlic powder
- 1 teaspoon onion powder
- ½ teaspoon salt
- 1 large egg, lightly beaten

Cooking spray

- ¼ cup (1 ounce) reduced-fat shredded cheddar cheese

FILLING:

- ½ cup prechopped onion
- ½ cup prechopped celery
- ½ cup prechopped red bell pepper
- 1 teaspoon bottled minced garlic
- 3 ounces andouille sausage or kielbasa, chopped (about ⅔ cup)
- ¾ cup egg substitute
- 2 large egg whites, lightly beaten
- ¼ cup plain fat-free yogurt
- ¼ teaspoon salt
- ¼ teaspoon hot pepper sauce (such as Tabasco)
- ¼ cup (1 ounce) reduced-fat shredded cheddar cheese

❶ Preheat oven to 375°.

❷ To prepare crust, combine first 5 ingredients. Spread into bottom and up sides of a 9-inch pie plate coated with cooking spray. Sprinkle bottom of crust evenly with ¼ cup cheese.

❸ To prepare filling, heat a medium nonstick skillet over medium-high heat; coat with cooking spray. Add onion and next 4 ingredients; sauté 5 minutes. Spoon filling into prepared crust.

❹ Combine egg substitute and next 4 ingredients; stir with a whisk. Pour egg substitute mixture over filling in crust. Sprinkle with ¼ cup cheese. Bake at 375° for 30 minutes or until center is set. Let stand 5 minutes before serving. Yield: 4 servings (serving size: 1 wedge).

CALORIES 291 (32% from fat); FAT 10.3g (sat 4.5g, mono 3.7g, poly 1.6g); PROTEIN 19.5g; CARB 29.4g; FIBER 0.9g; CHOL 79mg; IRON 2.8mg; SODIUM 623mg; CALC 181mg

Taste Tip: Adjust the amount of hot pepper sauce in the filling to suit your taste.

MENU *serves 4*

Cajun Quiche in a Rice Crust

Bibb-strawberry salad
Combine 4 cups torn Bibb lettuce leaves, 1 cup sliced strawberries, ½ cup sliced carrot, and 2 tablespoons chopped fresh mint in a large bowl. Drizzle with 1 tablespoon bottled poppy seed dressing; toss well to coat.

Low-fat butter pecan ice cream with low-fat caramel sauce

Game Plan

1 Prepare quiche crust.

2 Sauté onion, celery, bell pepper, garlic, and sausage for filling.

3 Prepare quiche filling.

4 While quiche bakes:

  • Slice and chop ingredients for salad.

  • Assemble and dress salad.

Poultry

Rotini with Chicken, Asparagus, and Tomatoes, page 318

Creamed Chicken

Using whole milk gives this dish a thick, rich texture that reduced-fat milk can't provide.

½ cup all-purpose flour
2¼ cups whole milk, divided
1 cup frozen green peas, thawed
2 teaspoons chopped fresh sage
1 teaspoon butter
1 (10-ounce) package roasted skinless, boneless chicken breast (such as Perdue Short Cuts), chopped
1 tablespoon fresh lemon juice
¼ teaspoon freshly ground black pepper
Sage sprigs (optional)

❶ Lightly spoon flour into a dry measuring cup, and level with a knife. Combine flour and ½ cup milk in a large saucepan over medium heat; stir with a whisk. Stir in 1¾ cups milk. Cook 4 minutes or until thick, stirring constantly with a whisk.
❷ Stir in peas, sage, butter, and chicken. Cook 2 minutes or until thoroughly heated. Remove from heat; stir in juice and pepper. Garnish with sage sprigs, if desired. Yield: 4 servings (serving size: about ¾ cup).

CALORIES 232 (23% from fat); FAT 6g (sat 3.6g, mono 1.8g, poly 0.4g); PROTEIN 20.9g; CARB 25.4g; FIBER 2.1g; CHOL 53mg; IRON 2.2mg; SODIUM 1,001mg; CALC 164mg

Ingredient Tip: If you can't find roasted skinless, boneless chicken breast, buy a whole roasted chicken and substitute 2¼ cups chopped cooked breast meat. Add the leftover chicken to a soup, pasta, or salad later in the week.

MENU serves 4

Creamed Chicken

Broiled tomatoes
Preheat broiler. Combine 2 tablespoons seasoned breadcrumbs, 1 tablespoon grated Parmesan cheese, ¼ teaspoon salt, and ¼ teaspoon freshly ground black pepper. Add 1½ teaspoons water and ½ teaspoon olive oil, stirring until moist. Halve 4 plum tomatoes lengthwise, and sprinkle evenly with breadcrumb mixture. Place tomato halves, cut sides up, in a baking pan coated with cooking spray. Broil 2 minutes or until golden brown.

Hot cooked rice

Game Plan

1 While water for rice comes to a boil:
 • Thaw peas.
 • Chop sage and chicken.

2 While rice cooks:
 • Prepare topping for tomatoes.
 • Prepare creamed chicken.
 • Preheat broiler.
 • Broil tomatoes.

Creamy Chicken and Mushroom Crepes

Broccoli with balsamic-butter sauce

Place 1 pound trimmed broccoli spears in a microwave-safe dish; add 1 tablespoon water. Cover with plastic wrap; vent. Microwave at HIGH 4 minutes or until crisp-tender; drain. Melt 1 tablespoon butter in a large nonstick skillet over medium-high heat. Add 2 tablespoons finely chopped shallots; sauté 2 minutes. Remove from heat. Stir in 2 tablespoons balsamic vinegar, ¼ teaspoon salt, and ¼ teaspoon freshly ground black pepper; drizzle over broccoli.

Hot cooked white and wild rice blend

Game Plan

1 While water for rice comes to a boil:

- Chop shallots for broccoli.

- Slice onion and mushrooms, and mince garlic for crepes.

- Shred chicken.

2 While rice cooks:

- Prepare filling for crepes.

- Prepare broccoli.

Creamy Chicken and Mushroom Crepes

Buy a rotisserie chicken from the deli counter of your supermarket, and use the breast meat for this recipe; you'll also have some leftover chicken for another meal later in the week. If you can't find baby portobello mushrooms, use cremini mushrooms instead. Look for packaged crepes in the produce aisle.

1 teaspoon butter
1 cup vertically sliced onion
1 garlic clove, minced
3 cups thinly sliced baby portobello mushroom caps (about 6 ounces)
¾ teaspoon salt
¼ teaspoon freshly ground black pepper
½ cup dry white wine
¾ cup fat-free, less-sodium chicken broth
2 teaspoons chopped fresh thyme
¼ cup crème fraîche
2 cups shredded skinless, boneless rotisserie chicken breast
6 (9-inch) packaged French crepes (such as Melissa's)
Thyme sprigs (optional)

❶ Melt butter in a large nonstick skillet over medium-high heat. Add onion and garlic to pan; sauté 2 minutes or until onion begins to brown. Add mushrooms, salt, and pepper; cook 3 minutes or until liquid evaporates and mushrooms are tender, stirring frequently. Add wine; cook 3 minutes or until liquid almost evaporates, stirring frequently. Add broth and chopped thyme; cook 2 minutes. Remove from heat; add crème fraîche, stirring until well blended. Add chicken to pan, tossing well to coat.

❷ Place 1 crepe on each of 6 plates. Spoon about ⅓ cup mushroom mixture into center of each crepe; roll up. Garnish with thyme sprigs, if desired. Serve immediately. Yield: 6 servings (serving size: 1 filled crepe).

CALORIES 272 (30% from fat); FAT 9.1g (sat 5g, mono 2.8g, poly 0.9g); PROTEIN 19.4g; CARB 27.5g; FIBER 0.8g; CHOL 66mg; IRON 2.1mg; SODIUM 643mg; CALC 66mg

Biscuit-Topped Chicken Potpie

This dish tastes like Mom's potpie, but we've taken a few shortcuts to slash the cooking time.

1 tablespoon butter
2 cups chopped leek
¼ cup chopped shallot
¾ teaspoon chopped fresh or ¼ teaspoon dried thyme
1½ cups refrigerated diced potatoes with onions (such as Simply Potatoes)
⅓ cup dry white wine
1 teaspoon Dijon mustard
1 (14-ounce) can fat-free, less-sodium chicken broth
2 cups chopped roasted chicken breast
1½ cups frozen mixed vegetables
¼ teaspoon salt
¼ teaspoon freshly ground black pepper
2 tablespoons water
1½ tablespoons cornstarch
⅔ cup half-and-half
Cooking spray
1¼ cups low-fat baking mix (such as Bisquick Heart Smart)
½ cup fat-free milk
1 large egg white, lightly beaten

❶ Preheat oven to 425°.
❷ Melt butter in a large nonstick skillet over medium-high heat. Add leek, shallot, and thyme to pan; sauté 2 minutes. Add potatoes to pan; sauté 2 minutes. Add wine to pan; cook 1 minute or until liquid evaporates. Stir in mustard and broth; bring to a boil. Cook 4 minutes, stirring occasionally. Stir in chicken, mixed vegetables, salt, and pepper; cook 1 minute. Combine 2 tablespoons water and cornstarch in a small bowl; stir with a whisk. Add cornstarch mixture and half-and-half; reduce heat, and simmer 2 minutes, stirring constantly. Spoon potpie mixture into a 13 x 9-inch baking dish coated with cooking spray.
❸ Lightly spoon baking mix into dry measuring cups; level with a knife. Combine baking mix, milk, and egg white in a medium bowl; stir with a whisk. Spoon batter evenly over chicken mixture. Bake at 425° for 20 minutes or until topping is golden and filling is bubbly. Let stand 10 minutes. Yield: 6 servings (serving size: 1½ cups).

CALORIES 348 (24% from fat); FAT 9.2g (sat 4.1g, mono 2.2g, poly 0.9g); PROTEIN 23.5g; CARB 43.3g; FIBER 4.4g; CHOL 55mg; IRON 3.1mg; SODIUM 634mg; CALC 131mg

Quick Tip: To clean leek, chop and place in a strainer; rinse under running water.

MENU *serves 6*

Biscuit-Topped Chicken Potpie

Sautéed baby spinach
Heat 1 tablespoon olive oil in a Dutch oven. Add 1 (10-ounce) bag baby spinach, and sauté 1 minute or until wilted; place cooked spinach in a medium bowl. Add another (10-ounce) bag baby spinach to Dutch oven; sauté 1 minute or until wilted. Add to spinach in bowl; sprinkle with ¼ teaspoon salt and ¼ teaspoon freshly ground black pepper. Serve with lemon wedges.

Mixed berries dolloped with vanilla yogurt

Game Plan

1 Chop leek, shallot, thyme, and chicken.

2 While oven heats:
  - Prepare chicken filling.
  - Prepare biscuit topping.

3 While potpie bakes:
  - Sauté spinach.
  - Cut lemon into wedges.
  - Wash berries.

MENU *serves 4*

Chicken Chilaquiles

Lime-cilantro coleslaw
Combine 3 tablespoons fresh lime juice, 1 tablespoon extra-virgin olive oil, and 2 teaspoons sugar in a small bowl. Combine ¼ cup chopped green onions, ¼ cup chopped fresh cilantro, and 1 (12-ounce) package coleslaw in a large bowl. Drizzle juice mixture over coleslaw mixture; toss well to coat.

Watermelon wedges

Game Plan

1 Shred chicken, and chop onions and cilantro.

2 While oven heats:
   • Combine chicken mixture.
   • Prepare tomatillo mixture.
   • Assemble casserole.

3 While casserole bakes:
   • Mix coleslaw.
   • Slice and refrigerate watermelon.

Chicken Chilaquiles

Jalapeño peppers, chili powder, and green chiles add heat to this dish. If you prefer it even hotter, add ¼ teaspoon ground red pepper to the tomatillo mixture.

2   cups shredded skinless, boneless rotisserie chicken breast
½   cup chopped green onions
½   cup (2 ounces) shredded Monterey Jack cheese with jalapeño peppers, divided
2   tablespoons grated Parmesan cheese
1   teaspoon chili powder
¼   teaspoon salt
¼   teaspoon black pepper
¾   cup 1% low-fat milk
¼   cup chopped fresh cilantro
1   (11-ounce) can tomatillos, drained
1   (4.5-ounce) can chopped green chiles, drained
12 (6-inch) corn tortillas
Cooking spray

❶ Preheat oven to 375°.
❷ Combine chicken, onions, ¼ cup Monterey Jack cheese, Parmesan cheese, chili powder, salt, and pepper in a medium bowl. Place milk and next 3 ingredients in a food processor or blender; process until smooth.
❸ Heat tortillas according to package directions. Pour ⅓ cup tomatillo mixture into bottom of an 11 x 7–inch baking dish coated with cooking spray. Arrange 4 tortillas in dish, and top with half of chicken mixture. Repeat layers with remaining tortillas and chicken mixture, ending with tortillas.
❹ Pour remaining tomatillo mixture over tortillas; sprinkle with ¼ cup Monterey Jack cheese. Bake at 375° for 20 minutes or until bubbly. Yield: 4 servings (serving size: 1½ cups).

CALORIES 347 (28% from fat); FAT 10.9g (sat 4.5g, mono 2.9g, poly 1.9g); PROTEIN 30.9g; CARB 33.3g; FIBER 5.9g; CHOL 79mg; IRON 1.5mg; SODIUM 560mg; CALC 272mg

Quick Tip: Purchase grated fresh Parmesan cheese at your supermarket.

BBQ Chicken Pizza

You'll love the contrast of flavors provided here by the combination of sweet tomato chutney, savory chicken, and extra-sharp cheddar cheese.

 1 (10-ounce) Italian cheese-flavored thin pizza crust (such as Boboli)
 ¾ cup tomato chutney
 2 cups chopped roasted skinless, boneless chicken breast (about 2 breasts)
 ⅔ cup chopped plum tomato
 ¾ cup (3 ounces) shredded extra-sharp white cheddar cheese
 ⅓ cup chopped green onions

❶ Preheat oven to 450°.
❷ Place crust on a baking sheet. Bake at 450° for 3 minutes. Remove from oven; spread chutney over crust, leaving a ½-inch border.
❸ Top chutney with chicken. Sprinkle tomato, cheese, and onions evenly over chicken. Bake at 450° for 9 minutes or until cheese melts. Cut pizza into 6 wedges. Yield: 6 servings (serving size: 1 wedge).

CALORIES 300 (26% from fat); FAT 8.5g (sat 3.9g, mono 2.9g, poly 1g); PROTEIN 21.3g; CARB 35.2g; FIBER 1.2g; CHOL 48mg; IRON 1.7mg; SODIUM 622mg; CALC 247mg

Ingredient Tip: If you can't find tomato chutney, you can quickly make your own: Combine 2 cups chopped plum tomato, 3 tablespoons brown sugar, 3 tablespoons cider vinegar, ⅛ teaspoon Jamaican jerk seasoning, and 1 minced garlic clove in a small saucepan; bring to a boil. Reduce heat to medium; cook 20 minutes or until thickened.

MENU serves 6

BBQ Chicken Pizza

Quick coleslaw
Combine 2 tablespoons white vinegar, 3 tablespoons low-fat mayonnaise, ½ teaspoon black pepper, and ⅛ teaspoon ground red pepper in a large bowl; stir with a whisk. Add 1 (10-ounce) package angel hair slaw; toss well to coat.

Corn on the cob

Game Plan

1 While oven heats:
 • Chop chicken, tomato, and onions.
 • Shred cheese.

2 While pizza bakes:
 • Prepare coleslaw.
 • Boil corn.

Cuban Chicken Pizza

Toasting the corn in a skillet brings out its natural sweetness and adds a smoky flavor note.

4 (8-inch) fat-free flour tortillas
Cooking spray
1 (11-ounce) can no-salt-added whole-kernel corn, drained
½ teaspoon cumin seeds
2 cups diced roasted chicken breast
1 (15-ounce) can black beans, rinsed and drained
1 garlic clove, minced
2 tablespoons fresh lime juice
¾ cup shredded Monterey Jack cheese with jalapeño peppers
4 teaspoons chopped fresh cilantro

1 Preheat oven to 350°.

2 Place flour tortillas on a baking sheet coated with cooking spray. Bake at 350° for 10 minutes or until edges are light brown. Remove tortillas from oven; stack tortillas and press down to flatten. Set aside.

3 Heat a large nonstick skillet over medium-high heat; coat with cooking spray. Add corn to pan, and cook 1 minute or until lightly charred. Add cumin seeds; cook 5 seconds, stirring constantly. Add chicken, black beans, and garlic; cook 2 minutes or until thoroughly heated. Remove from heat; stir in juice.

4 Place tortillas on baking sheet. Spoon ¾ cup bean mixture onto each tortilla; top each with 3 tablespoons cheese. Bake at 350° for 2 minutes or until cheese melts. Sprinkle each pizza with 1 teaspoon cilantro. Yield: 4 servings (serving size: 1 pizza).

CALORIES 460 (20% from fat); FAT 10.2g (sat 4.8g, mono 2.9g, poly 1.7g); PROTEIN 37.7g; CARB 54.3g; FIBER 8.4g; CHOL 78mg; IRON 3.6mg; SODIUM 760mg; CALC 210mg

Quick Tip: Use a rotisserie chicken from the deli counter of your supermarket, or thaw frozen cooked chicken breasts (such as Tyson).

Spicy Chicken with Poblano Peppers and Cheese

The sweet salad tames the heat of the casserole. Serve remaining chips on the side with salsa.

4 poblano chiles, halved and seeded
2 cups chopped cooked chicken breast
1 cup (4 ounces) reduced-fat shredded
   cheddar cheese
1 cup fresh corn kernels (about 2 ears)
½ cup chopped onion
½ cup chopped zucchini
½ cup chopped red bell pepper
2 tablespoons finely chopped fresh
   cilantro
½ teaspoon kosher salt
½ teaspoon ground cumin
½ teaspoon paprika
½ teaspoon freshly ground black
   pepper
½ teaspoon bottled minced garlic
¼ cup bottled salsa
Cooking spray
¾ cup crushed baked tortilla chips,
   divided

❶ Preheat broiler.
❷ Place chile halves, skin sides up, on a foil-lined baking sheet, and flatten with hand. Broil 8 minutes or until blackened. Place peppers in a zip-top plastic bag; seal. Let stand 15 minutes. Peel and discard skins.
❸ Reduce oven temperature to 375°.
❹ Combine chicken and next 11 ingredients in a large bowl; add salsa, stirring until well combined.
❺ Place peppers, cut sides up, in an 11 x 7-inch baking dish coated with cooking spray; top evenly with ¼ cup chips. Spoon chicken mixture evenly over chips; sprinkle with ½ cup chips. Lightly coat chips with cooking spray. Bake at 375° for 20 minutes or until cheese melts and casserole is thoroughly heated. Yield: 4 servings (serving size: 2 chile halves).

CALORIES 331 (30% from fat); FAT 11.1g (sat 4.9g, mono 1.5g, poly 1.5g); PROTEIN 32.4g; CARB 25.2g; FIBER 4.2g; CHOL 80mg; IRON 2mg; SODIUM 688mg; CALC 256mg

MENU *serves 4*

Spicy Chicken with Poblano Peppers and Cheese

Tossed salad with fruit
Combine 4 cups torn romaine lettuce, 1 cup fresh orange sections, 1 cup sliced kiwifruit, and ⅓ cup very thinly vertically sliced red onion in a large bowl. Combine 2 tablespoons fresh lime juice, 1 tablespoon honey, 2 teaspoons extra-virgin olive oil, 2 teaspoons Dijon mustard, ¼ teaspoon salt, and ⅛ teaspoon black pepper in a small bowl; stir with a whisk. Drizzle dressing over salad; toss gently to coat. Sprinkle with 2 tablespoons toasted slivered almonds.

Chips and salsa

Game Plan

1 While chiles broil and stand:
   • Chop chicken, onion, zucchini, bell pepper, and cilantro.
   • Shred cheese.
   • Remove kernels from corn cob.
2 Prepare casserole.
3 While casserole cooks:
   • Prepare salad.

Chicken Enchiladas with Salsa Verde

Spanish rice

Cook 2 slices bacon in a large nonstick skillet over medium heat until crisp. Remove bacon from pan; crumble. Add ½ cup chopped onion and 2 minced garlic cloves to drippings in pan; cook 4 minutes, stirring occasionally. Add 1 cup rice; 2 cups fat-free, less-sodium chicken broth; and 1 (14.5-ounce) can drained diced tomatoes. Stir to combine. Bring to a boil; cover, reduce heat, and simmer 20 minutes or until rice is tender. Stir in crumbled bacon and ⅓ cup sliced green onions just before serving.

Black beans

Game Plan

1 Cook bacon for rice.

2 Chop onion and mince garlic for enchiladas and rice.

3 While rice cooks:

• Preheat oven.

• Prepare enchiladas.

4 While enchiladas bake:

• Cook beans.

Chicken Enchiladas with Salsa Verde

A squeeze of lime juice brightens the flavor of this hearty Mexican dish. The enchiladas are mild, so serve them with hot sauce, if desired. If you can't find queso fresco, use ¼ cup shredded Monterey Jack cheese or Monterey Jack with jalapeño peppers.

1 cup chopped onion
¼ cup chopped fresh cilantro
2 garlic cloves, minced
1 (7-ounce) bottle salsa verde (such as Herdez)
2 cups shredded cooked chicken breast
⅓ cup (3 ounces) ⅓-less-fat cream cheese, softened
1 cup fat-free, less-sodium chicken broth
8 (6-inch) corn tortillas
Cooking spray
¼ cup (1 ounce) crumbled queso fresco
½ teaspoon chili powder
4 lime wedges
Cilantro sprigs (optional)

❶ Preheat oven to 425°.
❷ Place first 4 ingredients in a blender; process until smooth. Combine chicken and cream cheese in a large bowl. Stir in ½ cup salsa mixture. Reserve remaining salsa mixture.

❸ Bring broth to a simmer in a medium skillet. Working with 1 tortilla at a time, add tortilla to pan; cook 20 seconds or until moist, turning once. Remove tortilla; drain on paper towels. Spoon about ¼ cup chicken mixture down center of tortilla; roll up. Place tortilla, seam-side down, in an 11 x 7–inch baking dish coated with cooking spray. Repeat procedure with remaining tortillas, broth, and chicken mixture.

❹ Pour reserved salsa mixture over enchiladas; sprinkle evenly with queso fresco and chili powder. Bake at 425° for 18 minutes or until thoroughly heated. Serve with lime wedges. Garnish with cilantro sprigs, if desired. Yield: 4 servings (serving size: 2 enchiladas and 1 lime wedge).

CALORIES 327 (26% from fat); FAT 9.5g (sat 4.4g, mono 2.9g, poly 1.3g); PROTEIN 28.5g; CARB 31g; FIBER 3.3g; CHOL 78mg; IRON 1.8mg; SODIUM 493mg; CALC 149mg

Black Bean and Chicken Chilaquiles

A traditional Mexican breakfast favorite, *chilaquiles* (chee-lah-KEE-lays) is a sauté of day-old tortilla strips, fresh tomato sauce, cream, and cheese. This hearty version is baked.

Cooking spray
- 1 cup thinly sliced onion
- 5 garlic cloves, minced
- 2 cups shredded cooked chicken breast
- 1 (15-ounce) can black beans, rinsed and drained
- 1 cup fat-free, less-sodium chicken broth
- 1 (7¾-ounce) can salsa de chile fresco (such as El Pato)
- 15 (6-inch) corn tortillas, cut into 1-inch strips
- 1 cup shredded queso blanco (about 4 ounces)

1 Preheat oven to 450°.

2 Heat a large nonstick skillet over medium-high heat; coat with cooking spray. Add onion to pan; sauté 5 minutes or until lightly browned. Add garlic; sauté 1 minute. Add chicken; cook 30 seconds. Transfer chicken mixture to a medium bowl; stir in beans. Add broth and salsa to pan; bring to a boil. Reduce heat, and simmer 5 minutes, stirring occasionally; set aside.

3 Place half of tortilla strips in bottom of an 11 x 7-inch baking dish coated with cooking spray. Layer half of chicken mixture over tortillas; top with remaining tortillas and chicken mixture. Pour broth mixture evenly over chicken mixture. Sprinkle with cheese. Bake at 450° for 10 minutes or until tortillas are lightly browned and cheese is melted. Yield: 6 servings.

CALORIES 293 (15% from fat); FAT 4.9g (sat 1.7g, mono 1.5g, poly 1.2g); PROTEIN 22.9g; CARB 40g; FIBER 5.9g; CHOL 46mg; IRON 2.3mg; SODIUM 602mg; CALC 200mg

---

MENU *serves 6*

Black Bean and Chicken Chilaquiles

Green salad
Combine 11 cups torn red leaf lettuce, 2 cups plum tomato wedges, and ¾ cup thinly sliced green onions in a large bowl. Combine ¼ cup fresh lemon juice, 2 tablespoons sherry vinegar, 1 tablespoon extra-virgin olive oil, 1 tablespoon Dijon mustard, and ½ teaspoon salt in a small bowl; stir with a whisk. Drizzle dressing over lettuce mixture, tossing to coat. Serve immediately.

Store-bought angel food cake with sliced strawberries and fat-free whipped topping

Game Plan

1 While onion cooks:
- Shred chicken and cheese.
- Mince garlic.
- Rinse and drain beans.
- Cut tortillas into strips.

2 While chilaquiles bake:
- Tear lettuce, and slice tomatoes and onions.
- Prepare vinaigrette.
- Assemble salad.

3 Slice cake and strawberries.

MENU *serves 4*

**Fried Rice
(Nasi Goreng)**

Spinach soup

Heat a Dutch oven over medium-high heat; coat with cooking spray. Add ½ cup chopped onion, ½ cup chopped green bell pepper, ½ teaspoon salt, ¼ teaspoon freshly ground black pepper, and 1 minced garlic clove to pan; sauté 2 minutes. Add 4 cups fat-free, less-sodium chicken broth and 2 cups thawed frozen whole kernel corn. Bring to a boil; cook 10 minutes. Add 1 (6-ounce) package fresh baby spinach; cook until wilted.

Fresh pineapple cubes

Game Plan

1 Assemble ingredients for fried rice and soup.

2 While soup cooks:
  •Prepare fried rice.

Fried Rice (Nasi Goreng)

We recommend topping this fried rice with diced cucumbers and tomatoes; for a more traditional Indonesian accompaniment, top it with a fried egg. Sambal oelek is a spicy table condiment from southeast Asia; look for it in gourmet grocery stores and Asian markets.

2 teaspoons canola oil
⅓ cup minced shallots (about 3)
1 to 2 tablespoons minced serrano chile
1 tablespoon sambal oelek (chile paste with garlic)
2 teaspoons fish sauce
2 teaspoons low-sodium soy sauce
¼ teaspoon salt
4 garlic cloves, minced
2 cups diced cooked chicken breast
2 cups diced cooked shrimp (about 12 ounces)
3 cups cooked rice
½ cup diced cucumber
½ cup diced tomato

❶ Heat oil in a large nonstick skillet over medium-high heat. Add shallots and chile to pan; sauté 2 minutes or until shallots are lightly browned. Add chile paste, fish sauce, soy sauce, salt, and garlic to pan; cook 1 minute or until sauce becomes fragrant. Add chicken, shrimp, and rice to pan; stir well to coat with sauce. Cook 2 minutes or until thoroughly heated, stirring occasionally to prevent rice mixture from sticking to pan. Place about 1½ cups rice mixture on each of 4 plates, and sprinkle each serving with 2 tablespoons cucumber and 2 tablespoons tomato. Yield: 4 servings.

CALORIES 430 (13% from fat); FAT 6.2g (sat 1.2g, mono 2.5g, poly 1.7g); PROTEIN 44.1g; CARB 46.1g; FIBER 2.3g; CHOL 225mg; IRON 5.8mg; SODIUM 717mg; CALC 62mg

Flavor Tip: Use 2 tablespoons serrano chile if you prefer your rice to have more heat.

Chicken Potpies

The piecrust topping bakes on a baking sheet before being placed over the filling, so you don't need to use ovenproof bowls for the pies. Use the ramekin or bowl you'll be serving the potpies in as a guide for cutting the dough.

½ (15-ounce) package refrigerated pie dough (such as Pillsbury)
Cooking spray
⅛ teaspoon salt
2 tablespoons all-purpose flour
1 teaspoon dried rubbed sage
¼ teaspoon salt
¼ teaspoon black pepper
8 ounces chicken breast tenders, cut into bite-sized pieces
1¼ cups water
1½ cups frozen mixed vegetables
1 cup mushrooms, quartered
1 (10½-ounce) can condensed reduced-fat, reduced-sodium cream of chicken soup

1 Preheat oven to 425°.
2 Cut 3 (4-inch) circles out of dough; discard remaining dough. Place dough circles on a baking sheet coated with cooking spray. Lightly coat dough circles with cooking spray; sprinkle evenly with ⅛ teaspoon salt. Pierce top of dough with a fork. Bake at 425° for 8 minutes or until golden.
3 Combine flour, sage, ¼ teaspoon salt, and pepper in a zip-top plastic bag; add chicken. Seal bag, and toss to coat. Heat a large non-stick skillet over medium-high heat; coat with cooking spray. Add chicken mixture; cook 5 minutes, browning on all sides. Stir in water, scraping pan to loosen browned bits. Stir in vegetables, mushrooms, and soup; bring to a boil. Reduce heat, and cook 10 minutes. Spoon 1 cup chicken mixture into each of 3 (1-cup) ramekins or bowls; top each serving with 1 piecrust. Yield: 3 servings (serving size: 1 pie).

CALORIES 374 (27% from fat); FAT 11.4g (sat 4.8g, mono 4.2g, poly 1.2g); PROTEIN 24.1g; CARB 42.6g; FIBER 4.6g; CHOL 58mg; IRON 1.9mg; SODIUM 882mg; CALC 38mg

Ingredient Tip: Use 2 cups chopped leftover cooked chicken in place of chicken breast tenders.

MENU

Chicken Potpies

Spinach and orange salad

Combine 5 cups packaged baby spinach, 1 cup drained mandarin oranges in light syrup, and ¼ cup slivered red onion in a large bowl. Combine 2 tablespoons balsamic vinegar, 1 tablespoon honey, 2 teaspoons Dijon mustard, 1 teaspoon olive oil, ⅛ teaspoon salt, and ⅛ teaspoon black pepper in a small bowl; stir with a whisk. Drizzle vinaigrette over salad; toss gently to coat.

Chocolate low-fat ice cream with graham crackers

Game Plan

1 While oven heats for piecrusts:
- Prepare flour mixture for chicken.
- Cut chicken into bite-sized pieces.
- Prepare vinaigrette for salad.

2 While crusts bake:
- Cook chicken mixture.
- Toss salad.

MENU *serves 4*

Penne and Chicken Tenderloins with Spiced Tomato Sauce

Romaine salad with anchovy and fresh basil vinaigrette

Combine 1½ teaspoons anchovy paste, 1½ teaspoons Dijon mustard, and 1 tablespoon red wine vinegar in a small bowl. Add 2 tablespoons canola oil, stirring constantly with a whisk. Stir in 1 tablespoon chopped fresh basil. Place 8 cups torn romaine lettuce leaves in a large bowl. Add dressing, tossing to coat. Sprinkle salad with ¼ cup shredded Parmesan cheese.

Warm sourdough bread

Game Plan

1 Bring water for pasta to a boil.

2 While pasta sauce cooks:

- Cook pasta.
- Heat bread.
- Make salad dressing.
- Toss salad.

Penne and Chicken Tenderloins with Spiced Tomato Sauce

Ground fennel and coriander bring a welcome complexity to the chicken and sauce.

1 teaspoon ground fennel seed
1 teaspoon dried basil
½ teaspoon salt
½ teaspoon ground coriander
¼ teaspoon freshly ground black pepper
1 pound chicken breast tenders, cut into 1-inch pieces
1 tablespoon olive oil
4 garlic cloves, minced
4 cups canned diced tomatoes, undrained
1 cup white wine
8 ounces uncooked penne
¼ cup (1 ounce) freshly grated Parmigiano-Reggiano cheese
¼ cup chopped fresh basil

1 Combine first 5 ingredients in a small bowl; rub over chicken.

2 Heat oil in a large nonstick skillet over medium-high heat. Add chicken to pan; cook 4 minutes, turning once. Remove chicken from pan; set aside.

3 Reduce heat to medium. Add garlic to pan; sauté 30 seconds or until soft. Add tomatoes and wine to pan, scraping pan to loosen browned bits. Bring to a boil; reduce heat, and simmer 15 minutes. Add chicken back to pan; simmer 5 minutes.

4 Cook pasta according to package directions, omitting salt and fat. Drain. Toss pasta with chicken mixture in a large bowl. Sprinkle with cheese and basil. Yield: 4 servings (serving size: about 1½ cups).

CALORIES 356 (19% from fat); FAT 7.4g (sat 2g, mono 3.2g, poly 1.1g); PROTEIN 33.5g; CARB 38.4g; FIBER 4.3g; CHOL 72mg; IRON 3.1mg; SODIUM 527mg; CALC 106mg

Chicken and Noodles with Peanut Sauce

This dish works well served either at room temperature or cold; add a touch of warm water to loosen the noodles if serving them cold.

5   ounces uncooked Japanese curly noodles (chuka soba)
2   teaspoons dark sesame oil, divided
1   pound chicken breast tenders
1½ cups red bell pepper strips
½   cup fat-free, less-sodium chicken broth
⅓   cup hoisin sauce
¼   cup creamy peanut butter
2   tablespoons rice vinegar
2   tablespoons ketchup
¼   teaspoon crushed red pepper
1   tablespoon bottled ground fresh ginger (such as Spice World)
1   teaspoon bottled minced garlic
½   cup chopped green onions, divided

1 Cook noodles according to package directions; drain.

2 Heat 1 teaspoon oil in a large nonstick skillet over medium-high heat. Add chicken; sauté 4 minutes. Add bell pepper; sauté 3 minutes. Remove from heat. Combine chicken mixture and noodles in a large bowl.

3 Combine broth and next 5 ingredients in a bowl; stir with a whisk.

4 Heat 1 teaspoon oil in pan over medium heat. Add ginger and garlic; cook 15 seconds. Stir in broth mixture, and cook 30 seconds, stirring constantly. Add broth mixture and ¼ cup green onions to noodle mixture; toss well. Sprinkle with ¼ cup green onions. Yield: 5 servings (serving size: 1 cup).

CALORIES 353 (28% from fat); FAT 10.9g (sat 2g, mono 4.3g, poly 3.1g); PROTEIN 28.5g; CARB 36g; FIBER 2.3g; CHOL 53mg; IRON 1.5mg; SODIUM 663mg; CALC 21mg

Quick Tip: Using chicken breast tenders is ideal for hectic schedules. They don't need to be cut or trimmed, and the smaller pieces cook quicker than chicken breasts.

MENU *serves 5*

Chicken and Noodles with Peanut Sauce

Asian slaw
Combine 1 tablespoon sugar, 3 tablespoons rice vinegar, 1 tablespoon low-sodium soy sauce, and 2 teaspoons dark sesame oil. Pour dressing over 4 cups cabbage-and-carrot coleslaw; toss to coat. Chill until ready to serve.

Steamed broccoli spears

Game Plan

1   While water for pasta comes to a boil:

 •Prepare and refrigerate slaw.

 •Combine sauce ingredients for noodles.

 •Cut bell pepper into strips.

2   While chicken is sautéing:

 •Steam broccoli.

MENU *serves 4*

Herbed Chicken Parmesan

Roasted lemon-garlic broccoli

Preheat oven to 425°. Combine 6 cups broccoli florets, 1 teaspoon grated lemon rind, 2 teaspoons olive oil, ¼ teaspoon salt, ⅛ teaspoon black pepper, and 2 thinly sliced garlic cloves on a jelly-roll pan coated with cooking spray. Bake at 425° for 15 minutes or until crisp-tender and lightly browned, stirring occasionally.

Hot cooked orzo

Game Plan

1 While oven heats for broccoli and water for orzo comes to a boil:

- Prepare broccoli mixture.
- Combine ingredients for breadcrumb mixture.
- Shred provolone cheese.

2 While broccoli bakes:

- Cook chicken.
- Cook orzo.
- Prepare pasta sauce.

Herbed Chicken Parmesan

We recommend serving rice-shaped orzo with this saucy entrée, but you can also serve it over spaghetti or angel hair pasta.

- ⅓ cup (1½ ounces) grated fresh Parmesan cheese, divided
- ¼ cup dry breadcrumbs
- 1 tablespoon minced fresh parsley
- ½ teaspoon dried basil
- ¼ teaspoon salt, divided
- 1 large egg white, lightly beaten
- 1 pound chicken breast tenders
- 1 tablespoon butter
- 1½ cups bottled fat-free tomato-basil pasta sauce (such as Muir Glen Organic)
- 2 teaspoons balsamic vinegar
- ¼ teaspoon black pepper
- ⅓ cup (1½ ounces) shredded provolone cheese

❶ Preheat broiler.

❷ Combine 2 tablespoons Parmesan cheese, breadcrumbs, parsley, basil, and ⅛ teaspoon salt in a shallow dish. Place egg white in a shallow dish. Dip each chicken tender in egg white; dredge in breadcrumb mixture. Melt butter in a large nonstick skillet over medium-high heat. Add chicken; cook 3 minutes on each side or until done. Set aside.

❸ Combine ⅛ teaspoon salt, pasta sauce, vinegar, and pepper in a microwave-safe bowl. Cover with plastic wrap; vent. Microwave at HIGH 2 minutes or until thoroughly heated; pour over chicken. Sprinkle evenly with remaining Parmesan and provolone cheeses. Wrap handle of pan with foil; broil 2 minutes or until cheeses melt. Yield: 4 servings.

CALORIES 308 (30% from fat); FAT 10.4g (sat 5.7g, mono 3g, poly 0.6g); PROTEIN 35.9g; CARB 16.2g; FIBER 1.8g; CHOL 88mg; IRON 2.3mg; SODIUM 808mg; CALC 249mg

Chicken Saté with Peanut Sauce

Traditional Indonesian saté skewers are often broiled, so you can also broil the chicken in this recipe instead of grilling it. Place the skewers on a broiler pan coated with cooking spray; broil 8 to 10 minutes, turning once. To prevent the skewers from burning, be sure to soak them for 30 minutes in hot water before threading through the chicken. Serve the zesty peanut sauce either in condiment bowls or on individual serving plates.

SATÉ:
- 1 pound skinless, boneless chicken breast, cut into 8 strips
- 1 tablespoon light brown sugar
- 2½ tablespoons low-sodium soy sauce
- 2 teaspoons bottled ground fresh ginger (such as Spice World)
- 1 teaspoon grated lime rind
- ¼ teaspoon crushed red pepper
- 2 garlic cloves, minced

SAUCE:
- 1 tablespoon light brown sugar
- 1½ tablespoons low-sodium soy sauce
- 1 tablespoon fresh lime juice
- 2 tablespoons natural-style, reduced-fat creamy peanut butter (such as Smucker's)
- ¼ teaspoon crushed red pepper
- 1 garlic clove, minced

REMAINING INGREDIENT:
Cooking spray

❶ Prepare grill.

❷ To prepare saté, combine chicken and next 6 ingredients in a medium bowl. Let stand at room temperature for 10 minutes.

❸ To prepare sauce, combine 1 tablespoon brown sugar and next 5 ingredients in a medium bowl, stirring until sugar dissolves.

❹ Thread 1 chicken strip onto each of 8 (8-inch) skewers. Place chicken on grill rack coated with cooking spray; grill 5 minutes on each side or until chicken is done. Serve chicken with sauce. Yield: 4 servings (serving size: 2 skewers and 1 tablespoon sauce).

CALORIES 205 (20% from fat); FAT 4.5g (sat 1g, mono 0.4g, poly 0.4g); PROTEIN 29.3g; CARB 11.2g; FIBER 0.8g; CHOL 66mg; IRON 1.5mg; SODIUM 672mg; CALC 26mg

MENU *serves 4*

Chicken Saté with Peanut Sauce

Spicy cucumber salad
Combine ½ cup rice vinegar, 1 tablespoon sugar, 1 tablespoon minced seeded jalapeño pepper, and 1 teaspoon grated lime rind in a large bowl. Add 3 cups thinly sliced English cucumber and ½ cup thinly sliced red onion; toss to coat.

Rice noodles

Game Plan

1 While grill heats and water for noodles comes to a boil:
   - Marinate chicken for saté.
   - Soak wooden skewers in hot water.
   - Prepare peanut sauce.

2 While noodles cook:
   - Slice cucumber and red onion for salad.
   - Mince jalapeño pepper for salad.
   - Toss salad.

3 Thread chicken onto skewers, and grill.

Chicken, Peppers, Onions, and Mushrooms with Marsala Wine

The Greek salad complements the flavor of this quick-and-easy sautéed dish.

Cooking spray
1½ pounds chicken breast tenders
1½ cups thinly sliced onion
1 cup thinly vertically sliced red bell pepper (about 1 medium)
2 tablespoons olive oil
½ teaspoon salt
½ teaspoon black pepper
1 (8-ounce) package presliced exotic mushroom blend (such as shiitake, cremini, and oyster)
3 tablespoons Marsala wine

1 Heat a large nonstick skillet over medium-high heat; coat with cooking spray. Add chicken to pan; sauté 7 minutes or until chicken is done. Remove chicken from pan. Add onion and bell pepper to pan; sauté 5 minutes or until onion starts to brown. Add oil, salt, black pepper, and mushrooms to pan; sauté 3 minutes or until mushrooms are tender and onion starts to caramelize. Add wine and chicken to pan, and cook 1 minute or until thoroughly heated. Serve immediately. Yield: 4 servings (serving size: 1¾ cups).

CALORIES 295 (28% from fat); FAT 9.2g (sat 1.6g, mono 5.4g, poly 1.3g); PROTEIN 41.8g; CARB 8.9g; FIBER 1.8; CHOL 99mg; IRON 1.8mg; SODIUM 411mg; CALC 33mg

---

MENU *serves 4*

Chicken, Peppers, Onions, and Mushrooms with Marsala Wine

Greek salad
Combine 4 cups torn romaine lettuce, ½ cup thinly sliced red onion, ½ cup thinly sliced cucumber, ½ cup halved cherry tomatoes, and ½ cup crumbled feta cheese in a large bowl. Combine 1 tablespoon lemon juice, 2 teaspoons red wine vinegar, ½ teaspoon dried oregano, and ¼ teaspoon salt in a small bowl. Gradually add 1 tablespoon extra-virgin olive oil, stirring constantly with a whisk. Drizzle oil mixture over salad; toss well.

Warm crusty Italian bread

Game Plan

1 Prepare salad.

2 Slice onion and red bell pepper for chicken mixture.

3 While chicken mixture cooks:

•Warm bread.

Parmesan Chicken and Rice

Rice and broth are added to sautéed chicken, onion, garlic, and mushrooms for a simple and quick entrée that is also delicious.

MENU *serves 4*

Parmesan Chicken and Rice

Green beans amandine
Combine 1 (9-ounce) package frozen French-style green beans, 2 teaspoons butter, ¼ teaspoon garlic salt, and ¼ teaspoon black pepper in a medium, microwave-safe bowl. Microwave at HIGH 5 minutes or until tender. Top with 2 tablespoons toasted almonds.

Dinner rolls

Game Plan

1 While oil heats in skillet:
- Chop onion and parsley.
- Cut chicken into bite-sized pieces.

2 After stirring rice into chicken mixture:
- Microwave green beans.
- Toast almonds.

1 tablespoon olive oil
½ cup chopped onion
1 teaspoon bottled minced garlic
½ teaspoon dried thyme
1 (8-ounce) package presliced mushrooms
¾ pound skinless, boneless chicken breast, cut into bite-sized pieces
½ cup dry white wine
½ teaspoon salt
¼ teaspoon freshly ground black pepper
1 cup uncooked instant rice
1 cup fat-free, less-sodium chicken broth
½ cup (2 ounces) grated fresh Parmesan cheese
¼ cup chopped fresh parsley

❶ Heat oil in a large nonstick skillet over medium-high heat. Add onion, garlic, thyme, and mushrooms to pan; sauté 5 minutes or until onion is tender. Add chicken; sauté 4 minutes or until chicken is lightly browned. Add wine, salt, and pepper; cook 3 minutes or until liquid almost evaporates.

❷ Stir in rice and broth to chicken mixture in pan. Bring to a boil; cover, reduce heat, and simmer 5 minutes or until liquid is absorbed. Stir in cheese and parsley. Yield: 4 servings (serving size: about 1 cup).

CALORIES 395 (18% from fat); FAT 8g (sat 2.8g, mono 3.7g, poly 0.8g); PROTEIN 29.9g; CARB 44.4g; FIBER 2g; CHOL 57mg; IRON 4.1mg; SODIUM 656mg; CALC 171mg

Tarragon Chicken-in-a-Pot Pies

Popular in French cooking, tarragon adds anise flavor to the creamy chicken mixture.
Hollowed-out rolls serve as edible, individual vessels that absorb the flavorful sauce.

2 tablespoons all-purpose flour
1 cup 1% low-fat milk
½ cup fat-free, less-sodium chicken broth
½ cup dry white wine
1 tablespoon olive oil
⅔ cup chopped sweet onion
1 pound skinless, boneless chicken breast,
  cut into bite-sized pieces
1 cup sliced carrot
1 cup (⅛-inch-thick) slices zucchini
½ teaspoon salt
½ teaspoon dried tarragon
½ teaspoon black pepper
4 (4.5-ounce) country or peasant rolls

❶ Place flour in a small bowl; slowly add milk, stirring with a whisk to form a slurry (watery mixture). Add broth and wine.
❷ Heat oil in a large saucepan over medium-high heat; add onion and chicken to pan.

Sauté 2 minutes; stir in carrot and next 4 ingredients to pan. Cover, reduce heat, and cook 4 minutes. Stir slurry into chicken mixture in pan. Bring to a boil; cover, reduce heat, and simmer until thick (about 10 minutes), stirring occasionally.
❸ Cut rolls horizontally 1 inch from tops. Hollow out bottoms of rolls, leaving ¼-inch-thick shells; reserve torn bread and bread tops for another use. Spoon 1¼ cups chicken mixture into each bread shell. Yield: 4 servings.

CALORIES 413 (17% from fat); FAT 7.8g (sat 2.7g, mono 3g, poly 0.7g); PROTEIN 35.7g; CARB 48.8g; FIBER 3.5g; CHOL 68mg; IRON 4.2mg; SODIUM 865mg; CALC 199mg

Quick Tip: Make breadcrumbs for future use with the bread you remove from the rolls. Place the bread scraps in a food processor, and pulse 5 to 10 times. Freeze breadcrumbs in a heavy-duty zip-top plastic bag up to 6 months.

MENU *serves 4*

Tarragon Chicken-in-a-Pot Pies

Green salad

Caramel-coconut sundaes
Preheat oven to 325°. Sprinkle ¼ cup flaked sweetened coconut on a jelly-roll pan. Bake at 325° for 10 minutes or until golden brown, stirring occasionally. Scoop ½ cup vanilla low-fat ice cream into each of 4 dessert bowls; top each serving with 1 tablespoon fat-free caramel sundae syrup and about 1 tablespoon toasted coconut flakes.

Game Plan

1 Preheat oven for coconut.

2 While coconut bakes:
   - Chop onion, and slice carrot and zucchini.
   - Cut chicken into bite-sized pieces.

3 While chicken mixture cooks:
   - Hollow out rolls.
   - Prepare salad.

Chicken Soft Tacos with Sautéed Onions and Apples

MENU *serves 4*

Chicken Soft Tacos with Sautéed Onions and Apples

Spicy coleslaw

Combine 4 cups shredded cabbage, ⅓ cup thinly sliced red onion, ¼ cup chopped fresh cilantro, 2 tablespoons fresh lime juice, 2 tablespoons apple cider vinegar, ½ teaspoon salt, ¼ teaspoon ground red pepper, and ¼ teaspoon brown sugar in a large bowl. Toss well.

Canned refried beans

Game Plan

1 While oil heats in skillet:
  • Cut chicken into bite-sized pieces.
2 While onion mixture cooks:
  • Warm refried beans.
3 Prepare coleslaw.
4 Warm tortillas.

In this recipe, warm flour tortillas encase a savory-sweet taco filling that's sure to please.

1 tablespoon olive oil
1 pound skinless, boneless chicken breast, cut into bite-sized pieces
½ teaspoon salt
½ teaspoon ground nutmeg
½ teaspoon freshly ground black pepper
1 tablespoon butter
2 cups thinly sliced onion
2 cups thinly sliced peeled Granny Smith apple (about 2 apples)
2 garlic cloves, minced
8 (6-inch) flour tortillas

❶ Heat oil in a large nonstick skillet over medium-high heat. Sprinkle chicken evenly with salt, nutmeg, and pepper. Add chicken to pan; sauté 7 minutes or until golden. Remove chicken from pan; keep warm.

❷ Melt butter in pan over medium heat. Add onion; cook 4 minutes or until tender, stirring frequently. Add apple; cook 6 minutes or until golden, stirring frequently. Add garlic; sauté 30 seconds. Return chicken to pan; cook 2 minutes or until thoroughly heated, stirring frequently.

❸ Heat tortillas according to package directions. Arrange ½ cup chicken mixture over each tortilla. Yield: 4 servings (serving size: 2 tacos).

CALORIES 454 (25% from fat); FAT 12.6g (sat 3.8g, mono 6.1g, poly 1.5g); PROTEIN 32.9g; CARB 51.5g; FIBER 4.8g; CHOL 73mg; IRON 3.3mg; SODIUM 705mg; CALC 116mg

Quick Tip: If you're making the entire menu, use bagged shredded cabbage to save a step in the preparation.

Thai-Style Stir-Fried Chicken

Once the chicken and vegetables are prepped, the cooking goes quickly. Have all of the ingredients close at hand to whip up this sweet-hot dinner on a busy evening.

¼ cup rice vinegar
2 tablespoons brown sugar
2 tablespoons fresh lime juice
2 teaspoons red curry paste
⅛ teaspoon crushed red pepper
1 pound skinless, boneless chicken breast, cut into bite-sized pieces
1½ tablespoons canola oil, divided
1 cup chopped onion
1 cup chopped carrot
1 (8-ounce) package presliced mushrooms
½ cup light coconut milk
1 tablespoon fish sauce
½ teaspoon salt
1 cup fresh bean sprouts
¼ cup chopped fresh cilantro

1 Combine first 5 ingredients in a large zip-top plastic bag. Add chicken; seal and marinate in refrigerator 15 minutes, turning once.

2 Remove chicken from bag, and reserve marinade. Heat 1 tablespoon oil in a large non-stick skillet or wok over medium-high heat. Add chicken; stir-fry 4 minutes. Remove chicken from pan; keep warm. Add remaining 1½ teaspoons oil to pan. Add onion and carrot; stir-fry 2 minutes. Add mushrooms; stir-fry 3 minutes. Add reserved marinade, scraping pan to loosen browned bits. Add coconut milk and fish sauce; bring to a boil. Reduce heat, and simmer 1 minute. Stir in chicken and salt; cook 1 minute. Top with sprouts and cilantro. Yield: 4 servings (serving size: 1 cup chicken mixture, ¼ cup sprouts, and 1 tablespoon cilantro).

CALORIES 271 (28% from fat); FAT 8.4g (sat 2.2g, mono 1.6g, poly 3.4g); PROTEIN 29.7g; CARB 19.6g; FIBER 2.9g; CHOL 66mg; IRON 2.2mg; SODIUM 767mg; CALC 43mg

Quick Tip: Look for prechopped onion in the produce section of your supermarket.

MENU *serves 4*

Thai-Style Stir-Fried Chicken

Rice noodles
Place 6 ounces thin rice vermicelli (thin rice noodles) in a large bowl; cover with boiling water. Let stand 20 minutes. Drain; serve chicken over noodles.

Green tea

Game Plan

1 While rice noodles soak:
- Prepare marinade for chicken.
- Chop chicken into bite-sized pieces.

2 While chicken marinates:
- Chop onion, carrot, and cilantro.

MENU *serves 4*

Rotini with Chicken, Asparagus, and Tomatoes

Spinach salad
Combine 2 tablespoons minced shallots, 1 tablespoon olive oil, 1 tablespoon balsamic vinegar, ⅛ teaspoon salt, and a dash of black pepper in a large bowl, stirring with a whisk. Add 6 cups fresh baby spinach; toss well.

Italian bread

Game Plan

1 While water boils for pasta:

  • Prepare ingredients for chicken mixture.

2 While pasta cooks:

  • Cook chicken mixture.

  • Prepare salad.

Rotini with Chicken, Asparagus, and Tomatoes

Reminiscent of pasta salad, this recipe calls for coating rotini and colorful vegetables with a basil-flecked balsamic vinaigrette.

　8　ounces uncooked rotini (corkscrew pasta)
　　Cooking spray
　1　pound skinless, boneless chicken breast, cut into ¼-inch strips
　½　teaspoon kosher salt
　½　teaspoon freshly ground black pepper
　1　cup (1-inch) slices asparagus
　2　cups cherry tomatoes, halved
　2　garlic cloves, minced
　2　tablespoons chopped fresh basil
　2　tablespoons balsamic vinegar
　1　tablespoon extra-virgin olive oil
　¼　cup (1 ounce) crumbled goat cheese

❶ Cook pasta according to package directions, omitting salt and fat.

❷ Heat a large nonstick skillet over medium-high heat; coat with cooking spray. Sprinkle chicken with salt and pepper. Add chicken and asparagus to pan; sauté 5 minutes. Add tomatoes and garlic to pan; sauté 1 minute. Remove from heat. Stir in pasta, basil, vinegar, and oil to chicken mixture in pan. Arrange 2 cups pasta mixture on each of 4 plates; top each serving with 1 tablespoon goat cheese. Yield: 4 servings.

CALORIES 419 (20% from fat); FAT 9.5g (sat 3.2g, mono 4.1g, poly 1.6g); PROTEIN 33.9g; CARB 48.5g; FIBER 3.4g; CHOL 70mg; IRON 3.2mg; SODIUM 324mg; CALC 105mg

Prep Tip: Slice the chicken across the grain into strips so the pieces will be tender and retain their shape after cooking.

Kung Pao Chicken

The menu's slightly sweet cucumber salad nicely balances this traditionally spicy Szechuan dish. If you prefer fiery flavors, add up to 1 teaspoon crushed red pepper. Speed up dinner by using bottled ground fresh ginger, bottled minced garlic, and packaged precut broccoli florets.

1 tablespoon canola oil, divided
4 cups broccoli florets
1 tablespoon ground fresh ginger (such as Spice World), divided
2 tablespoons water
½ teaspoon crushed red pepper
1 pound skinless, boneless chicken breast, cut into ¼-inch strips
½ cup fat-free, less-sodium chicken broth
2 tablespoons hoisin sauce
2 tablespoons rice wine vinegar
2 tablespoons low-sodium soy sauce
1 teaspoon cornstarch
4 garlic cloves, minced
2 tablespoons coarsely chopped salted peanuts

❶ Heat 1 teaspoon oil in a large nonstick skillet over medium-high heat. Add broccoli and 2 teaspoons ginger to pan; sauté 1 minute. Add water; cover and cook 2 minutes or until broccoli is crisp-tender. Remove broccoli from pan; keep warm.

❷ Heat remaining 2 teaspoons oil in pan; add remaining 1 teaspoon ginger, crushed red pepper, and chicken. Cook 4 minutes or until chicken is lightly browned, stirring frequently.

❸ Combine broth and next 5 ingredients in a small bowl; stir with a whisk. Add broth mixture to pan; cook 1 minute or until mixture thickens, stirring constantly. Return broccoli to pan; toss to coat. Sprinkle with peanuts. Yield: 4 servings (serving size: about 1 cup chicken mixture and 1½ teaspoons peanuts).

CALORIES 239 (30% from fat); FAT 7.9g (sat 1.1g, mono 3.7g, poly 2.3g); PROTEIN 30.9g; CARB 11.4g; FIBER 3g; CHOL 66mg; IRON 1.8mg; SODIUM 589mg; CALC 60mg

Quick Tip: To make it easier to cut chicken into thin strips, freeze 15 minutes before slicing. Look for bags of cut-up broccoli florets in the produce section of your supermarket.

MENU *serves 4*

Kung Pao Chicken

Cool cucumber salad
Whisk together 1 tablespoon sugar, 2 tablespoons rice wine vinegar, ½ teaspoon salt, and ¼ teaspoon black pepper in a medium bowl. Add ¼ cup chopped fresh mint; 2 tablespoons chopped fresh basil; 2 peeled, seeded, and sliced cucumbers; 1 medium tomato, cut into wedges; and 2 chopped green onions. Toss to combine. Refrigerate until ready to serve.

Short-grain or sticky rice

Game Plan

1 While water boils for rice:
   • Prepare and chill salad.

2 While rice cooks:
   • Cut chicken into strips.
   • Mince garlic.
   • Chop peanuts.

3 Cook chicken and vegetables.

Chicken Saté with Spicy Peanut Sauce

Classic Indonesian saté features skewered meat, fish, or poultry that is grilled or broiled.

MENU *serves 4*

Chicken Saté with Peanut Sauce

Assorted vegetable sauté

Heat 1 tablespoon canola oil over medium-high heat in a large skillet. Add 2 cups snow peas, 2 cups julienne-cut shiitake mushrooms, and 1 cup julienne-cut red bell pepper to pan. Stir in 1 tablespoon low-sodium soy sauce, 1 teaspoon lime juice, ½ teaspoon crushed red pepper, ¼ teaspoon salt, and a dash of sugar; sauté 5 minutes or until vegetables just begin to soften.

Hot white rice with green onions

Game Plan

1 While broiler heats:

- Soak skewers 30 minutes in hot water to prevent burning.

- Prepare shallot mixture for chicken.

- Cook rice.

2 While chicken marinates:

- Prepare peanut sauce.

3 While chicken broils:

- Sauté vegetables.

SATÉ:

½ cup chopped shallots (about 4)
2 tablespoons dark brown sugar
1 tablespoon minced fresh ginger
1 tablespoon sambal oelek (chile paste with garlic)
1 tablespoon low-sodium soy sauce
2 teaspoons coriander seeds
2 teaspoons canola oil
1 teaspoon fish sauce
½ teaspoon turmeric
½ teaspoon black peppercorns
Dash of freshly ground nutmeg
4 garlic cloves
2 whole cloves
1½ pounds chicken breast tenders

PEANUT SAUCE:

½ cup reduced-fat creamy peanut butter
⅓ cup water
3 tablespoons lime juice
1 tablespoon low-sodium soy sauce
2 teaspoons dark brown sugar
1 teaspoon hot paprika
1 teaspoon Sriracha (hot chile sauce, such as Huy Fong)

REMAINING INGREDIENT:

Cooking spray

❶ Preheat broiler.
❷ To prepare saté, place first 13 ingredients in a food processor, and process until smooth. Place shallot mixture and chicken in a large zip-top plastic bag; seal and marinate in refrigerator 10 minutes.
❸ To prepare peanut sauce, combine peanut butter and next 6 ingredients in a medium bowl; stir well with a whisk.
❹ Remove chicken from bag; discard marinade. Thread chicken onto 8 (12-inch) wooden skewers. Place skewers on a broiler or roasting pan rack coated with cooking spray. Broil 12 minutes or until done. Serve with peanut sauce. Yield: 4 servings (serving size: 2 skewers and about ¼ cup sauce).

CALORIES 424 (33% from fat); FAT 15.5g (sat 3.2g, mono 1.3g, poly 0.9g); PROTEIN 47.2g; CARB 23.7g; FIBER 2.7g; CHOL 99mg; IRON 2.6mg; SODIUM 745mg; CALC 37mg

Chicken Picadillo

Reheat leftover chicken mixture, and serve it in hot tortillas. Top each serving with shredded lettuce, chopped tomatoes, and light sour cream for a quick weeknight meal.

1 pound skinless, boneless chicken breast
2 teaspoons olive oil
1 cup chopped onion
1½ teaspoons ground cumin
½ teaspoon salt
¼ teaspoon ground cinnamon
3 garlic cloves, minced
1 cup bottled salsa
⅓ cup golden raisins
¼ cup slivered almonds, toasted
¼ cup chopped fresh cilantro
Cilantro sprigs (optional)

1 Place chicken in a food processor; pulse until ground.
2 Heat oil in a large nonstick skillet over medium-high heat. Add onion to pan; cook 3 minutes, stirring occasionally. Add chicken, cumin, salt, cinnamon, and garlic to pan; cook 3 minutes or until chicken is done, stirring frequently. Stir in salsa and raisins to chicken mixture in pan; cover, reduce heat, and simmer 5 minutes or until thoroughly heated. Remove pan from heat; stir in almonds and chopped cilantro. Garnish with cilantro sprigs, if desired. Yield: 4 servings (serving size: about 1 cup).

CALORIES 257 (26% from fat); FAT 7.5g (sat 1g, mono 4.2g, poly 1.5g); PROTEIN 29.6g; CARB 19g; FIBER 3.2g; CHOL 66mg; IRON 2.2mg; SODIUM 762mg; CALC 74mg

Quick Tip: To toast nuts quickly, place them on a paper plate and microwave at HIGH 1 to 2 minutes, or until nuts smell toasted.

MENU *serves 4*

Chicken Picadillo

Black beans and rice
Bring 1¼ cups fat-free, less-sodium chicken broth to a boil in a medium saucepan. Add ¾ cup long-grain rice; cover, reduce heat, and simmer 18 minutes or until liquid is absorbed. Stir in 1 cup rinsed and drained canned black beans and ¼ cup chopped fresh cilantro; cook until heated. Stir in ¼ teaspoon salt.

Flour tortillas

Game Plan

1 While broth for rice comes to a boil:
   • Assemble ingredients for picadillo.
2 While rice cooks:
   • Prepare picadillo.
   • Warm tortillas.

MENU   *serves 4*

Swedish Meatballs

Green peas

Buttered poppy seed noodles

Cook 8 ounces wide egg noodles according to package directions, omitting salt and fat; drain. Place noodles in a large bowl. Add 2 tablespoons chopped fresh parsley, 1½ tablespoons butter, 1 teaspoon poppy seeds, ¼ teaspoon salt, and ¼ teaspoon pepper; toss to coat.

Game Plan

1 While water for noodles comes to a boil:

  •Prepare meatballs.

2 While noodles cook:

  •Cook meatballs.

3 While meatballs simmer in sauce:

  •Prepare peas.

  •Chop parsley for noodles.

Swedish Meatballs

Substitute white or whole wheat bread for the rye to bind the meatballs, if you like.

2 (1-ounce) slices rye bread
1 pound skinless, boneless chicken breast
¾ teaspoon salt, divided
¼ teaspoon ground nutmeg
¼ teaspoon freshly ground black pepper
1 large egg white, lightly beaten
1 tablespoon canola oil
1 cup fat-free, less-sodium chicken broth
1 tablespoon all-purpose flour
1 (8-ounce) carton fat-free sour cream
2 tablespoons chopped fresh parsley

1 Place bread slices in a food processor, and pulse 10 times or until coarse crumbs measure 1 cup. Place breadcrumbs in a medium bowl; set aside.

2 Place chicken in food processor, and pulse until ground. Add ground chicken, ½ teaspoon salt, nutmeg, pepper, and egg white to breadcrumbs in bowl; stir well. Shape mixture into 16 (1½-inch) meatballs.

3 Heat oil in a large nonstick skillet over medium-high heat. Add meatballs; cook 6 minutes, browning on all sides. Remove meatballs from pan. Add ¼ teaspoon salt, broth, and flour to pan, stirring with a whisk. Bring to a boil, and cook 1 minute or until slightly thickened, stirring constantly. Stir in sour cream, and return meatballs to pan. Reduce heat to medium-low; cook 10 minutes or until meatballs are done and sauce is thick. Sprinkle with parsley. Yield: 4 servings (serving size: 4 meatballs and ⅓ cup sauce).

CALORIES 269 (21% from fat); FAT 6.3g (sat 1.2g, mono 2.6g, poly 1.5g); PROTEIN 32.3g; CARB 18.6g; FIBER 1g; CHOL 72mg; IRON 1.5mg; SODIUM 783mg; CALC 117mg

Prep Tip: Since the meat mixture is very moist, lightly coat your hands with cooking spray to keep the meat from sticking to your hands.

Spicy Chicken Cakes with Horseradish Aïoli

Aïoli (ay-OH-lee) is a garlic mayonnaise from the Provence region in France, where it is a popular condiment for meat and vegetables. Prepare it in advance and keep refrigerated until serving time.

CAKES:

- 2 (1½-ounce) slices whole wheat bread
- 1 pound skinless, boneless chicken breast
- ¼ cup chopped fresh chives
- 3 tablespoons low-fat mayonnaise
- 1 teaspoon Cajun seasoning
- ¼ teaspoon salt
- 2 large egg whites
- 2 teaspoons canola oil

AÏOLI:

- 2 tablespoons low-fat mayonnaise
- 2 teaspoons prepared horseradish
- 1 teaspoon bottled minced garlic
- ⅛ teaspoon salt

1 To prepare cakes, place bread in a food processor; pulse 10 times or until coarse crumbs measure 1 cup (freeze remaining breadcrumbs for another use). Set breadcrumbs aside.

2 Place chicken in food processor; pulse until ground. Combine breadcrumbs, chicken, chives, and next 4 ingredients in a medium bowl; mix well (mixture will be wet). Divide mixture into 8 equal portions, shaping each into a ½-inch-thick patty.

3 Heat oil in a large nonstick skillet over medium heat. Add patties; cook 7 minutes on each side or until done.

4 To prepare aïoli, combine 2 tablespoons mayonnaise and remaining 3 ingredients in a small bowl. Serve with cakes. Yield: 4 servings (serving size: 2 chicken cakes and about 1½ teaspoons aïoli).

CALORIES 242 (26% from fat); FAT 7.1g (sat 1.3g, mono 1.8g, poly 1.3g); PROTEIN 29.5g; CARB 12.5g; FIBER 0.5g; CHOL 66mg; IRON 1.6mg; SODIUM 749mg; CALC 44mg

Quick Tip:

Use day-old bread to make breadcrumbs for future use. Freeze the breadcrumbs in a zip-top plastic bag up to 6 months.

MENU *serves 4*

Spicy Chicken Cakes with Horseradish Aïoli

Steamed asparagus

Mashed sweet potatoes

Peel and dice 1½ pounds sweet potatoes. Cook in boiling water 10 minutes or until tender; drain and place in a large bowl. Add ¼ cup fat-free milk and ¼ teaspoon salt. Mash with a potato masher to desired consistency.

Game Plan

1 While water for potatoes comes to a boil:
- Peel and dice potatoes.

2 While potatoes cook:
- Prepare chicken cakes.

3 While chicken cakes cook:
- Steam asparagus.
- Prepare aïoli.

Greek Chicken with Angel Hair Pasta

Leftovers of this pasta taste great either cold or warmed. Coffee-flavored ice cream makes a nice finale to this meal because it offers a contrast to the tangy pasta and salad.

1 pound uncooked angel hair pasta
1 tablespoon olive oil
4 (6-ounce) skinless, boneless chicken breast halves, each cut in half
2 cups chopped red onion
1 cup chopped yellow bell pepper
6 tablespoons fresh lemon juice
1 teaspoon dried basil
½ teaspoon dried oregano
2 (14.5-ounce) cans diced tomatoes with basil, garlic, and oregano
¾ cup (3 ounces) feta cheese, crumbled

❶ Cook pasta according to package directions, omitting salt and fat.

❷ Heat oil in a large nonstick skillet over medium-high heat. Add chicken to pan; sauté 3 minutes on each side. Add onion and next 5 ingredients to pan; stir well. Cover, reduce heat, and simmer 25 minutes or until chicken is done. Remove from heat; sprinkle with cheese. Serve with pasta. Yield: 8 servings (serving size: ½ chicken breast, about ½ cup tomato mixture, and about 1 cup pasta).

CALORIES 400 (16% from fat); FAT 7.3g (sat 2.7g, mono 2.7g, poly 1.5g); PROTEIN 30g; CARB 54.3g; FIBER 3.1g; CHOL 60mg; IRON 3.9mg; SODIUM 694mg; CALC 148mg

Chicken Saté with Ponzu Sauce

To prevent wooden skewers from burning while grilling, soak them for 30 minutes in hot water before using.

4 (6-ounce) skinless, boneless chicken breast halves
¼ cup packed light brown sugar
¼ cup sake (rice wine)
¼ cup rice vinegar
¼ cup fresh lime juice
2 teaspoons low-sodium soy sauce
1 teaspoon dark sesame oil
¼ teaspoon crushed red pepper
1 garlic clove, minced
Cooking spray

❶ Prepare grill.
❷ Cut each chicken breast half lengthwise into 4 strips. Combine sugar and next 7 ingredients in a small bowl; stir until sugar dissolves. Combine chicken and half of sake mixture in a large bowl; let stand 10 minutes. Reserve remaining sake mixture.

❸ Drain chicken, discarding marinade. Thread 1 chicken strip onto each of 16 (8-inch) skewers. Place chicken on grill rack coated with cooking spray; grill 2 minutes on each side or until done. Serve with remaining sake mixture. Yield: 4 servings (serving size: 4 skewers and about 1½ tablespoons sake mixture).

CALORIES 267 (12% from fat); FAT 3.5g (sat 0.7g, mono 0.5g, poly 0.5g); PROTEIN 39.6g; CARB 13.3g; FIBER 0.1g; CHOL 99mg; IRON 1.6mg; SODIUM 216mg; CALC 30mg

Ingredient Tip:
Sesame oil provides a distinctive nutty flavor. Since its shelf life is shorter than that of canola or vegetable oil, purchase it in a small bottle and store in the refrigerator after opening. It will become cloudy and partially solid when chilled but clear and fluid as it returns to room temperature.

MENU *serves 4*

Chicken Saté with Ponzu Sauce

Asian slaw
Combine 2 tablespoons rice vinegar, 2 tablespoons low-sodium soy sauce, 2 teaspoons light brown sugar, and 1 teaspoon sesame oil in a large bowl, stirring with a whisk. Add 1 (16-ounce) package cabbage-and-carrot coleslaw, ¼ cup minced fresh cilantro, ¼ cup chopped green onions, and 2 tablespoons chopped dry-roasted peanuts; toss to coat.

Raspberry sorbet

Game Plan

1 While grill heats:
  • Soak skewers in hot water for 30 minutes.
  • Slice chicken; combine with sake mixture.
  • Prepare slaw; chill.

2 Thread chicken on skewers; grill.

325

MENU *serves 4*

Chicken Scallopini

Orzo, tomato, and zucchini toss

Heat 1 teaspoon olive oil in a medium skillet over medium-high heat. Add 1 cup halved cherry tomatoes, 1 cup chopped zucchini, and 2 minced garlic cloves; sauté 2 minutes. Stir in ½ teaspoon Italian seasoning and ¼ teaspoon red pepper flakes; sauté 1 minute or until zucchini is crisp-tender. Combine tomato mixture, 3 cups hot cooked orzo, and ¼ teaspoon salt; toss well.

Garlic bread

Game Plan

1 While orzo cooks:

- Pound chicken.
- Season and dredge chicken in breadcrumbs.
- Cut tomatoes, chop zucchini, and mince garlic.

2 While chicken cooks:

- Cook tomato mixture.
- Heat garlic bread.

Chicken Scallopini

Pounding the chicken breast halves to thin "scallops" cuts the cooking time in half and leaves the chicken moist and tender. If you don't have orzo, substitute rice in the side dish.

4 (6-ounce) skinless, boneless chicken breast halves
2 teaspoons fresh lemon juice
¼ teaspoon salt
¼ teaspoon black pepper
⅓ cup Italian-seasoned breadcrumbs
Cooking spray
½ cup fat-free, less-sodium chicken broth
¼ cup dry white wine
4 teaspoons capers
1 tablespoon butter

1 Place each chicken breast half between 2 sheets of heavy-duty plastic wrap; pound chicken to ¼-inch thickness using a meat mallet or rolling pin. Brush chicken with lemon juice; sprinkle with salt and pepper. Dredge chicken in breadcrumbs.

2 Heat a large nonstick skillet over medium-high heat; coat with cooking spray. Add chicken to pan; cook 3 minutes on each side or until chicken is done. Remove chicken from pan; keep warm.

3 Add broth and wine to pan; cook 30 seconds, stirring constantly. Remove pan from heat. Stir in capers and butter until butter melts. Serve sauce over chicken. Yield: 4 servings (serving size: 1 chicken breast half and 1 tablespoon sauce).

CALORIES 206 (20% from fat); FAT 4.6g (sat 2.2g, mono 1.3g, poly 0.5g); PROTEIN 29.2g; CARB 7.7g; FIBER 0.6g; CHOL 76mg; IRON 1.6mg; SODIUM 657mg; CALC 27mg

Lemon and Oregano-Rubbed Chicken Paillards

To create paillards, pound the chicken breast halves with a meat mallet or rolling pin until they are very thin; the increased surface area of the chicken will allow you to apply even more of the flavorful rub.

4   (6-ounce) skinless, boneless chicken breast halves
5   teaspoons grated lemon rind
1   tablespoon olive oil
1½ teaspoons dried oregano
¾   teaspoon kosher salt
½   teaspoon freshly ground black pepper
¼   teaspoon water
2   garlic cloves, minced
Cooking spray
4   lemon wedges
2   tablespoons chopped fresh parsley

❶ Prepare grill.
❷ Place each chicken breast half between 2 sheets of heavy-duty plastic wrap, and pound chicken to ¼-inch thickness using a meat mallet or rolling pin.
❸ Combine lemon rind and next 6 ingredients; rub evenly over both sides of chicken. Place chicken on a grill rack coated with cooking spray, and grill 3 minutes on each side or until chicken is done. Remove from heat. Squeeze 1 lemon wedge evenly over each chicken breast half. Sprinkle parsley evenly over chicken. Yield: 4 servings (serving size: 1 chicken breast half).

CALORIES 226 (22% from fat); FAT 5.6g (sat 1g, mono 3g, poly 0.8g); PROTEIN 39.6g; CARB 2.2g; FIBER 0.7g; CHOL 99mg; IRON 1.8mg; SODIUM 465mg; CALC 38mg

Quick Tip: Using the pounding technique on the chicken not only tenderizes the meat, but also shortens the cooking time.

MENU *serves*

Lemon and Oregano-Rubbed Chicken Paillards

Greek farmer's salad
Combine 2 tablespoons red wine vinegar, 2 teaspoons Dijon mustard, 1 teaspoon extra-virgin olive oil, ½ teaspoon dried oregano, ¼ teaspoon salt, ¼ teaspoon crushed red pepper, and 2 minced garlic cloves, stirring with a whisk. Combine 3 cups coarsely chopped English cucumber, 2 cups halved cherry tomatoes, 1 cup chopped yellow bell pepper, ¼ cup finely chopped red onion, and ¼ cup halved kalamata olives. Drizzle dressing over salad; toss to coat. Refrigerate until ready to serve.

Basmati rice

Game Plan

1 While grill heats:
- Prepare and chill salad.
- Bring water for rice to a boil.
- Pound chicken breasts.
- Prepare rub for chicken.

2 While rice cooks:
- Grill chicken.
- Chop parsley for chicken.

MENU *serves 4*

Chicken with Lime Sauce

Cumin-flavored roasted potatoes
Preheat oven to 500°. Cut 2 large unpeeled baking potatoes into ½-inch slices. Arrange slices on a baking sheet coated with cooking spray. Combine 1 table-spoon extra-virgin olive oil, 1 teaspoon ground cumin, 1 teaspoon bottled minced garlic, ½ teaspoon salt, and ¼ teaspoon ground red pepper in a small bowl. Spoon mixture over potato slices, tossing well to coat. Bake at 500° for 20 minutes or until done.

Green beans

Game Plan

1 While oven heats:
- Cut potatoes, and coat with oil mixture.

2 While potatoes bake:
- Prepare chicken.
- Cook green beans.

Chicken with Lime Sauce

A silky sauce coats the chicken with rich, tangy flavor. Substitute lemon juice if you don't have a lime on hand. For a splash of color, garnish with chopped parsley or chives.

4 (6-ounce) skinless, boneless chicken breast halves
¼ teaspoon salt
¼ teaspoon freshly ground black pepper
2 teaspoons olive oil
Cooking spray
¾ cup fat-free, less-sodium chicken broth
1 tablespoon brown sugar
3 tablespoons lime juice, divided
2 teaspoons Dijon mustard
2 tablespoons water
1 teaspoon cornstarch
1 tablespoon butter

1 Place each chicken breast half between 2 sheets of heavy-duty plastic wrap; pound to ¼-inch thickness using a meat mallet or small heavy skillet. Sprinkle chicken with salt and pepper.

2 Heat oil in a large nonstick skillet coated with cooking spray over medium-high heat. Add chicken; cook 4 minutes on each side or until browned. Remove from pan; keep warm.

3 Add broth, sugar, 2 tablespoons juice, and mustard to pan, and cook over medium heat, scraping pan to loosen browned bits.

4 Combine 2 tablespoons water and cornstarch in a small bowl. Add cornstarch mixture to pan; stir with a whisk. Bring to a boil over medium-high heat; cook 1 minute or until slightly thick. Add 1 tablespoon lime juice and butter, stirring with a whisk until butter melts. Return chicken to pan; simmer 2 min-utes or until chicken is thoroughly heated. Yield: 4 servings (serving size: 1 chicken breast half and 2 tablespoons sauce).

CALORIES 260 (26% from fat); FAT 7.5g (sat 2.7g, mono 3.1g, poly 0.8g); PROTEIN 40.7g; CARB 5.4g; FIBER 0.1g; CHOL 106mg; IRON 1.8mg; SODIUM 382mg; CALC 32mg

MENU *serves 4*

Orange Chicken

Couscous pilaf
Bring 1½ cups fat-free, less-sodium chicken broth to a boil in a medium sauce-pan. Stir in 1 cup Israeli couscous. Cover, reduce heat, and simmer 10 minutes or until al dente; fluff with a fork. Stir in ¼ cup chopped fresh flat-leaf parsley, ¼ cup finely chopped red onion, ¼ cup toasted pine nuts, ¼ teaspoon salt, and ⅛ teaspoon freshly ground black pepper.

Sautéed Broccolini

Game Plan

1 Chop parsley and red onion for pilaf.

2 Pound chicken, and dredge in flour.

3 While couscous simmers:

 • Cook chicken and sauce.

 • Toast pine nuts for pilaf.

 • Sauté Broccolini.

4 Toss together pilaf ingredients.

Orange Chicken

Israeli couscous is pearl-sized pasta. If you can't find it in your local supermarket, use regular couscous for the pilaf: its cook time will vary, so follow the package directions.

4 (6-ounce) skinless, boneless chicken breast halves
¼ teaspoon salt
¼ teaspoon freshly ground black pepper
1½ ounces all-purpose flour (about ⅓ cup)
2 teaspoons olive oil
2 teaspoons butter
½ cup white wine
½ cup fresh orange juice (about 2 oranges)

❶ Place each chicken breast half between 2 sheets of heavy-duty plastic wrap; pound each piece to ½-inch thickness using a meat mallet or small heavy skillet. Sprinkle both sides of chicken evenly with salt and pepper; dredge chicken in flour.
❷ Heat oil and butter in a large nonstick skillet over medium-high heat; cook 1 minute or until lightly browned, stirring occasionally. Add chicken to pan; cook 4 minutes on each side or until done. Remove chicken; cut into thin slices, and keep warm. Add wine and juice to pan; cook until reduced to ½ cup (about 4 minutes). Serve sauce over chicken. Yield: 4 servings (serving size: 1 chicken breast half and 2 tablespoons sauce).

CALORIES 261 (22% from fat); FAT 6.4g (sat 2.1g, mono 2.7g, poly 0.8g); PROTEIN 40.2g; CARB 8.2g; FIBER 0.3g; CHOL 104mg; IRON 1.7mg; SODIUM 274mg; CALC 26mg

MENU *serves 4*

Chicken and Asparagus in White Wine Sauce

Parmesan-chive mashed potatoes

Heat 1 (20-ounce) package refrigerated mashed potatoes (such as Simply Potatoes) according to package directions. Stir in ¼ cup grated fresh Parmesan cheese, 2 tablespoons chopped fresh chives, and ½ teaspoon freshly ground black pepper.

Soft breadsticks

Game Plan

1 Pound chicken breasts.

2 While butter melts in pan:
- •Dredge chicken in flour.
- •Grate cheese for potatoes.

3 While chicken cooks:
- •Mince garlic.
- •Wash and trim asparagus.
- •Chop parsley and chives.
- •Squeeze lemon for juice for sauce.

4 While asparagus cooks:
- •Prepare potatoes.

Chicken and Asparagus in White Wine Sauce

This recipe also works well with green beans or haricots verts in place of the asparagus.

    4   (6-ounce) skinless, boneless chicken
        breast halves
    ¾   teaspoon salt
    ¼   teaspoon freshly ground black pepper
    2   tablespoons butter
    2¼ ounces all-purpose flour (about ½ cup)
    ½   cup dry white wine
    ½   cup fat-free, less-sodium chicken broth
    2   garlic cloves, minced
    1   pound asparagus spears, trimmed
    2   tablespoons chopped fresh parsley
    1   tablespoon fresh lemon juice

❶ Place each chicken breast half between 2 sheets of heavy-duty plastic wrap; pound to ¼-inch thickness using a meat mallet or small heavy skillet. Sprinkle chicken evenly with salt and pepper.

❷ Melt butter in a large nonstick skillet over medium-high heat. Place flour in a shallow dish; dredge chicken in flour. Add chicken to pan; cook 3 minutes on each side or until done. Remove chicken from pan; keep warm. Add wine, broth, and garlic to pan, scraping pan to loosen browned bits; cook 2 minutes. Add asparagus; cover and cook 3 minutes or until asparagus is crisp-tender. Remove from heat; stir in parsley and juice. Serve asparagus and sauce with chicken. Yield: 4 servings (serving size: 1 chicken breast half, about 5 asparagus spears, and about 2 tablespoons sauce).

CALORIES 289 (25% from fat); FAT 8g (sat 4.2g, mono 2g, poly 0.8g); PROTEIN 43g; CARB 10.5g; FIBER 2.8g; CHOL 114mg; IRON 4.3mg; SODIUM 648mg; CALC 59mg

Quick Tip: To speed up pounding the chicken, purchase thinly sliced chicken breast halves (sometimes labeled chicken cutlets or chicken breast fillets).

Chicken Breasts Stuffed with Artichokes, Lemon, and Goat Cheese

Browning the chicken on the stove top and finishing it in the oven frees you to put the final touches on the pilaf before serving. Wilt the spinach just before the chicken is done.

2½ tablespoons Italian-seasoned breadcrumbs
2 teaspoons grated lemon rind
¼ teaspoon salt
¼ teaspoon freshly ground black pepper
1 (6-ounce) jar marinated artichoke hearts, drained and chopped
1 (3-ounce) package herbed goat cheese, softened
4 (6-ounce) skinless, boneless chicken breast halves
Cooking spray

❶ Preheat oven to 375°.
❷ Combine first 6 ingredients; stir well.
❸ Place each chicken breast half between 2 sheets of heavy-duty plastic wrap; pound to ¼-inch thickness using a meat mallet or rolling pin. Top each chicken with 2 tablespoons goat cheese mixture; roll up jelly-roll fashion. Tuck in sides; secure each roll with wooden picks.
❹ Heat a large nonstick skillet over medium-high heat; coat with cooking spray. Add chicken to pan, and cook 3 minutes on each side or until browned. Wrap handle of pan with foil, and bake at 375° for 15 minutes or until chicken is done. Yield: 4 servings (serving size: 1 stuffed chicken breast half).

CALORIES 234 (30% from fat); FAT 7.8g (sat 3.5g, mono 1.4g, poly 0.5g); PROTEIN 33g; CARB 7.2g; FIBER 1.5g; CHOL 78mg; IRON 1.6mg; SODIUM 545mg; CALC 49mg

Quick Tip: You can stuff the chicken breast halves and chill them up to 4 hours before baking.

MENU *serves 4*

Chicken Breasts Stuffed with Artichokes, Lemon, and Goat Cheese

Wilted spinach

Bulgur pilaf with pine nuts

Heat 2 teaspoons olive oil in a medium skillet over medium-high heat. Add 1 cup coarse bulgur, ⅓ cup sliced green onions, ⅓ cup chopped shiitake mushrooms, and ⅛ teaspoon salt; sauté 5 minutes. Stir in 1 (14-ounce) can fat-free, less-sodium chicken broth; bring to a boil. Cover, reduce heat, and simmer 15 minutes. Remove from heat; let stand, covered, 5 minutes. Stir in 2 tablespoons pine nuts and 2 tablespoons chopped fresh parsley.

Game Plan

1 While bulgur cooks:
   - Combine cheese mixture for chicken.
   - Pound chicken.
   - Stuff chicken.
2 While chicken cooks:
   - Finish pilaf.
   - Prepare spinach.

MENU *serves 4*

Chicken Breasts Stuffed with Italian Sausage and Breadcrumbs

Sautéed zucchini and tomatoes

Heat a large skillet coated with cooking spray over medium-high heat. Cut 1 pound zucchini into ¼-inch slices; add zucchini and ½ cup chopped onion to pan. Sauté 5 minutes or until vegetables are tender. Add 1½ cups chopped tomato; cook 5 minutes. Remove from heat; stir in ½ teaspoon dried basil, ¼ teaspoon salt, and ¼ teaspoon pepper.

Mixed greens with bottled Italian dressing

Game Plan

1 Chop onion and celery, and mince parsley for chicken

2 While sausage mixture cooks:

- Pound chicken.

- Slice zucchini, and chop onion and tomato.

3 Stuff chicken breasts with sausage mixture.

4 While chicken cooks:

- Sauté zucchini mixture.

- Toss greens with dressing.

Chicken Breasts Stuffed with Italian Sausage and Breadcrumbs

Tangy sourdough bread adds an intriguing flavor element to this herbed sausage mixture.

1   (4-ounce) Italian sausage link
¼   cup finely chopped onion
2   tablespoons finely chopped celery
¼   cup dry white wine
1   (1½-ounce) slice sourdough bread, toasted and crusts removed
1   garlic clove, halved
1   tablespoon minced fresh parsley
½   teaspoon salt, divided
¼   teaspoon freshly ground black pepper
2   (6-ounce) skinless, boneless chicken breast halves
Cooking spray
½   cup fat-free, less-sodium chicken broth

❶ Remove casing from sausage; crumble sausage. Heat a large nonstick skillet over medium-high heat. Add sausage, onion, and celery to pan; sauté 5 minutes or until sausage is browned and onion is golden. Add wine; cook 1 minute or until most of liquid evaporates.

❷ Rub each side of bread with cut sides of garlic; discard garlic. Coarsely crumble bread; add to sausage mixture. Stir in parsley, ¼ teaspoon salt, and pepper. Let sausage mixture stand 5 minutes or until liquid is absorbed; toss to combine.

❸ Place each chicken breast half between 2 sheets of plastic wrap; pound to ¼-inch thickness using a meat mallet or rolling pin. Place half of stuffing on 1 side of each chicken breast half, leaving a 1-inch border around sides. Fold remaining half of each chicken breast over stuffing, and secure with wooden picks. Sprinkle chicken with ¼ teaspoon salt.

❹ Heat a large skillet over medium-high heat; coat with cooking spray. Add stuffed chicken breast halves to pan; cook 3 minutes on each side. Add broth, scraping pan to loosen browned bits. Cover, reduce heat, and simmer 5 minutes or until chicken is done. Remove wooden picks; slice breasts in half. Serve immediately. Yield: 4 servings (serving size: ½ chicken breast).

CALORIES 233 (29% from fat); FAT 7.6g (sat 2.5g, mono 0.5g, poly 0.4g); PROTEIN 21.9g; CARB 11.5g; FIBER 0.9g; CHOL 65mg; IRON 1.6mg; SODIUM 774mg; CALC 47mg

Chicken with Sherry Vinegar Sauce

Simple and luscious, this dish comes together quickly. Pan-sautéed chicken, mashed potatoes, and green beans form a classic taste combination.

- 4 (6-ounce) skinless, boneless chicken breast halves
- ½ teaspoon salt
- ¼ teaspoon black pepper
- 1 teaspoon butter
- 1 teaspoon olive oil
- ½ cup minced shallots
- ¾ cup fat-free, less-sodium chicken broth
- 3 tablespoons sherry vinegar
- 2 tablespoons whipping cream
- 1 tablespoon chopped fresh parsley

1 Sprinkle chicken with salt and pepper. Heat butter and oil in a large nonstick skillet over medium-high heat. Add chicken; cook 4 minutes on each side. Remove from pan; keep warm. Add shallots to pan; sauté 1 minute. Stir in broth and vinegar; cook 2 minutes. Add whipping cream; cook 1 minute. Serve sauce with chicken. Sprinkle with parsley. Yield: 4 servings (serving size: 1 chicken breast half and 1 tablespoon sauce).

CALORIES 194 (29% from fat); FAT 6.3g (sat 2.9g, mono 2.2g, poly 0.6g); PROTEIN 27.4g; CARB 5.6g; FIBER 0.4g; CHOL 78mg; IRON 1.3mg; SODIUM 457mg; CALC 33mg

MENU *serves 4*

Chicken with Sherry Vinegar Sauce

Rustic mashed potatoes

Place 3 cups refrigerated new potato wedges (such as Simply Potatoes) in a medium saucepan. Cover with water; bring to a boil over high heat. Reduce heat to medium; cook 5 minutes or until tender. Drain potatoes. Mash with 1 tablespoon butter, ½ teaspoon salt, and ¼ teaspoon pepper.

Steamed green beans

Game Plan

1 While chicken cooks:
- Mince shallots.
- Chop parsley.

2 While potatoes boil:
- Make sauce for chicken.
- Steam green beans.

Chicken with Balsamic-Fig Sauce

The simple preparation of this menu's side dishes means that the chicken—and its rich, sweet-tart sauce—is the star of this meal.

4 (6-ounce) skinless, boneless chicken breast halves
1½ tablespoons fresh thyme leaves, divided
½ teaspoon salt, divided
¼ teaspoon freshly ground black pepper
1 tablespoon olive oil
1 tablespoon butter
¾ cup chopped onion
½ cup fat-free, less-sodium chicken broth
¼ cup balsamic vinegar
2 teaspoons low-sodium soy sauce
½ cup finely chopped dried figs (such as Mission)

❶ Sprinkle both sides of chicken evenly with 1½ teaspoons thyme, ¼ teaspoon salt, and pepper. Heat oil in a large nonstick skillet over medium-high heat. Add chicken; cook 6 minutes on each side or until done. Remove from pan; keep warm.

❷ Reduce heat to medium; add butter to pan. Add onion; sauté 3 minutes. Add broth, vinegar, soy sauce, and figs. Simmer until sauce is reduced to 1 cup (about 3 minutes). Add 1 tablespoon thyme and ¼ teaspoon salt. Cut chicken breast halves lengthwise on diagonal into slices. Serve sauce over chicken. Yield: 4 servings (serving size: 4 ounces chicken and ¼ cup sauce).

CALORIES 355 (28% from fat); FAT 11g (sat 3.6g, mono 4.9g, poly 1.5g); PROTEIN 41.3g; CARB 21.6g; FIBER 3g; CHOL 116mg; IRON 2.1mg; SODIUM 563mg; CALC 71mg

Chicken in Cherry Marsala Sauce

If you can't find dried cherries, use regular dried cranberries. Pleasantly bitter broccoli rabe complements the sweet fruit sauce; blanching lessens its bite.

⅓ cup dried cherries
⅓ cup Marsala
2 teaspoons olive oil
4 (6-ounce) skinless, boneless chicken breast halves
½ teaspoon salt, divided
½ teaspoon black pepper, divided
1 teaspoon butter
¼ cup finely chopped shallots
1 tablespoon chopped fresh thyme
½ cup fat-free, less-sodium chicken broth

❶ Combine cherries and Marsala in a small microwave-safe bowl. Microwave at HIGH 45 seconds, and set aside.
❷ Heat oil in a large nonstick skillet over medium-high heat. Add chicken to pan, and cook 4 minutes on each side or until done. Remove chicken from pan; sprinkle with ¼ teaspoon salt and ¼ teaspoon pepper. Cover and keep warm.
❸ Add butter to pan; cook until butter melts. Add shallots and thyme; sauté 1 minute or until tender. Stir in broth, scraping pan to loosen browned bits. Add cherry mixture, ¼ teaspoon salt, and ¼ teaspoon pepper; bring to a boil. Reduce heat to medium, and simmer 2 minutes or until sauce is slightly thick. Serve chicken with sauce. Yield: 4 servings (serving size: 1 chicken breast half and about ¼ cup sauce).

CALORIES 297 (16% from fat); FAT 5.4g (sat 1.4g, mono 2.6g, poly 0.8g); PROTEIN 40.5g; CARB 13.7g; FIBER 1.1g; CHOL 101mg; IRON 2.1mg; SODIUM 464mg; CALC 33mg

---

MENU *serves 4*

Chicken in Cherry Marsala Sauce

Broccoli rabe with garlic

Cook 8 cups coarsely chopped broccoli rabe in boiling water 2 minutes; drain. Melt 2 teaspoons butter in a large nonstick skillet over medium heat. Add 3 thinly sliced garlic cloves; cook 1 minute, stirring frequently. Add blanched broccoli rabe, ½ teaspoon salt, and ¼ teaspoon freshly ground black pepper; toss to combine. Serve with lemon wedges.

Buttered egg noodles

Game Plan

1 While water for noodles comes to a boil:

- Chop broccoli rabe, slice garlic, and cut lemon into wedges.

- Chop shallots and thyme for chicken.

- Microwave cherry mixture.

2 While egg noodles cook:

- Prepare chicken dish.

- Bring water to boil for broccoli rabe.

3 Prepare broccoli rabe.

MENU *serves 4*

Curried Chicken with Mango Chutney

Minted cucumber salad

Combine 2 cups chopped seeded cucumber, ¼ cup chopped red onion, 2 tablespoons rice vinegar, 1 teaspoon sugar, ½ teaspoon salt, and ½ teaspoon freshly ground black pepper in a large bowl; toss well. Add 1 cup plain fat-free yogurt and 3 tablespoons chopped fresh mint, stirring well to combine.

Hot basmati rice

Game Plan

1 While chutney cooks:

- •Cook rice.
- •Marinate chicken.
- •Chop cucumber, red onion, and fresh mint for salad.

2 While chicken cooks:

- •Prepare cucumber salad.

Curried Chicken with Mango Chutney

A grill pan will score the chicken nicely, but using a skillet to cook the chicken works just as well. Substitute fresh or frozen peaches, plums, or nectarines for the mango in the chutney.

MANGO CHUTNEY:

- 2 cups chopped peeled mango
- 1 cup apple juice
- ⅓ cup diced dried apricots
- 2 teaspoons cider vinegar
- 1 teaspoon grated peeled fresh ginger
- ¼ teaspoon ground allspice
- ⅛ teaspoon ground red pepper

CHICKEN:

- ⅓ cup low-sodium soy sauce
- ⅓ cup fresh lime juice
- 1 teaspoon curry powder
- 4 (6-ounce) skinless, boneless chicken breast halves

Cooking spray

REMAINING INGREDIENT:

Lime wedges (optional)

❶ To prepare chutney, combine first 7 ingredients in a saucepan, and bring to a boil. Reduce heat; simmer 20 minutes, stirring occasionally.
❷ To prepare chicken, combine soy sauce, juice, curry, and chicken in a zip-top plastic bag; seal bag and shake. Marinate chicken in refrigerator 10 minutes, turning once. Heat a grill pan over medium-high heat; coat with cooking spray.
❸ Remove chicken from bag; discard marinade. Add chicken to pan; cook 5 minutes on each side or until chicken is done. Serve with chutney. Garnish with lime wedges, if desired. Yield: 4 servings (serving size: 1 chicken breast half and about ½ cup chutney).

CALORIES 257 (7% from fat); FAT 1.9g (sat 0.5g, mono 0.5g, poly 0.4g); PROTEIN 29.6g; CARB 30.6g; FIBER 2.8g; CHOL 68mg; IRON 1.7mg; SODIUM 880mg; CALC 35mg

Tandoori Chicken

Although it's not cooked in a tandoor oven, this vibrant entrée has all the flavors of the traditional Indian dish, due to its long marinating time.

¾ cup coarsely chopped onion
1 teaspoon coarsely chopped peeled fresh ginger
2 garlic cloves, peeled
½ cup plain low-fat yogurt
1 tablespoon fresh lemon juice
1 teaspoon paprika
1 teaspoon ground cumin
1 teaspoon ground coriander seeds
½ teaspoon salt
½ teaspoon chili powder
¼ teaspoon black pepper
Dash of ground nutmeg
4 (4-ounce) skinless, boneless chicken breast halves
Cooking spray

1 Place onion, ginger, and cloves in a food processor; process until finely chopped. Add yogurt and next 8 ingredients to onion mixture in food processor; pulse 4 times or until blended.

2 Make 3 diagonal cuts ¼ inch deep across top of each chicken breast half. Combine chicken and yogurt mixture in a large zip-top plastic bag. Seal bag and marinate chicken in refrigerator 8 hours or overnight, turning occasionally.

3 Prepare grill or preheat broiler.

4 Remove chicken breast halves from bag; discard marinade. Place chicken on grill rack or broiler pan rack coated with cooking spray; cook 6 minutes on each side or until done. Yield: 4 servings (serving size: 1 chicken breast half).

CALORIES 146 (12% from fat); FAT 1.9g (sat 0.6g, mono 0.4g, poly 0.4g); PROTEIN 27.4g; CARB 3.4g; FIBER 0.7g; CHOL 67mg; IRON 1.1mg; SODIUM 234mg; CALC 50mg

MENU *serves 4*

Tandoori Chicken

Tabbouleh

Soak 1 cup uncooked bulgur in 2 cups boiling water 20 minutes or until just tender. Combine bulgur, 1½ cups chopped fresh flat-leaf parsley, 1 cup chopped tomato, and ¼ cup chopped green onions in a large bowl. Combine ¼ cup fresh lemon juice, 1½ tablespoons olive oil, ½ teaspoon salt, and ¼ teaspoon black pepper in a small bowl; stir with a whisk. Drizzle dressing over bulgur mixture; toss gently to combine.

Pita wedges

Game Plan

1 Prepare marinade, and marinate chicken 8 hours or overnight.

2 While grill or broiler heats for chicken:
- Bring water for bulger to a boil.
- Chop parsley, tomato, and green onions for tabbouleh.

3 While bulgur soaks:
- Cook chicken.
- Prepare dressing for tabbouleh.
- Cut pita into wedges.

Grilled Chicken Tostadas

Fried tortillas usually form the shells for tostadas, but grilling them lowers the fat. Prepared salsa, canned beans, and preshredded coleslaw make this recipe come together in a snap.

4 (6-ounce) skinless, boneless chicken breast halves
1 tablespoon fresh lime juice
1 tablespoon 40%-less-sodium taco seasoning (such as Old El Paso)
½ teaspoon sugar
Cooking spray
6 (8-inch) flour tortillas
6 cups packaged coleslaw
1 (7-ounce) can green salsa
4 cups chopped tomato
¼ cup sliced ripe olives, chopped
1¼ cups fat-free refried beans
½ cup (2 ounces) crumbled feta cheese
6 tablespoons reduced-fat sour cream
¼ cup fresh cilantro leaves
¼ cup unsalted pumpkinseed kernels, toasted (optional)

1 Prepare grill, or heat a grill pan over medium-high heat.

2 Brush chicken with juice; sprinkle with seasoning and sugar. Place chicken on grill rack or grill pan coated with cooking spray; grill 4 minutes on each side or until done. Cool slightly. Cut chicken into ¼-inch strips; set aside. Place tortillas on grill rack or grill pan coated with cooking spray; grill 30 seconds on each side or until golden brown.

3 Combine coleslaw and salsa; toss to coat. Combine tomato and olives; toss gently.

4 Spread about 3 tablespoons beans over each tortilla; divide chicken evenly among tortillas. Top each serving with about ⅔ cup slaw mixture, ⅔ cup tomato mixture, 4 teaspoons cheese, 1 tablespoon sour cream, and 2 teaspoons cilantro. Sprinkle each serving with 2 teaspoons pumpkinseeds, if desired. Yield: 6 servings (serving size: 1 tostada).

CALORIES 361 (23% from fat); FAT 9.2g (sat 3.6g, mono 1.5g, poly 1.2g); PROTEIN 28.7g; CARB 43g; FIBER 6.8g; CHOL 65mg; IRON 3.7mg; SODIUM 844mg; CALC 221mg

Roasted Chicken with Dried Plums and Shallots

Bone-in chicken breast halves work well for roasting because the meat stays moist in the oven's high heat. Substitute dried apricot halves for dried plums, if you prefer.

2 teaspoons olive oil
4 bone-in chicken breast halves (about 2 pounds)
¾ teaspoon salt, divided
½ teaspoon black pepper, divided
8 garlic cloves, peeled
4 large shallots, peeled and halved (about 8 ounces)
2 thyme sprigs
1 large fennel bulb, cut into 8 wedges
16 pitted dried plums
¾ cup fat-free, less-sodium chicken broth, divided
1/4 cup dry white wine
1 tablespoon all-purpose flour
2 teaspoons chopped fresh thyme

❶ Preheat oven to 450°.
❷ Drizzle oil in a small roasting pan or bottom of a broiler pan; place pan in oven 5 minutes or until oil is hot. Sprinkle chicken with ¼ teaspoon salt and ¼ teaspoon pepper. Place chicken, skin sides down, in pan. Arrange garlic, shallots, thyme sprigs, and fennel around chicken; sprinkle vegetables with ¼ teaspoon salt and ⅛ teaspoon pepper. Bake at 450° for 20 minutes. Remove pan from oven. Turn chicken over; stir vegetables. Add plums to pan. Bake an additional 15 minutes or until chicken is done. Remove chicken and vegetable mixture from pan; discard thyme sprigs. Discard skin. Loosely cover chicken and vegetable mixture; keep warm.
❸ Place pan over medium-high heat. Add ½ cup broth and wine, stirring to loosen browned bits. Combine flour and ¼ cup broth; stir with a whisk until smooth. Add flour mixture to pan; stir until well blended. Bring to a boil; cook 1 minute or until slightly thick. Stir in chopped thyme, ¼ teaspoon salt, and ⅛ teaspoon pepper. Serve sauce with chicken and vegetable mixture. Yield: 4 servings (serving size: 1 chicken breast half, about ⅓ cup vegetable mixture, and 3 tablespoons sauce).

CALORIES 384 (30% from fat); FAT 13g (sat 3.3g, mono 5.8g, poly 2.4g); PROTEIN 36.6g; CARB 31g; FIBER 5.1g; CHOL 96mg; IRON 3.1mg; SODIUM 632mg; CALC 95mg

Ingredient Tip: Look for jars of peeled garlic cloves in the produce section of your supermarket.

MENU *serves 4*

Roasted Chicken with Dried Plums and Shallots

Brussels sprouts with garlic and honey
Melt 1 tablespoon butter in a large nonstick skillet over medium-high heat. Add 1 pound trimmed and quartered Brussels sprouts, ¼ teaspoon salt, and ¼ teaspoon black pepper. Sauté 3 minutes. Add 3 thinly sliced garlic cloves; sauté 2 minutes or until lightly browned. Add 3 tablespoons water; cover and cook 3 minutes or until Brussels sprouts are tender. Drizzle with 1 tablespoon honey; toss to coat.

Israeli couscous

Game Plan

1 Prepare garlic, shallots, and fennel for chicken.

2 While chicken roasts:
  • Combine flour and broth.
  • Chop thyme.
  • Cook couscous.
  • Prepare Brussels sprouts.

MENU *serves 4*

Chicken Paprikash-Topped Potatoes

Roasted Brussels sprouts

Preheat oven to 425°. Combine 4 cups trimmed and halved Brussels sprouts, 2 teaspoons melted butter, ½ teaspoon salt, and ¼ teaspoon black pepper on a jelly-roll pan coated with cooking spray. Bake at 425° for 25 minutes or until crisp-tender.

Garlic breadsticks

Game Plan

1 While Brussels sprouts roast:

•Microwave potatoes.

•Prepare chicken mixture for potatoes.

•Warm breadsticks.

2 Assemble potatoes.

Chicken Paprikash-Topped Potatoes

The traditional Hungarian dish of chicken and onion in a creamy paprika sauce makes for a hearty topping on baked potatoes.

 4 baking potatoes (about 1½ pounds)
 4 skinless, boneless chicken thighs (about 12 ounces), cut into bite-sized pieces
 2 tablespoons all-purpose flour
 2 teaspoons paprika
 ¾ teaspoon salt
 ¼ teaspoon ground red pepper
 1 tablespoon butter
 ½ cup coarsely chopped onion
 1 (8-ounce) package presliced mushrooms
 2 garlic cloves, minced
 ½ cup fat-free, less-sodium chicken broth
 ¼ cup reduced-fat sour cream
 2 tablespoons chopped fresh parsley

❶ Pierce potatoes with a fork; arrange in a circle on paper towels in microwave oven. Microwave at HIGH 16 minutes or until done, rearranging potatoes after 8 minutes. Let stand 5 minutes.

❷ Combine chicken, flour, paprika, salt, and pepper in a large zip-top plastic bag; seal bag and shake to coat.

❸ Melt butter in a large nonstick skillet over medium-high heat. Add chicken mixture, onion, mushrooms, and garlic; sauté 5 minutes. Add broth, and bring to a boil. Cook 6 minutes or until chicken is done and sauce thickens, stirring frequently. Remove from heat; stir in sour cream.

❹ Split potatoes open with fork; fluff pulp. Divide chicken mixture evenly over potatoes; sprinkle with parsley. Yield: 4 servings (serving size: 1 potato and ½ cup chicken mixture).

CALORIES 311 (25% from fat); FAT 8.6g (sat 3.9g, mono 1.9g, poly 1.2g); PROTEIN 22.9g; CARB 36.3g; FIBER 3.4g; CHOL 86mg; IRON 2.6mg; SODIUM 619mg; CALC 56mg

Chicken and Potatoes over Sautéed Spinach

This recipe exemplifies the Chinese technique of red cooking: braising meat in a flavorful combination of soy sauce, ginger, alcohol, and spices. Serve this dish in shallow-rimmed soup bowls so you can enjoy all the broth. Sautéed mustard greens would be another good side dish option to offer here. The refreshing salad provides a textural contrast.

4 cups thinly sliced leek (about 4 large)
1 cup thinly sliced celery
6 tablespoons low-sodium soy sauce
¼ cup julienne-cut peeled fresh ginger
¼ cup dry vermouth or dry sherry
2 teaspoons sugar
1 teaspoon five-spice powder
1 (14-ounce) can fat-free, less-sodium chicken broth
1½ pounds skinless, boneless chicken thighs, cut into thirds
1½ pounds peeled white potatoes, cut into 1-inch pieces
¼ cup chopped fresh cilantro
½ teaspoon freshly ground black pepper
2 teaspoons canola oil
1 teaspoon dark sesame oil
2 (10-ounce) packages fresh spinach

1 Combine leek, celery, soy sauce, and next 5 ingredients in a large Dutch oven over medium-high heat; bring to a boil. Add chicken; return to a boil. Cover, reduce heat, and simmer 10 minutes, stirring occasionally.
2 Add potatoes; return to a simmer. Cover and cook 25 minutes or until potatoes are tender, stirring occasionally. Stir in cilantro and pepper.
3 Heat oils in a large skillet over medium-high heat. Add half of spinach; cook 1 minute, tossing constantly. Add remaining spinach; cook 2 minutes or until spinach wilts, tossing constantly. Serve chicken mixture over spinach. Yield: 6 servings (serving size: 1⅓ cups chicken mixture and about ⅓ cup spinach).

CALORIES 343 (20% from fat); FAT 7.6g (sat 1.5g, mono 2.7g, poly 2.2g); PROTEIN 29.6g; CARB 39.4g; FIBER 6.1g; CHOL 94mg; IRON 6.2mg; SODIUM 846mg; CALC 170mg

MENU *serves 6*

Chicken and Potatoes over Sautéed Spinach

Asian salad
Combine 6 cups chopped romaine lettuce heart, 1 cup grated carrot, 1 cup chopped cucumber, and 1 cup halved grape tomatoes in a large bowl. Combine ¼ cup rice wine vinegar, 2 tablespoons soy sauce, 1½ teaspoons miso, 1 teaspoon minced garlic, and 1 teaspoon grated peeled fresh ginger in a small bowl. Add 1 tablespoon sesame oil and 1 teaspoon peanut oil, stirring constantly with a whisk. Drizzle dressing over greens; toss gently.

Pineapple chunks with ground red pepper

Game Plan

1 Prepare leek, celery, ginger, and chicken.

2 While chicken mixture simmers:
  • Cut potatoes.

3 While chicken and potato mixture simmers:
  • Chop cilantro.
  • Prepare salad.
  • Prepare pineapple.

4 Cook spinach mixture.

Margarita-Braised Chicken Thighs

Green rice

Bring 2 cups fat-free, less-sodium chicken broth to a boil in a medium sauce-pan; stir in 1 cup long-grain white rice. Cover and cook 20 minutes or until liquid is absorbed and rice is tender. Stir in 2 tablespoons butter and ½ teaspoon salt. Combine ¾ cup chopped fresh cilantro, ¾ cup sliced green onions, and 2 tablespoons fresh lime juice. Add to rice; stir well.

Pineapple sherbet

Game Plan

1 While chicken browns:

- Slice onion and mince garlic.

- Combine fruit, juice, and tequila.

2 While chicken bakes:

- Chop cilantro and onions for rice.

- Squeeze lime for juice for rice.

Margarita-Braised Chicken Thighs

This juicy, fruity chicken dish received rave reviews from our Test Kitchens staff.

- ½ cup flour (about 2¼ ounces)
- 1 tablespoon paprika
- 2 teaspoons garlic powder
- 8 skinless, boneless chicken thighs (about 1½ pounds)
- ½ teaspoon salt
- 1 tablespoon olive oil
- Cooking spray
- 1 cup thinly sliced onion (about 1 medium)
- 5 garlic cloves, minced
- ½ cup dried tropical fruit
- ½ cup fresh orange juice
- ¼ cup tequila
- 1 lime, thinly sliced

1 Preheat oven to 400°.

2 Combine first 3 ingredients in a small baking dish. Sprinkle chicken with salt; dredge chicken in flour mixture.

3 Heat oil in a large nonstick skillet over medium-high heat. Add chicken to pan; cook 4 minutes on each side or until lightly browned. Transfer chicken to an 11 x 7-inch baking dish coated with cooking spray. Add onion to pan; cook 3 minutes. Add garlic, and sauté 1 minute.

4 Combine fruit, juice, and tequila in a microwave-safe dish, and microwave at HIGH 2 minutes. Pour fruit mixture into pan; bring to a boil, scraping pan to loosen browned bits. Cook 1 minute. Pour onion mixture over chicken; top with lime slices. Bake at 400° for 20 minutes or until chicken is done. Yield: 4 servings (serving size: 2 thighs and about ¹/₃ cup fruit mixture).

CALORIES 350 (25% from fat); FAT 9.9g (sat 2.2g, mono 4.3g, poly 2.1g); PROTEIN 25.1g; CARB 37.9g; FIBER 2.7g; CHOL 94mg; IRON 2.7mg; SODIUM 416mg; CALC 55mg

Quick Tip: Purchase boneless, skinless chicken thighs; presliced onion; and bottled minced garlic to slash your prep time in half.

Chicken Thighs with Roasted Apples and Garlic

Baking and then mashing the apples creates a flavorful, chunky sauce for the chicken—and allows you to sneak more fruit into your diet, too. Feel free to leave bits of peel on the apples to make this rustic dish even more colorful and rich in fiber.

5 cups chopped peeled Braeburn apple
(about 1½ pounds)
1 teaspoon chopped fresh sage
¼ teaspoon ground cinnamon
⅛ teaspoon ground nutmeg
4 garlic cloves, chopped
½ teaspoon salt, divided
Cooking spray
8 chicken thighs (about 2 pounds), skinned
¼ teaspoon black pepper

❶ Preheat oven to 475°.
❷ Combine first 5 ingredients. Add ¼ teaspoon salt; toss to coat. Spread apple mixture on a jelly-roll pan coated with cooking spray.

❸ Sprinkle chicken with ¼ teaspoon salt and pepper, and arrange on top of apple mixture. Bake at 475° for 25 minutes or until chicken is done and apple is tender. Remove chicken from pan; keep warm.
❹ Partially mash apple mixture with a potato masher; serve with chicken. Yield: 4 servings (serving size: 2 thighs and about ⅔ cup apple mixture).

CALORIES 257 (20% from fat); FAT 5.7g (sat 1.4g, mono 1.6g, poly 1.4g); PROTEIN 25.9g; CARB 26.6g; FIBER 3.5g; CHOL 107mg; IRON 1.7mg; SODIUM 405mg; CALC 30mg

Quick Tip: To save prep time, look for bone-in chicken thighs that are already skinned.

MENU *serves 4*

Chicken Thighs with Roasted Apples and Garlic

Browned Brussels sprouts

Heat 1 tablespoon olive oil in a large nonstick skillet over medium heat. Add 1½ pounds trimmed and halved Brussels sprouts, ¼ teaspoon salt, and 3 thinly sliced garlic cloves; cook 15 minutes or until lightly browned, stirring occasionally. Stir in 2 teaspoons balsamic vinegar; cook 1 minute.

Dinner rolls

Game Plan

1 While oven heats for chicken:
   • Prepare apple mixture.
   • Skin chicken thighs.
2 While chicken bakes:
   • Prepare and cook Brussels sprouts.
   • Warm dinner rolls.

Parmesan Chicken and Rice Casserole

Parmesan cheese provides a nutty, salty flavor. Garnish the dish with a thyme sprig, if you like.

Cooking spray
 1 cup chopped onion
 2 garlic cloves, minced
 2 (3½-ounce) bags boil-in-bag brown rice
 ⅓ cup dry white wine
 8 skinless, boneless chicken thighs (about 1¾ pounds)
 1½ teaspoons chopped fresh thyme
 ½ teaspoon salt
 2 cups fat-free, less-sodium chicken broth
 3 tablespoons whipping cream
 ⅓ cup (1½ ounces) shredded Parmesan cheese

1 Preheat oven to 450°.
2 Heat a large nonstick skillet over medium-high heat; coat with cooking spray. Add onion to pan; sauté 2 minutes. Add garlic, and sauté 30 seconds. Remove rice from bags; add to pan. Sauté 30 seconds. Stir in wine; cook 30 seconds or until liquid almost evaporates. Spoon rice mixture in an even layer into a 13 x 9–inch baking dish coated with cooking spray.
3 Arrange chicken thighs in a single layer over rice mixture; sprinkle evenly with thyme and salt. Combine broth and cream, stirring well; pour over chicken and rice mixture.
4 Bake at 450° for 15 minutes. Sprinkle with cheese. Bake an additional 5 minutes or until chicken is done. Yield: 4 servings (serving size: 2 chicken thighs and 1 cup rice).

CALORIES 498 (35% from fat); FAT 19.1g (sat 7.5g, mono 6.7g, poly 3.1g); PROTEIN 38.2g; CARB 43.8g; FIBER 5.6g; CHOL 122mg; IRON 3mg; SODIUM 765mg; CALC 198mg

MENU *serves 4*

Parmesan Chicken and Rice Casserole

Green beans with warm bacon dressing
Cook 1 pound trimmed fresh green beans in boiling water 3 minutes or until crisp-tender; drain. Cook 2 strips bacon in a skillet over medium heat until crisp. Remove bacon from pan; crumble. Add ¼ cup chopped shallots to drippings in pan; cook 3 minutes, stirring frequently. Add 2 tablespoons white wine vinegar; cook 1 minute, stirring constantly. Add green beans; toss to coat. Sprinkle with crumbled bacon.

Broiled plum tomatoes

Game Plan

1 While oven heats:
 •Prepare ingredients for casserole.
 •Prepare ingredients for green beans.
 •Halve plum tomatoes; sprinkle with salt and pepper.

2 While casserole bakes:
 •Cook green beans.

3 Broil tomatoes.

MENU *serves 4*

Oven-Fried Chicken

Garlic mashed potatoes

Place 4 cups cubed peeled Yukon gold potatoes in a saucepan; cover with water. Bring to a boil; cook 6 minutes or until tender. Drain. Return potatoes to pan. Add ¼ cup fat-free, less-sodium chicken broth; ¼ cup reduced-fat sour cream; 2 tablespoons butter; ½ teaspoon salt; and 3 minced garlic cloves. Mash with a potato masher to desired consistency.

Green peas

Game Plan

1 While oven heats:
- •Combine buttermilk and egg whites.
- •Combine flour, cornmeal, and seasoning.

2 While chicken bakes:
- •Prepare potatoes.
- •Prepare green peas.

Oven-Fried Chicken

You can prepare the garlic mashed potatoes on the stove top while the chicken bakes in the oven. Dipping the chicken pieces into buttermilk not only tenderizes the meat, but also adds a pleasant, tangy flavor.

　1　cup low-fat buttermilk
　2　large egg whites, beaten
4½　ounces all-purpose flour (about 1 cup)
　⅓　cup cornmeal
　1　teaspoon salt, divided
　¾　teaspoon freshly ground black pepper
　¼　teaspoon ground red pepper
　2　chicken breast halves, skinned (about 1 pound)
　2　chicken thighs, skinned (about ½ pound)
　2　chicken drumsticks, skinned (about ½ pound)
　2　tablespoons canola oil
Cooking spray

❶ Preheat oven to 425°.
❷ Cover a large baking sheet with parchment paper. Combine buttermilk and egg whites in a shallow dish; stir with a whisk. Combine flour, cornmeal, ½ teaspoon salt, black pepper, and red pepper in a separate shallow dish; stir well to combine. Sprinkle chicken breast halves, thighs, and drumsticks evenly with ½ teaspoon salt. Dip chicken in buttermilk mixture; dredge in flour mixture.
❸ Heat oil in a large nonstick skillet over medium-high heat. Add chicken to pan; cook 4 minutes on each side or until lightly browned. Place chicken on prepared baking sheet; lightly coat chicken with cooking spray. Bake at 425° for 30 minutes or until chicken is done. Yield: 4 servings (serving size: 1 chicken breast half or 1 drumstick and 1 thigh).

CALORIES 450 (28% from fat); FAT 13.8g (sat 2.5g, mono 6.1g, poly 3.6g); PROTEIN 43.5g; CARB 35.3g; FIBER 1.7g; CHOL 109mg; IRON 3.2mg; SODIUM 803mg; CALC 88mg

Orange-Ginger Glazed Cornish Hens

Roasting small Cornish hens at a high temperature means that these fruit-glazed beauties will be cooked to perfection after only 25 minutes in the oven.

¾ cup fresh orange juice (about 3 oranges)
2 tablespoons minced peeled fresh ginger
2 tablespoons honey
1 tablespoon low-sodium soy sauce
1 tablespoon water
2 teaspoons cornstarch
2 (1½-pound) Cornish hens, skinned and halved
Cooking spray
½ teaspoon salt
½ teaspoon ground ginger

❶ Preheat oven to 475°.
❷ Combine first 4 ingredients in a small saucepan; bring to a boil. Combine water and cornstarch in a small bowl; stir with a whisk. Add to juice mixture in pan, stirring with a whisk. Cook 2 minutes or until thick and glossy, stirring constantly.

❸ Place hen halves, meaty sides up, on a foil-lined jelly-roll pan coated with cooking spray; sprinkle hen halves with salt and ground ginger. Spoon juice mixture evenly over hen halves.
❹ Insert a meat thermometer into meaty part of a thigh, making sure not to touch bone. Bake at 475° for 25 minutes or until thermometer registers 165°. Yield: 4 servings (serving size: 1 hen half).

CALORIES 188 (18% from fat); FAT 3.8g (sat 1g, mono 1.2g, poly 0.9g); PROTEIN 22.5g; CARB 15.6g; FIBER 0.3g; CHOL 99mg; IRON 1mg; SODIUM 487mg; CALC 19mg

Quick Tip: Lining the pan with foil makes cleanup easy. Don't worry if the sweet glaze burns on the foil; it won't burn on the hens. Cooking the hens and green beans in the oven together saves time and ensures that everything will be ready at the same time.

MENU *serves 4*

Orange-Ginger Glazed Cornish Hens

Oven-roasted green beans

Preheat oven to 475°. Combine 1 pound trimmed green beans, 2 teaspoons olive oil, ½ teaspoon salt, and ⅛ teaspoon black pepper. Arrange in a single layer on a baking sheet coated with cooking spray; place in oven on rack below hens. Bake at 475° for 10 minutes or until tender, turning once. Remove from oven; toss with 2 teaspoons fresh lemon juice.

Hot long-grain and wild rice blend

Game Plan

1 While oven heats:
   - Prepare glaze for hens.
   - Split and skin hens.
   - Bring water for rice to a boil.

2 While hens roast:
   - Cook rice.
   - Prepare green beans.
   - Place beans in oven during final 10 minutes of the hens' cook time.

MENU *serves 6*

Rosemary-Scented Cornish Hens with Red Wine Reduction

Double-walnut rice pilaf

Heat 2 teaspoons olive oil in a large saucepan over medium-high heat. Add ¼ cup chopped fresh shallots to pan; sauté 3 minutes. Add 2 minced garlic cloves; sauté 1 minute. Add 1 cup uncooked long-grain rice; sauté 1 minute. Stir in 2 cups fat-free, less-sodium chicken broth; bring to a boil. Cover, reduce heat, and cook 20 minutes or until liquid is absorbed. Stir in 2 tablespoons chopped fresh chives and 2 tablespoons toasted walnut oil. Top with ¼ cup toasted walnuts.

Sautéed Broccolini

Game Plan

1 Mince rosemary and garlic.

2 Prepare and bake hens.

3 While drippings stand:

- Sauté shallot, garlic, and rice.

- Bring rice mixture to a boil.

4 While rice simmers:

- Chop chives and toast walnuts.

- Prepare sauce for hens.

- Sauté Broccolini.

Rosemary-Scented Cornish Hens with Red Wine Reduction

These hens will need only a small drizzle of the intensely flavorful sauce. Try this menu for your next dinner party.

- 3 (1¼-pound) Cornish hens
- 3 tablespoons stone-ground mustard
- 2 teaspoons minced fresh rosemary
- ¾ teaspoon kosher salt
- ½ teaspoon freshly ground black pepper
- 5 garlic cloves, minced and divided
- Cooking spray
- ½ cup dry red wine
- ½ cup fat-free, less-sodium chicken broth
- 2 tablespoons fresh lemon juice
- 2 teaspoons honey

❶ Remove and discard giblets and necks from hens; trim excess fat. Split hens in half lengthwise. Starting at neck cavity, loosen skin from hens by inserting fingers, gently pushing between skin and meat. Combine mustard, rosemary, salt, pepper, and 3 garlic cloves to form a paste; rub mustard mixture under loosened skin. Place hen halves, meaty sides up, on a broiler pan rack coated with cooking spray. Chill 30 minutes.

❷ Preheat oven to 425°.

❸ Bake hens at 425° for 30 minutes or until a thermometer registers 165°. Place hens on a platter; keep warm.

❹ Place a zip-top plastic bag inside a 2-cup glass measure. Pour drippings from pan into bag; let stand 10 minutes (fat will rise to the top). Seal bag; snip off 1 bottom corner of bag. Drain drippings into a nonstick skillet, stopping before fat layer reaches opening; discard fat and zip-top bag.

❺ Add wine to drippings in pan; bring to a boil over medium-high heat. Cook until reduced to ¼ cup (about 3 minutes). Stir in broth, juice, honey, and 2 garlic cloves; cook until reduced to ¼ cup (about 2 minutes). Remove mixture from heat.

❻ Remove skin from hens; discard. Drizzle each hen with 2 teaspoons wine mixture. Serve immediately. Yield: 6 servings (serving size: ½ hen).

CALORIES 345 (25% from fat); FAT 9.5g (sat 2.4g, mono 3g, poly 2.3g); PROTEIN 57.3g; CARB 3.7g; FIBER 0.2g; CHOL 258mg; IRON 2.3mg; SODIUM 565mg; CALC 42mg

Apricot Grilled Duck Breasts

You can serve this savory-sweet entrée over couscous, brown or white rice, or even pasta.

½ cup apricot preserves
2½ tablespoons sherry vinegar
¼ teaspoon salt
¼ teaspoon ground cumin
⅛ teaspoon ground red pepper
4 (6-ounce) boneless duck breast halves, skinned
Cooking spray

❶ Combine first 5 ingredients in a large bowl; stir with a whisk. Add duck; cover and marinate in refrigerator 20 minutes.
❷ Prepare grill.
❸ Remove duck from marinade, reserving marinade. Bring marinade to a boil in a small saucepan over medium-high heat; boil marinade 1 minute. Remove from heat.
❹ Place duck on grill rack coated with cooking spray. Grill 6 minutes on each side or until a thermometer inserted into thickest portion registers 165°, basting occasionally with reserved marinade. Yield: 4 servings (serving size: 1 duck breast half).

CALORIES 299 (11% from fat); FAT 3.7g (sat 0.8g, mono 1.3g, poly 0.5g); PROTEIN 39.4g; CARB 26.8g; FIBER 0.2g; CHOL 203mg; IRON 6.7mg; SODIUM 311mg; CALC 23mg

MENU *serves 4*

Apricot Grilled Duck Breasts

Sautéed green beans with pecans
Cook 1 (12-ounce) package prewashed cut green beans in boiling water 1½ minutes or until crisp-tender. Drain and plunge green beans into ice water; drain. Melt 2 teaspoons butter in a large nonstick skillet over medium-high heat. Add ¼ cup chopped shallots; sauté 5 minutes or until lightly browned. Add green beans, ¼ cup chopped pecans, ¼ teaspoon salt, and ¼ teaspoon freshly ground black pepper. Cook 1 minute or until thoroughly heated.

Israeli couscous

Game Plan

1 While duck marinates:
  • Prepare grill.
  • Chop shallots and pecans for green beans.

2 While duck grills:
  • Prepare couscous.
  • Sauté green beans.

Game Plan

1 While oven heats:

- Cut potatoes.

- Chop herbs and mince garlic for potatoes.

- Prepare cherry mixture for duck.

2 While potatoes bake:

- Cook duck.

Duck with Dried Cherries and Rosemary

We used pinot noir for the red wine in this sauce. You can substitute beef broth to make a nonalcoholic version. Use sweetened dried cranberries instead of cherries, if desired.

½   cup dried sweet cherries
½   cup dry red wine
2   tablespoons raspberry vinegar
1   tablespoon chopped fresh rosemary
2   teaspoons grated peeled fresh ginger
⅛   teaspoon sugar
2   teaspoons olive oil
4   (6-ounce) boneless duck breast halves, skinned
¼   teaspoon salt
¼   teaspoon freshly ground black pepper
Rosemary sprigs (optional)

❶ Combine first 6 ingredients in a medium bowl; set aside.

❷ Heat oil in a large nonstick skillet over medium-high heat. Sprinkle both sides of duck breast halves with salt and pepper. Add duck to pan; cook 3 minutes on each side or until a thermometer inserted into thickest portion registers 165°. Place duck on a cutting board; cover with foil.

❸ Add cherry mixture to pan; cook over medium-low heat 5 minutes. Remove pan from heat. Cut duck into thin slices; spoon cherry mixture over duck. Garnish with rosemary sprigs, if desired. Yield: 4 servings (serving size: 1 duck breast half and 2 tablespoons cherry sauce).

CALORIES 279 (27% from fat); FAT 8.3g (sat 2.2g, mono 3.4g, poly 1.1g); PROTEIN 28.7g; CARB 16.8g; FIBER 2.2g; CHOL 109mg; IRON 7mg; SODIUM 230mg; CALC 29mg

Turkey Curry

Serve this dish with basmati rice and a selection of chutneys, raisins, bell peppers, tomato, pineapple, papaya, and roasted almonds. Leftovers taste even better the next day.

2 tablespoons butter
3 cups finely chopped peeled Golden Delicious apple (about 2)
2 cups finely chopped onion (about 1 large)
2 garlic cloves, minced
1 tablespoon curry powder
½ teaspoon salt
¼ teaspoon ground red pepper
½ cup fat-free milk
2 tablespoons cornstarch
2 cups fat-free, less-sodium chicken broth
6 cups chopped cooked turkey breast (about 1 pound)
1½ tablespoons fresh lemon juice

1 Melt butter in a large Dutch oven over medium-low heat. Add apple, onion, and garlic to pan; cover and cook 12 minutes or until onion is tender. Add curry powder, salt, and pepper. Combine milk and cornstarch in a small bowl; stir with a whisk, and add to pan. Stir in broth. Reduce heat, and cook 4 minutes or until slightly thick, stirring constantly. Add turkey and juice to pan; cook 5 minutes or until turkey is thoroughly heated. Yield: 8 servings (serving size: 1 cup).

CALORIES 143 (21% from fat); FAT 3.4g (sat 2g, mono 0.9g, poly 0.3g); PROTEIN 18.3g; CARB 9.7g; FIBER 1.2g; CHOL 55mg; IRON 1.2mg; SODIUM 316mg; CALC 37mg

MENU *serves 8*

Turkey Curry

Summer squash sauté
Melt 2 tablespoons butter in a large nonstick skillet over medium-high heat. Add 3 cups julienne-cut zucchini, 3 cups julienne-cut yellow squash, 1 cup red bell pepper strips, 1 cup vertically sliced onion, ½ teaspoon salt, and ½ teaspoon freshly ground black pepper; sauté 5 minutes. Remove from heat, and sprinkle with 2 tablespoons chopped fresh cilantro.

Hot basmati rice

Game Plan

1 Chop apple and onion, and mince garlic for curry.

2 While apple mixture cooks:
- Cook rice.
- Chop turkey and squeeze lemon for juice for curry.
- Julienne zucchini and squash.
- Slice red bell pepper and onion.
- Chop cilantro.

3 While turkey cooks:
- Sauté squash ingredients.

Turkey-Sausage Paella

Use smoked Spanish paprika for this recipe; regular paprika will not impart the same rich, hearty flavor.

2¾ cups fat-free, less-sodium chicken broth
¼ teaspoon saffron threads
Cooking spray
2 ounces Spanish chorizo sausage
½ cup chopped onion
½ cup chopped red bell pepper
3 garlic cloves, minced
¾ cup uncooked Arborio rice
¼ cup dry white wine
½ teaspoon smoked Spanish paprika
1 (14.5-ounce) can petite diced tomatoes, drained
2 cups shredded cooked turkey breast (about 8 ounces)
½ cup frozen peas, thawed
2 tablespoons chopped fresh parsley

❶ Combine broth and saffron in a small saucepan over low heat; bring to a simmer. Remove from heat.

❷ Heat a large nonstick skillet over medium-high heat; coat with cooking spray. Add sausage to pan; cook 5 minutes or until browned, stirring to crumble. Remove sausage from pan with a slotted spoon, and drain on paper towels. Add onion and pepper to pan; cook 5 minutes or until lightly browned. Add garlic to pan; cook 2 minutes. Add rice to pan; cook 3 minutes, stirring constantly. Add wine and paprika to pan; cook 1 minute or until liquid evaporates, scraping pan to loosen browned bits. Stir in broth mixture and tomatoes; bring to a boil. Cover, reduce heat, and simmer 20 minutes or until rice is tender and liquid is absorbed, stirring occasionally. Gently stir in sausage, turkey, peas, and parsley; cook 2 minutes or until thoroughly heated. Yield: 4 servings (serving size: 1½ cups).

CALORIES 297 (30% from fat); FAT 9.8g (sat 3.3g, mono 4g, poly 1.6g); PROTEIN 25.5g; CARB 26.2g; FIBER 3.1g; CHOL 54mg; IRON 2.6mg; SODIUM 746mg; CALC 61mg

Ingredient Tip: Look for saffron and smoked Spanish paprika in the spice aisle of your supermarket.

Turkey Alfredo Pizza

Collard greens and leftover turkey meld beautifully with commercial Alfredo sauce and nutty fontina cheese, resulting in an easy yet inventive meal.

1 cup shredded cooked turkey breast
1 cup frozen chopped collard greens or spinach, thawed, drained, and squeezed dry
2 teaspoons lemon juice
½ teaspoon salt
¼ teaspoon black pepper
1 garlic clove, halved
1 (1-pound) Italian cheese-flavored thin pizza crust (such as Boboli)
½ cup light Alfredo sauce (such as Contadina)
¾ cup (3 ounces) shredded fontina cheese
½ teaspoon crushed red pepper

❶ Preheat oven to 450°.
❷ Combine first 5 ingredients; toss well. Rub cut sides of garlic over crust; discard garlic. Spread Alfredo sauce evenly over crust; top with turkey mixture. Sprinkle with cheese and red pepper. Bake at 450° for 12 minutes or until crust is crisp. Cut into 6 wedges. Yield: 6 servings (serving size: 1 wedge).

CALORIES 316 (29% from fat); FAT 10.3g (sat 5.2g, mono 3.5g, poly 1.1g); PROTEIN 19.2g; CARB 35.6g; FIBER 0.6g; CHOL 39mg; IRON 2.5mg; SODIUM 837mg; CALC 351mg

Quick Tip: Rubbing the pizza crust with a halved garlic clove imparts a boost of flavor.

MENU *serves 6*

Turkey Alfredo Pizza

Herbed tomato-mozzarella salad
Combine 3 cups halved grape tomatoes and 1 cup cubed fresh mozzarella cheese in a large bowl. Combine 2 tablespoons white balsamic vinegar, 1 teaspoon bottled minced garlic, 1 teaspoon olive oil, ¼ teaspoon salt, ¼ teaspoon dried basil, and ¼ teaspoon dried oregano in a small bowl; stir well with a whisk. Pour dressing over salad; toss well. Serve chilled or at room temperature.

Peach sorbet

Game Plan

1 While oven heats:
- •Thaw and drain collards or spinach.
- •Shred turkey and cheese.
- •Halve garlic.
- •Place toppings on pizza crust.

2 While pizza bakes:
- •Prepare salad.

MENU *serves 6*

Sesame Turkey Cakes with Sweet Chili Sauce

Asian slaw

Combine 8 cups shredded napa (Chinese) cabbage, 1 cup red bell pepper strips, ¼ cup chopped green onions, and ¼ cup shredded carrot in a large bowl. Combine 3 tablespoons rice vinegar, 1 tablespoon roasted peanut oil, 1 teaspoon chile paste with garlic, and ¼ teaspoon salt in a small bowl; stir with a whisk. Drizzle vinaigrette over slaw; toss to combine.

Steamed sugar snap peas

Game Plan

1 While rice for turkey cakes cooks:

  • Chop green onions for patties and slaw.

  • Chop water chestnuts and celery, and mince garlic.

  • Lightly beat egg whites.

  • Prepare slaw.

2 Prepare patties.

3 While patties cook:

  • Steam sugar snap peas.

Sesame Turkey Cakes with Sweet Chili Sauce

These Asian-flared cakes are best served just out of the skillet. Their texture is similar to that of crab cakes but a bit denser. The patties can be made earlier in the day and refrigerated until you're ready to cook. Prepare the slaw within an hour of serving. Look for sweetened chili sauce in Asian markets.

2   cups chopped cooked turkey or chicken
1   cup cooked basmati rice
½   cup finely chopped green onions
½   cup chopped water chestnuts
¼   cup finely chopped celery
¼   cup light mayonnaise
1   teaspoon ground cumin
⅛   teaspoon ground red pepper
⅛   teaspoon freshly ground black pepper
2   large egg whites, lightly beaten
1   garlic clove, minced
½   cup dry breadcrumbs
2   teaspoons sesame seeds, toasted
1   tablespoon canola oil, divided
½   cup sweetened chili sauce

❶ Combine the first 11 ingredients in a large bowl. Add dry breadcrumbs and sesame seeds; stir until well blended. Divide the turkey mixture into 6 equal portions, shaping each portion into a ¾-inch-thick patty.

❷ Heat 1½ teaspoons oil in a large nonstick skillet over medium heat. Add 3 patties; cook 3 minutes. Carefully turn patties; cook 3 minutes or until golden. Repeat procedure with remaining oil and patties. Serve with chili sauce. Yield: 6 servings (serving size: 1 patty and about 1½ tablespoons sauce).

CALORIES 295 (28% from fat); FAT 9.1g (sat 1.8g, mono 2.4g, poly 4g); PROTEIN 17.3g; CARB 36.6g; FIBER 1.2g; CHOL 39mg; IRON 2.1mg; SODIUM 419mg; CALC 45mg

Spicy Turkey Soft Tacos

Be careful while browning the turkey; it will spatter from time to time in the pan.

MOLE:

- 1 (7-ounce) can chipotle chiles in adobo sauce
- ½ medium onion, peeled and quartered
- 2 garlic cloves, peeled
- ⅓ cup fat-free, less-sodium chicken broth
- ⅓ cup orange juice
- 2 tablespoons cider vinegar
- ½ teaspoon ground cumin
- ½ teaspoon dried oregano
- ½ teaspoon ground red pepper
- ¼ teaspoon salt
- ¼ teaspoon ground cinnamon
- ¼ teaspoon black pepper

REMAINING INGREDIENTS:

- 1 teaspoon canola oil
- 2 cups shredded cooked turkey
- 8 (6-inch) corn tortillas
- ½ cup bottled salsa
- ½ cup diced peeled avocado
- 4 lime wedges

❶ Preheat oven to 400°.

❷ To prepare mole, drain chipotle chiles in a colander over a bowl, reserving ½ teaspoon adobo sauce. Remove 1 chile; chop to measure 1½ teaspoons. Reserve remaining adobo sauce and chiles for another use.

❸ Place onion and garlic in a small, shallow baking dish; bake at 400° for 15 minutes.

❹ Combine ½ teaspoon adobo sauce, chopped chile, broth, and next 8 ingredients in a blender; add onion and garlic to blender. Process until smooth.

❺ Heat oil in a large nonstick skillet over medium-high heat. Add turkey, and sauté 12 minutes or until browned. Add mole; cook 4 minutes or until liquid is absorbed, stirring occasionally.

❻ Heat tortillas in microwave according to package directions. Spoon ¼ cup turkey mixture onto each tortilla; fold tortilla over turkey mixture. Top each tortilla evenly with salsa and avocado. Serve with lime wedges. Yield: 4 servings (serving size: 2 tacos, 2 tablespoons salsa, 2 tablespoons avocado, and 1 lime wedge).

CALORIES 318 (29% from fat); FAT 10.1g (sat 2.1g, mono 3.8g, poly 2.7g); PROTEIN 25g; CARB 33.7g; FIBER 3.5g; CHOL 54mg; IRON 2.6mg; SODIUM 532mg; CALC 129mg

MENU *serves 4*

Spicy Turkey Soft Tacos

Baked sweet potatoes
Pierce 4 small sweet potatoes (about 1½ pounds) with a fork. Microwave at HIGH 10 minutes or until done, rearranging potatoes after 5 minutes. Combine 2 tablespoons each softened butter and brown sugar. Top each potato with about 2 teaspoons butter mixture.

Game Plan

1 Prepare mole sauce.

2 While potatoes cook:
- •Sauté turkey.
- •Peel and dice avocado.
- •Warm tortillas.
- •Combine sugar and butter for potatoes.

3 Assemble tacos.

MENU *serves 4*

Shredded Five-Spice Turkey with Herb and Noodle Salad

Edamame

Bring 2 quarts water and 1 teaspoon salt to a boil in a large saucepan. Add 1 (1-pound) package frozen edamame in pods; cook 3 minutes. Drain. Place edamame in a bowl; sprinkle with kosher or other coarse-grain salt.

Green tea sorbet

Game Plan

1 While water for edamame boils:

- Prepare vegetables and herbs for turkey mixture and salad.
- Prepare dressing.
- Bring water for noodles to a boil.

2 While noodles cook:

- Assemble turkey mixture.

Shredded Five-Spice Turkey with Herb and Noodle Salad

If you don't have leftover turkey, shredded rotisserie chicken makes a great substitute.

TURKEY:

- 1 tablespoon dark sesame oil
- 1 cup thinly sliced shiitake mushrooms (about 2 ounces)
- ¾ cup chopped onion
- 2 cups shredded cooked skinless dark-meat turkey (about 8 ounces)
- ½ cup fat-free, less-sodium chicken broth
- 1 tablespoon rice wine vinegar
- 1 tablespoon low-sodium soy sauce
- ½ teaspoon five-spice powder
- ¼ teaspoon kosher salt

DRESSING:

- 2 tablespoons rice wine vinegar
- 1 tablespoon low-sodium soy sauce
- 1 tablespoon oyster sauce
- 1 tablespoon fresh lime juice
- 1 teaspoon hot chili sauce with garlic
- 1 teaspoon dark sesame oil
- 3 garlic cloves, minced

SALAD:

- 4 ounces uncooked rice vermicelli
- 4 cups torn butter lettuce
- 2 cups thinly sliced red bell pepper
- 1 cup chopped green onions
- ½ cup chopped fresh basil
- ½ cup chopped fresh cilantro
- ½ cup chopped fresh mint

Mint sprigs (optional)

❶ To prepare turkey, heat 1 tablespoon oil in a large nonstick skillet over medium-high heat. Add mushrooms and ¾ cup onion to pan; sauté 5 minutes or until lightly browned. Add turkey and next 5 ingredients to pan; cook 5 minutes or until liquid evaporates.

❷ To prepare dressing, combine 2 tablespoons vinegar and next 6 ingredients in a small bowl; stir with a whisk.

❸ To prepare salad, cook pasta according to package directions, omitting salt and fat; drain. Combine lettuce and next 5 ingredients. Place about 2 cups lettuce mixture into each of 4 bowls. Top lettuce with 1 cup noodles and 1½ cups turkey mixture; drizzle turkey with 1½ tablespoons dressing. Garnish with mint sprigs, if desired. Yield: 4 servings.

CALORIES 315 (26% from fat); FAT 9.2g (sat 2.1g, mono 2.9g, poly 3.3g); PROTEIN 21.2g; CARB 35.3g; FIBER 3.2g; CHOL 48mg; IRON 3.9mg; SODIUM 570mg; CALC 75mg

Turkey Jambalaya

Andouille sausage adds a kick to this colorful post-Thanksgiving twist on the Cajun classic. Rice and shredded turkey absorb a mixture of tomatoes and spices until they're bursting with flavor.

- 1 tablespoon olive oil
- 1½ cups chopped onion
- 1 teaspoon bottled minced garlic
- 1 cup chopped green bell pepper
- 1 cup chopped red bell pepper
- 2½ teaspoons paprika
- ½ teaspoon salt
- ½ teaspoon dried oregano
- ½ teaspoon ground red pepper
- ½ teaspoon black pepper
- 1 cup uncooked long-grain rice
- 2 cups fat-free, less-sodium chicken broth
- 1 (14.5-ounce) can diced tomatoes, undrained
- 2 cups shredded cooked turkey
- 6 ounces andouille sausage, chopped
- 2 tablespoons sliced green onions

1 Heat oil in a large Dutch oven over medium-high heat. Add chopped onion and garlic to pan; sauté 6 minutes or until lightly browned. Stir in bell peppers and next 5 ingredients to pan; sauté 1 minute. Add rice to pan; sauté 1 minute. Stir in broth and tomatoes to pan; bring to a boil. Cover, reduce heat, and simmer 15 minutes. Add turkey and sausage to pan; cover and cook 5 minutes. Sprinkle with green onions. Yield: 8 servings (serving size: 1 cup).

CALORIES 249 (27% from fat); FAT 7.6g (sat 2.4g, mono 3.4g, poly 1.3g); PROTEIN 17.3g; CARB 27.4g; FIBER 2.7g; CHOL 42mg; IRON 2.7mg; SODIUM 523mg; CALC 37mg

Ingredient Tip: You can substitute cooked chicken for the turkey in this recipe, if you prefer.

MENU *serves 8*

Turkey Jambalaya

Stewed okra

Combine 4 cups frozen cut okra; 1 (14.5-ounce) can stewed tomatoes, undrained; ½ teaspoon sugar; and ¼ teaspoon crushed red pepper in a saucepan. Bring to a boil; cover, reduce heat, and simmer 10 minutes or until done.

French bread

Game Plan

1 Chop onion and bell peppers.

2 While broth and tomato mixture simmers:
- Prepare okra.
- Shred turkey and chop sausage.

3 While turkey and sausage cook:
- Warm bread.
- Slice green onions.

MENU *serves 6*

Turkey Tamale Potpie

Tossed salad with poppy seed dressing and orange sections

Warm spiced apples with vanilla frozen yogurt

Toss 3 cups sliced peeled apple with 2 teaspoons lemon juice. Melt 2 teaspoons butter in a large nonstick skillet over medium-high heat. Add apple; sauté 6 minutes or until tender. Stir in 1 tablespoon maple syrup, ¼ teaspoon ground cinnamon, and ⅛ teaspoon ground nutmeg; cook 1 minute. Scoop ½ cup vanilla frozen yogurt into each of 6 bowls; top evenly with spiced apples.

Game Plan

1 While oven heats:

- Make potpie filling.

- Prepare corn bread topping.

- Scoop yogurt into dessert dishes; place in freezer.

2 While potpie bakes:

- Toss salad.

- Sauté apple for dessert; keep warm.

Turkey Tamale Potpie

This dish has all the ingredients of tamales, but the meat filling is topped with a cornmeal batter and baked instead of being wrapped in a corn husk.

FILLING:
Cooking spray
1   cup chopped onion
¾   cup chopped red bell pepper
4   garlic cloves, minced
1   pound ground turkey breast
1   tablespoon chili powder
1   teaspoon dried oregano
½   teaspoon salt
1   (14.5-ounce) can no-salt-added diced tomatoes, undrained
1   (15-ounce) can kidney beans, rinsed and drained

TOPPING:
4½ ounces all-purpose flour (about 1 cup)
¾   cup yellow cornmeal
1   teaspoon sugar
1   teaspoon baking powder
½   teaspoon salt
¼   teaspoon baking soda
1   cup low-fat buttermilk
1   large egg, lightly beaten

1 Preheat oven to 425°.

2 To prepare filling, heat a large nonstick skillet over medium-high heat; coat with cooking spray. Add onion, bell pepper, garlic, and turkey to pan; cook 5 minutes or until turkey loses its pink color and vegetables are tender. Add chili powder and next 4 ingredients to pan; cook 3 minutes. Spoon turkey mixture into an 11 x 7–inch baking dish coated with cooking spray.

3 To prepare topping, lightly spoon flour into a dry measuring cup; level with a knife. Combine flour, cornmeal, and next 4 ingredients in a medium bowl. Combine buttermilk and egg in a separate bowl; add to dry ingredients, stirring just until moist. Spread cornmeal mixture evenly over turkey mixture. Bake at 425° for 18 minutes or until topping is golden. Yield: 6 servings (serving size: 1¾ cups).

CALORIES 329 (8% from fat); FAT 3g (sat 0.9g, mono 0.5g, poly 0.4g); PROTEIN 27.6g; CARB 47.6g; FIBER 6.8g; CHOL 67mg; IRON 2.4mg; SODIUM 705mg; CALC 120mg

Turkey Mini Meat Loaves

This menu's appeal lies in its straightforward flavors. For a bolder taste, add ½ teaspoon chipotle chile powder to the potatoes. You can make 6 servings of these loaves by doubling the ingredients and shaping the mixture into 1 (8 x 4-inch) loaf. The bake time may increase to about 45 to 50 minutes; use a thermometer to check for an internal temperature of 165°.

Cooking spray
½ cup chopped onion
3 tablespoons dry breadcrumbs
1 tablespoon chopped fresh parsley
1 teaspoon Worcestershire sauce
¼ teaspoon salt
¼ teaspoon dried oregano
⅛ teaspoon freshly ground black pepper
8 ounces ground turkey breast
1 large egg white, lightly beaten
3 tablespoons ketchup, divided
¼ teaspoon hot pepper sauce (such as Tabasco)

❶ Preheat oven to 350°.
❷ Heat a small skillet over medium-high heat; coat with cooking spray. Add onion to pan; sauté 5 minutes or until lightly browned. Remove from heat; cool slightly.
❸ Combine onion, breadcrumbs, and next 7 ingredients in a large bowl. Stir in 2 tablespoons ketchup. Spoon about ½ cup meat mixture into each of 3 muffin cups coated with cooking spray; place muffin pan on a baking sheet. Combine 1 tablespoon ketchup and hot pepper sauce in a small bowl; brush ketchup mixture over meat loaf tops. Bake at 350° for 30 minutes or until a thermometer registers 165°. Yield: 3 servings (serving size: 1 loaf).

CALORIES 142 (10% from fat); FAT 1.5g (sat 0.4g, mono 0.1g, poly 0.2g); PROTEIN 20.2g; CARB 12g; FIBER 0.8g; CHOL 30mg; IRON 1.2mg; SODIUM 508mg; CALC 28mg

MENU *serves 3*

Turkey Mini Meat Loaves

Smashed cheddar new potatoes
Place 1½ pounds quartered new potatoes in a medium saucepan; cover with water. Bring to a boil; reduce heat, and simmer 20 minutes or until tender. Drain. Place potatoes in a medium bowl. Add ¾ cup 2% reduced-fat milk, ⅓ cup shredded extrasharp white cheddar cheese, 1 tablespoon butter, ½ teaspoon salt, and ½ teaspoon freshly ground black pepper; mash with a potato masher to desired consistency.

Green salad

Game Plan
1 Chop onion and parsley.
2 Prepare meat loaves.
3 While meat loaves cook:
   • Prepare potatoes.
   • Prepare salad.

Turkish Turkey Pizza

Pomegranate molasses may be sold as concentrated pomegranate juice. Look for it in Middle Eastern markets, gourmet shops, and some large supermarkets. Its unique flavor makes it well worth seeking out, and a bottle lasts indefinitely in the refrigerator. If you can't find it, combine 2 tablespoons fresh lemon juice and 2 teaspoons honey, stirring until blended.

  1   tablespoon olive oil
  ¾   cup chopped red onion
  ½   cup chopped red bell pepper
  ½   pound lean ground turkey
  1   cup diced canned tomatoes, drained
  ¼   cup chopped fresh flat-leaf parsley, divided
  1   tablespoon tomato paste
1½   teaspoons pomegranate molasses
  ¼   teaspoon ground cumin
  ⅛   teaspoon ground allspice
  4   (4-inch) pitas
  ¼   cup plain low-fat yogurt
  ½   teaspoon salt
  ½   teaspoon freshly ground black pepper
  ½   teaspoon ground red pepper

1 Preheat oven to 450°.

2 Heat oil in a large nonstick skillet over medium-high heat. Add onion and bell pepper; cook 2 minutes or until tender. Add turkey; cook 3 minutes. Add tomato, 2 tablespoons parsley, tomato paste, and next 3 ingredients to pan; reduce heat to medium. Cook 5 minutes or until liquid almost evaporates.

3 Place pitas on a baking sheet. Combine yogurt, salt, black pepper, and red pepper in a small bowl; spread evenly over pitas. Divide turkey mixture evenly among pitas; sprinkle evenly with 2 tablespoons parsley. Bake at 450° for 5 minutes; serve immediately. Yield: 4 servings (serving size: 1 pizza).

CALORIES 248 (30% from fat); FAT 8.3g (sat 1.7g, mono 2.8g, poly 0.5g); PROTEIN 15.7g; CARB 27.4g; FIBER 2.5g; CHOL 49mg; IRON 2.7mg; SODIUM 667mg; CALC 109mg

---

MENU *serves 4*

Turkish Turkey Pizza

Minted cucumber and cherry tomato salad
Combine 1 tablespoon extra-virgin olive oil, 2 teaspoons red wine vinegar, ¼ teaspoon salt, and ¼ teaspoon freshly ground black pepper in a small bowl; stir with a whisk. Combine 2 cups thinly sliced English cucumber and 2 cups halved cherry tomatoes in a serving bowl. Drizzle dressing over cucumber and tomato, tossing to coat. Sprinkle with ¼ cup chopped fresh mint.

Iced grapes

Game Plan

1 While oven heats:
  • Cook topping for pizza.
  • Combine salad ingredients (except mint).

2 While pizza bakes:
  • Sprinkle mint over salad.
  • Freeze grapes.

MENU *serves 6*

Chipotle Meat Loaf

Pineapple-pepper salsa

Combine 1 cup chopped pineapple, 1 cup chopped papaya, and 3 tablespoons diced red onion in a medium bowl. Stir in 3 tablespoons chopped cilantro, 2 table-spoons vinegar, ¼ teaspoon salt, and ⅛ teaspoon ground red pepper. Toss well to combine.

Whipped sweet potatoes

Game Plan

1 Chop onion, cilantro, and parsley; mince garlic.

2 Prepare meatloaf.

3 While meatloaf cooks:

•Prepare potatoes.

•Prepare salsa.

•Prepare topping for meatloaf.

Chipotle Meat Loaf

Mellow sweet potatoes balance the spiciness of the meat loaf and the tangy-sweet salsa. You can use extra-lean ground beef instead of turkey, if you prefer.

MEAT LOAF:

- 1 (7-ounce) can chipotle chiles in adobo sauce
- ½ cup finely chopped onion
- ½ cup coarsely chopped fresh cilantro
- ¼ cup regular oats
- ¼ cup dry breadcrumbs
- ¼ cup tomato sauce
- 2 teaspoons chopped fresh parsley
- 1 teaspoon salt
- ½ teaspoon ground cumin
- ½ teaspoon dried oregano
- ¼ teaspoon dried basil
- ¼ teaspoon freshly ground black pepper
- 2 garlic cloves, minced
- 2 large egg whites
- 1 pound ground turkey
- 1 pound ground turkey breast

Cooking spray

TOPPING:

- ¼ cup tomato sauce
- 1 tablespoon ketchup
- ½ teaspoon hot sauce

❶ Preheat oven to 350°.

❷ To prepare meat loaf, remove 1 chipotle chile and 1 teaspoon adobo sauce from can; reserve remaining chiles and sauce for another use. Chop chile. Combine chile, sauce, onion, and next 14 ingredients in a large bowl, stirring well. Place turkey mixture in a 9 x 5-inch loaf pan coated with cooking spray. Bake, uncovered, at 350° for 30 minutes.

❸ To prepare topping, combine ¼ cup tomato sauce, ketchup, and hot sauce in a small bowl; brush mixture evenly over meat loaf. Cover and bake an additional 30 minutes or until thermometer registers 160°. Let stand 10 minutes before slicing. Yield: 6 servings (serving size: 1 slice).

CALORIES 239 (24% from fat); FAT 7.1g (sat 1.9g, mono 2.5g, poly 1.9g); PROTEIN 36.3g; CARB 8.4g; FIBER 1.3g; CHOL 94mg; IRON 2.1mg; SODIUM 753mg; CALC 55mg

Turkey Tetrazzini

This soothing supper is great to make ahead and refrigerate. Then just pop it in the oven, bake, and serve.

10   ounces uncooked vermicelli
2   teaspoons canola oil
1   pound turkey breast cutlets
¾   teaspoon onion powder, divided
½   teaspoon salt, divided
¼   teaspoon black pepper, divided
2   tablespoons dry sherry
2   (8-ounce) packages presliced mushrooms
¾   cup frozen green peas, thawed
¾   cup fat-free milk
⅔   cup fat-free sour cream
⅓   cup (about 1½ ounces) grated fresh Parmesan cheese
1   (10¾-ounce) can reduced-fat cream of chicken soup (such as Healthy Choice)
    Cooking spray
⅓   cup dry breadcrumbs
2   tablespoons butter, melted

❶ Preheat oven to 450°.
❷ Cook pasta according to package directions, omitting salt and fat. Drain.
❸ Heat oil in a large nonstick skillet over medium-high heat. Sprinkle turkey with ½ teaspoon onion powder, ¼ teaspoon salt, and ⅛ teaspoon pepper. Add turkey to pan; cook 2 minutes on each side or until done. Remove turkey from pan.
❹ Add ¼ teaspoon onion powder, sherry, and mushrooms to pan. Cover and cook 4 minutes or until mushrooms are tender.
❺ Combine peas and next 4 ingredients in a large bowl. Chop turkey. Add ¼ teaspoon salt, ⅛ teaspoon pepper, pasta, turkey, and mushroom mixture to soup mixture, tossing gently to combine. Spoon mixture into a 13 x 9-inch baking dish coated with cooking spray.
❻ Combine breadcrumbs and butter in a small dish; toss to combine. Sprinkle breadcrumb mixture over pasta mixture. Bake at 450° for 12 minutes or until bubbly and thoroughly heated. Yield: 6 servings (serving size: about 1⅔ cups).

CALORIES 459 (29% from fat); FAT 14.8g (sat 5.9g, mono 4.4g, poly 2.8g); PROTEIN 30.5g; CARB 48.1g; FIBER 3.1g; CHOL 69mg; IRON 4mg; SODIUM 716mg; CALC 199mg

MENU *serves 6*

Turkey Tetrazzini

Green beans with almonds

Cook 1 pound trimmed green beans in boiling water 2 minutes or until crisp-tender; drain. Toast 2 tablespoons sliced almonds in a nonstick skillet over medium-high heat 2 minutes, stirring frequently. Add 2 teaspoons butter to pan; cook 30 seconds or until lightly browned. Add green beans, ½ teaspoon salt, and ¼ teaspoon black pepper; toss to coat.

Garlic bread

Game Plan

1 While water for pasta and water for green beans come to a boil:
  • Trim green beans.
  • Heat oil in skillet for turkey.

2 While pasta and beans cook:
  • Cook turkey.
  • Cook mushroom mixture.
  • Preheat oven.

3 While turkey mixture bakes:
  • Prepare garlic bread.
  • Toast almonds.
  • Finish preparing green beans.

Sausage and Bean Casserole

MENU *serves 8*

Sausage and Bean Casserole

Mustard cheesy toasts
Preheat broiler. Spread 1 teaspoon whole-grain Dijon mustard over each of 8 (1-inch-thick) slices French bread. Top each slice with 1 tablespoon Italian blend shredded cheese. Place on a baking sheet. Broil 2 minutes or until cheese melts.

Green salad

Game Plan

1 Chop onion and parsley, mince garlic, and slice sausage.

2 While sausage mixture simmers:

• Prepare bread crumbs.

3 While casserole bakes:

• Prepare toasts.

• Prepare salad.

Simple and satisfying, this hearty casserole comes together fast enough to prepare on a busy evening. Inspired by the classic French cassoulet, the quick prep and cook times make this dish an easy, light dinner option.

Cooking spray
- 1 cup chopped onion (about 1 medium)
- 1 (16-ounce) package light smoked turkey sausage (such as Hillshire Farm), cut into ¼-inch-thick slices
- 2 garlic cloves, minced
- 1 (14-ounce) can fat-free, less-sodium chicken broth
- 2 tablespoons brown sugar
- 2 tablespoons tomato paste
- ½ teaspoon dried thyme
- ½ teaspoon freshly ground black pepper
- 3 (16-ounce) cans cannellini beans or other white beans, rinsed and drained
- 1 bay leaf
- ⅛ teaspoon ground red pepper (optional)
- 3 (1-ounce) slices white bread
- 2 tablespoons chopped fresh parsley

❶ Preheat oven to 375°.

❷ Heat an ovenproof Dutch oven over medium-high heat; coat with cooking spray. Add onion and sausage to pan; sauté 5 minutes or until browned. Add garlic, and sauté 2 minutes. Stir in broth, scraping pan to loosen browned bits. Stir in brown sugar and next 5 ingredients. Add red pepper, if desired. Bring to a boil; cover, reduce heat, and simmer 5 minutes. Remove from heat. Discard bay leaf.

❸ Place bread in a food processor, and pulse 10 times or until coarse crumbs measure 1½ cups.

❹ Sprinkle breadcrumbs evenly over sausage mixture, and lightly coat with cooking spray. Bake at 375° for 15 minutes or until browned. Sprinkle with parsley. Yield: 8 servings (serving size: about 1 cup).

CALORIES 205 (14% from fat); FAT 3.3g (sat 1.1g, mono 0.1g, poly 0.5g); PROTEIN 12.1g; CARB 30g; FIBER 4.4g; CHOL 25mg; IRON 2.7mg; SODIUM 823mg; CALC 77mg

Slow-Cooker Red Beans and Rice

This recipe is the ultimate in thriftiness and convenience. For a longer slow–cooker time, you can cook this dish on LOW heat for 8 hours. Sweet–and–sour slaw is a choice complement.

3   cups water
1   cup dried red kidney beans
1   cup chopped onion
1   cup chopped green bell pepper
¾   cup chopped celery
1   teaspoon dried thyme
1   teaspoon paprika
¾   teaspoon ground red pepper
½   teaspoon black pepper
½   (14-ounce) package turkey, pork, and beef smoked sausage (such as Healthy Choice), thinly sliced
1   bay leaf
5   garlic cloves, minced
½   teaspoon salt
3   cups hot cooked long-grain rice
¼   cup chopped green onions

❶ Combine first 12 ingredients in an electric slow cooker. Cover with lid; cook on HIGH 5 hours. Discard bay leaf; stir in salt. Serve over rice; sprinkle servings with green onions. Yield: 4 servings (serving size: 1 cup bean mixture, ³/₄ cup rice, and 1 tablespoon green onions).

CALORIES 413 (5% from fat); FAT 2.5g (sat 0.7g, mono 0.2g, poly 0.5g); PROTEIN 21.1g; CARB 76.3g; FIBER 10.1g; CHOL 18mg; IRON 6mg; SODIUM 749mg; CALC 102mg

MENU *serves 4*

Sausage, Pepper, and Onion Pizza

Pickle spears

Strawberry-anise sundaes
Bring ¼ cup light-colored corn syrup, 2 tablespoons sugar, 2 teaspoons fresh lemon juice, and ⅛ teaspoon salt to a boil in a small saucepan. Cook 1 minute or until sugar dissolves, stirring constantly. Remove from heat; stir in 1 tablespoon anise-flavored liqueur. Place ½ cup vanilla low-fat ice cream in each of 4 bowls. Top each serving with ¼ cup sliced strawberries; drizzle each serving with about 1 tablespoon anise syrup.

Game Plan

1 While oven heats:

   • Prepare pizza topping.

   • Cut French bread in half.

2 While pizza bakes, prepare anise syrup for dessert.

Sausage, Pepper, and Onion Pizza

This recipe uses mild Italian turkey sausage and, for a little heat, a touch of crushed red pepper. Use hot Italian turkey sausage if you want even more kick.

Cooking spray
1½ cups vertically sliced onion
  1 cup green bell pepper strips
  4 ounces mild Italian turkey sausage
  ¼ teaspoon crushed red pepper
  1 (14.5-ounce) can diced tomatoes, undrained
  1 (8-ounce) loaf French bread, cut in half horizontally
  1 cup (4 ounces) shredded part-skim mozzarella cheese

1 Preheat oven to 450°.
2 Heat a large nonstick skillet over medium-high heat; coat with cooking spray. Add onion and bell pepper; sauté 6 minutes or until tender.

3 Remove casings from sausage. Add sausage to pan, and cook 5 minutes or until lightly browned, stirring to crumble. Add red pepper and tomatoes, and cook 5 minutes or until mixture thickens.
4 Spread sausage mixture evenly over cut sides of bread, and sprinkle evenly with cheese. Place bread halves on a baking sheet. Bake at 450° for 5 minutes or until cheese melts. Cut each pizza in half. Yield: 4 servings (serving size: 1 piece).

CALORIES 375 (29% from fat); FAT 12g (sat 5.1g, mono 4.2g, poly 2.2g); PROTEIN 24.6g; CARB 42g; FIBER 4.9g; CHOL 63mg; IRON 2.7mg; SODIUM 967mg; CALC 280mg

Rosemary-Scented Lentils and Sausage

Radicchio adds color and agreeable bitterness to the side salad. Substitute peppery arugula for the radicchio or clementines for the oranges, if you prefer. To make this sausage dish even spicier, use hot Italian turkey sausage.

4 cups water
4 cups fat-free, less-sodium chicken broth
2 cups petite green lentils
2 teaspoons olive oil
2 cups minced yellow onion (about 1 large)
½ cup minced carrot (about 1 medium)
2 teaspoons minced fresh rosemary
2 garlic cloves, minced
8 ounces mild Italian turkey sausage, casings removed
1 tablespoon tomato paste
½ teaspoon salt
¼ teaspoon freshly ground black pepper
⅛ teaspoon hot paprika
Dash of ground red pepper

❶ Combine first 3 ingredients in a large saucepan over medium heat. Bring to a simmer. Cook 30 minutes or until almost tender.
❷ Heat oil in a saucepan over medium-high heat. Add onion, carrot, rosemary, and garlic to pan; sauté 10 minutes or until tender. Add sausage; cook 5 minutes, stirring to crumble. Add tomato paste and remaining 4 ingredients; cook 1 minute or until heated. Add sausage mixture to lentils; bring to a boil. Cook 30 minutes or until lentils are tender. Yield: 6 servings (serving size: about 1 cup).

CALORIES 341 (19% from fat); FAT 7g (sat 1.6g, mono 2.5g, poly 1.7g); PROTEIN 26.4g; CARB 43.6g; FIBER 7.7g; CHOL 33mg; IRON 5.8mg; SODIUM 731mg; CALC 38mg

MENU *serves 6*

Rosemary-Scented Lentils and Sausage

Winter salad
Combine 5 cups baby spinach leaves, 3 cups chopped radicchio, and 3 cups chopped endive in a large bowl. Combine 3 tablespoons red wine vinegar, 2 tablespoons extra-virgin olive oil, 1 teaspoon Dijon mustard, ¼ teaspoon salt, and ¼ teaspoon freshly ground black pepper in a small bowl; stir with a whisk. Drizzle vinegar mixture over greens; toss well to combine. Top salad with ½ cup orange sections.

Syrah/Shiraz

Game Plan

1 While lentils cook:
  • Mince onion, carrot, rosemary, and garlic.

2 While sausage and lentils cook:
  • Prepare salad.

MENU *serves 4*

San Francisco–Style Scrambled Eggs

Crisp oven potatoes
Preheat oven to 450°. Combine 2¼ cups frozen hash brown potatoes with onions and peppers (such as Ore-Ida Potatoes O'Brien), 1 tablespoon vegetable oil, 1 teaspoon bottled minced garlic, ½ teaspoon salt, ¼ teaspoon hot paprika, and ¼ teaspoon black pepper on a jelly-roll pan coated with cooking spray. Bake at 450° for 20 minutes or until browned, stirring once.

Beer

Game Plan

1 While oven heats for potatoes:
- Combine potato mixture.
- Chop chard for scrambled eggs.
- Toast bread.

2 While potatoes cook:
- Finish preparing scrambled eggs.

San Francisco–Style Scrambled Eggs

This San Francisco specialty turns straightforward scrambled eggs into a deliciously distinctive dish. To stay true to the recipe's roots, serve with slices of toasted sourdough bread.

- ½ teaspoon dried basil
- ¼ teaspoon salt
- 4 large egg whites
- 3 large eggs
- 4 ounces hot Italian turkey sausage
- 2 cups chopped onion
- 6 cups chopped Swiss chard (about ½ pound)
- 4 (1½-ounce) slices sourdough bread, toasted

1 Combine first 4 ingredients in a medium bowl; stir with a whisk. Set aside.

2 Remove casings from sausage. Cook sausage in a large nonstick skillet over medium-high heat until lightly browned; stir sausage to crumble. Add onion to crumbled sausage in pan; cook 3 minutes or until onion is tender. Stir in chopped chard to sausage mixture in pan; cover and cook 3 minutes or until chard wilts, stirring occasionally. Uncover and cook 1 minute or until liquid evaporates. Stir in egg mixture to pan; cook 3 minutes or until eggs are set, stirring frequently. Serve scrambled eggs with toast. Yield: 4 servings (serving size: 1 cup scrambled egg mixture and 1 toast slice).

CALORIES 335 (23% from fat); FAT 8.6g (sat 2.4g, mono 3.3g, poly 1.8g); PROTEIN 20.9g; CARB 43.2g; FIBER 4.3g; CHOL 183mg; IRON 3.7mg; SODIUM 931mg; CALC 116mg

Farfalle with Sausage, Cannellini Beans, and Kale

Use a vegetable peeler to shave fresh Parmesan cheese to top this rustic pasta dish.

8 ounces uncooked farfalle (bow tie pasta)
¼ cup oil-packed sun-dried tomatoes
1½ cups chopped onion
8 ounces hot Italian turkey sausage, casings removed
6 garlic cloves, minced
1 teaspoon dried Italian seasoning
¼ teaspoon crushed red pepper
1 (14-ounce) can fat-free, less-sodium chicken broth
1 (16-ounce) package fresh kale
1 (15-ounce) can cannellini beans, rinsed and drained
1 ounce shaved fresh Parmesan cheese (about ¼ cup)

❶ Cook pasta according to package directions, omitting salt and fat. Drain, reserving 1 cup cooking liquid; keep warm.
❷ Drain tomatoes in a small sieve over a bowl, reserving 2 teaspoons oil; slice tomatoes. Heat a large Dutch oven over medium heat. Add sliced tomatoes, reserved 2 teaspoons tomato oil, onion, and sausage to pan; cook 10 minutes or until sausage is browned, stirring to crumble. Add garlic to pan; cook 1 minute. Add seasoning, pepper, and broth to pan. Stir in kale; cover and simmer 5 minutes or until kale is tender. Stir in pasta, reserved 1 cup cooking liquid, and beans. Sprinkle with cheese. Yield: 6 servings (serving size: 1¾ cups pasta mixture and 2 teaspoons cheese).

CALORIES 329 (25% from fat); FAT 9g (sat 2.2g, mono 3g, poly 2.3g); PROTEIN 18.7g; CARB 45.7g; FIBER 5g; CHOL 26mg; IRON 4mg; SODIUM 669mg; CALC 204mg

MENU *serves 6*

Farfalle with Sausage, Cannellini Beans, and Kale

Garlic toast
Preheat broiler. Coat tops of 12 (½-inch-thick) slices diagonally cut French bread baguette with cooking spray; sprinkle evenly with ½ teaspoon garlic powder and ½ teaspoon dried Italian seasoning. Place bread slices on a baking sheet; broil 2 minutes or until golden brown.

Sliced pears with amaretti cookies

Game Plan

1 While water for pasta boils:
  • Prepare ingredients for sausage mixture.
2 While pasta cooks:
  • Preheat broiler.
3 While sausage mixture simmers:
  • Prepare garlic toast.
  • Slice pears.
4 Add pasta and remaining ingredients to sausage mixture.

French-Style Shrimp Salad, page 384

Weekend Menus

From Saturday brunch to Sunday supper, these easy menus let you prepare healthful, flavorful meals with minimal effort.

Individual Potato-Bacon Frittatas, page 377

Peppercorn-Crusted Flank Steak, page 390

Shortcakes with Fresh Berries, page 399

Late Saturday Breakfast

serves 6

*Grits Casserole with Mushrooms,
Prosciutto, and Provolone*

Fruit Salad with Honey-Yogurt Sauce

Whole Wheat Apricot Muffins

Grits Casserole with Mushrooms, Prosciutto, and Provolone

Use yellow grits for the best presentation here. To get a head start on the recipe, cook the grits in advance and spoon them into a prepared baking dish; cover and refrigerate overnight. Let the baking dish stand at room temperature while you prepare the mushroom topping the next day; top the grits, and bake as directed.

    5   cups water
 1¼   cups stone-ground yellow grits
  ¾   cup (3 ounces) shredded sharp provolone
           cheese, divided
    1   teaspoon salt, divided
Cooking spray
 1½   teaspoons butter
  ¾   cup chopped onion
    2   garlic cloves, minced
    4   cups thinly sliced portobello mushrooms
           (about 6 ounces)
    3   cups thinly sliced shiitake mushroom caps
           (about 4½ ounces)
    1   teaspoon dried herbes de Provence
  ¼   teaspoon freshly ground black pepper
    1   cup chopped prosciutto (about 3 ounces)
  ⅓   cup dry white wine
    3   large eggs, lightly beaten
    2   large egg whites, lightly beaten
    1   tablespoon minced fresh parsley

1 Bring 5 cups water to a boil in a large saucepan; gradually stir in grits. Reduce heat, and simmer 30 minutes or until thick, stirring frequently. Remove grits from heat. Stir in ¼ cup cheese and ½ teaspoon salt. Spoon grits mixture into an 11 x 7–inch baking dish coated with cooking spray.
2 Preheat oven to 350°.
3 Melt butter in a large nonstick skillet over medium-high heat. Add chopped onion and garlic; sauté 3 minutes or until tender. Add remaining ½ teaspoon salt, mushrooms, herbes de Provence, and pepper; cook 6 minutes or until mushrooms are tender, stirring frequently. Stir in prosciutto and wine; cook 5 minutes or until liquid almost evaporates. Remove from heat; cool slightly. Stir in eggs and egg whites. Spread mushroom mixture over grits mixture, and sprinkle with remaining ½ cup cheese. Bake at 350° for 30 minutes or until cheese melts and grits are thoroughly heated; let stand 5 minutes before serving. Sprinkle with parsley. Yield: 6 servings.

CALORIES 287 (30% from fat); FAT 9.6g (sat 4.4g, mono 3.1g, poly 0.9g); PROTEIN 16.3g; CARB 35.7g; FIBER 2.3g; CHOL 131mg; IRON 2.9mg; SODIUM 832mg; CALC 136mg

Fruit Salad with Honey-Yogurt Sauce

    1   cup vanilla low-fat yogurt
    1   tablespoon honey
 1½   teaspoons grated lime rind
    3   cups cubed pineapple (about 1 medium)
 1½   cups chopped Braeburn apple (about 1 large)
    1   cup orange sections (about 2 oranges)
    1   cup chopped peeled kiwi (about 2 large)
  ⅓   cup flaked sweetened coconut
    1   medium banana, sliced
  ¼   cup slivered almonds, toasted

1 Combine yogurt, honey, and rind in a small bowl.
2 Combine cubed pineapple and next 4 ingredients in a large bowl; toss gently to combine. Just before serving, stir in banana. Top fruit mixture with yogurt sauce; sprinkle with almonds. Yield: 6 servings (serving size: 1¼ cups fruit mixture, 2 tablespoons sauce, and 2 teaspoons almonds).

CALORIES 196 (22% from fat); FAT 4.8g (sat 1.8g, mono 1.7g, poly 0.8g); PROTEIN 4.3g; CARB 37.9g; FIBER 4.7g; CHOL 2mg; IRON 0.9mg; SODIUM 40mg; CALC 111mg

Whole Wheat Apricot Muffins

You can substitute dried cherries or dates for the apricots.

 4½   ounces all-purpose flour (about 1 cup)
  ⅔   cup whole wheat flour (about 3 ounces)
  ½   cup sugar
 1¼   teaspoons grated orange rind
    1   teaspoon baking soda
  ¼   teaspoon salt
    1   cup low-fat buttermilk
  ¼   cup butter, melted
  ½   teaspoon vanilla extract
    1   large egg
    1   cup finely chopped dried apricots
Cooking spray

1 Preheat oven to 375°.
2 Lightly spoon flours into dry measuring cups; level with a knife. Combine flours, sugar, orange rind, soda, and salt in a large bowl, stirring with a whisk; make a well in center of mixture. Combine buttermilk, butter, vanilla, and egg; add to flour mixture, stirring just until moist. Fold in apricots.
3 Spoon batter into 12 muffin cups coated with cooking spray. Bake at 375° for 15 minutes or until muffins spring back when touched lightly in center. Remove muffins from pan; place on a wire rack. Yield: 1 dozen (serving size: 1 muffin).

CALORIES 167 (25% from fat); FAT 4.7g (sat 2.6g, mono 1.3g, poly 0.3g); PROTEIN 3.6g; CARB 29g; FIBER 1.9g; CHOL 29mg; IRON 1.1mg; SODIUM 221mg; CALC 37mg

Sunday Brunch

serves 4

Poached Eggs with White Corn Polenta

Strawberry Bellinis

*Fresh Fruit Salad with
Nutmeg-Cinnamon Syrup*

Whole-grain toast

Poached Eggs with White Corn Polenta

This dish uses white cornmeal to form a creamy polenta. If you can find it, use imported Italian white cornmeal, since the grain is very fine and will result in a soft texture. You can prepare the salsa up to an hour ahead but not much longer; its flavor and form are best served at room temperature.

SALSA:
- ⅓ cup chopped bottled roasted red bell peppers
- 1 tablespoon chopped fresh basil
- ½ teaspoon extra-virgin olive oil
- ⅛ teaspoon salt
- 1 large plum tomato, seeded and diced (about ⅓ cup)

POLENTA:
- 4 cups water
- 1½ cups frozen white corn kernels, thawed
- 1 cup white cornmeal or dry polenta
- ½ teaspoon salt, divided
- 3 tablespoons grated fresh Parmesan cheese
- 1 teaspoon butter
- ¼ teaspoon freshly ground black pepper

EGGS:
- 4 large eggs
- Cooking spray

REMAINING INGREDIENT:
- 2 slices bacon, cooked and crumbled

❶ To prepare salsa, combine first 5 ingredients. Set aside.
❷ To prepare polenta, bring 4 cups water to a boil in a medium saucepan over medium-high heat. Add corn, cornmeal, and ¼ teaspoon salt. Cook 2 minutes or until cornmeal mixture comes to a boil, stirring constantly. Reduce heat to low; cook 20 minutes or until thick, stirring frequently. Stir in remaining ¼ teaspoon salt, cheese, butter, and black pepper. Cover and keep warm.
❸ To prepare eggs, while polenta cooks, add water to a large skillet, filling two-thirds full; bring to a boil. Reduce heat; simmer. Break 1 egg into each of 4 (6-ounce) custard cups coated with cooking spray. Place custard cups in simmering water in pan. Cover pan; cook 6 minutes. Remove custard cups from water; carefully remove eggs from custard cups.
❹ Spoon about 1 cup polenta onto each of 4 plates; top each serving with about 3 tablespoons salsa and 1 poached egg. Sprinkle evenly with bacon. Yield: 4 servings.

CALORIES 307 (30% from fat); FAT 10.3g (sat 3.4g, mono 4g, poly 1.6g); PROTEIN 14.2g; CARB 40.5g; FIBER 4.6g; CHOL 221mg; IRON 1.9mg; SODIUM 664mg; CALC 78mg

Strawberry Bellinis

Strawberries take the place of peaches in this version of a classic Italian drink. The recipe yields enough to allow for refills.

- ¼ cup sugar
- 2 tablespoons water
- 3 cups hulled strawberries
- 2 tablespoons fresh lemon juice
- 1 (750-milliliter) bottle prosecco or other sparkling wine, chilled

❶ Combine ¼ cup sugar and 2 tablespoons water in a small saucepan, stirring until sugar dissolves. Bring sugar mixture to a boil over medium-high heat. Remove from heat.
❷ Place sugar mixture, strawberries, and juice in a blender; process until smooth. Pour pureed strawberry mixture through a sieve over a medium bowl, reserving liquid. Discard solids.
❸ Place 3 tablespoons strawberry mixture into each of 8 champagne flutes. Pour ⅓ cup wine into each flute. Yield: 8 servings (serving size: about ½ cup).

CALORIES 110 (2% from fat); FAT 0.2g (sat 0g, mono 0g, poly 0.1g); PROTEIN 0.6g; CARB 12.3g; FIBER 0.5g; CHOL 0mg; IRON 0.6mg; SODIUM 8mg; CALC 17mg

Fresh Fruit Salad with Nutmeg-Cinnamon Syrup

The spiced maple syrup takes just minutes to cook on the stove top. Substitute your favorite apple for Granny Smith, if desired.

- 2 cups thinly sliced Granny Smith apple (about 1 large apple)
- 2 cups thinly sliced ripe pear (about 1 large pear)
- 1 cup sliced strawberries
- ½ cup orange sections (about 1 orange)
- ½ cup sliced banana (about 1 medium)
- ¼ cup fresh lemon juice
- ¼ cup maple syrup
- ⅛ teaspoon ground nutmeg
- ⅛ teaspoon ground cinnamon

❶ Combine first 5 ingredients in a large bowl. Drizzle with juice; toss gently.
❷ Combine syrup, nutmeg, and cinnamon in a small saucepan. Cook 10 minutes over low heat, stirring occasionally. Spoon syrup mixture over fruit; toss gently. Serve immediately. Yield: 4 servings (serving size: 1 cup).

CALORIES 152 (2% from fat); FAT 0.4g (sat 0.1g, mono 0.1g, poly 0.2g); PROTEIN 1.2g; CARB 39.8g; FIBER 4.6g; CHOL 0mg; IRON 0.8mg; SODIUM 4mg; CALC 38mg

Make-Ahead Brunch

serves 6

Individual Potato-Bacon Frittatas

Mocha-Spiced Coffee

Blueberry-Pecan Scones

Melon wedges

Individual Potato-Bacon Frittatas

To make brunch preparation even faster and easier, you can sauté the onion, red bell pepper, and garlic the night before. Buy precooked bacon and preshredded cheese to save even more time.

¾ pound small red potatoes (about 6)
Cooking spray
½ cup chopped onion
½ cup chopped red bell pepper
2 garlic cloves, minced
¾ cup (3 ounces) shredded reduced-fat Swiss cheese
4 bacon slices, cooked and crumbled
1¾ cups egg substitute
¼ teaspoon salt
¼ teaspoon freshly ground black pepper

1 Place red potatoes in a large saucepan; cover with water. Bring to a boil, and cook 25 minutes or until tender. Drain; cool slightly. Cut potatoes into ¹/₂-inch cubes.
2 Preheat oven to 375°.
3 Heat a medium nonstick skillet over medium heat; coat with cooking spray. Add onion, bell pepper, and garlic; sauté 5 minutes or until tender. Remove from heat. Stir in potato, cheese, and bacon.
4 Combine egg substitute, salt, and black pepper. Spoon vegetable mixture evenly into 12 (6-ounce) ramekins or muffin cups coated with cooking spray. Pour egg mixture evenly over vegetable mixture. Bake at 375° for 18 minutes or until set. Remove from ramekins, and cool slightly. Yield: 6 servings (serving size: 2 frittatas).

CALORIES 184 (25% from fat); FAT 5.2g (sat 1.6g, mono 1.6g, poly 1.4g); PROTEIN 16g; CARB 17.8g; FIBER 1.8g; CHOL 10mg; IRON 2.6mg; SODIUM 366mg; CALC 188mg

Mocha-Spiced Coffee

Use a high-quality unflavored coffee, such as French roast, for a properly robust cup; the aroma is sure to arouse late risers. You can prepare the ingredients for the frittatas while the coffee brews.

½ cup ground coffee
1½ teaspoons ground cinnamon
½ teaspoon ground nutmeg
5 cups water
1 cup fat-free milk
¼ cup packed brown sugar
⅓ cup light chocolate syrup
1 teaspoon vanilla extract
Whipped cream (optional)

1 Place first 3 ingredients in a coffee filter or filter basket of a coffeemaker. Add 5 cups water to coffeemaker, and brew according to the manufacturer's instructions.
2 Combine milk, brown sugar, and chocolate syrup in a heavy saucepan. Cook over low heat, stirring constantly, until sugar dissolves; remove from heat. Stir in brewed coffee and vanilla extract. Serve with whipped cream, if desired. Serve immediately. Yield: 6 servings (serving size: 1 cup).

CALORIES 83 (18% from fat); FAT 1.7g (sat 0.1g, mono 0g, poly 0g); PROTEIN 1.8g; CARB 16.8g; FIBER 0.4g; CHOL 1mg; IRON 0.7mg; SODIUM 39mg; CALC 56mg

Blueberry-Pecan Scones

Make these scones up to 2 days ahead, and store them in an airtight container. Resist the temptation to knead the dough to avoid breaking apart the tender blueberries. Any leftover scones make a tasty accompaniment to chicken salad.

½ cup 2% reduced-fat milk
¼ cup sugar
2 teaspoons grated lemon rind
1 teaspoon vanilla extract
1 large egg
9 ounces all-purpose flour (about 2 cups)
1 tablespoon baking powder
½ teaspoon salt
3 tablespoons chilled butter, cut into small pieces
1 cup fresh or frozen blueberries
¼ cup finely chopped pecans, toasted
Cooking spray
1 large egg white, lightly beaten
2 tablespoons sugar

1 Preheat oven to 375°.
2 Combine first 5 ingredients in a medium bowl; stir with a whisk. Lightly spoon flour into dry measuring cups; level with a knife. Combine flour, baking powder, and salt in a large bowl; stir with a whisk. Cut in butter with a pastry blender or 2 knives until mixture resembles coarse meal. Gently fold in blueberries and pecans. Add milk mixture, stirring just until moist (dough will be sticky).
3 Turn dough out onto a floured surface, and pat into an 8-inch circle. Cut the dough into 10 wedges; place dough wedges on a baking sheet coated with cooking spray. Brush egg white over dough wedges; sprinkle evenly with 2 tablespoons sugar. Bake at 375° for 18 minutes or until golden. Serve warm. Yield: 10 servings (serving size: 1 scone).

CALORIES 196 (30% from fat); FAT 6.6g (sat 2.2g, mono 2.9g, poly 1g); PROTEIN 4.4g; CARB 30.2g; FIBER 1.4g; CHOL 31mg; IRON 1.5mg; SODIUM 308mg; CALC 107mg

Alfresco
Brunch

serves 8

Sparkling Fruit Gelées

Fresh Mozzarella, Sun-Dried Tomato,
and Prosciutto Strata

Mixed Greens Salad with
Honey-Orange Dressing

Sparkling Fruit Gelées

These stylish individual fruit cups can be prepared and refrigerated up to 2 days before the gathering. You can substitute your favorite summer fruits in any combination.

    3½ teaspoons unflavored gelatin
    2⅔ cups sparkling wine, divided
     ⅔ cup sugar
     4 teaspoons fresh lemon juice
     2 cups sliced strawberries
    1⅓ cups fresh blueberries
     ⅔ cup sliced banana
     ⅔ cup fresh raspberries

❶ Sprinkle gelatin over ⅔ cup sparkling wine in a small saucepan; let stand 5 minutes. Place saucepan over low heat; cook 5 minutes or until gelatin dissolves, stirring constantly.
❷ Combine sugar and ⅔ cup wine in a medium saucepan over medium heat; cook 5 minutes or until sugar dissolves, stirring frequently. Remove from heat; stir in remaining 1⅓ cups wine. Add gelatin mixture and juice, stirring well.
❸ Divide mixture evenly among 8 (6-ounce) champagne flutes or wine glasses. Combine strawberries, blueberries, banana, and raspberries. Stir about ½ cup fruit mixture into each flute; cover and chill 6 hours or overnight. Yield: 8 servings (serving size: 1 gelée).

CALORIES 166 (2% from fat); FAT 0.3g (sat 0g, mono 0g, poly 0.2g); PROTEIN 1.7g; CARB 28.3g; FIBER 2.4g; CHOL 0mg; IRON 0.6mg; SODIUM 7mg; CALC 19mg

Fresh Mozzarella, Sun-Dried Tomato, and Prosciutto Strata

Stratas are great make-ahead entrées. Assemble all of the ingredients the day before, chill overnight, and bake the strata in the morning. If you do not have enough time to refrigerate it overnight, chill it for at least 3 hours.

    1 pound rosemary focaccia, cut into
       ¾-inch cubes (about 15 cups)
    3¼ cups fat-free milk
    ¼ cup (2 ounces) crème fraîche or reduced-fat
       sour cream
    1 (8-ounce) carton egg substitute
    ¼ cup oil-packed sun-dried tomatoes, drained
       and chopped
    1 garlic clove, minced
Cooking spray
    4 ounces prosciutto, chopped
    4 ounces fresh mozzarella cheese, cut into
       ¼-inch-wide strips
    ½ cup (2 ounces) grated fresh Parmesan cheese

❶ Preheat oven to 350°.
❷ Arrange bread cubes in a single layer on a large baking sheet. Bake at 350° for 10 minutes or until toasted, stirring once halfway through baking.
❸ Combine milk, crème fraîche, and egg substitute in a large bowl; stir with a whisk until smooth. Add sun-dried tomatoes and garlic; stir with a whisk. Add bread; stir gently to combine; let stand 5 minutes.
❹ Pour half of bread mixture into a 13 x 9-inch baking dish coated with cooking spray. Arrange prosciutto and mozzarella evenly over bread mixture. Top with remaining bread mixture. Cover and chill at least 3 hours or up to overnight.
❺ Preheat oven to 350°.
❻ Uncover dish. Bake at 350° for 20 minutes. Sprinkle evenly with Parmesan. Bake an additional 20 minutes. Remove from oven; let stand 5 minutes. Serve warm. Yield: 8 servings.

CALORIES 325 (30% from fat); FAT 11g (sat 5.4g, mono 4.3g, poly 0.7g); PROTEIN 20.3g; CARB 36.9g; FIBER 1.2g; CHOL 36mg; IRON 3.2mg; SODIUM 738mg; CALC 263mg

Mixed Greens Salad with Honey-Orange Dressing

This easy salad complements almost any summer entrée. The sweetness of its citrus-based dressing balances the bitterness of the radicchio. Prepare and refrigerate the dressing up to a day before the brunch; stir well, and toss over the salad just before serving.

DRESSING:
    3 tablespoons fresh orange juice
    1 tablespoon honey
    2 teaspoons minced shallots
    2 teaspoons white wine vinegar
    ½ teaspoon Dijon mustard
    ¼ teaspoon salt
    ¼ teaspoon freshly ground black pepper
SALAD:
    4 cups chopped romaine lettuce
    4 cups torn radicchio
    3 cups bagged baby spinach leaves

❶ To prepare dressing, combine first 7 ingredients in a large bowl; stir with a whisk.
❷ To prepare salad, combine lettuce, radicchio, and spinach in a large bowl. Add dressing to salad in bowl; toss gently to coat. Yield: 8 servings (serving size: about 1 cup).

CALORIES 24 (8% from fat); FAT 0.2g (sat 0g, mono 0g, poly 0.1g); PROTEIN 1.1g; CARB 5.3g; FIBER 1.1g; CHOL 0mg; IRON 0.8mg; SODIUM 97mg; CALC 26mg

Soup and Sandwich Lunch

serves 4

Summer Squash and Pasta Soup

Green Salad with Apples and
Maple-Walnut Dressing

Feta-Basil Sandwiches

Chewy Chocolate-Coconut Macaroons

Summer Squash and Pasta Soup

This soup is a light and refreshing accompaniment to the sandwiches and salad.

- 2 teaspoons butter
- ¾ cup chopped onion
- 1 garlic clove, minced
- 1½ cups small yellow squash, halved lengthwise and thinly sliced
- ¼ cup dry white wine
- 2 cups organic vegetable broth (such as Swanson Certified Organic)
- 1 cup water
- ⅔ cup uncooked ditalini (very short tube-shaped macaroni)
- 1 tablespoon fresh lemon juice
- ½ teaspoon chopped fresh thyme
- ¼ teaspoon salt
- ¼ teaspoon freshly ground black pepper

1 Melt butter in a large saucepan over medium-high heat. Add onion and garlic; sauté 3 minutes. Add squash; sauté 2 minutes. Add wine; cook 1 minute or until liquid almost evaporates. Add broth and water; bring to a boil. Add pasta; cook 10 minutes or until pasta is done. Stir in juice, thyme, salt, and pepper. Yield: 4 servings (serving size: about 1 cup).

CALORIES 124 (17% from fat); FAT 2.3g (sat 1.1g, mono 0.8g, poly 0.1g); PROTEIN 3.8g; CARB 22.7g; FIBER 1.6g; CHOL 5mg; IRON 1mg; SODIUM 450mg; CALC 21mg

Green Salad with Apples and Maple-Walnut Dressing

This salad contains sweet, spicy, nutty, and salty notes. Walnut oil adds depth, but you can substitute extra-virgin olive oil, albeit with milder results.

- 6 cups gourmet salad greens
- 1 cup (2-inch) julienne-cut Braeburn apple
- 2 tablespoons cider vinegar
- 2 tablespoons maple syrup
- 2 teaspoons whole-grain Dijon mustard
- 1½ teaspoons walnut oil
- ⅛ teaspoon salt
- ⅛ teaspoon ground red pepper

1 Combine salad greens and apple in a large bowl.
2 Combine vinegar and remaining ingredients; stir with a whisk. Drizzle dressing over salad; toss gently to coat. Yield: 4 servings (serving size: about 1¼ cups).

CALORIES 73 (27% from fat); FAT 2.2g (sat 0.2g, mono 0.5g, poly 1.3g); PROTEIN 1.6g; CARB 13.7g; FIBER 2.5g; CHOL 0mg; IRON 1.4mg; SODIUM 159mg; CALC 58mg

Feta-Basil Sandwiches

Prepare the cheese filling up to a day in advance; cover and chill. The sandwiches take very little time to assemble.

- 1 cup (4 ounces) crumbled feta cheese
- ¼ cup chopped fresh basil
- ¼ cup fat-free mayonnaise
- ¼ teaspoon freshly ground black pepper
- 8 (1½-ounce) slices firm white bread (such as Pepperidge Farm Hearty White), toasted
- 8 (¼-inch-thick) slices tomato

1 Combine first 4 ingredients, tossing with a fork until well combined. Spread about 2½ tablespoons cheese mixture onto each of 4 bread slices; top each with 2 tomato slices and 1 bread slice. Yield: 4 servings (serving size: 1 sandwich).

CALORIES 313 (28% from fat); FAT 9.6g (sat 4.3g, mono 2.7g, poly 0.9g); PROTEIN 14.4g; CARB 44.8g; FIBER 0.9g; CHOL 27mg; IRON 1.9mg; SODIUM 954mg; CALC 227mg

Chewy Chocolate-Coconut Macaroons

Leftover cookies are best stored in an airtight container.

- 2 ounces unsweetened chocolate, chopped
- 2 ounces sifted cake flour (about ½ cup)
- 2 tablespoons unsweetened cocoa
- ⅛ teaspoon salt
- 2½ cups lightly packed flaked sweetened coconut
- 1 teaspoon vanilla extract
- 1 (14-ounce) can fat-free sweetened condensed milk

1 Preheat oven to 250°.
2 Line a large baking sheet with parchment paper; secure with masking tape.
3 Place chocolate in a small microwave-safe bowl. Microwave at HIGH 1 minute or until almost melted, stirring until smooth.
4 Lightly spoon flour into a dry measuring cup; level with a knife. Combine flour, cocoa, and salt in a large bowl. Add coconut, and toss well. Stir in melted chocolate, vanilla, and milk (mixture will be stiff). Drop by level tablespoons 2 inches apart onto prepared pan. Bake at 250° for 45 minutes or until edges of cookies are firm and centers of cookies are soft, rotating baking sheet once during baking time. Remove from oven; cool 10 minutes on pan on a wire rack. Remove cookies from parchment paper; cool completely on wire racks. Store in an airtight container. Yield: 3 dozen (serving size: 1 cookie).

CALORIES 84 (38% from fat); FAT 3.7g (sat 3.3g, mono 0.3g, poly 0g); PROTEIN 1.9g; CARB 11.7g; FIBER 0.9g; CHOL 1mg; IRON 0.2mg; SODIUM 45mg; CALC 33mg

Casual Vegetarian Lunch

serves 4

Southwestern Falafel with Avocado Spread

Chickpea and Hearts of Palm Salad

Velvety Fudge Pudding

Lemon and Mint Iced Tea

Southwestern Falafel with Avocado Spread

PATTIES:
- 1 (15-ounce) can pinto beans, rinsed and drained
- ½ cup (2 ounces) shredded Monterey Jack cheese
- ¼ cup finely crushed baked tortilla chips
- 2 tablespoons finely chopped green onions
- 1 tablespoon finely chopped cilantro
- ⅛ teaspoon ground cumin
- 1 large egg white
- 1½ teaspoons canola oil

SPREAD:
- ¼ cup mashed peeled avocado
- 2 tablespoons finely chopped plum tomato
- 1 tablespoon finely chopped red onion
- 2 tablespoons fat-free sour cream
- 1 teaspoon fresh lime juice
- ⅛ teaspoon salt
- 2 (6-inch) pitas, each cut in half crosswise

❶ To prepare patties, place pinto beans in a medium bowl; mash with a fork. Add cheese and next 5 ingredients; stir until well blended. Form into 4 (½-inch-thick) oval patties.
❷ Heat oil in a large nonstick skillet over medium-high heat. Add patties; cook 3 minutes on each side or until patties are browned and thoroughly heated.
❸ To prepare spread, combine avocado, tomato, onion, sour cream, juice, and salt. Place 1 patty in each pita half. Spread about 2 tablespoons avocado mixture over patty in each pita half. Yield: 4 servings (serving size: 1 stuffed pita half).

CALORIES 281 (30% from fat); FAT 9.5g (sat 3.4g, mono 3.9g, poly 1.5g); PROTEIN 12.2g; CARB 37.4g; FIBER 5.9g; CHOL 13mg; IRON 2.4mg; SODIUM 625mg; CALC 188mg

Chickpea and Hearts of Palm Salad

- 1 cup drained canned chickpeas (garbanzo beans)
- ½ cup chopped plum tomato
- ⅓ cup (about 1½ ounces) diced provolone cheese
- ¼ cup finely chopped red onion
- 1 (14-ounce) can hearts of palm, drained and cut crosswise into ½-inch slices
- 1 tablespoon minced fresh parsley
- 2 tablespoons red wine vinegar
- 1 teaspoon olive oil

❶ Combine first 5 ingredients in a medium bowl.
❷ Combine parsley, vinegar, and oil; stir with a whisk. Drizzle dressing over salad; toss well. Yield: 4 servings (serving size: about ¾ cup).

CALORIES 149 (31% from fat); FAT 5.2g (sat 2.2g, mono 1.9g, poly 0.7g); PROTEIN 8g; CARB 19.4g; FIBER 5g; CHOL 7mg; IRON 3.5mg; SODIUM 479mg; CALC 151mg

Velvety Fudge Pudding

This pudding has a very thick consistency.

- 1 cup 1% low-fat milk, divided
- 1 cup fat-free half-and-half
- ⅓ cup sugar
- ⅔ cup semisweet chocolate chips
- 3 tablespoons cornstarch
- 1 large egg
- 1 large egg white
- 1½ teaspoons vanilla extract

❶ Combine ½ cup milk, half-and-half, and sugar in a medium saucepan over medium heat. Cook 2 minutes or just until mixture begins to simmer, stirring constantly. Remove from heat; add chocolate chips. Let stand 5 minutes; stir until smooth.
❷ Place chocolate mixture over low heat; return to a simmer, stirring frequently. Combine remaining ½ cup milk, cornstarch, egg, and egg white in a medium bowl; stir with a whisk. Gradually add 1 cup hot chocolate mixture to cornstarch mixture, stirring constantly with a whisk. Return mixture to pan; cook, stirring constantly, over low heat 4 minutes or until thickened. Stir in vanilla. Serve warm, or cover and chill. Yield: 4 servings (serving size: ½ cup).

CALORIES 314 (30% from fat); FAT 10.3g (sat 5.8g, mono 3.5g, poly 0.5g); PROTEIN 5.7g; CARB 49.1g; FIBER 1.7g; CHOL 55mg; IRON 1.2mg; SODIUM 126mg; CALC 132mg

Lemon and Mint Iced Tea

This twist on sweet iced tea is refreshingly tart.

- 8 cups cold water, divided
- 3 family-sized tea bags
- 1 sprig fresh mint (about ¼ cup leaves)
- ¾ cup sugar
- ¼ cup fresh lemon juice

❶ Bring 4 cups water to a boil in a medium saucepan. Add tea bags and mint; steep 10 minutes. Strain tea mixture, and discard tea bags and mint.
❷ Combine sugar and juice in a glass measuring cup. Add ½ cup hot tea mixture; stir until sugar dissolves. Pour sugar mixture into a 2-quart pitcher; add remaining hot tea mixture. Add 4 cups cold water, and stir. Serve over ice. Yield: 8 servings (serving size: 1 cup).

CALORIES 75 (0% from fat); FAT 0g; PROTEIN 0g; CARB 19.4g; FIBER 0g; CHOL 0mg; IRON 0mg; SODIUM 5mg; CALC 5mg

Lunch on the Deck
serves 6

French-Style Shrimp Salad

Sparkling Cassis Aperitif

French bread

Vanilla Crème with Fresh Berry Jam

French-Style Shrimp Salad

This dish offers a twist on the classic salade niçoise. Assemble the salad in individual servings, or arrange on a platter and serve family-style. Niçoise olives are a small purplish black variety; you can substitute kalamata, if you prefer.

VINAIGRETTE:
- 6 garlic cloves, halved
- ⅔ cup fat-free, less-sodium chicken broth
- ¼ cup chopped fresh basil
- ¼ cup chopped fresh parsley
- 2 tablespoons fresh lemon juice
- 2 tablespoons tarragon vinegar
- 2 tablespoons extra-virgin olive oil
- 2 teaspoons Dijon mustard
- ½ teaspoon freshly ground black pepper

SALAD:
- 2 pounds peeled and deveined large shrimp
- 12 small red potatoes (about ¾ pound)
- ½ pound haricots verts or green beans

Cooking spray
- 5 cups gourmet salad greens
- 4 cups torn romaine lettuce
- 1 cup (¼-inch-thick) slices red bell pepper (about 1 medium)
- 3 medium tomatoes, each cut into 6 wedges
- 1 (14-ounce) can quartered artichoke hearts, drained
- 3 hard-cooked large eggs, each cut into quarters
- ½ cup niçoise olives
- 2 tablespoons capers

1 To prepare vinaigrette, drop garlic through food chute with food processor on; process until minced. Add broth and next 7 ingredients; process until well blended.

❷ To prepare salad, combine 2 tablespoons of the vinaigrette and shrimp in a large zip-top plastic bag. Seal and marinate in refrigerator 20 minutes, turning bag occasionally.

❸ Place potatoes in a large saucepan; cover with water. Bring to a boil; cook 8 minutes. Add haricots verts; cook 2 minutes or until haricots verts are crisp-tender and potatoes are tender. Drain and rinse with cold water; drain. Cut potatoes into 1/4-inch-thick slices; set aside.

❹ Heat a large grill pan over medium-high heat; coat with cooking spray. Remove shrimp from bag; discard marinade. Add shrimp to pan; cook 3 minutes on each side or until shrimp are done.

❺ Combine potato slices, haricots verts, salad greens, lettuce, red bell pepper, tomato, and artichoke in a large bowl. Add the remaining vinaigrette, tossing gently to coat. Place lettuce mixture on a serving platter. Arrange shrimp and eggs over lettuce mixture; sprinkle with olives and capers. Serve immediately. Yield: 6 servings (serving size: about 2 1/2 cups salad mixture, 5 ounces shrimp, 2 pieces egg, 4 teaspoons olives, and 1 teaspoon capers).

CALORIES 366 (30% from fat); FAT 12g (sat 2.2g, mono 6g, poly 2.2g); PROTEIN 39.3g; CARB 26.1g; FIBER 6.4g; CHOL 336mg; IRON 6.7mg; SODIUM 798mg; CALC 179mg

Sparkling Cassis Aperitif

An aperitif is a light alcoholic beverage enjoyed before a meal; many are made with Champagne.

    4 cups currant juice (such as Looza)
    3/4 cup crème de cassis (black currant–flavored liqueur)
    2 tablespoons fresh lemon juice
    2 cups chilled sparkling water
    1 (750-milliliter) bottle chilled Champagne
    1 cup fresh blackberries

❶ Combine first 3 ingredients in a large pitcher. Chill until ready to serve.

❷ Before serving, add sparkling water and Champagne to currant mixture; stir well. Divide blackberries evenly among 9 glasses. Pour about 1 cup Champagne mixture over blackberries in each glass. Serve immediately. Yield: 9 servings.

CALORIES 199 (0% from fat); FAT 0.1g (sat 0g, mono 0g, poly 0g); PROTEIN 0.7g; CARB 24.5g; FIBER 0.8g; CHOL 0mg; IRON 0.4mg; SODIUM 6mg; CALC 29mg

Vanilla Crème with Fresh Berry Jam

Prepare the strawberry jam and custard up to a day ahead, and refrigerate separately. Assemble the desserts just before serving. The jam is also good with toast, pancakes, or pound cake.

JAM:
    1/3 cup water
    3 tablespoons sugar
    2 cups coarsely chopped strawberries, divided
CRÈME:
    2 teaspoons unflavored gelatin
    1 1/4 cups whole milk
    1 (6-inch) piece vanilla bean, split lengthwise
    6 tablespoons sugar
    2 cups buttermilk
  Mint sprigs (optional)

❶ To prepare jam, combine 1/3 cup water and 3 tablespoons sugar in a small saucepan over medium heat. Cook 3 minutes or until sugar dissolves. Add 1 cup coarsely chopped strawberries; bring to a boil. Reduce heat, and simmer 10 minutes or until mixture is syrupy, mashing strawberries with a fork. Remove from heat; stir in remaining 1 cup chopped strawberries. Pour into a bowl, and cool completely. Cover and chill.

❷ To prepare crème, sprinkle gelatin over whole milk in a small saucepan; let stand 10 minutes. Scrape seeds from vanilla bean; add seeds and bean to milk mixture. Place over medium-low heat; cook 10 minutes or until gelatin dissolves, stirring constantly with a whisk. Increase heat to medium; add 6 tablespoons sugar, stirring until sugar dissolves. Remove from heat. Remove and discard vanilla bean. Stir in buttermilk.

❸ Spoon about 1/2 cup buttermilk mixture into each of 6 small glasses. Cover and chill 6 hours or until set. Top each serving with 3 tablespoons jam. Garnish with mint sprigs, if desired. Yield: 6 servings.

CALORIES 178 (23% from fat); FAT 4.6g (sat 2.6g, mono 0.4g, poly 0.3g); PROTEIN 5.5g; CARB 30g; FIBER 2.7g; CHOL 17mg; IRON 0.3mg; SODIUM 119mg; CALC 69mg

Picnic in the Park

serves 4

Antipasto Chicken Sandwich

Papaya-Carrot Slaw

Ginger Limeade

Oatmeal-Walnut Cookies

Antipasto Chicken Sandwich

To speed preparation, purchase rotisserie chicken breasts and shred the meat. Build the sandwich the morning of your picnic, and wrap it tightly in foil. Refrigerate it until you're ready to pack the cooler.

- 2 tablespoons olive paste
- 1 (10-ounce) loaf round focaccia, cut in half horizontally
- 2 cups shredded roasted skinless, boneless chicken breast
- 1/2 cup coarsely chopped drained marinated artichoke hearts
- 1/2 cup chopped drained oil-packed sun-dried tomato halves
- 1/2 cup coarsely chopped bottled roasted red bell peppers
- 2 ounces thinly sliced prosciutto
- 1/2 cup (2 ounces) shredded fontina cheese

1 Spread olive paste over bottom half of focaccia. Arrange chicken on top of paste. Arrange artichokes, tomatoes, bell peppers, and prosciutto over chicken. Sprinkle with cheese. Top with top half of focaccia; press gently.
2 Heat a large nonstick skillet over medium heat. Add sandwich to pan. Place a cast-iron or heavy skillet on top of sandwich, and press gently to flatten. Cook 2 minutes on each side or until bread is lightly toasted (leave cast-iron skillet on sandwich while cooking). Cut sandwich into 4 wedges. Yield: 4 servings (serving size: 1 wedge).

CALORIES 447 (29% from fat); FAT 14.5g (sat 5g, mono 4.2g, poly 2.1g); PROTEIN 36.8g; CARB 42.1g; FIBER 3.8g; CHOL 89mg; IRON 3.6mg; SODIUM 986mg; CALC 156mg

Papaya-Carrot Slaw

Prepare this slaw up to a day in advance; store in an airtight container in the refrigerator.

- 1 cup shredded peeled green papaya
- 1/2 cup shredded carrot
- 1/2 cup red bell pepper strips
- 1 tablespoon grated peeled fresh ginger
- 1 teaspoon grated lime rind
- 2 tablespoons fresh lime juice
- 1/4 teaspoon salt
- 1/4 teaspoon pepper

1 Combine all ingredients in a medium bowl. Stir well; cover and refrigerate. Yield: 4 servings (serving size: 1/2 cup).

CALORIES 29 (4% from fat); FAT 0.1g (sat 0g, mono 0g, poly 0.1g); PROTEIN 0.6g; CARB 7.2g; FIBER 1.4g; CHOL 0mg; IRON 0.2mg; SODIUM 158mg; CALC 17mg

Ginger Limeade

This sweet-tart beverage is refreshing on a hot day.

- 6 cups cold water, divided
- 1/2 cup sugar
- 3 tablespoons chopped peeled fresh ginger
- 3 tablespoons grated lime rind
- 10 mint leaves
- 1 1/4 cups fresh lime juice (about 6 limes)
- 4 lime wedges (optional)

1 Combine 1/4 cup water, sugar, ginger, lime rind, and mint leaves in a blender; process until well blended. Cover and chill 2 hours.
2 Add remaining 5 3/4 cups water and juice, and stir to combine. Garnish with lime wedges, if desired. Yield: 4 servings (serving size: 2 cups).

CALORIES 124 (1% from fat); FAT 0.1g (sat 0g, mono 0g, poly 0g); PROTEIN 0.6g; CARB 33.5g; FIBER 0.9g; CHOL 0mg; IRON 0.1mg; SODIUM 9mg; CALC 21mg

Oatmeal-Walnut Cookies

After removing the baked cookies from the baking sheet, wipe it with a paper towel; recoat it with cooking spray before baking the second batch of cookies.

- 1/2 cup granulated sugar
- 1/3 cup packed dark brown sugar
- 1/4 cup butter, softened
- 1 teaspoon vanilla extract
- 1 large egg
- 3 1/3 ounces all-purpose flour (about 3/4 cup)
- 1 cup regular oats
- 1/4 teaspoon salt
- 2/3 cup golden raisins
- 1/4 cup chopped toasted walnuts
- Cooking spray

1 Preheat oven to 350°.
2 Combine granulated sugar, dark brown sugar, butter, vanilla, and egg in a large bowl; beat with a mixer at medium speed until well blended. Lightly spoon flour into a dry measuring cup; level with a knife. Add flour, oats, and salt to sugar mixture; beat well. Stir in raisins and walnuts.
3 Drop dough by level tablespoons, 1 1/2 inches apart, onto a baking sheet coated with cooking spray. Bake at 350° for 12 minutes or until lightly browned. Remove from oven; let stand 2 minutes. Remove cookies from baking sheet; cool on wire racks. Yield: 2 dozen (serving size: 1 cookie).

CALORIES 109 (28% from fat); FAT 3.4g (sat 1.4g, mono 0.9g, poly 0.9g); PROTEIN 2.1g; CARB 18.3g; FIBER 1.1g; CHOL 14mg; IRON 0.7mg; SODIUM 24mg; CALC 12mg

Family Favorites Menu

serves 6

Sloppy Joes

Millionaire Salad

Baby carrots

Marble Cheesecake Squares

Sloppy Joes

Kids and adults alike will love these sweet-savory sandwiches. Baby carrots and vegetable chips make great side options.

- ¾ cup chopped onion
- ½ cup chopped green bell pepper
- ¾ pound ground round
- 2 cups no-salt-added tomato sauce
- 2 tablespoons tomato paste
- 1 tablespoon prepared mustard
- 1 teaspoon chili powder
- 2 teaspoons Worcestershire sauce
- ½ teaspoon salt
- ½ teaspoon sugar
- ½ teaspoon dried oregano
- ⅛ teaspoon black pepper
- 6 (2½-ounce) whole wheat hamburger buns, split

❶ Heat a large nonstick skillet over medium heat. Add chopped onion, green bell pepper, and beef. Cook until beef is browned, stirring to crumble. Add tomato sauce and next 8 ingredients; stir until combined.

❷ Cover, reduce heat, and cook 15 minutes, stirring occasionally; uncover and cook an additional 5 minutes. Spoon about ½ cup of beef mixture over bottom half of each bun; cover with top halves of buns. Yield: 6 servings (serving size: 1 sandwich).

CALORIES 300 (17% from fat); FAT 5.9g (sat 1.4g, mono 1.7g, poly 1.8g); PROTEIN 18.8g; CARB 46.2g; FIBER 6.9g; CHOL 30mg; IRON 3.5mg; SODIUM 699mg; CALC 89mg

Millionaire Salad

Also known as 5-cup salad, this creamy dish serves a crowd. Leftovers will keep in the refrigerator for 2 to 3 days.

- 2 cups miniature marshmallows
- 1 cup flaked sweetened coconut
- 2 (11-ounce) cans mandarin oranges in light syrup, drained
- 1 (20-ounce) can crushed pineapple in juice, drained
- 1 (8-ounce) carton low-fat sour cream
- 1 (8-ounce) carton plain fat-free yogurt

❶ Combine all ingredients in a large bowl. Cover and chill. Yield: 12 servings (serving size: ½ cup).

CALORIES 151 (30% from fat); FAT 5g (sat 4.2g, mono 0.2g, poly 0.1g); PROTEIN 2.9g; CARB 24.8g; FIBER 1g; CHOL 6mg; IRON 0.5mg; SODIUM 60mg; CALC 67mg

Marble Cheesecake Squares

If you forget to set out the cream cheese to soften before-hand, arrange unwrapped blocks in a single layer in a large bowl and microwave at HIGH for 1 minute.

- 1 cup chocolate graham cracker crumbs (about 9 cookie sheets)
- Cooking spray
- 1 tablespoon butter, melted
- 2 (8-ounce) blocks fat-free cream cheese, softened
- 1 (8-ounce) block ⅓-less-fat cream cheese, softened
- 1 cup sugar
- 3 tablespoons all-purpose flour
- 1 tablespoon vanilla extract
- 3 large egg whites
- 1 large egg
- 1 ounce semisweet chocolate

❶ Preheat oven to 325°.

❷ Place crumbs in a 9-inch square baking pan coated with cooking spray; drizzle with butter. Toss with a fork until moist, and press into bottom of pan. Bake at 325° for 8 minutes; cool on a wire rack.

❸ Place cheeses in a large bowl; beat with a mixer at high speed until smooth. Add sugar and flour; beat well. Add vanilla, egg whites, and egg; beat until well blended. Pour cheese mixture into prepared pan.

❹ Place chocolate in a small microwave-safe bowl, and microwave at HIGH 1½ minutes or until soft, stirring after 45 seconds (chocolate should not completely melt). Stir until smooth. Drop melted chocolate onto cheese mixture to form 9 mounds. Swirl chocolate into batter using tip of a knife. Bake at 325° for 35 minutes or until almost set. Cool on a wire rack; cover and chill at least 4 hours. Yield: 12 servings.

CALORIES 239 (29% from fat); FAT 7.6g (sat 4.1g, mono 2.1g, poly 0.2g); PROTEIN 9.7g; CARB 31.4g; FIBER 0.6g; CHOL 41mg; IRON 0.6mg; SODIUM 355mg; CALC 124mg

Easy Steak House Menu

serves 4

Peppercorn-Crusted Flank Steak

Caesar Salad

Asiago, Potato, and Bacon Gratin

Peach and Raspberry Pavlova Parfaits

Peppercorn-Crusted Flank Steak

We call for flank steak in this recipe, but the dry rub seasoning works well on any cut of meat. For a special occasion, try it on filet mignon. Toasting and grinding the peppercorns is a worthwhile step that provides deep flavor.

RUB:

- 1 tablespoon whole black peppercorns
- 1 teaspoon kosher salt
- 1 teaspoon dry mustard
- ½ teaspoon garlic powder
- ¼ teaspoon dried thyme

REMAINING INGREDIENTS:

- 1 (1-pound) flank steak, trimmed

Cooking spray

1 To prepare rub, heat a small skillet over medium heat. Add black peppercorns, and cook 1 minute or until fragrant. Transfer toasted peppercorns to a spice grinder; grind until fine. Combine ground peppercorns, salt, mustard, garlic powder, and thyme in a small bowl. Rub peppercorn mixture evenly over steak; let stand 10 minutes.

2 Heat a nonstick grill pan over medium-high heat. Coat steak with cooking spray; cook 7 minutes on each side or until desired degree of doneness. Let stand 5 minutes. Yield: 4 servings (serving size: 3 ounces).

CALORIES 171 (34% from fat); FAT 6.5g (sat 2.4g, mono 2.4g, poly 0.3g); PROTEIN 25g; CARB 1.6g; FIBER 0.5g; CHOL 37mg; IRON 2mg; SODIUM 533mg; CALC 36mg

Caesar Salad

Prepare the salad dressing ahead of time; cover and chill. Double the recipe if you'd like to have extra on hand.

- 1 hard-cooked large egg
- 2 tablespoons fresh lemon juice
- 1 tablespoon olive oil
- 1 tablespoon water
- 2 teaspoons red wine vinegar
- 1½ teaspoons anchovy paste
- 1 teaspoon Dijon mustard
- ½ teaspoon Worcestershire sauce
- ⅛ teaspoon pepper
- 1 garlic clove, minced
- 8 cups torn romaine lettuce
- 1 cup fat-free Caesar croutons
- 8 teaspoons grated fresh Parmesan cheese

❶ Cut egg in half lengthwise; remove and reserve yolk for another use. Mince egg white.
❷ Combine juice and next 8 ingredients in a small bowl; stir with a whisk. Combine egg white, juice mixture, and lettuce in a large bowl; toss well. Place 1½ cups salad mixture on each of 4 plates; top each with ¼ cup croutons and 2 teaspoons cheese. Yield: 4 servings.

CALORIES 134 (35% from fat); FAT 6.7g (sat 1.3g, mono 2.9g, poly 0.4g); PROTEIN 6.7g; CARB 13g; FIBER 1.9g; CHOL 3mg; IRON 1.3mg; SODIUM 538mg; CALC 99mg

Asiago, Potato, and Bacon Gratin

Cook the potatoes first and set them aside while you prepare the cheese sauce for the gratin.

- 1½ pounds peeled Yukon gold potatoes, cut into ¼-inch-thick slices
- 1 teaspoon salt, divided
- Cooking spray
- 2 tablespoons minced shallots
- 1 ounce all-purpose flour (about ¼ cup)
- 2 cups 1% low-fat milk, divided
- ¾ cup (3 ounces) grated Asiago cheese
- ¼ cup chopped fresh chives
- ¼ teaspoon freshly ground black pepper
- 4 bacon slices, cooked and crumbled
- ¼ cup (1 ounce) grated fresh Parmesan cheese

❶ Preheat oven to 350°.
❷ Place potatoes in a large saucepan; cover with water, and bring to a boil. Reduce heat; simmer 5 minutes or until potatoes are almost tender. Drain. Sprinkle potatoes evenly with ¼ teaspoon salt; keep warm.

❸ Heat a medium saucepan over medium heat; coat with cooking spray. Add shallots, and cook 2 minutes or until tender, stirring frequently. Lightly spoon flour into a dry measuring cup, and level with a knife. Sprinkle flour over shallots. Gradually add ½ cup milk, stirring with a whisk until well blended. Gradually add remaining 1½ cups milk, stirring with a whisk. Cook over medium heat 9 minutes or until mixture is thick, stirring frequently. Remove from heat; stir in ¾ teaspoon salt, Asiago, chives, pepper, and bacon.
❹ Arrange half of potato slices in an 8-inch square baking dish coated with cooking spray. Pour half of cheese sauce over potato slices. Top with remaining potato slices and cheese sauce; sprinkle with Parmesan. Bake at 350° for 35 minutes or until cheese is bubbly and lightly browned. Yield: 6 servings.

CALORIES 250 (30% from fat); FAT 8.2g (sat 4.6g, mono 2.7g, poly 0.5g); PROTEIN 12.3g; CARB 31.9g; FIBER 2.3g; CHOL 23mg; IRON 0.9mg; SODIUM 618mg; CALC 306mg

Peach and Raspberry Pavlova Parfaits

You can make this light, refreshing summer dessert entirely in advance and refrigerate it until ready to serve.

- ½ cup (4 ounces) ⅓-less-fat cream cheese
- ¼ cup sugar, divided
- 1 cup vanilla fat-free yogurt
- 2 cups sliced peeled peaches (about 6 to 7 peaches)
- 1 cup fresh raspberries
- 1 cup vanilla meringue cookie crumbs (such as Miss Meringue Minis; about 12 cookies, coarsely crushed)
- 12 vanilla meringue mini-cookies

❶ Place cream cheese and 3 tablespoons sugar in a medium bowl; beat with a mixer at high speed for 2 minutes or until smooth. Add vanilla fat-free yogurt, and beat until blended.
❷ Combine remaining 1 tablespoon sugar, peaches, and raspberries in a large bowl; toss to coat. Let stand 5 minutes.
❸ Spoon 2 tablespoons cheese mixture into each of 6 (8-ounce) glasses; top each with ¼ cup peach mixture and about 2½ tablespoons cookie crumbs. Repeat layers once with remaining cheese mixture and remaining peach mixture. Cover and chill. To serve, top each parfait with 2 mini cookies. Yield: 6 servings.

CALORIES 193 (22% from fat); FAT 4.7g (sat 2.9g, mono 1.3g, poly 0.2g); PROTEIN 5.1g; CARB 34.7g; FIBER 2.5g; CHOL 15mg; IRON 0.3mg; SODIUM 111mg; CALC 94mg

Italian-Inspired Menu

serves 4

Grilled Halibut with Lemon-Caper Vinaigrette

Mediterranean Couscous

Steamed Broccolini

Tuscan Almond Biscotti

Grilled Halibut with Lemon-Caper Vinaigrette

This simple vinaigrette perfectly complements halibut—which is a light-textured white fish—but you can use it on any grilled fish.

VINAIGRETTE:
1½ tablespoons fresh lemon juice
1 tablespoon extra-virgin olive oil
1½ teaspoons finely chopped shallots
1 teaspoon chopped capers
¼ teaspoon kosher salt
¼ teaspoon freshly ground black pepper

FISH:
Cooking spray
4 (6-ounce) halibut fillets
½ teaspoon kosher salt
2 tablespoons chopped fresh chives

① To prepare vinaigrette, combine juice, oil, shallots, capers, ¼ teaspoon salt, and pepper in a small bowl; stir with a whisk.
② To prepare fish, heat a nonstick grill pan over medium-high heat; coat with cooking spray. Sprinkle fish with ½ teaspoon salt. Add fish to pan; cook 4 minutes on each side or until fish flakes easily when tested with a fork. Spoon vinaigrette over fish. Sprinkle with chives. Yield: 4 servings (serving size: 1 fillet, about 2 teaspoons vinaigrette, and 1½ teaspoons chives).

CALORIES 221 (30% from fat); FAT 7.4g (sat 1.1g, mono 4g, poly 1.6g); PROTEIN 35.6g; CARB 0.5g; FIBER 0.1g; CHOL 54mg; IRON 1.5mg; SODIUM 531mg; CALC 83mg

Mediterranean Couscous

Quick-cooking couscous is now even better, since it's available in a whole wheat version. Fresh sage gives this side dish an earthy taste and aroma, but you can use other fresh herbs, such as basil, cilantro, or mint.

1¾ cups fat-free, less-sodium chicken broth
¾ cup whole wheat couscous
1 cup grape tomatoes, halved
½ cup chopped seeded peeled cucumber
½ cup chopped red bell pepper
¼ cup sliced green onions
1 tablespoon chopped fresh sage
¼ teaspoon grated lemon rind
2 tablespoons fresh lemon juice
4 teaspoons extra-virgin olive oil
½ teaspoon salt
½ teaspoon freshly ground black pepper

① Bring broth to a boil in a medium saucepan; gradually stir in couscous. Remove from heat; cover and let stand 5 minutes. Fluff with a fork. Combine couscous, tomatoes, and remaining ingredients in a large bowl. Yield: 4 servings (serving size: about 1 cup).

CALORIES 150 (32% from fat); FAT 5.4g (sat 0.7g, mono 3.7g, poly 0.5g); PROTEIN 4.8g; CARB 22.1g; FIBER 4.4g; CHOL 0mg; IRON 1.2mg; SODIUM 467mg; CALC 25mg

Tuscan Almond Biscotti

These crunchy cookies are a specialty of Prato, a city in Tuscany, where they are called *cantucci*. They are typically served at the end of a meal with a glass of vin santo, a sweet dessert wine. Keep leftover biscotti in air-tight tins up to a week.

7¾ ounces all-purpose flour (about 1¾ cups)
1 cup sugar
1 teaspoon baking powder
¼ teaspoon salt
1 cup whole almonds, toasted
2 large eggs
½ teaspoon almond extract
Cooking spray

① Preheat oven to 375°.
② Lightly spoon flour into dry measuring cups; level with a knife. Combine flour, sugar, baking powder, and salt in a large bowl. Place almonds in a food processor; pulse 10 times. Stir nuts into flour mixture.
③ Combine eggs and extract; stir with a whisk. Add egg mixture to flour mixture, stirring just until blended (dough will be crumbly). Turn dough out onto a lightly floured surface; knead lightly 7 or 8 times. Divide dough into 2 equal portions; shape each portion into a 6-inch-long roll. Place rolls 6 inches apart on a baking sheet coated with cooking spray, and pat to 1-inch thickness. Bake at 375° for 25 minutes or until lightly browned. Cool 5 minutes on a wire rack.
④ Cut each roll crosswise into 12 (½-inch) slices. Stand slices upright on pan. Bake 14 minutes (cookies will be slightly soft in the center but will harden as they cool). Remove from pan, and cool completely on a wire rack. Yield: 2 dozen (serving size: 1 biscotto).

CALORIES 102 (30% from fat); FAT 3.4g (sat 0.4g, mono 2.1g, poly 0.8g); PROTEIN 2.7g; CARB 15.7g; FIBER 0.9g; CHOL 18mg; IRON 0.8mg; SODIUM 51mg; CALC 28mg

Caribbean Menu

serves 4

Jerk Pork Tenderloin with Fresh Pineapple Chutney

Mint-Cilantro-Coconut Rice

Skillet Onions, Peppers, and Garlic

Banana-Mango Crisp

Jerk Pork Tenderloin with Fresh Pineapple Chutney

For more heat and spice flavor, use up to 1 tablespoon Easy Jerk Seasoning. Store remaining seasoning in a small jar or plastic container with a tight-fitting lid.

PORK:
- 1 teaspoon olive oil
- 1 (1¼-pound) pork tenderloin, trimmed
- 2 teaspoons Easy Jerk Seasoning

CHUTNEY:
- Cooking spray
- ½ cup finely chopped onion
- 2 cups finely chopped fresh pineapple (about ½ cored pineapple)
- 1 tablespoon dark brown sugar
- 1 tablespoon cider vinegar
- ⅛ teaspoon salt
- Dash of freshly ground black pepper

❶ Preheat oven to 425°.

❷ To prepare pork, heat oil in a large ovenproof skillet over medium-high heat. Rub pork with 2 teaspoons Easy Jerk Seasoning. Add pork to pan; cook 3 minutes, turning to brown all sides. Place pan in the oven; bake at 425° for 25 minutes or until a thermometer registers 160° (slightly pink). Let stand 10 minutes before slicing.

❸ To prepare chutney, heat a medium saucepan over medium-high heat; coat pan with cooking spray. Add onion; cook 5 minutes or until lightly browned. Add pineapple and remaining ingredients. Cover, reduce heat, and simmer 15 minutes or until thickened, stirring occasionally. Serve over pork. Yield: 4 servings (serving size: 3 ounces pork and about ½ cup chutney).

CALORIES 276 (32% from fat); FAT 9.8g (sat 3.2g, mono 4.3g, poly 0.9g); PROTEIN 31.5g; CARB 14.8g; FIBER 1.6g; CHOL 97mg; IRON 1.9mg; SODIUM 377mg; CALC 25mg

Easy Jerk Seasoning:

- 1 tablespoon garlic powder
- 2½ teaspoons kosher salt
- 2 teaspoons dried thyme
- 1½ teaspoons apple-pie spice
- 1 teaspoon ground red pepper

❶ Combine all ingredients in a small bowl. Yield: 5 teaspoons (serving size: about ½ teaspoon).

CALORIES 5 (0% from fat); FAT 0.1g (sat 0g, mono 0g, poly 0g); PROTEIN 0.2g; CARB 1.1g; FIBER 0.4g; CHOL 0mg; IRON 0.3mg; SODIUM 471mg; CALC 6mg

Mint-Cilantro-Coconut Rice

Basmati rice is naturally nutty in flavor and is delicious when combined with fresh herbs.

- 2 teaspoons olive oil
- 1 cup uncooked basmati rice
- ¼ cup sliced green onions
- ¾ cup fat-free, less-sodium chicken broth
- ¼ cup light coconut milk
- ½ teaspoon kosher salt
- ¼ teaspoon freshly ground black pepper
- 2 tablespoons chopped fresh mint
- 2 tablespoons chopped fresh cilantro

❶ Heat oil in a medium saucepan over medium-high heat. Add rice; sauté 3 minutes. Add onions; sauté 1 minute. Add broth, milk, salt, and pepper; stir. Bring to a boil; cover, reduce heat, and simmer 17 minutes or until liquid is absorbed and rice is tender, stirring once after 10 minutes. Stir in mint and cilantro; cover and let stand 5 minutes. Yield: 4 servings (serving size: about ½ cup).

CALORIES 290 (16% from fat); FAT 5g (sat 1.7g, mono 2.6g, poly 0.5g); PROTEIN 6.1g; CARB 54.7g; FIBER 0.9g; CHOL 0mg; IRON 0.5mg; SODIUM 423mg; CALC 13mg

Skillet Onions, Peppers, and Garlic

- 2 teaspoons olive oil
- 1 cup thinly sliced red bell pepper
- 1 cup thinly sliced yellow bell pepper
- 1 cup vertically sliced sweet onion
- 1 teaspoon minced garlic
- ½ teaspoon dried rosemary
- ¼ teaspoon salt
- ¼ teaspoon freshly ground black pepper

❶ Heat oil in a large nonstick skillet over medium-high heat. Add bell peppers and onion; cook 13 minutes or until onion is tender, stirring frequently. Add garlic, rosemary, salt, and black pepper; cook 2 minutes, stirring frequently. Yield: 4 servings (serving size: about ½ cup).

CALORIES 55 (40% from fat); FAT 2.4g (sat 0.3g, mono 1.7g, poly 0.2g); PROTEIN 1g; CARB 7.5g; FIBER 1.9g; CHOL 0mg; IRON 0.4mg; SODIUM 119mg; CALC 24mg

Banana-Mango Crisp

- 5 cups sliced banana (about 6 bananas)
- 3 cups chopped peeled mango (about 3 mangoes)
- ¼ cup dark rum
- Cooking spray
- 1 ounce all-purpose flour (about ¼ cup)
- ¾ cup regular oats
- ½ cup flaked sweetened coconut, toasted
- 6 tablespoons brown sugar
- 3 tablespoons chopped crystallized ginger
- ¼ teaspoon salt
- 3 tablespoons chilled butter, cut into small pieces

❶ Preheat oven to 375°.
❷ Combine first 3 ingredients in an 11 x 7–inch baking dish coated with cooking spray. Lightly spoon flour into a dry measuring cup; level with a knife. Combine flour, oats, coconut, sugar, ginger, and salt in a bowl; cut in butter with a pastry blender or 2 knives until the mixture resembles coarse meal.
❸ Add ⅓ cup oat mixture to banana mixture, stirring gently to combine. Sprinkle remaining oat mixture over banana mixture.
❹ Bake at 375° for 30 minutes or until the crisp is lightly browned and bubbly. Yield: 8 servings (serving size: about 1 cup).

CALORIES 276 (23% from fat); FAT 6.9g (sat 4.3g, mono 1.5g, poly 0.5g); PROTEIN 3g; CARB 50g; FIBER 4.4g; CHOL 12mg; IRON 1.2mg; SODIUM 134mg; CALC 27mg

A Taste of Provence

serves 6

Oven-Poached Halibut Provençal

Green beans

Herbed Potato Salad

Strawberry-Black Pepper Sorbet

Oven-Poached Halibut Provençal

Herbes de Provence (EHRB duh proh-VAWNS) is a traditional blend of fragrant dried herbs. It is especially good when added to olive oil and used to coat raw meat before cooking.

1 tablespoon olive oil
3 garlic cloves, minced
2 cups chopped fennel bulb
1½ cups chopped onion
1 teaspoon salt, divided
4 cups diced tomato
⅓ cup chopped fresh basil
⅓ cup chopped fresh flat-leaf parsley
6 (6-ounce) halibut fillets
1 cup dry white wine
⅓ cup dry breadcrumbs
2 tablespoons chopped pitted kalamata olives
1 teaspoon dried herbes de Provence
1 teaspoon olive oil
½ teaspoon coarsely ground black pepper
Fresh flat-leaf parsley sprigs (optional)

❶ Preheat oven to 450°.
❷ Heat 1 tablespoon oil in a large nonstick skillet over medium-high heat. Add garlic; sauté 30 seconds. Add fennel, onion, and ½ teaspoon salt; sauté 8 minutes or until lightly browned. Stir in diced tomato; cook 2 minutes. Remove from heat; stir in basil and parsley.
❸ Spoon half of tomato mixture into a 13 x 9–inch baking dish. Place fillets over tomato mixture. Pour wine into dish; sprinkle fillets with ¼ teaspoon salt. Spoon remaining tomato mixture over fillets. Bake at 450° for 15 minutes or until fish flakes easily when tested with a fork or until desired degree of doneness.
❹ Preheat broiler.
❺ Combine remaining ¼ teaspoon salt, dry breadcrumbs, olives, herbes de Provence, 1 teaspoon oil, and pepper in a small bowl. Sprinkle breadcrumb mixture over fillets. Broil 5 minutes or until lightly browned. Garnish with parsley sprigs, if desired. Serve immediately. Yield: 6 servings (serving size: 1 fillet and about ½ cup tomato mixture).

CALORIES 315 (26% from fat); FAT 9g (sat 1.3g, mono 4.6g, poly 2g); PROTEIN 38.8g; CARB 19.3g; FIBER 4.4g; CHOL 54mg; IRON 3.1mg; SODIUM 653mg; CALC 158mg

Herbed Potato Salad

3 pounds Yukon gold potatoes
1 cup dry white wine
3 tablespoons white wine vinegar
2 tablespoons extra-virgin olive oil
1 tablespoon whole-grain Dijon mustard
¾ teaspoon salt
¾ teaspoon freshly ground black pepper
2 garlic cloves, minced
½ cup thinly sliced chives
2 tablespoons chopped fresh parsley
1 teaspoon chopped fresh tarragon

❶ Place potatoes in a large saucepan; cover with water. Bring to a boil; reduce heat, and simmer 20 minutes or until tender. Drain; cool 10 minutes. Slice each potato in half lengthwise; cut each half crosswise into ½-inch-thick slices. Place potato slices in a large bowl.
❷ Place wine in a small saucepan over medium-high heat; bring to a boil. Cook until reduced to ½ cup (about 6 minutes). Transfer wine to a bowl. Add vinegar, oil, mustard, salt, pepper, and garlic; stir with a whisk. Drizzle wine mixture over potatoes; sprinkle with chives, parsley, and tarragon. Toss gently to combine. Serve warm or chilled. Yield: 6 servings (serving size: about 1 cup).

CALORIES 239 (18% from fat); FAT 4.7g (sat 0.7g, mono 3.6g, poly 0.4g); PROTEIN 6.2g; CARB 42.3g; FIBER 3g; CHOL 0mg; IRON 2.3mg; SODIUM 374mg; CALC 14mg

Strawberry-Black Pepper Sorbet

1 cup sugar
1 cup water
2 tablespoons coarsely crushed black peppercorns
6 cups sliced strawberries (about 2 pounds), divided
2 tablespoons fresh lemon juice, divided

❶ Combine sugar and 1 cup water in a small saucepan; bring to a boil, stirring occasionally until sugar dissolves. Remove from heat. Stir in peppercorns; let stand 20 minutes.
❷ Drain sugar syrup through a fine sieve into a bowl; discard solids. Place half of sugar syrup, 3 cups strawberries, and 1 tablespoon juice in a blender; process until smooth. Pour pureed mixture into a bowl. Repeat procedure with remaining sugar syrup, strawberries, and juice.
❸ Pour mixture into freezer can of an ice-cream freezer; freeze according to manufacturer's instructions. Spoon sorbet into a freezer-safe container; cover and freeze 4 hours or until firm. Yield: 12 servings (serving size: ½ cup).

CALORIES 93 (3% from fat); FAT 0.3g (sat 0g, mono 0.1g, poly 0.2g); PROTEIN 0.6g; CARB 23.4g; FIBER 2.2g; CHOL 0mg; IRON 0.6mg; SODIUM 2mg; CALC 17mg

Sunday Night Chicken Dinner

serves 8

Roasted Chicken with Lemons and Thyme

Green Beans with Bacon-Balsamic Vinaigrette

Romaine Salad with Oranges

Dinner rolls

Shortcakes with Fresh Berries

Roasted Chicken with Lemons and Thyme

Paprika, lemon, and thyme lend fresh flavor to this simple roasted chicken. You can substitute oregano for thyme.

1 (6-pound) roasting chicken
2 teaspoons Hungarian paprika or paprika
2 tablespoons chopped fresh thyme, divided
1 teaspoon salt, divided
1 teaspoon freshly ground black pepper, divided
2 lemons
Cooking spray
1 teaspoon olive oil
2 tablespoons all-purpose flour
½ cup dry white wine (such as sauvignon blanc)
1 cup fat-free, less-sodium chicken broth
1 tablespoon fresh lemon juice
2 teaspoons sugar

❶ Preheat oven to 425°.

❷ Remove and discard giblets and neck from chicken, and trim excess fat. Starting at neck cavity, loosen skin from breast and drumsticks by inserting fingers, gently pushing between skin and meat. Combine paprika, 1 tablespoon thyme, ½ teaspoon salt, and ¼ teaspoon pepper; rub under loosened skin. Thinly slice 1 lemon; arrange slices under loosened skin. Cut remaining lemon into quarters, and place inside chicken cavity. Add remaining 1 tablespoon thyme to chicken cavity.

❸ Place chicken on a broiler pan or roasting pan rack coated with cooking spray. Brush oil over skin. Cover chicken with foil. Place rack in pan. Bake at 425° for 30 minutes. Uncover and bake 50 minutes or until an instant-read thermometer inserted into thigh registers 165°. Transfer chicken to a cutting board; cover with foil, and let stand 15 minutes before carving.

❹ Place a zip-top plastic bag in a 2-cup glass measure. Pour drippings into bag; let stand 10 minutes (fat will rise to the top). Seal bag; carefully snip off 1 bottom corner of bag. Drain drippings into measuring cup, stopping before fat layer reaches opening; discard fat. Place pan on stove top over medium heat. Sprinkle flour into pan. Add white wine; bring to a boil, stirring constantly with a whisk. Add drippings, broth, juice, sugar, remaining ¾ teaspoon pepper, and remaining ½ teaspoon salt, stirring constantly with a whisk until slightly thickened. Remove from heat.

❺ Remove skin and lemon slices from chicken, and remove lemon wedges from cavity; discard. Carve chicken, and arrange on a serving platter. Serve with gravy. Yield: 8 servings (serving size: about 3 ounces chicken and 3 tablespoons gravy).

CALORIES 174 (35% from fat); FAT 6.7g (sat 1.8g, mono 2.7g, poly 1.5g); PROTEIN 23.5g; CARB 3.2g; FIBER 0.1g; CHOL 69mg; IRON 1.3mg; SODIUM 417mg; CALC 21mg

Green Beans with Bacon-Balsamic Vinaigrette

2 pounds green beans, trimmed
2 bacon slices
¼ cup minced shallots
3 tablespoons coarsely chopped almonds
2 tablespoons brown sugar
¼ cup white balsamic vinegar

❶ Cook beans in boiling water 2 minutes. Drain and rinse under cold water; drain and set aside.
❷ Cook bacon in a small skillet over medium-high heat until crisp. Remove bacon from skillet; crumble and set aside. Add minced shallots to drippings in skillet; sauté 1 minute. Add chopped almonds; sauté 1 minute. Remove and cool. Add sugar and vinegar; stir until sugar dissolves. Add crumbled bacon.
❸ Pour vinaigrette over beans, tossing gently to coat. Yield: 8 servings (serving size: ³/₄ cup).

CALORIES 75 (31% from fat); FAT 2.6g (sat 0.5g, mono 1.4g, poly 0.5g); PROTEIN 3.4g; CARB 11.8g; FIBER 2.8g; CHOL 0mg; IRON 1.4mg; SODIUM 50mg; CALC 54mg

Romaine Salad with Oranges

Honey and oranges lend sweetness to this salad. You'll find yourself preparing it often, as it goes well with any main dish.

½ cup thinly sliced red onion
¼ cup thinly sliced fresh basil
2 navel oranges, peeled, halved, and sliced
1 (10-ounce) package prewashed romaine lettuce, torn
½ English cucumber, peeled, halved lengthwise, and sliced (about 1 cup)
3 tablespoons red wine vinegar
1 tablespoon canola oil
1 tablespoon honey
¼ teaspoon kosher salt
¼ teaspoon freshly ground black pepper
1 small garlic clove, minced

❶ Place first 5 ingredients in a large bowl. Combine vinegar and next 5 ingredients in a small bowl; stir with a whisk. Drizzle over lettuce mixture; toss to coat. Serve immediately. Yield: 8 servings (serving size: 1¹/₂ cups).

CALORIES 53 (34% from fat); FAT 2g (sat 0.2g, mono 1.1g, poly 0.6g); PROTEIN 1g; CARB 9g; FIBER 1.8g; CHOL 0mg; IRON 0.5mg; SODIUM 63mg; CALC 34mg

Shortcakes with Fresh Berries

Make the shortcakes up to 2 days ahead, and store them in an airtight container. Use a serrated knife to cut them in half before adding the filling. You can prepare the berry filling up to 12 hours ahead; refrigerate until ready to serve. (Pictured on page 371.)

9 ounces all-purpose flour (about 2 cups)
3 tablespoons granulated sugar, divided
2 teaspoons baking powder
¼ teaspoon salt
3 tablespoons chilled butter, cut into small pieces
²/₃ cup reduced-fat buttermilk
1 tablespoon canola oil
1 teaspoon vanilla extract
1 large egg
Cooking spray
3½ teaspoons turbinado sugar, divided
½ cup apple jelly
3 tablespoons fresh lemon juice
3 cups fresh strawberries, quartered
2½ cups fresh blackberries
1 cup fat-free whipped topping

❶ Preheat oven to 425°.
❷ Lightly spoon flour into dry measuring cups; level with a knife. Combine flour, 2 tablespoons granulated sugar, baking powder, and salt in a large bowl; stir with a whisk. Cut in butter with a pastry blender or 2 knives until the mixture resembles coarse meal.
❸ Combine buttermilk, oil, vanilla, and egg in a small bowl; stir with a whisk. Add to flour mixture, stirring just until moist (dough will be sticky).
❹ Turn dough out onto a baking sheet coated with cooking spray. Pat dough into an 8-inch circle; cut into 8 wedges, cutting into, but not through, dough. Sprinkle 1¹/₂ teaspoons turbinado sugar over dough. Bake at 425° for 15 minutes or until golden. Cool 15 minutes.
❺ Combine jelly, juice, and remaining 1 tablespoon granulated sugar in a microwave-safe bowl; microwave at HIGH 1 minute. Stir with a whisk until smooth. Combine jelly mixture, strawberries, and blackberries in a large bowl; toss to coat berries. Cover and chill.
❻ Cut shortcake into 8 wedges. Cut each wedge in half horizontally; spoon ¹/₂ cup berry mixture over bottom half of each shortcake. Replace top half of shortcake. Top each serving with 2 tablespoons whipped topping, and sprinkle each evenly with remaining 2 teaspoons turbinado sugar. Yield: 8 servings (serving size: 1 filled shortcake).

CALORIES 306 (22% from fat); FAT 7.5g (sat 3.2g, mono 2.4g, poly 1.1g); PROTEIN 5.7g; CARB 53.5g; FIBER 3.9g; CHOL 39mg; IRON 2.1mg; SODIUM 264mg; CALC 117mg

Tex-Mex Dinner for a Crowd

serves 12

Black Bean Dip

Baked corn chips

Chicken Poblano Casserole

Tossed green salad

Piña Colada Sherbet with Pineapple Sauce

Black Bean Dip

Offer this dip with baked corn chips as the perfect party-starter for any Spanish-themed dinner menu.

1 (15-ounce) can black beans, drained
1 teaspoon canola oil
½ cup chopped onion
2 garlic cloves, minced
½ cup diced tomato
⅓ cup mild picante sauce
½ teaspoon ground cumin
½ teaspoon chili powder
¼ cup (1 ounce) shredded reduced-fat Monterey Jack cheese
¼ cup chopped fresh cilantro
1 tablespoon fresh lime juice

❶ Place beans in a bowl, and partially mash until chunky. Set aside.

❷ Heat canola oil in a medium nonstick skillet over medium heat. Add onion and garlic; sauté 4 minutes or until tender. Add beans, tomato, picante sauce, cumin, and chili powder; cook 5 minutes or until thick, stirring constantly. Remove from heat; add cheese, cilantro, and juice, stirring well. Serve warm or at room temperature. Yield: 1⅔ cups (serving size: 2 tablespoons).

CALORIES 42 (21% from fat); FAT 1g (sat 0.4g, mono 0.2g, poly 0.2g); PROTEIN 2.6g; CARB 6.2g; FIBER 1g; CHOL 2mg; IRON 0.6mg; SODIUM 136mg; CALC 30mg

Chicken Poblano Casserole

You can save time preparing this recipe by roasting the peppers and shucking and broiling the corn in advance.

- 3 poblano chiles (about 12 ounces)
- 1 large red bell pepper (about 8 ounces)
- 3 ears shucked corn
- 1½ ounces all-purpose flour (about ⅓ cup)
- 1 teaspoon salt, divided
- ¼ teaspoon freshly ground black pepper
- 3½ cups 1% low-fat milk
- 3 cups (12 ounces) preshredded reduced-fat 4-cheese Mexican blend cheese, divided
- ⅓ cup chopped red onion
- ⅓ cup chopped fresh cilantro
- 2 large eggs, lightly beaten
- 1 (15-ounce) carton part-skim ricotta cheese
- Cooking spray
- 18 (6-inch) white corn tortillas
- 3¾ cups chopped cooked chicken breast
- 1 cup thinly sliced green onions, divided

1 Preheat broiler.
2 Cut poblanos and bell pepper in half lengthwise; discard seeds and membranes. Place poblanos and bell pepper, skin sides up, on a foil-lined baking sheet; flatten with hand. Place corn on baking sheet. Broil for 10 minutes or until poblanos and bell pepper are blackened and corn is lightly browned. Place poblanos and bell pepper in a zip-top plastic bag; seal and let stand 10 minutes. Peel and coarsely chop; set poblanos and bell pepper aside separately. Remove corn kernels from cobs.
3 Lightly spoon flour into a dry measuring cup; level with a knife. Place flour, ½ teaspoon salt, and black pepper in a large saucepan. Gradually add milk, stirring with a whisk. Cook over medium heat until slightly thick (about 12 minutes), stirring constantly; remove from heat. Combine 1 cup milk mixture and poblanos in a blender; process until smooth. Stir pureed poblano mixture into remaining milk mixture.
4 Preheat oven to 350°.
5 Combine bell pepper, corn, remaining ½ teaspoon salt, 1 cup Mexican cheese, red onion, cilantro, eggs, and ricotta.
6 Coat bottom of a 13 x 9–inch baking dish with cooking spray. Spread ½ cup sauce in bottom of dish. Arrange 6 tortillas over sauce, overlapping slightly. Spread half of ricotta mixture over tortillas; top with half of chicken. Sprinkle with ⅓ cup green onions and ⅔ cup Mexican cheese. Pour about 1 cup sauce over cheese. Repeat layers with 6 tortillas, remaining ricotta mixture, remaining chicken, ⅓ cup green onions, ⅔ cup Mexican cheese, 1 cup sauce, and 6 tortillas. Pour remaining sauce over tortillas. Coat 1 side of foil with cooking spray; place foil, coated side down, over casserole. Bake at 350° for 30 minutes or until bubbly.
7 Uncover; sprinkle with remaining ⅔ cup Mexican cheese and ⅓ cup green onions. Bake, uncovered, 15 minutes or until cheese melts. Let stand 15 minutes. Yield: 12 servings.

CALORIES 369 (29% from fat); FAT 11.9g (sat 6.1g, mono 2.9g, poly 1.2g); PROTEIN 33.1g; CARB 33.8g; FIBER 3.6g; CHOL 98mg; IRON 1.8mg; SODIUM 594mg; CALC 536mg

Piña Colada Sherbet with Pineapple Sauce

This frozen treat combines all of the favorite flavors found in a tropical beverage but is served in a bowl. Look for cans of cream of coconut near the drink mixes in your supermarket.

- 5 cups pineapple sherbet
- ⅔ cup cream of coconut
- ⅓ cup white rum
- 2½ tablespoons fresh lime juice
- Pineapple Sauce
- ¼ cup shredded coconut, toasted

1 Place a large bowl in freezer. Let pineapple sherbet stand at room temperature 45 minutes or until softened.
2 Combine softened sherbet, cream of coconut, rum, and juice in chilled bowl; blend well with a rubber spatula or stand mixer. Cover and freeze to desired consistency. Place ½ cup sherbet in each of 12 bowls; top each serving with 2 tablespoons pineapple sauce and 1 teaspoon coconut. Yield: 12 servings (serving size: ½ cup sherbet, 2 tablespoons pineapple sauce, and 1 teaspoon coconut).

CALORIES 190 (19% from fat); FAT 4g (sat 2.9g, mono 0.4g, poly 0.1g); PROTEIN 1g; CARB 33.9g; FIBER 2.7g; CHOL 0mg; IRON 0.3mg; SODIUM 37mg; CALC 40mg

Pineapple Sauce:

This simple sauce places fresh pineapple at the forefront of this dessert. And since it requires no cooking, the sauce can be ready in a flash.

- 3 cups coarsely chopped pineapple
- 2 tablespoons brown sugar
- ¼ teaspoon vanilla extract

1 Place pineapple, sugar, and extract in a food processor; pulse 10 times or until finely chopped. Cover and chill. Yield: 1¾ cups (serving size: 2 tablespoons).

CALORIES 24 (4% from fat); FAT 0.1g (sat 0g, mono 0g, poly 0.1g); PROTEIN 0.1g; CARB 6g; FIBER 0.4g; CHOL 0mg; IRON 0.2mg; SODIUM 1mg; CALC 4mg

Elegant Summer Dinner

serves 4

*Broiled Salmon with
Roasted Tomato Sauce*

Mushroom Duxelles on Bruschetta

*Gourmet salad greens with
red wine vinaigrette*

*Figs and Prosciutto with Mint
and Shaved Parmigiano-Reggiano*

Broiled Salmon with Roasted Tomato Sauce

Roasting the tomatoes imbues them with a flavor that's a delicious match to the rich fish.

- 1 pound plum tomatoes, quartered
- ½ small onion, peeled and quartered
- 2 garlic cloves
- Cooking spray
- ¼ teaspoon salt
- ¼ teaspoon freshly ground black pepper
- 2 tablespoons tomato paste
- 1 cup organic vegetable broth (such as Swanson Certified Organic)
- 2 tablespoons water
- 1 teaspoon cornstarch
- 4 (6-ounce) salmon fillets, skinned
- ⅛ teaspoon salt
- ¼ cup thinly sliced fresh basil
- Coarsely ground black pepper (optional)
- 4 oregano sprigs (optional)

1 Preheat broiler.

2 Arrange tomatoes, onion, and garlic in an even layer on a jelly-roll pan coated with cooking spray. Sprinkle evenly with ¼ teaspoon salt and pepper. Broil 8 minutes; stir gently. Broil an additional 5 minutes or until vegetables begin to blacken at the edges.

3 Place tomato mixture and tomato paste in a blender or food processor; process until smooth. Place tomato mixture in a saucepan over medium heat. Stir in broth; bring to a simmer. Cook 10 minutes, stirring frequently; remove from heat. Strain mixture through a sieve into a large bowl; discard solids. Return tomato mixture to saucepan over medium heat.

4 Combine 2 tablespoons water and 1 teaspoon cornstarch in a small bowl; stir into tomato mixture. Increase heat to medium-high, and bring to a boil. Cook 1 minute, stirring constantly. Remove from heat.

5 Place fish on a broiler pan lightly coated with cooking spray. Sprinkle evenly with ⅛ teaspoon salt. Broil 6 minutes or until fish flakes easily when tested with a fork or until desired degree of doneness.

6 Place about ¼ cup tomato mixture on each of 4 deep plates; top each with 1 salmon fillet. Sprinkle each with 1 tablespoon basil. Garnish each serving with coarsely ground black pepper and a sprig of oregano, if desired. Yield: 4 servings.

CALORIES 324 (38% from fat); FAT 13.5g (sat 3.2g, mono 5.7g, poly 3.4g); PROTEIN 37.9g; CARB 11.7g; FIBER 2.2g; CHOL 87mg; IRON 1.5mg; SODIUM 520mg; CALC 43mg

Mushroom Duxelles on Bruschetta

Duxelles (dook-SEHL) is a mixture of finely chopped mushrooms cooked to the consistency of a pâté.

- 16 (½-inch-thick) slices diagonally cut French bread baguette
- 4 cups cremini mushrooms (about 8 ounces)
- 4 cups shiitake mushroom caps (about 8 ounces)
- Cooking spray
- 3 garlic cloves, minced
- 2 tablespoons chopped fresh parsley
- 3 tablespoons whipping cream
- 2 teaspoons chopped fresh thyme
- ½ teaspoon kosher salt
- ¼ teaspoon freshly ground black pepper

1 Prepare grill or preheat broiler.

2 Place bread on a grill rack or baking sheet; cook 1 minute on each side or until toasted.

3 Place mushrooms in a food processor, and pulse 10 times or until finely chopped.

4 Heat a large nonstick skillet over medium-high heat; coat pan with cooking spray. Add mushrooms and garlic; sauté 10 minutes or until most of liquid evaporates. Add parsley and remaining ingredients; cook 2 minutes, stirring occasionally. Spoon 1 tablespoon duxelles onto each bread slice. Serve immediately. Yield: 8 servings (serving size: 2 bread slices and 2 tablespoons duxelles).

CALORIES 117 (30% from fat); FAT 3.9g (sat 1.6g, mono 1.1g, poly 1g); PROTEIN 3.7g; CARB 16.4g; FIBER 2.1g; CHOL 8mg; IRON 1.1mg; SODIUM 244mg; CALC 12mg

Figs and Prosciutto with Mint and Shaved Parmigiano-Reggiano

Make sure to use ripe figs when preparing this dessert.

- 4 fresh figs, quartered
- 1 teaspoon extra-virgin olive oil
- ⅛ teaspoon cracked black pepper
- ½ ounce fresh Parmigiano-Reggiano cheese, thinly shaved
- 6 mint leaves, thinly sliced
- 2 ounces thinly sliced prosciutto

1 Place figs in a bowl; drizzle with oil. Sprinkle figs with pepper, and toss gently. Place fig mixture in the center of a platter; top with cheese and mint. Top with prosciutto. Yield: 4 servings (serving size: 4 fig quarters, about ½ ounce prosciutto, and ⅛ ounce cheese).

CALORIES 90 (34% from fat); FAT 3.4g (sat 1.2g, mono 1.8g, poly 0.3g); PROTEIN 4.8g; CARB 9.5g; FIBER 1.4g; CHOL 11mg; IRON 0.3mg; SODIUM 270mg; CALC 64mg

Summer Celebration Menu

serves 8

Striped Bass with Fennel Relish over Sautéed Spinach

Mixed Bean–Cherry Tomato Salad with Basil Vinaigrette

Corn Pudding

Peanut Butter–Banana Ice Cream
(page 406)

Mocha Ice Cream
(page 406)

Striped Bass with Fennel Relish over Sautéed Spinach

Prepare the fennel relish up to an hour in advance, and set aside. It can be served at room temperature.

RELISH:
4 cups diced fennel bulb (about 1 pound)
2 cups diced red onion
2 teaspoons olive oil
½ teaspoon salt
½ teaspoon freshly ground black pepper
Cooking spray
2 teaspoons sugar
2 teaspoons capers, drained
1 tablespoon balsamic vinegar

BASS:
8 (6-ounce) striped bass fillets without skin
2 teaspoons olive oil
½ teaspoon salt
½ teaspoon freshly ground black pepper

SPINACH:
2 teaspoons olive oil
6 garlic cloves, thinly sliced
2 pounds fresh spinach, trimmed
½ teaspoon salt
¼ teaspoon freshly ground black pepper

❶ Preheat oven to 450°.
❷ To prepare relish, combine first 5 ingredients, tossing well to coat. Arrange fennel mixture in a single layer on a jelly-roll pan coated with cooking spray. Bake at 450° for 30 minutes or until lightly browned, stirring once. Place fennel mixture in a bowl; stir in sugar, capers, and vinegar.
❸ Preheat grill to medium-high heat.
❹ To prepare fish, place fillets on grill rack coated with cooking spray. Brush fillets evenly with 2 teaspoons oil; sprinkle evenly with ½ teaspoon salt and ½ teaspoon pepper. Grill 4 minutes on each side or until fish flakes easily when tested with a fork or until desired degree of doneness. Keep warm.
❺ To prepare spinach, heat 2 teaspoons oil in a Dutch oven over medium-high heat. Add garlic; cook 2 minutes or until golden, stirring frequently. Add half of spinach; cook 1 minute, stirring constantly. Add remaining spinach, and cook 2 minutes or until wilted, stirring frequently. Sprinkle with ½ teaspoon salt and ¼ teaspoon pepper.
❻ Place ½ cup spinach mixture on each of 8 plates; top each with 1 fillet and about ¼ cup relish. Yield: 8 servings.

CALORIES 287 (24% from fat); FAT 7.8g (sat 1.4g, mono 3.9g, poly 1.7g); PROTEIN 34.7g; CARB 21.5g; FIBER 7.4g; CHOL 140mg; IRON 5.6mg; SODIUM 779mg; CALC 142mg

Mixed Bean–Cherry Tomato Salad with Basil Vinaigrette

This salad can be made early in the day and refrigerated until ready to serve.

1 pound green beans, trimmed
1 pound wax beans, trimmed
¼ cup balsamic vinegar
2 tablespoons extra-virgin olive oil
½ teaspoon kosher salt
½ teaspoon freshly ground black pepper
3 cups cherry tomatoes, halved (2 pints)
1 cup loosely packed basil leaves, coarsely chopped
½ cup finely chopped red onion

❶ Cook green and wax beans in boiling water 5 minutes. Drain and plunge beans into ice water; drain.
❷ Combine vinegar, olive oil, kosher salt, and pepper. Add beans, tomatoes, basil, and onion; toss gently. Cover and chill. Yield: 8 servings (serving size: ¾ cup bean mixture).

CALORIES 86 (38% from fat); FAT 3.6g (sat 0.5g, mono 2.5g, poly 0.4g); PROTEIN 2.1g; CARB 11.2g; FIBER 4.4g; CHOL 0mg; IRON 1mg; SODIUM 132mg; CALC 57mg

Corn Pudding

If you use frozen corn, thaw it before using. If you don't have fresh chives, chop off the green part of green onions. Let the pudding bake while you finish preparing the rest of the meal.

3 cups fresh corn kernels (about 6 ears)
¼ cup chopped fresh chives
1 tablespoon chopped fresh thyme
¾ teaspoon salt
¼ teaspoon freshly ground black pepper
1½ cups 1% low-fat milk
½ cup egg substitute
2 tablespoons ⅓-less-fat cream cheese
1 large egg, lightly beaten
Cooking spray

❶ Preheat oven to 350°.
❷ Combine corn, chives, thyme, salt, and pepper in a medium bowl. Combine milk, egg substitute, cream cheese, and egg in a medium bowl. Add milk mixture to corn mixture, and stir well to combine. Pour corn mixture into an 11 x 7–inch baking dish coated with cooking spray. Bake at 350° for 55 minutes or until top of pudding is golden. Yield: 8 servings (serving size: 1 square).

CALORIES 113 (32% from fat); FAT 4.1g (sat 1.3g, mono 1.1g, poly 1.4g); PROTEIN 6.5g; CARB 14.4g; FIBER 1.7g; CHOL 31mg; IRON 0.8mg; SODIUM 308mg; CALC 80mg

Peanut Butter–Banana Ice Cream

Chunky peanut butter adds a pleasing crunch, while the banana imparts a fruity sweetness.

- 4 cups vanilla low-fat ice cream
- 1 cup mashed ripe banana (about 2 small bananas)
- ¼ cup chunky peanut butter

❶ Place a large bowl in freezer. Let vanilla ice cream stand at room temperature about 45 minutes or until softened.
❷ Combine banana and peanut butter in a small bowl; mash with a fork until well blended.
❸ Combine banana mixture and softened ice cream in chilled bowl; blend well with a rubber spatula or stand mixer. Cover and freeze to desired consistency. Yield: 8 servings (serving size: ½ cup).

CALORIES 183 (30% from fat); FAT 6.1g (sat 1.8g, mono 1.9g, poly 1.2g); PROTEIN 5.2g; CARB 27.3g; FIBER 2.2g; CHOL 5mg; IRON 0.2mg; SODIUM 84mg; CALC 105mg

Mocha Ice Cream

- 4 cups chocolate low-fat ice cream
- ¼ cup Kahlúa (coffee-flavored liqueur)
- 1 tablespoon instant coffee granules
- 2 ounces bittersweet chocolate, finely chopped

❶ Place a large bowl in freezer. Let ice cream stand at room temperature 45 minutes or until softened.
❷ Combine liqueur and coffee granules in a small bowl. Microwave at HIGH 30 seconds; stir until coffee dissolves. Cool slightly.
❸ Combine softened ice cream, coffee mixture, and chopped chocolate in chilled bowl; blend well with a rubber spatula or stand mixer. Cover and freeze to desired consistency. Yield: 8 servings (serving size: ½ cup).

CALORIES 206 (30% from fat); FAT 6.9g (sat 4.5g, mono 1.5g, poly 0.2g); PROTEIN 3.6g; CARB 30.5g; FIBER 0.6g; CHOL 15.3mg; IRON 0.4mg; SODIUM 101mg; CALC 101mg

HOW TO USE IT AND WHY Glance at the end of any *Cooking Light* recipe, and you'll see how committed we are to helping you make the best of today's light cooking. With chefs, registered dietitians, home economists, and a computer system that analyzes every ingredient we use, *Cooking Light* gives you authoritative dietary detail like no other magazine. We go to such lengths so you can see how our recipes fit into your healthful eating plan. If you're trying to lose weight, the calorie and fat figures will probably help most. But if you're keeping a close eye on the sodium, cholesterol, and saturated fat in your diet, we provide those numbers, too. And because many women don't get enough iron or calcium, we can help there, as well. Finally, there's a fiber analysis for those of us who don't get enough roughage.

Here's a helpful guide to put our nutrition analysis numbers into perspective. Remember, one size doesn't fit all, so take your lifestyle, age, and circumstances into consideration when determining your nutrition needs. For example, pregnant or breast-feeding women need more protein, calories, and calcium. And women older than 50 need 1,200 mg of calcium daily, 200 mg more than the amount recommended for younger women.

IN OUR NUTRITIONAL ANALYSIS, WE USE THESE ABBREVIATIONS:

sat	saturated fat	**CHOL**	cholesterol
mono	monounsaturated fat	**CALC**	calcium
poly	polyunsaturated fat	**g**	gram
CARB	carbohydrates	**mg**	milligram

Daily Nutrition Guide

	WOMEN AGES 25 TO 50	WOMEN OVER 50	MEN AGES 25 TO 50	MEN OVER 50
Calories	2,000	2,000*	2,700	2,500
Protein	50 g	50 g	63 g	60 g
Fat	65 g*	65 g*	88 g*	83 g*
Saturated Fat	20 g*	20 g*	27 g*	25 g*
Carbohydrates	304 g	304 g	410 g	375 g
Fiber	25 g to 35 g	25 g to 35 g	25 g to 35 g	25 g to 35 g
Cholesterol	300 mg*	300 mg*	300 mg*	300 mg*
Iron	18 mg	8 mg	8 mg	8 mg
Sodium	2,300 mg*	1,500 mg*	2,300 mg*	1,500 mg*
Calcium	1,000 mg	1,200 mg	1,000 mg	1,000 mg

The nutritional values used in our calculations either come from The Food Processor, Version 7.5 (ESHA Research), or are provided by food manufacturers. *or less, for optimum health

METRIC EQUIVALENTS

The information in the following charts is provided to help cooks outside the United States successfully use the recipes in this book. All equivalents are approximate.

Equivalents for Different Types of Ingredients

Standard Cup	Fine Powder (ex. flour)	Grain (ex. rice)	Granular (ex. sugar)	Liquid Solids (ex. butter)	Liquid (ex. milk)
1	140 g	150 g	190 g	200 g	240 ml
¾	105 g	113 g	143 g	150 g	180 ml
⅔	93 g	100 g	125 g	133 g	160 ml
½	70 g	75 g	95 g	100 g	120 ml
⅓	47 g	50 g	63 g	67 g	80 ml
¼	35 g	38 g	48 g	50 g	60 ml
⅛	18 g	19 g	24 g	25 g	30 ml

Liquid Ingredients by Volume

¼ tsp						=	1 ml	
½ tsp						=	2 ml	
1 tsp						=	5 ml	
3 tsp	=	1 tbl			= ½ fl oz	=	15 ml	
		2 tbls	=	⅛ cup	= 1 fl oz	=	30 ml	
		4 tbls	=	¼ cup	= 2 fl oz	=	60 ml	
		5⅓ tbls	=	⅓ cup	= 3 fl oz	=	80 ml	
		8 tbls	=	½ cup	= 4 fl oz	=	120 ml	
		10⅔ tbls	=	⅔ cup	= 5 fl oz	=	160 ml	
		12 tbls	=	¾ cup	= 6 fl oz	=	180 ml	
		16 tbls	=	1 cup	= 8 fl oz	=	240 ml	
		1 pt	=	2 cups	= 16 fl oz	=	480 ml	
		1 qt	=	4 cups	= 32 fl oz	=	960 ml	
					33 fl oz	=	1000 ml	= 1l

Dry Ingredients by Weight

(To convert ounces to grams, multiply the number of ounces by 30.)

1 oz	=	⅟₁₆ lb	=	30 g
4 oz	=	¼ lb	=	120 g
8 oz	=	½ lb	=	240 g
12 oz	=	¾ lb	=	360 g
16 oz	=	1 lb	=	480 g

Length

(To convert inches to centimeters, multiply the number of inches by 2.5.)

1 in =			2.5 cm
6 in =	½ ft	=	15 cm
12 in =	1 ft	=	30 cm
36 in =	3 ft = 1 yd	=	90 cm
40 in =			100 cm = 1 m

Cooking/Oven Temperatures

	Fahrenheit	Celsius	Gas Mark
Freeze Water	32° F	0° C	
Room Temperature	68° F	20° C	
Boil Water	212° F	100° C	
Bake	325° F	160° C	3
	350° F	180° C	4
	375° F	190° C	5
	400° F	200° C	6
	425° F	220° C	7
	450° F	230° C	8
Broil			Grill

Index

Index

Index

Index

Index